**HURON COUNTY PUBLIC LIBRARY**

## Date Due

| BC 2'81 | | | |
|---|---|---|---|
| June 27 | | | |
| | | | |
| | | | |
| | | | |
| | | | |
| | | | |
| | | | |
| | | | |
| | | | |
| | | | |
| | | | |
| | | | |

51537

```
971        Down North: the book of Cape Breton's
.69002        magazine.  Ronald Caplan, editor.
Dow           Toronto, Doubleday, 1980.
              241 p.  illus., maps.
              Articles previously published in Cape
           Breton's magazine.

           1. Cape Breton - Miscellanea.  2. Canadians
           - Interviews.  I. Caplan, Ronald.
           II. Cape Breton's magazine.
           038514475X                      0717347
           0385144768 pb                   0717363
```

# Down North

DOUBLEDAY CANADA LIMITED, Toronto, Ontario
DOUBLEDAY & COMPANY, INC., Garden City, New York
1980

# Down North
## The Book of Cape Breton's Magazine

RONALD CAPLAN, editor

Library of Congress Catalog Card Number 78-68351

Copyright © 1980 by Ronald Caplan

Most of the material in this book appeared in much the same form in *Cape Breton's Magazine*

The maps on pages ix, 72, 185, and 187 are by Sam Daniel

The picture on page xiii is of Malcolm Angus MacLeod

Design by Robert Burgess Garbutt

Printed and bound in Canada by T. H. Best Company Ltd.

**Canadian Cataloguing in Publication Data**

Main entry under title:

Down North

Articles previously published in Cape Breton's magazine.

ISBN 0-385-14475-X bd.   ISBN 0-385-14476-8 pa.

1. Cape Breton Island, N.S.—Miscellanea.
2. Canadians—Interviews. I. Caplan, Ronald.
II. Cape Breton's magazine.

FC2343.42.D69       971.6'9'002       C79-094776-5
F1039.C2D69

*This book unquestionably belongs to all Cape Bretoners, as does the magazine from which it comes; but I want to dedicate it particularly to people who especially have made my work possible:*

*Roddy Hector and Jenny MacDonald, and Bessie Ann MacDonald (1882-1976), Wreck Cove*

*Jeff and Christiane Tanner, and their children Isabelle, Rachèle and Geoffrey, Westmount*

*and Bonnie Thompson, Indian Brook*

# Introduction

I got a call today that Sandy Kenny Morrison died. Another time it was Murdoch MacAskill. Malcolm Angus MacLeod disappeared. Maisie Morrison has died. Red Dan Smith has died. Dear Fermin Fleet and Johnny Murphy. And several others beside. People whom I have loved. People who have been more generous with me than I ever had right to expect. People who talked with me, talked with me—who took me seriously and made meaningful the work I was doing, even on days when I myself was uncertain as to the meaning or worth of what I was up to. How can I talk to you about the people in this book, living and dead, without in some manner standing in their way, getting in between them and you, the very thing I have not wanted to do?

These past seven years I have offered the stories I collected in *Cape Breton's Magazine* with very little editorial comment. I continue to feel that in presenting certain things I have said as much about them as I wish. My touch is already very much there. I once thought I would prefer not to be seen in this book at all, that I somehow could offer the materials *that* pure—but I know now that this is neither possible, nor right. *Down North* is a selection taken mostly from the early issues of *Cape Breton's Magazine*. It is an accurate though far-from-complete word-and-picture portrait of elements of Cape Breton life. It is also a portrait of *my* Cape Breton, the rooms I was in and the people I talked with, the questions I thought to ask. This book could not have been essentially different unless another person had done it—and given the choice I'm happy that I have been the one to pass my days this way, to have made those visits and met those people who have made my own life possible these several years.

I went out one day searching for the old cemetery at White Point. The land beyond the village juts out into the Atlantic, a narrow resistant finger forming the southeastern arc of Aspy Bay. I left the houses and the wharf behind, followed a rough road that eventually disappeared in the tough grass, and wondered the whole walk out why the sea hadn't torn this bit of land away. And far out there—high above the bay on my left and the ocean to the right; St. Paul's Island a hazy blue form at the horizon and everything else sky—there is a cemetery. In recent years a cross has been raised and a fence put around, or it would be easy to miss. It's difficult to tell the rough headstones from rocks tossed up by the frost. They are a little smoother, some obviously set on edge, here and there in the grass.

And I sat down there and I thought about what I took to be the stark reality of that place. I imagined a small group of mourners, probably the entire village, coming out along this ridge of land, the coffin made by themselves and in among them, the body dressed and waked by neighbors and family—carrying one of their small number out to this beautiful, forlorn place. I thought of cold wind and backs bent against both wind and the weight of the community's loss, of no protection but what their own hands and prayers could work, the water ripping in at both sides.

Bob Fitzgerald belonged to White Point. I told him some days later I had been out to the old cemetery. But why, I asked him, why did they bury them so far from the village? "Oh, no, no, no, no," he said. "You can't see it now, but that *was* the village. People lived out there. There were fishing shacks at the shore, and stores—not just one store—and a post office. And when the telegraph came, that's where it went. You just think that was the end of the world because you travel by car. In those days they travelled by boat. Came from communities all around. White Point was the center of the world."

So it was a romantic view of the world that took me out and gave me my first reading of White Point, and it was Bob Fitzgerald brought me home, made me focus more accurately on what I thought I knew, and thus made White Point more real. It was that same romantic capacity that first brought me to Cape Breton and eventually to the idea of staying and making *Cape Breton's Magazine*.

I remember an early interview, perhaps the idea of doing the magazine was barely formed. I came close to arguing with Annie Margaret Morrison—it's all on tape and there's no denying it—she was trying to tell me about the difficulties of farm/fishing lives on the North Shore of Cape Breton fifty years ago. And I was saying, "But you were independent" (probably "self-sufficient" was the word I was using then), "you had your own land, you had your own potatoes," and so on. "I suppose so," she said softly, knowing and thus unconvinced.

Mrs. MacAskill rammed it home. She told a young woman

who was collecting information for a local archives: "I'll tell you about the old way. The only difference between us and the cattle was that come tomorrow morning we knew which field we'd be in."

This life newcomers dare to call "traditional," "the old way," to which we imagine some possible return.

I know there was joy. I know there was vigor. But how hard it was—we forget that or no one tells us or we refuse to hear. And going back, re-reading early issues, I realize that I was time and again being told, that I was gently being given a portrait of Cape Breton to that extent more accurate and real.

Cape Breton seems to be one of the touchstones of North America. I think people come here for some reminder, if not of their own former lives at least of their own capacities. Even those Cape Bretoners who return summer after summer from Upper Canada and the Boston States to visit the countryside or the coal mining districts or the little fishing communities, they seem to me to be looking to Cape Bretoners who remained behind for qualities they hope are still within themselves, for something of which they are still capable, regardless of where they now live or how they live out their lives. They are looking for something they might, if pressed, call "the authentic." They are happy to find even remnants of a bit more manageable world, evidences of a time when life was simpler and more direct. And on occasion they meet someone who is more than a remnant, who is, you might say, the real thing.

You cannot imagine how much respect there is for these people in every community I know, how little ridicule I find for those who have held to traditional modes of thinking and working and treating others. I have heard an auto mechanic referred to as one who will deal with you as an oldtime Acadian would—and it was the highest form of respect.

There exist here communities of regard. Economics alone is clearly not the explanation. Dan Murdoch Morrison would make as fine an axe handle for himself as for another—and there is a way in which the community depends on him to do his work just that well. They look to him, speak of him—he is a touchstone and his existence means that this quality is still in among them. Not just that he takes great care. He is, in a certain sense, *beyond* care.

I remember going across the hill to Roddy Hector MacDonald's. I had heard him splitting wood and I wanted to watch. I came through the fence after he had gone into the house for tea. It was a workman's place: meticulous, split spruce at one side, unsplit stove-length chunks piled at the other side, the splitting block itself clean in the cold autumn light with the axe head flat on it, Roddy Hector's gloves neatly crossed on the axe head. I know it was not a presentation. It was in every respect impeccable. For Roddy Hector, there was just no other way to do it. He had simply left his workplace and gone in for tea. And I came through the fence and found things this way.

But I don't want to overstate this. Neither Cape Breton nor its people is a living museum. While the older ways are highly regarded and Gaelic and Acadian French and Micmac languages to varying degrees survive here, the modern world is both encroaching and fully welcomed. While Red Dan Smith twisted wood into rope or Alex Matheson beat out blades for a pair of stock skates, a supertanker inched its way up the Strait of Canso, heading for the oil refinery at Point Tupper. The steel plant and coke ovens fill the skies over the industrial area and enormous harvesters are pulping out the heart of the Highlands. Cape Breton today is a complex occasion with a tremendous amount to resolve in terms of how much it will give over, how much it will hold onto that is its own. But it is one of the North American places that still has an "own" to consider, to defend or to barter. It still has a way of doing things, a shared lore and way of speaking and regarding one another which is a people and a place. Sometime between 1790 and 1900, various peoples and the place emerged as one. To say Cape Breton is to say both land *and* people. And to a Cape Bretoner there are only two places on earth: Cape Breton Island and that other place, Away.

For seven years now I have been making *Cape Breton's Magazine*, traveling the island in all kinds of weather with a camera and tape recorder, visiting with Cape Bretoners, talking and taking pictures. I spend time in various local archives and libraries, and supplement my work with that of specialists (particularly in the case of natural history articles, none of which are included, and French and Gaelic stories, examples of which are here.) It's been essentially a one-man job. Three times a year I stop and (in recent years with the help of Bonnie Thompson) I make transcriptions from tapes, edit and organize the material and make an issue of *Cape Breton's Magazine*.

I am an American who came here to change my life— simple as that. The choice of the magazine as support was a happy accident that has used me well. My concern was not this book or an archival collection or even what is called "oral history" and preservation of the old way—though these might be consequences, my real concern was to keep alive this form, a magazine, which gave me access to a people and a place I wanted to draw more close to, a magazine that is not only a form of personal support but a way of organizing the materials and giving them back. The magazine has been extraordinarily good to me in the quantity of decent people with whom I have been permitted to spend my time, in the landscape I drive through and take as my workspace. I have been talked to and fed and have had little fear for a place to sleep. I have been a stranger on the road, and I have been welcomed and warmed.

Finally, the title of this book. *Down North* doesn't really speak for all of Cape Breton, but I haven't yet come up with a single word or phrase that does. "Down North" is a distinctive phrase commonly heard here, and it holds for me a good deal of the tough, sweet contrariness I find everywhere in Cape Breton. When I first came to the island I asked Jenny MacDonald about it. I had often heard people say that a truck went down, heading for Cape North. I told her that north is usually at the top of a map and I would think "Up North" would be right. "Well," Jenny said straight out, "that may be the way it is on a map, but here in Cape Breton it's *Down* North." And so it is.

Ronald Caplan<br>
Cape Breton's Magazine<br>
Wreck Cove<br>
Cape Breton Island<br>
Canada<br>
1979

# Contents

*Introduction* / vii

An Orange in Cheticamp / 1
Trap Fishing with Mike MacDougall / 2
Red Dan Smith Makes Rope from Wood / 11
A Visit with Jack Sam Hinkley / 15
A Milling Frolic on the North Shore / 18
Hilda MacDonald and Glendyer Mills / 24
A Céilidh at Malcolm Campbell's / 28
Mary Ann Beaton Makes Country Cheese / 33
Lee Cremo and Scottish Fiddling / 36
Deux Contes Merveilleux pour les Enfants / 39
Tius Tutty and Handpick Mining / 42
The "Pluck Me": Life and Death of the Company Store / 47
The Eyestone / 50
Rita and Rory Murphy Remember Moonshining Days / 51
Waltes: An Ancient Micmac Game / 54
Reitach: A Scottish Engagement Rite / 58
Chandeleur: An Acadian Feast / 60
Oidhche Na Calluinn / 64
Dan Murdoch Morrison Makes an Axe Handle / 66
How I Learned to Smoke / 71
Remembering St. Paul's Island / 72
How Leather Was Sewn / 76
Joe MacNeil Tells a Wonderful Story / 83
This Was Swordfishing / 96
John Joseph LeBlanc Shears Sheep / 102
Remembering Rum Running Days / 104
How to Make Spruce Beer / 114
Willy Petrie: A Man Who Finds Water / 115
In the North River Lumber Woods / 118

A Pair of Stock Skates / 123
How We Cured Ourselves / 128
Dr. MacPherson, the Cancer Doctor / 134
Wild Archie Plays the Bones / 135
Ellen Googoo Makes a Micmac Basket / 139
Hector Carmichael: A Maker of Songs / 144
Maisie Morrison Hooks a Rag Rug / 148
Fishing for Gaspereaux on the Southwest Margaree / 154
Cleve Townsend of Louisbourg / 161
How to Make Ceann Groppi / 166
The Life and Death of the *Aspy* / 168
John R. and Bessie MacLeod Tell Stories of Their Old Home / 176
Evidence of Early Man on Cape Breton / 180
A Theory of Vikings on Cape Breton / 184
Pirate Shipyard on the Mira River / 189
Sowing Oats and Hay / 193
The Dump Cart and Hay Truck / 197
A Story of Christmas Island / 204
A Visit with Marguerite Gallant / 205
The Sinking of the *Caribou* / 212
The Berthing of Supertankers / 217
Johnny Murphy of North East Margaree / 226
How We Buried Our Dead / 231

*Acknowledgments* / 241

# Down North

# An Orange in Cheticamp

*by Mrs. William D. Deveau*

There was no paper in my time. I'm not too old. I'm seventy. That's not too old. I bet that maybe the richest ones that lived down here maybe had the paper once in a while. There was nothing like the *Cape Breton Post*. The only paper we had was the *Dr. Chase Almanac*. We never used to have any Christmas cards. Maybe two or three cards. I remember my uncle sent me one. Well, look, I had that card in my clothes box for I don't know how many years.

And when we used to have oranges—it was *so* rare. I remember we used to go to picnics. Under tents at the church. My mother and my brother and me. Before we'd go in the picnic ground, we used to meet the orange papers. You know, the orange papers that were kind of gallivanting to the wind. And we used to jump on them and smell them and say, "Oooh, doesn't it smell good." But there were no oranges in them. We weren't without fruit, in season. But no oranges, no bananas, and no grapes. So, before we'd go home, Mama would say, "I'll buy an orange."

She bought an orange. We didn't peel it as we do today. I remember that so well. Mama made a hole in it. Then she kind of squeezed the orange, took a little, then she gave it to us. One after the other, we had each our turn. I used to squeeze and get the juice. My lips were so sore. Then I used to pass the orange to my brother. Okay, my brother had a suck for a while. Then he'd pass it back to me. We were walking from the church. We had that orange all the way home.

When we got home Mama would say, "Now, don't throw that orange away. I'm going to make you some drink with it." There was the peeling and the pulp. She used to cut it in little bits. Then she took that orange peeling and put it in a jar with water and sugar. She said, "Now, it won't be ready for fifteen days or three weeks." But once in a while, I used to beg her to go with the spoon to taste if it was getting strong. Well, after a few days it *was* getting to have a good taste.

So, nothing was lost. We got that drink and what was left was no good at all. Mama said, "You better go throw it away." It was all soft, and it had given all its strength in the water. And we drank it. And it was good.

Mrs. Willy Deveau.

# Trap Fishing with Mike MacDougall

*Mike and his brother Gabe in the powerboat tow the crew and the rest of the boats out to the fish trap.*

You have to have four boats to do the job. You have the tow boat—some people call it the powerboat—it's the only one that has a motor. It tows the fleet of boats behind. The next we call the door boat because it goes underneath the strongback [the main rope from shore to anchor; see drawing] to pull up your door and close the fish off. The third one is called the cut boat because she's the one that all the men go into and cut the twine around [haul up netting into the boat, making the trap smaller] and bring the fish around to wherever they're going to be taken up. The dory is something a fellow like myself has to have for rowing around, seeing to this or that—then if you need her, placing her onto a strengthener in a corner to pen off fish.

To get ready for mackerel season, it's almost a year-round job. You'll put your stuff away the last of August and then come January or at least February, you start thinking about

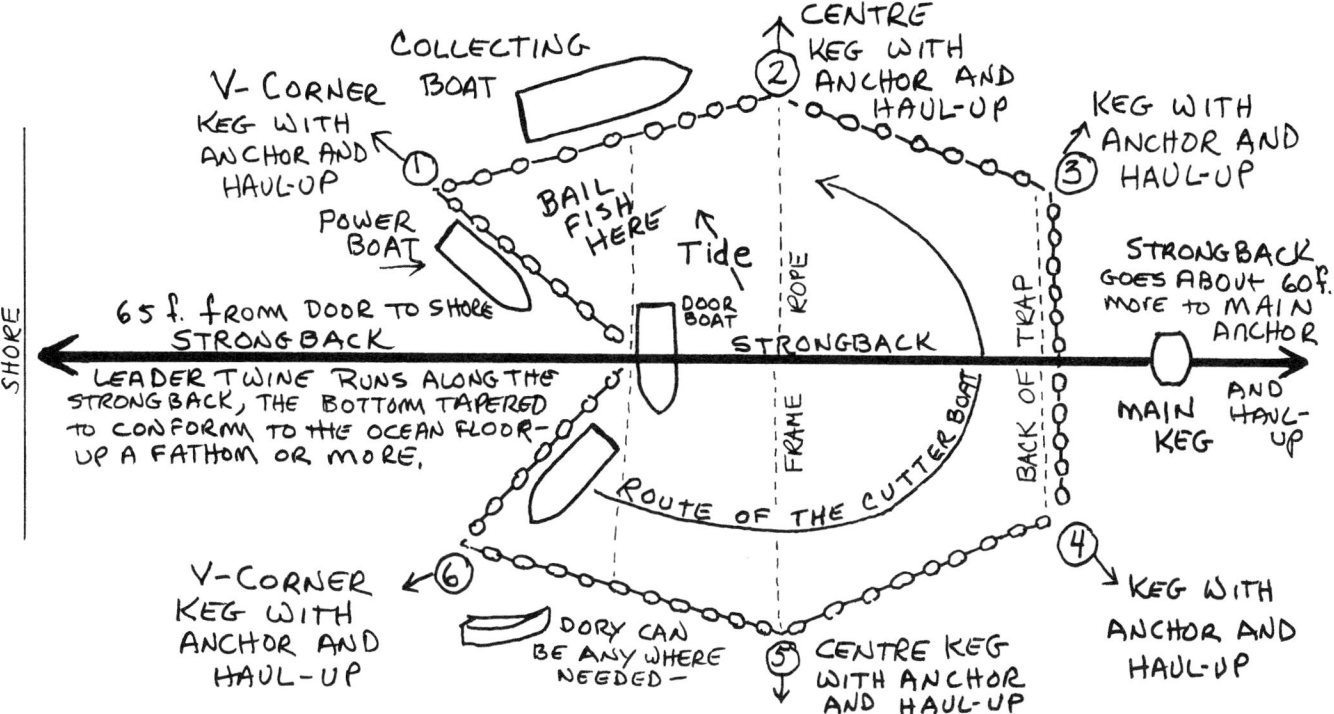

mending the nets. Then when the weather gets fine—probably the last week of April to the fifteenth of May—you can paint and caulk your boats. You want to be ready to set your twine [the trap] by the twenty-fourth of May. This year was supposed to be a late spring. It wasn't. The drift ice stayed around till just about lobster fishing time [May 15] but I'm sure there were mackerel missed here. They figured the mackerel would be late because of the drift ice, but they were here about the twenty-seventh or twenty-eighth of May. You can count on their coming. You hear that they're getting them in Hubbard's and Lunenburg—then Petit-de-Grat and L'Ardoise. Within the next two days after L'Ardoise you're going to get mackerel here. Definitely. You're not going to get a big catch. You'll start probably with two or three. They call them the leaders. Next thing you know you're in the thousands.

And winds are very very important. Mackerel is a windward fish. They go against the wind. And to get mackerel coming in along the shore you need the westerly winds—winds off of the land—the northwest winds or the southwest winds bring them on the shore and hold them on the shore. If you get easterly the fish head into it and they go out and down outside and you miss the bulk of the mackerel. And in the fall

*The door boat, cut boat, and dory under tow.*

straight out off of the shore with this rope with a main anchor on the end. That anchor is much heavier than any other that goes on the trap; it holds all the strain of everything. You go out first sixty-five fathoms—and that's where your leader mesh [net twine] will come out along the strongback to the door of the trap. Then you go another ten to eleven fathoms—and that's where the back of your trap will tie on the strongback. And back of that two more fathom, you have what we call the main keg. The strongback ties on the keg, is cut, and

*Below: With the anchors already set out (see drawing) the trap and leader are loaded aboard and taken out to the fishing grounds. Bottom: The trap is tied onto kegs.*

they make the return trip—but they don't take the exact road back. Mackerel, in the fall, are a hooking fish. You can jig them. Nobody has tried to trap them then. See, the difference in the fall and in the spring—mackerel is a schooling fish. They are a surface fish, on top of the water, schooling a lot. A fine evening you'll see the water black with pods of them. When they're coming back in the fall, they don't school. You have to use what we call tollins or pogey—people often grind up mackerel and mix in salt. When it hits the water the salt'll take it down quicker. That attracts mackerel. Then there's this: in the early part of the year, right from the time you start getting them in May, up until about the fifteenth or twentieth of June, mackerel has the eye completely covered with a scale. The first or second week of fishing you see the scale starting to leave the corner of the eye. It'll gradually come right off. By the end of the season they know where they're going, and they're a lot harder to trap. And that's when they can see the jig.

The first thing you do is tie on your strongback—it's about 115 fathoms of heavy rope. You tie that on the shore and go then ties on the other side of the keg—then runs out about another sixty fathoms from the main keg to the main anchor. You set your main anchor—and on the claw you have a haul-up, a rope with a big ball float onto the end of it. It's a trip line for tripping your anchor. We take hold of that haul-up and pull it out as tight as we can get it with the boat. Then you come back in and put a tackle on between the strongback and the main keg—and the boys haul on that tackle till we get the strongback singing tight like a fiddle string.

*Part of the crew hauls the gate boat along the strongback rope, while the trap is put overboard.*

Next, we use a set of frame-ropes [see drawing], half-hitched onto the strongback so they are divided in half. One goes where the back of the trap will finally be. One goes where the door will be, and one in the center. When you go out to set your anchors, you throw the keg to two men in the dory and they tie the end of the frame-rope to the keg—and you steam out with the haul-up until everything comes just tight—not singing tight—then you drop your anchor. Each anchor has a keg and a haul-up [1, 2, 3, 4, 5, 6]. Your haul-ups vary according to the depth of the water. If you've got thirteen fathom of water you put a haul-up onto it of fourteen fathoms. We call the keg ropes the moorings. So there's a keg at every corner, center kegs and a main keg. And with the frame-ropes you've got your kegs pretty well in position, so when you set your trap you're not going to have too much pulling and tugging to shape it.

You bring your twine [net mesh] out and start tying it on. It will shape up into a diamond-shaped trap. Your finished trap has roughly sixty-two to sixty-four fathom of twine around. When you get the trap set you take the frame-ropes out. And your trap is simply a room—a floor underneath with walls surrounding you. It is open at the trap door, about six to seven feet wide. It has a bar, a piece of pipe—sometimes they fill it with sand. It goes right to the bottom. When you're fishing, the first thing you do in the morning, the men in the door boat hook the strongback with a gaff and bring it over the bow of the boat. Then they have to haul her in as close to the door as they need her. They tie the door boat onto the strongback.

*The trap begins to take shape.*

*Trap Fishing with Mike MacDougall*

When actually fishing, the powerboat does not go over the trap. The other boats are cut loose and allowed to drift over. A man in the door boat gaffs the strongback which is raised and the boat drifts under it.

Below: The door-bar is hauled up, closing the trap. Bottom (left to right): The wall of the trap is hauled up into the door boat; Mike takes the dory over the trap, watching for fish as the trap gets smaller; Mike signals to the collecting boat to come in, there's fish in the trap.

*Leaving a man or two or in the door boat, the rest of the crew get in the cut boat and continue hauling in twine, pursing around, the trap getting smaller and smaller.*

Then they bring the ropes from the door around the bow and the stern so they can haul the door bar up on the inside of the trap. You get that up and tie it in the door boat. Then you're ready to purse your trap.

They start hauling as much twine as possible into that door boat. They take an awful lot of twine in. And they have what they call strengtheners—a piece of rope tied onto the twine that runs from the corner down the mesh a piece. They have to take all this twine into the boat so they can get hold of this strengthener. There's three men on each end of the boat. They each get to a strengthener, get it tight across from the kegs [1 and 6]—and they take a piece of rope—we call them stops—and tie it on. I put the power boat at the corner where the fish will be gathered and tie on to that first strengthener [1]. That will pen off the fish when the men cut it around. They just keep on pursing, hauling twine into the boat—and the next thing you know each group of three men has another strengthener coming from the next kegs [2 and 5]. They pull till they get these tied. Then they both get their third strengthener. They are taking up the whole bottom of that trap, plus the walls from this side, into that boat. When those six strengtheners are tied into that door boat, and they've got the bottom leads in over the gunwale of the boat—all but one man leave and get into the cut boat—and they are going to cut all this twine right around [see arrow showing the path of the cut boat]. If there's any fish in the mesh, they'll shake and clean her out, taking the net in and shoving it overboard, and it's going underneath the boat.

*Trap Fishing with Mike MacDougall*

*Top (left): The trap is so small fish begin to come up with the net. They are shaken back into the trap. Above: Mike has gone aboard the collecting boat. A portion of the trap has been taken aboard and tied. The men in the cut boat continue pulling in twine, drawing the cut boat to the collecting boat. Right (top to bottom): The bailing net is sent out, dipped and hauled back aboard the collecting boat.*

*The collecting boat has left with a hold full of mackerel for the fish plant, and the trap-fishing crew heads back in to Ingonish.*

They have to cross the strongback, put it over the boat and take a rope from the strongback and tie it on the cut boat. They give themselves lots of slack. But if there's any wind or tide, this rope keeps the cut boat from going down on the door boat and beating your boats up. They keep cutting as far as they can get twine, pulling it—driving the fish to the corner where the collecting boat is. We purse with the tide and we put the collecting boat to where the tide is going. The collecting boat takes up a V-keg [a corner keg] and a center keg. Then he takes all the cork [floats] between them and ties it along the rail.

Then the collecting boat sends out a bailer—just a scoop that would hold about eight hundred pounds of fish. And as they bail out the fish the boys have to draw that twine in more, get it singing tight again, to keep bringing the fish up so they don't go too deep for bailing. When we finish bailing, the collecting boat cuts loose, drifts away with the tide. When it's clear of our moorings, he starts his motor and he's away. Then the boys untie everything and throw the twine over and the trap is set back again. It falls into the right place. The fellow left on the door boat has all this time been letting his twine down. Now he unties his stops and lets the door down.

Good mackerel fishing—25,000 pounds would be a small day. That's a man with two fish traps. Two fish traps for the first two weeks, if things go right and you get the right kind of weather and wind, you could easily land 100,000. I've had in three days 101,000 on Monday, 105,000 on Tuesday and 109,000 on Wednesday for a total of 315,000 pounds for three days. The biggest catch of fish that ever was weighed in this harbor in mackerel—I can't go back to the days of haddock—I had it in 1974. I had 114,985 pounds—one day. In 1970, which was the crack year, I had a million and 35,000 pounds of fish for the month of June to the fifteenth of July. We had two traps in the water. We had two collecting boats—good service—but the two boats couldn't handle what we were taking out of the two traps. They could just look after one. The other trap below was loaded every morning and every evening with fish—and we just had to let her sit there most of the season.

# Red Dan Smith Makes Rope from Wood

There are very few men who know how to make rope from wood, and there are even fewer who would bother to try. Red Dan Smith of Jersey Cove, Victoria County, is one of those who has had actual experience making and using wood rope, and continues to make it. "I call this curiosity work," Red Dan said, twisting wood strips into the beginnings of rope. "When father made it it was not made for curiosity as this is made. I made a lot of it with father. Every spring we made rope moorings for the nets. March and April. Ten, fifteen fathoms for the harbor. Outside, they made them twenty-five fathoms long." In Red Dan's time this seems to have been the one use for rope made from wood: as moorings to hold the nets, one end of the rope tied to a *kellic*, an anchor made of a heavy stone affixed into the fork of a tree.

It looks quite simple, watching the rope being made. But that simplicity is deceptive. According to Red Dan, here's how it's made.

Go to the woods and find a *perfect* piece of yellow birch. The right one will be straight and without knots—about four feet long—and the grain will permit you to pull off long, thin strips of wood, one right after the other—and they'll run off three to four feet long, and between an eighth and a thirty-second of an inch thick, and from three-eighths to an inch wide. Perhaps the hardest part of making rope is finding that tree. The old fellows used to sit with the birch across their knees and a pocketknife in their right hand, holding the wood steady at the center with their left. They'd use the knife to start the strip at one end, catch it with their fingers and draw it off to the center, exchange hands and let the right hand hold while the left pulled the strip off the other end. Dan Smith uses a vice to hold the wood and works standing up when pulling off strips.

You pull off one strip after another, and when you have a batch you bundle it together and tie it with a strip and put it aside. You can work a piece of yellow birch six or eight inches thick down to perhaps one or two inches. When it got down that far, some men would start a broom, running the strips only two-thirds of the way along the wood and leaving them attached. Then they would turn them back and tie them. And many women still remember taking up one of those bundles of wood strips and using it with soft soap and salt to scrub a wood floor.

*Red Dan twisting rope into wood, a board at his foot on which the rope is wound, a pail of water to keep his materials damp, a bundle of wet, wood strips ready for twisting-in underneath him on the bench.*

But we're making rope. For equipment you'll need a sturdy bench to sit on, a piece of plank about a foot square to tie the beginnings of rope to and to hold firm with your foot, a bucket of water to soak your strips if they are dry, a piece of plastic to cover the wet strips which you sit on on the bench, pulling them out from under you as you work—and a piece of wood perhaps three or four inches long and whittled to a point on one end to push through the ends of the rope for "finishing." That's all it takes—that, and powerful hands. Because the trick is to twist and twist and twist—not turn but *twist*—keeping a firm grip at all times so that it does not unravel and watching every inch of the way so that you bury all loose ends in the center of the rope and maintain a constant thickness all the way along.

You start making the rope by twisting together five or six strips—really quite roughly—the idea being to have something you can tie around the board and leave an end free. This piece will stay on the board. It will never actually become rope. It is the place where you start the rope. Each time you make rope you will begin at that piece, twisting in fresh strips. And each time you finish you'll cut away what's made, leaving behind the old piece tied to the board.

And that's how it is done—twisting—adding one strip after another, trying to keep five or six strips *of different lengths* going at one time, gripping it tight with thumb and forefinger and inching forward, twisting fiercely with the right and constantly watching for the time to bury the shortest strip or to add a new one. You keep your foot down hard on the board, the twisted piece taut along your leg and over your knee—now

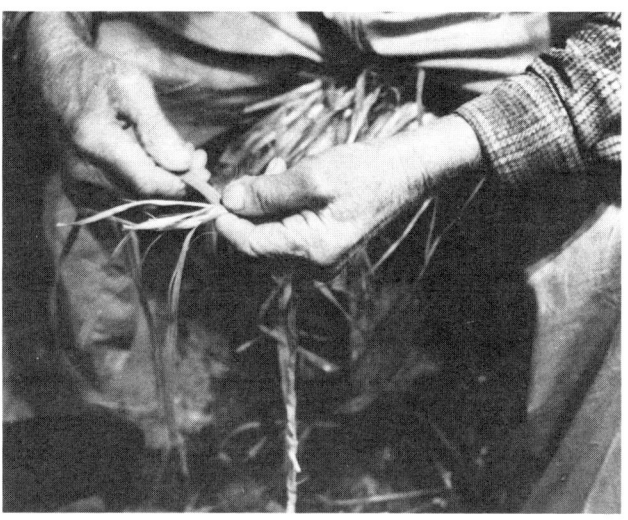

*Fitting a strip of wood into the rough beginning of a rope.*

*Both hands twisting the strips together.*

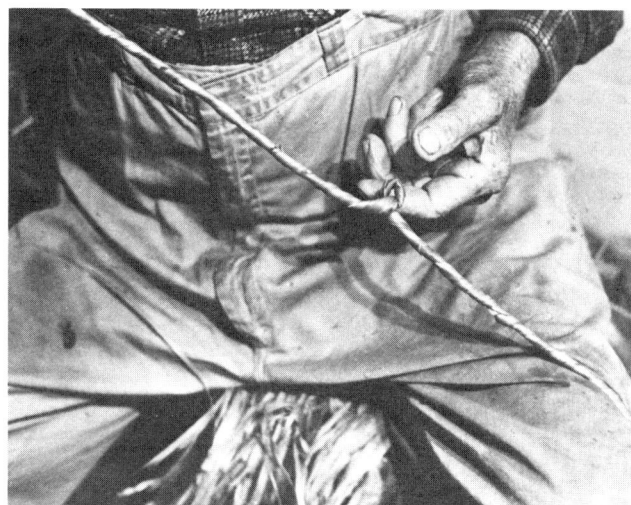

*Turning back, the beginning of doubling the thickness.*

*The rope is now two thicknesses.*

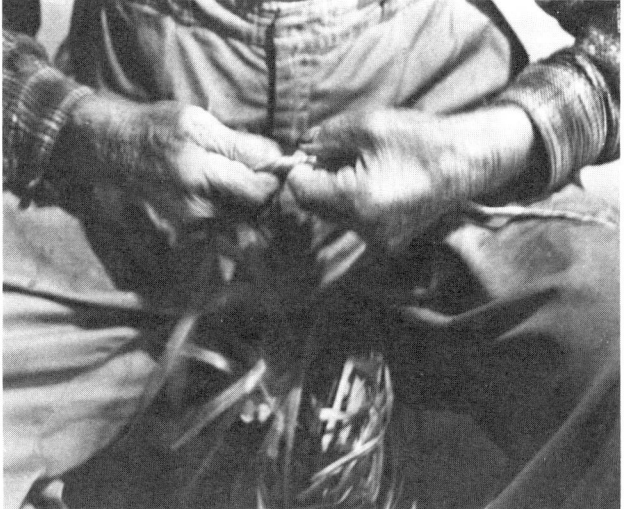

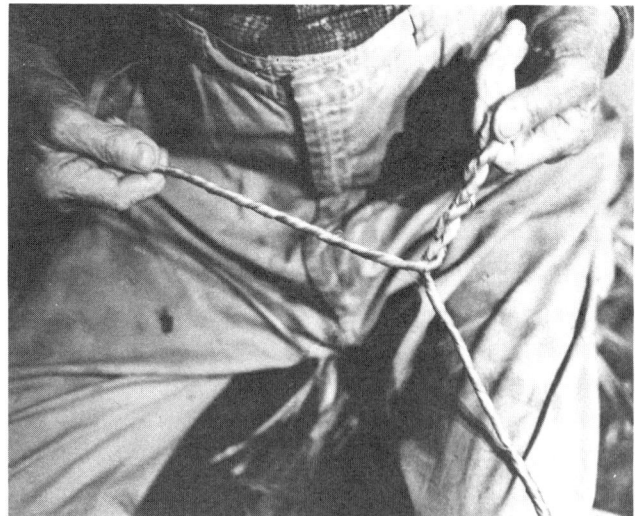

*Red Dan Smith Makes Rope from Wood*

*Turning back again, the third thickness is made and twisted into the rope.*

*The end of the rope is forced open for finishing.*

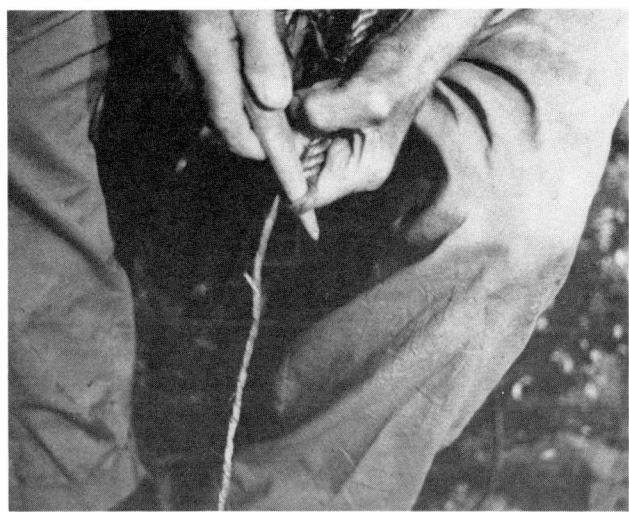

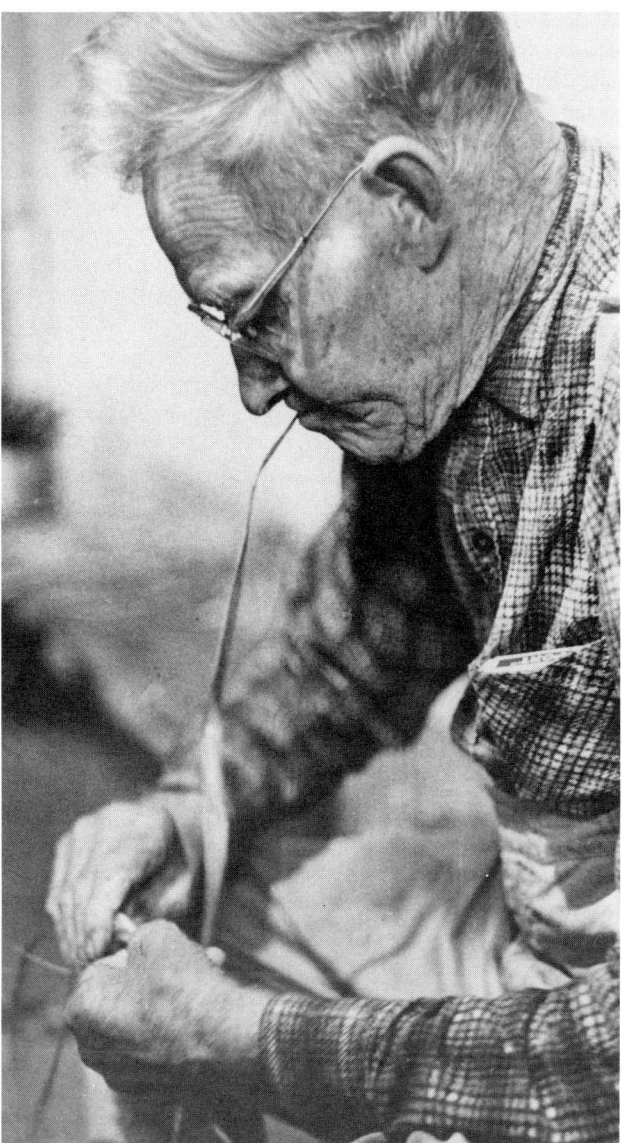

and then turning the board over to wind on and take up slack. And soon you'll have four or five feet of line—you could as well have one hundred feet—if done right it will all be about the same thickness.

This line is only one of the three lines thickness you'll end up with. Because you now turn back, working in the direction of your twist so as not to unravel, winding into a single strand of two thicknesses. But notice that you are not simply winding, you are still twisting and using the tension of each twist to get the strands to grip one another. As you double back you will also stop now and then to add strips on. And you are doing it in a way that keeps everything taut, nothing unravels—which seems impossible without three hands but can be done. And done so neatly that the turns will all be the same length.

Your third strand will come from the few feet of line you were winding on the board. It has to be twisted into place along the other two. Try to remember what rope *looks* like. "Just put it in so it'll be in its right place," Dan Smith said. "Loosen it so it'll fit and keep it tight enough so it'll fit." You are *not* setting strands side by side. You are working the third line in so that it is slightly grabbed by the twists of the first two strands. Remember: it is not three separate strands but one strand with a terrific amount of twist in it, turned back on itself and twisted (so that you have hard twists pushing in opposite directions and thus gripping one another), then turned once again—the "third" strand being twisted against and slightly into the groove of the first two strands, making a powerful piece of rope. You finish off with the whittled piece of wood—forcing an opening at each end and pulling the single strand through—twisting it closed and tight again. Cut away from the board and trim off any loose bits. "The length doesn't matter, only time. I can make a foot of rope in about fifteen minutes, but if I've got to make a hundred feet it will take me some days to make it."

The finished rope is amazingly resilient, and is three strands with only two raw ends. It is said that one would last a man two season's fishing. Some say that they could be tarred and made to last much longer but Dan Smith doesn't think there was much of this going on.

*Mary and Red Dan Smith, Jersey Cove.*

# A Visit with Jack Sam Hinkley

I'll tell you about a fellow one time got in contact with a bear. There was a man down here, down in the lower part of the settlement here—a bear came and killed his pig. And they set a gun. Ever hear about setting a gun for an animal? They fix a gun up—make a house and put a gun into it—aimed about the height a bear would be—his breast, you know. And then they had an old muzzle loader—balls in her, I suppose—and they had a string from the trigger of the gun and they had a bait tied to the string. When the bear'd come in and give a jerk on the bait, he'd put the gun off and kill him. Anyway, the bear came in in the middle of the night—and the gun went off and it hit him in the hip—broke his hip. Well, there was a bunch went down. And there was a man down here, Sandy Moore, a big husky man, and he was scared of nothing—not even scared of a bear. A fellow had a gun there. The bear was up on the hill and he was going to shoot the bear. And Sandy Moore said, "No, no, don't shoot him at all—I'm going to kill him with my bare hands. I read in a book, a magazine," he said, "where an Indian tackled a bear. He killed him with his bare hands. Said he got his hand in his mouth and choked him by the tongue—and I'm going to try it." So he did. He went after the bear. He had a little stick and he hit the bear on the nose and this made him mad and when he opened his mouth Sandy Moore drove his hand in to about the wrist and he got the tongue and the bear got him by the wrist and away they went, down the mountain, the two of them, end over end. And this is true because there was a man there when it happened told me, and he wasn't lying. Alex Timmons. Down the mountain they went. And they couldn't shoot the bear. They were frightened they'd shoot Sandy Moore. And the bear chawed him on the legs and arms, chawed him real bad. And there was a Fraser fellow—Duncan Fraser—he had a great big stone and he watched his chance and he struck the bear on the side of the head and he kind of knocked him out—and they got Sandy Moore clear of him. Now wasn't that a terrible trick for a man to do? And that's a true story.

I ran the mail to Cheticamp with dogs. I mushed her with snowshoes and dog team when there was no road. Only a little trail. In the summertime I used a horse, horseback—the trail wouldn't be cut out any more than six or seven feet. Not that. In the winter with dog team and snowshoes. Dog sleigh. Oh,

yes. I had most Newfoundland dogs. I had one Great Dane, female, around eighty-eight or eighty-five pounds. I had five dogs, I think. Always had a spare one in case there was something wrong with one. Generally only take four. The first years I ran it all the way through from Red River to Cheticamp. Then the last two years I ran it halfway—a Frenchman from Cheticamp would meet me with the mail and take my mail the other way. He'd have two of my dogs and I'd have the other two—and then I could be home every night. I ran twice a week. I started on the first of April in 1919 and I ran it till the last of July in 1923.

Spring—that's the worst time of the year. Half the road would be bare and half snow on it. It was hard for the dogs to haul the mail. And you couldn't get through it with a horse or anything. The month of April was the worst month of the year. The month of April and the month of December I found the two worst months. December days were short and the weather was dark and overcast and snowing all the time in December. Three o'clock it's coming dark some days. And it'd get dirty. I was out in a snowstorm it was snowing a foot an hour. Made it—but that was all. You couldn't stop, once you were on that road—you had to keep going. There wasn't a farm between here and Cape Rouge. I stayed at Aucoin's. Oh, I had a nice place to stay. Nice clean bed to sleep in and plenty good food. Aw, they were lovely people. Makes me lonely going by that Cape Rouge yet—they're all gone out of there. Park [Cape Breton Highlands National Park] drove them out. Anyway, I'd come back fresh the next day. Walked on snowshoes. The dogs when it was good going on the down grade, I'd ride on the load—but most of the time I walked. Lots of times I had to break a road ahead of the dogs with the snowshoes. And when crust was on it I'd have to have a shovel and sometimes shovel a path for me and the dogs to get through.

And summertime on horseback and these corduroy bridges —you know, poles laid on the mud—maybe the poles would be broken—well, if he'd go down two feet in that you'd think you were never coming out of it if you were on his back. But I liked it all right. Yeah. I wish I was smart enough to do it again. I'm going on ninety. I was born February 19, 1888.

I used to trap all over these mountains—halfway to Ingonish. My father used to trap way back there. They used to call it the Everlasting Barrens back there. I don't suppose you ever heard anybody talking about the Everlasting Barrens. That's the highest place in Cape Breton. My father used to trap there and when he didn't feel like going I'd go out with another man. We were able to catch martens that time, and lynx and foxes and weasel—you'd do all right. You'd get ten or fifteen dollars for marten at that time—be as good as 125 dollars today. That's seventy years ago. They were quite plentiful. Have three or four every trip you'd go out. Metal traps for martens and weasels and lynx but the foxes you generally caught in snares on the river. In the first of the fall you'd have a log on the brook and the fox would cross on the log and you'd have a snare on it and you'd get him. Sometimes get a lynx that way too. You'd want bait for the marten—use rabbit or any kind of bait. They're easy to trap, the marten— right easy to trap. I don't think there's any anymore. If there are you don't see any of them. Ever see one? Aw, they're beautiful little animals. You saw minks? Well, they're bigger than a mink and they have orange on their throat—bright orange strip. They're the prettiest fur that's going—the marten. They kept way back in the heart of the country. It was no trouble to clean them out. They were so easy to trap.

Stayed in a camp way back there on the barrens. Made out of logs and we had birch bark on the roof of it. Tight. It was great. Yeah. With one of those old fashioned box heating stoves. Oh, it was great. Perhaps you'd be out there three days. A day going out. And then the next day all day and perhaps the third day you'd come home. Three days on a trip. Loved that. Better'n a trip to New York.

Used to hunt caribou back there too. Yes, lots of them. My father—many's the one he killed. Haul them out of there on a hand sled—tabagin—in the wintertime. It was against the law doing it but he used to do it. Not a toboggan, no. A toboggan is right flat, turned up in the front. A tabagin sleigh has runners and it's quite light and the sides came together flat and you could carry it under your arm. And my father could make them great, boy. When you wanted to use it you could square

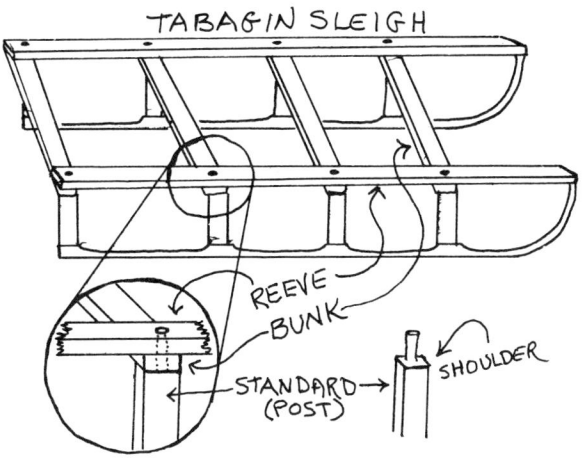

JACK SAM: Tabagin sleigh. You could carry it under your arm. There were three beams into it and the beams [the bunk] were on standards [the posts]. You'd have three or perhaps four posts. The post would have a collar so the bunk wouldn't go down. Then you'd have the reeve fit over that. The bunk has a hole in it—inch or three-quarters hole—and the top of the post had a kind of pin that goes up there through the bunk and the reeve. The bottom part is the runner. I suppose it's four inches wide and where the standard would be, about an inch thick. It would thin out to about half inch between the standards, to make it light. You see, there's nothing to keep it from coming right together—pull one side back and the other ahead and it went flat. When you wanted to use it you could square it out and tie two little pieces of wood—little spruce or hardwood—tie them on across the bunk to keep it straightened.

*Bernard G. Hoffman in his excellent thesis on the Micmac Indians, goes to some length to show that there is an important difference between* tobakun *("sled") and* tobakunas-kool *("sleds with broad bottoms or 'toboggans'") and what LeClerc (1691) called* tabagannes. *Perhaps in the form of this light, collapsible hunting sled Jack Sam has saved not only a name but the basic structure of this tool.*

it out. When you're hunting caribou you'd have two or three of them. When I was a kid there'd be three or four hunting in a bunch—maybe kill six or eight. Have you ever eaten caribou meat? Well, you'll never eat meat like it in your life. I ate moose meat and deer meat and there's nothing like caribou. They say it's something sweet on the barren they eat that makes them taste so good.

You'd clean the caribou right there. And if there was a lot of snow on you'd skin him and quarter him up and you'd dig a hole in the snow away down and put some perhaps boughs underneath him; then you'd pack him down there and put some boughs over him and cover him with snow. Then you'd put a flag on a tree or something—so you wouldn't have trouble finding him. Sometimes you'd save the skin but it wasn't very often you would bother with them. The hide wasn't much good, to tan them. The water would go through it just like a piece of rag. No good for leather. Sometimes take one in to dry it and clean it to have in a sleigh—an odd one. For a seat of a sleigh. But the bloody hair would come out. Worse than deer. They have been gone a long while. Since sixty years the last caribou was killed that I know of.

I've seen myself eight or nine in one school. But I heard my father say he counted forty one time, long years ago.

*A Visit with Jack Sam Hinkley*

# A Milling Frolic on the North Shore

*The milling frolic has played an important role in the survival of Gaelic songs associated with that event. Weaving as a necessity went out as soon as inexpensive factory goods were readily available. The old looms which took up a room in themselves, went on the rock pile or into the fire—very few were saved—and most of the weavers were grateful to be free of them. But the milling frolic continued in form at least—organized for tourists or for Cape Bretoners home for the summer. An old blanket would be milled over and over, and the community hall would be used instead of a home—but the songs were to be heard as beautiful as ever, and people had a chance to gather together. But we wanted to experience a traditional milling and neighbors along the North Shore set up the one shown here. Josie Tommy MacDonald offered her home and Gwennie Pottie supplied newly woven cloth. Neighbors donated the traditional foods—salt herring, blue potatoes, oatcakes,* bannoch *and strong black tea—and they sang and milled and had a meal in the harrow in a home for the first time since 1939.*

JOHN ALEX JOHN X. MACDONALD: You'd hear songs in the homes. Yes. My father was a great singer, and he had a wonderful memory. Everybody talked about him even after

*Neighbors at the milling board, pounding cloth and singing Gaelic songs.*

*Three of the North Shore Gaelic Singers: John Alex John X. MacDonald, Thomas A. (Tommy Peggy) MacDonald, and John Shaw.*

he was dead, you know. He'd remember everything. And if he'd go to a milling and hear a song for the first time—he'd sing the whole thing for you the next day, and just heard it once. Sing every verse of it. As far as singing is concerned, it was quite common to go to three millings a week. I was to four millings one week. And the homespun was five times as hard to mill as the blankets—the blankets were light, you know. They used to have some millings in the daytime and there'd be nobody there but women. And there were so many women then that could sing, beautiful singers and a lot of songs—no end. I remember millings right in this house—and the house was packed tight. They'd be in the kitchen—the harrow [milling board—*cliath*] would be right here. And people sitting around the room, and upstairs. And where the beams are cut there for the stairway, my father was quite nervous one night—there were so many up there in the hall there, that he was scared that the header would give way with the weight that went on it. But it didn't.

My father would be sitting there where the cat is there. He'd be so tired every night he'd be there—but if we'd start singing a song, part of one we'd heard at a milling—he'd start over there and he'd finish it off—perhaps there'd be thirteen or fourteen verses. So there was no trouble to learn. He had them there in bushels. He learned songs though I don't think he ever composed any. But he told me one time there was a milling up at Donny's place and he was only fourteen— and boys of that age were to be home at ten o'clock. Up till eighteen or nineteen you weren't out on the road, you were home. Really they were too young to go to the milling. They walked three miles. They went to the window to look in. The window was up—the house so warm and a big fire on. And there was a fellow there singing a song that Murdoch MacDermid had composed from Wreck Cove. He made a song for a girl he had been going with and she had been in Boston and when she came back she had lost her Gaelic—it's in the songbook here—and my father outside the window. He had heard the tune but never heard the song. He told me himself that when he woke up in the morning, he was lying in bed, and

*Left: Gwennie Pottie wrings out her newly woven blanket, preparing it for milling. Middle: Murdoch MacAskill, another North Shore Gaelic Singer, leads a song. Right: Jessie Mary MacLeod with a traditional oatcake, made simply of standard oats, a little salt and shortening and baking soda, and just enough lukewarm water to mix it. It is shaped gently by hand, never with a rolling pin, to about a quarter inch thick—and it gets about half an hour in the oven at moderate heat. It's not supposed to get brown like other bread.*

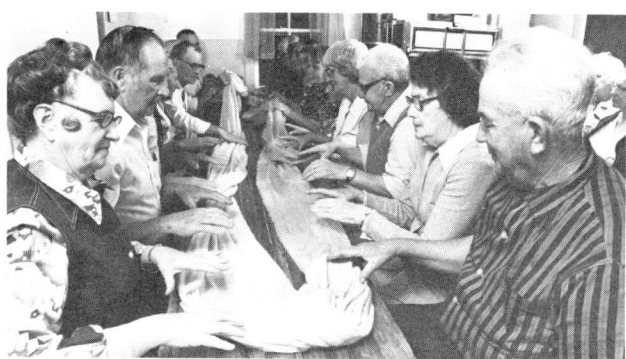 

*Above: In the early portion of the milling the cloth is taken up and passed along, gently brushing across the grooves of the harrow in rhythm to the song. Right: Thomas A. MacDonald in his fish shed at the shore.*

he had the whole fourteen verses. Now I couldn't do anything like that. My father at ninety, when he died—two weeks before he died, if you came to the house and asked him to sing a song he would, he'd remember it that well. If there was anyone to sing the chorus, good and well; if not, he was going to sing it for you anyway.

I don't think they'd be singing anywhere else, only in the house. But I heard Malcolm Angus MacLeod talking about it up in Ontario. His father was a beautiful singer and his mother was still better. And they both had songs to no end. And he said there used to be this composer—this Norman MacDonald, he used to go to visit there—come in and have a smoke and then start singing songs. And it was quite common, he said, to sing for two hours, one after the other, one after the other. His mother would sing a song and his father would sing a song and this MacDonald fellow would sing. Most of the good singers learned the songs from end to end at home, from their parents. And that Norman MacDonald was pretty sharp, you know. If anything would happen, you know, he'd make a song. He made a song once about a milling frolic that was up the road somewhere, one fellow wanted to have a girl friend. Anyhow, I think what happened they all piled on the sleigh and when they were going down the road the sleigh broke and the horse ran away—and that was enough to start a song, you know. And he made another song, I don't know it, but I heard it sung, of fellows that used to trap out in the woods and they went out—R. J.'s father and another Urquhart, he was my uncle—and they were supposed to have got lost out in the fog and snowing and what-not—and pretty hard up before they got back. They had some dogfish out there for bait. Dogfish, you know, it's not edible as far as we're

concerned. But they used to take it ashore and split it up and dry it and take it out to the woods—use it for bait for lynx traps and the like of that. So the grub ran out on them and as a last resort they had to start eating the dogfish. And it was put together good. I know only three or four verses of it. How the events happened, how they got lost and all.

THOMAS A. MACDONALD: The custom was to have the cloth—the blankets and the homespun—soaked in warm water and oatmeal. I don't know why the oatmeal. Then when the crowd came, they'd bring it out—they wouldn't wring it out dry at all—just dry enough so it wouldn't drip on your knees. And then as the milling went on, after three or four songs, the water would be pretty well out of it. And they'd come around and sprinkle more water over it.

In some instances, like down at Wreck Cove where they had a regular milling board, with the big grooves, they used to have that and put it up in the different places where they'd have millings. But in most places all along here the people that were going to have a milling would always have lumber and make a milling board themselves. These would not have grooves. There weren't too many of the ones with grooves. They were just milling boards made on the same principle as the old time homemade washboards, ridges in them. That was the idea of it. It would mill the cloth more uniform, better. If you have a bunch of smooth boards on the milling board, well, if they wouldn't be good old-time millers on it, they'd just swish the cloth along and it wouldn't have too much effect on it. The old-time millers, they'd usually start off by giving it a light pounding first, give it a hit and pass it, rub it along, passing it to the next fellow, he'd do the same—and that was bringing

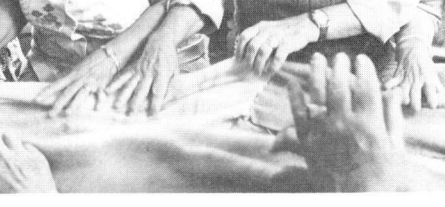
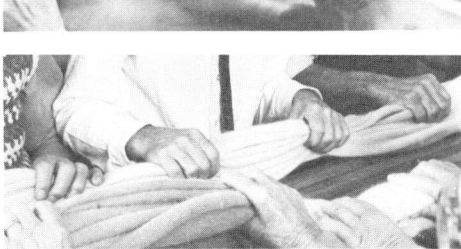
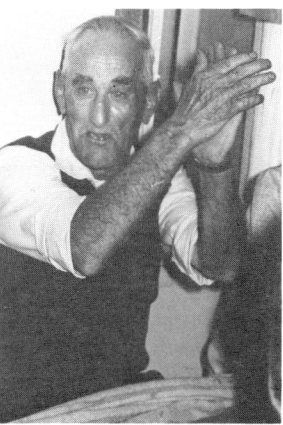

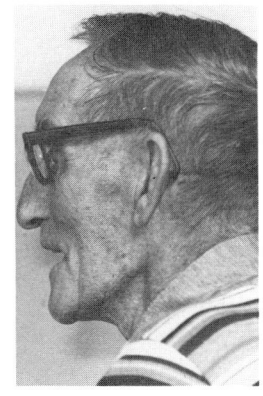

*A Milling Frolic on the North Shore*

the nap out and shrinking it. And then when they'd come to the last part, the finishing it up, they'd just hold it in their hands and pound it on the table—not pass it along at all, just pound it—that really shrunk it, you know, that last going off. I think the idea of not giving it too much pounding in the start, it would shrink it too much in a hurry and not bring the nap out.

*Who would make the decision to change from pound and pass to holding it in place and pounding it?*

Well, the fellow who was leading the singing. When they'd get to that point, he'd hang on and then everybody would hang onto the cloth and pound and pound it instead of passing. No one would tell us. He'd just hold tight and that was the signal.

The table would be set up in the kitchen. The milling board was always put in the biggest room. And in some instances, I didn't see too many but it was quite common—when time came to have something to eat—usually the milling tables were pretty big because they'd all have a long piece of cloth probably—you'd have probably ten or perhaps twelve on each side of the milling board—and the women would tell them to have a rest, we're going to eat. They'd take the whole thing to the milling board, take the cloth away, and they didn't have to move out of there. Very often they'd have baked beans, sometimes potatoes and meat, potatoes and fish—but very often a great big pot of nicely baked beans. Eat it right at the milling

*Rolling milled cloth.*

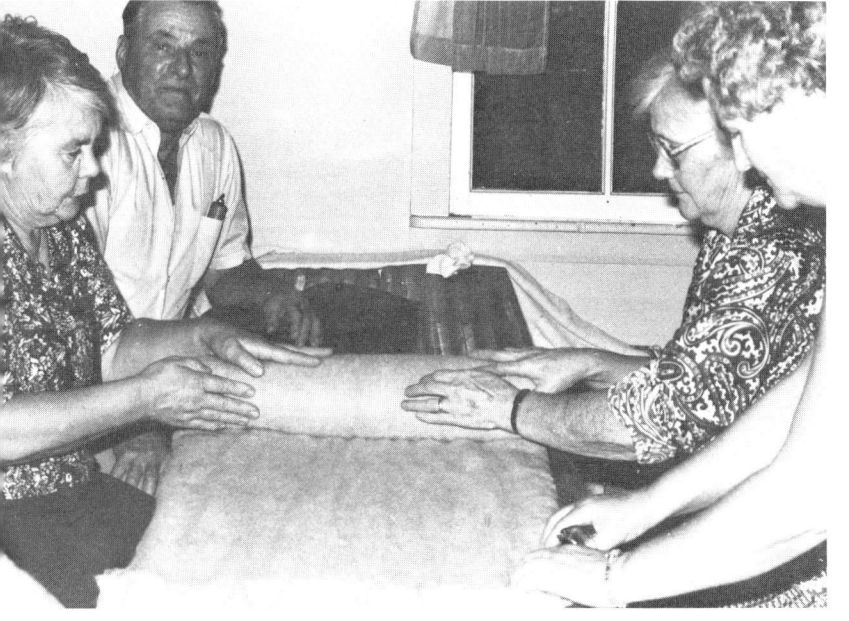

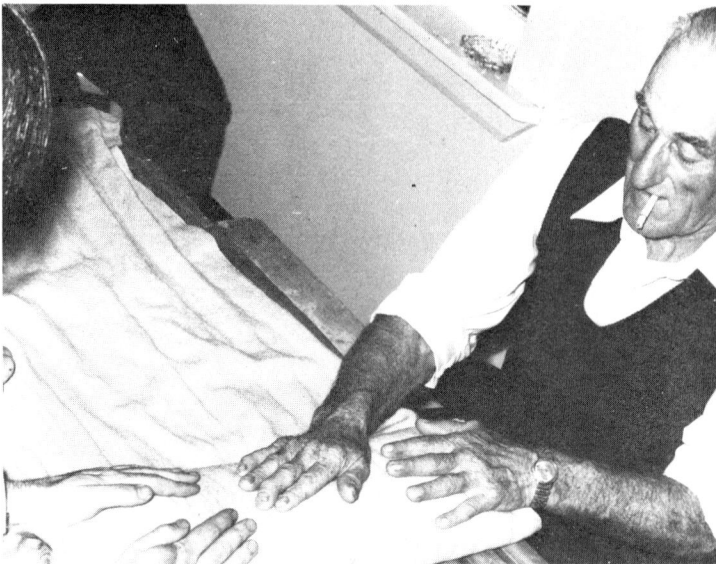

*John Shaw shows how the hands are held when slapping the cloth, driving the water out.*

board. Biscuits and perhaps brown baked, Boston baked beans—brown bread. Then when they'd be through, another bunch would sit up to the milling board and have a feed.

Milling would start in some cases very early in the evening—and usually some of the women would have perhaps thirty yards of homespun. That is for trousers and jackets. And that required three or four, perhaps five hours of milling. And then perhaps thirty or forty yards of blankets, which didn't require so much milling. In that case they'd very often have to start four or five o'clock in the evening in the fall of the year. Getting dark then, you know. And that would continue on till sometimes two and three o'clock in the morning. Because that old homespun, boy, required a lot of pounding and milling. Heavier stuff. When that was milled, it was that thick and stiff you could almost stand it up on the end. Great stuff. But the blankets, you know, I think the women watched that pretty closely so you wouldn't mill them too much—around an hour or a little better than an hour.

And millings were so common then. I remember the only time I was ever away from home working was in 1924—and I came home in November. And my mother had been weaving I guess most of the fall. I don't know just how much she had woven. And we were supposed to have a milling the following week. I came home on a Monday, and the following week there were three millings, and all in the same district. And the next week the same way, two or three millings. That went on

till perhaps the latter part of December and it had started perhaps in October. Because everybody was weaving and they wanted to get the blankets milled. That was the pattern: probably every second household had their batch of cloth to be milled.

After you finish milling, there'd be two fellows get on one end of the milling board, two on the other end. The cloth was one long single strip, just as it came from the loom. If it had been sewn together at the end for passing around the table, it was taken apart for this. But very often where there was a great bunch of millers they didn't need to sew the ends together— they'd just watch for the end and pass it. Anyhow, they'd stretch the blanket out, and then just roll it up tight on the table—fellows on one end holding it back tight and the other two fellows rolling it up tight, right up to the finish. Then, when that was done, they turned it sideways, two strapping

*Left: Gwennie with her finished cloth. Top: Talking at the milling board, waiting for a meal. Above: A traditional milling frolic meal served in the harrow: salt herring, blue potatoes, oatcakes, bannoch, and good strong tea.*

fellows now, one on each side of the board. Each gave the roll two or three whacks from the center out. Then they unrolled it some—perhaps three or four feet—did the same thing—all the way till the end—just driving all the water out of it. And that finished it. After that they'd be washing it.

The same principle finished off the homespun. Roll it up right tight then start to unroll it. Two fellows, one on each side, banging it as they were unrolling it, and that would be it— two o'clock in the morning, sometimes quite a lot later than that. See, the women were pretty meticulous about that. It

*A Milling Frolic on the North Shore*

had to be shrunk to a certain width—I think it's twenty-eight inches or twenty-seven was it. And it was pretty hard to get to that last going off, because it was shrunk so much. But some of them insisted it had to be shrunk to that—keep singing, milling—three or four o'clock in the morning before they'd get it shrunk enough to satisfy. Kept measuring—a *cromadh*, they called it—that's the measure. That meant from the tip of the finger to the knuckle. Most of them figured that, I think, as five inches. The one that owned the cloth would do that measuring—her finger. She had to be the boss to see that it was done to her satisfaction. Even if somebody else thought it was pretty good, if she didn't think so you'd have to go at it again. Three or four o'clock in the morning. And we wouldn't think anything of it then. And there was such a lot of them, you know. It would be hard work with that heavy homespun, swinging that around, perhaps a fellow would have a song with twenty-five or thirty verses in it—by the time that would be finished a fellow's tongue would be hanging out.

*But you wouldn't think of not going?*

Oh, no. We'd go. It was great fun.

*And all you got out of it was a plate of beans?*

Plate of beans. Lots to eat, whatever they had—they always had lots to eat. If the milling was going on later than the usual hour, they would come around with tea perhaps one or two o'clock in the morning.

And you know, that song John Shaw sang the other night at the milling [at Josie Tommy MacDonald's, French River]—I haven't heard it since years and years till he sang it that night. That was the song they would sing when they were rolling the cloth. The singer started off, and he'd sing the chorus: *O co chuireas sinn anns an luing Eireannach?* Oh, who will we put in the Irish ship? Then if there were nine or ten around the milling board, you'd start at one end. Like if I was singing it and John Shaw was sitting there, I'd sing: It's John Shaw that we'll put in the Irish ship. [*Gur e John Shaw chuireas sinn anns an luing Eireannach.*] After that comes: *Cò fear tè òg a theid ri thaobh anns an luing Eireannach?* Who's the young girl that we'll put there with him on the ship? Then name one of the girls at the milling board, that she'd go with him. And it follows all around the milling board. One fellow would name the girl and the boy and all the rest would take in the chorus. We used to call them "Oran Leannanachd" [Courtship Song]. I remember when there were two or three of those kinds of songs. And some people would take offense if you'd name them and name a certain girl to go with them. Perhaps some fellow would do it for devilment. If there was a young fellow and his name was mentioned, then when it came to who were they going to put with him in the ship—perhaps they'd name an old crow of seventy or eighty years old. Used to get some of them wild.

# Hilda MacDonald and Glendyer Mills

I was born right here in Glendyer on November the ninth, 1885—the same year as the C.P.R. was born. My grandfather [Donald MacLean MacDonald] came here from Pictou County. And his grandfather [Donald MacDonald of Kilmorack] came from Scotland on the famous ship *Hector* in 1773. I suppose he was a crofter, likely. But my grandfather—his grandson—apprenticed, when he was a boy, to a miller and learned the milling business from the bottom up. At that time Cape Breton hadn't anybody to as they say "dress" their homespun. They would do the weaving but they hadn't anybody to dye the material for men's suitings and so on, or to press it. And they had to go to the mainland of Nova Scotia to get anything like that done. So they were writing and beseeching the people there to find somebody who would come to Cape Breton. My grandfather had apprenticed in Pictou County but he came to work in Antigonish County, just outside of Antigonish in a place called Trotter's Mills. Mr. Trotter had so many letters, he

*Hilda MacDonald in her garden at Glendyer.*

*A view of the mills at their height.*

said to young MacDonald, "Why don't you go to Cape Breton?" So he came here on foot, prospecting for waterpower—because it had to be waterpower. He walked all the way—crossed of course on a small boat at the Strait of Canso—walked all the way up the coast. He found some power in Judique. But he decided to keep on, and he came to the mouth of Mabou Harbour and followed the river up, walking up and up and up, until he came to a division—one stream went to the right and one to the left—and he decided to follow the one to the left which brought him to what later became Glendyer. And that was in 1847.

He found suitable waterpower. Next was to try to buy the land. This was dense woods here. And it was owned by a local gentleman named Mr. Smith. One of the early settlers. And he had a large family. He didn't want to sell really, but finally my grandfather persuaded him. He came back the next year and with him came two bachelor brothers and an unmarried sister and they started operations. They had to start from scratch. Absolutely. Out of the woods. They built a log house—and my grandfather used that log house until all the family were born—six altogether. One of them died when just a small boy. He was engaged to be married when he came—he was established in '48 and he was married in '49. That was Nancy. She was a MacDonald too. When his wife came his sister went back to her home. And I think by that time both brothers had gone. So it was just the young married couple—Donald MacLean MacDonald and his wife Nancy. Pretty much alone.

I think the mill they built first was the dying mill, and in association with that there had to be a mill where woven material was put through a process of thickening—they call that "fulling" or "milling" or "waulking." That's the very same thing as a milling frolic. They'd wet the material and soap it and pound it—and it would get all thick with a nap on it. And they also did carding. People would bring their wool and they had a machine that would card it, and the wool comes out in rolls. Makes it easy for the women who were doing the spinning. And then later—soon too—he built a gristmill and a sawmill. There's a hill over here—I'm probably the only person at present that calls it The Sawmill Hill. Though I never saw the sawmill. It was gone a long long time before I arrived on the scene. But the sawmill was at the base of this hill, on the water. All those things were run by water. And the shingle mill. There were two dams. There was one above the bridge—the railway bridge goes right over it—and there's still tiny traces of some of the old logs. And then the other one was farther up. And every night, one of the chores—I can see my father's partner, he'd go up every night—he would go and shut the water off so there'd be a good head the next day.

*Hilda MacDonald and Glendyer Mills* **25**

26  Hilda MacDonald and Glendyer Mills

As time went by they couldn't depend on water so they got a dynamo, and they created their own electricity. In latter years it was all coal. The coal was hauled in by teams from Inverness, before the train came. Then when the railroad came through after 1900, there was a siding at the mill and the coal cars would be put there. My grandfather came when he was twenty-three and he died when he was forty-one—and he built those six mills. And his first and only frame house—that was his home. He died in 1863—so that frame house must have been built in the 1850s. *Must* have been. Because he was a sick man for some time before he died. He had a heart condition. And Nancy—she had to take over. She was a busy woman. She was a great lover of flowers, the garden—and in order to keep her garden she had to get up at four o'clock in the morning and she'd garden for an hour or two before the day began. She never went away without bringing back a package of plants—that's what they call "slips." She had to take over. My father was just sixteen when his father died. And he had to become a grown-up man immediately. Under his mother's guidance they carried on the business. She was just a young woman, you see. She'd only be the same age as her husband. He was just forty-one when he died.

People would come from all over Cape Breton, even from Newfoundland. And this was called The Dyer's Glen or Dan the Dyer's Glen. And grandfather just transposed the words and named it Glendyer. I can remember the mills that my father and his brothers operated. My grandfather never manufactured woolen goods. He just processed, you see. But his sons began manufacture. And so they built quite a large mill—one big building—and they didn't do any of these other things—grinding or sawing—they just went in for woolen manufacturing. Blankets, rugs, suitings. That mill was burned around 1880. And they rebuilt one which was operating until the works closed down, in 1913. Altogether, there'd be twenty-five or thirty people working here at one time. There were men with families, some unmarried men and quite a lot of unmarried women who were weavers. The weaving was entirely mechanized. And oh, yes, there was a sound to it. All those machines. The mill was built on a sort of side hill. The looms were below the ground. On the first floor were the carding machines and the office. Then on the next floor were the spinning jennies. To begin with there were the spinning jennies—Arkwright's machine—and then later on there was a similar machine which they called the mule. They began work at seven o'clock in the morning and they worked till six, with an hour off at noon. They all lived in the glen during the week, sometimes they'd go home for weekends. Today, just two families live in the glen all year round. Last winter there were fourteen people—eight of them children. There would have been sixty or seventy when I was small. Four houses are gone now completely. And the wool—nearly all was from local people. They'd come in with their wool and sell some of it, and some of it they'd have carded and take it home as rolls to be spun—and the rest of it they would sell. They came from all over Cape Breton. And they were paid in cash, not by barter. This was the first industry to do this.

The mills closed because shipping became too expensive. To begin with, in the early days, in order to ship their

*Nancy MacDonald.*

*Opposite (top left): A view inside the loom room and (top right) a view of the upper dam. Opposite (center and bottom): samples of fabrics woven at Glendyer. The spinner seated at the back of the sheep is the symbol of Glendyer, indicating wool so pure it was right off the sheep's tail.*

*Monument honoring the Glendyer pioneers.*

*Donald MacLean MacDonald.*

materials out, their finished goods, they had to ship it by stage from here to the Strait of Canso—forty miles by stage. That would be expensive. Then as time went by a railroad went through Cape Breton called the I.C.R.—the Intercolonial Railway. And there was a station at Orangedale—about seven miles out of Whycocomagh—and that was only twenty-five miles. So then the goods were shipped to Orangedale and that was a little less expensive. And then at the beginning of this century this little line was pushed through to Inverness. The Inverness and Richmond Railway. They could load their material right down here at the station. But that wasn't inexpensive either, because if they shipped from here they had to pay two freights. They had to pay the freight on this line, and the freight on the line that took it over on the other side of the strait. So it was an expensive operation from the very beginning. And then my father died in 1910. He was just sixty. The operation carried on till 1913 under his partner, who was not one of the family. His name was Macdonald too. But he spelled it *M-a-c* and a small *d*.

# A Céilidh at Malcolm Campbell's

MALCOLM CAMPBELL: Did you ever hear any stories of this one had a charm for taking the milk from her neighbor's cow? Man, you haven't lived. Say now Sadie there had the charm and our neighbor had a cow down the road; maybe two or three cows and we would have one. But our cow would be producing more milk than all these three because we'd be getting the milk from our neighbor's cows. And apparently the old women who had this charm—I never heard tell of a man being able to do it—it was always women that were supposed to be witches or something—they would go May

*28  Hilda MacDonald and Glendyer Mills*

Day—first day of May—borrow something, and whatever you do you weren't supposed to loan them anything because then they would surely take the virtue from your land and from your cattle. They would take the good from your land and from you. She would get the benefit of whatever you were doing. Particularly your cattle. And they used to tie a red string on the cow's tail to combat this, so that they couldn't take this from you. There was a family—two or three old women over at Margaree—I often heard my mother talking about it—and the boys would be going just for hellery and cutting this thing off. And every time they'd do it the next time you'd come the cow would have the red string on again. But these women were supposed to be witches themselves. I remember them telling this story about this one: They sent her to the store—to the market—with butter and the merchant wouldn't take it, said she had more than her own and he wouldn't take it from her. There was this fellow was taking her butter on horseback, and he had his own. And he had a bag slung across his saddle, if he had a saddle. And as he was going along, her package of butter was getting heavier and heavier and he had to put stones in the other bag to counteract the weight of it.

HELEN HOWATT: They claim that these people who were supposed to have the witchcraft, one of them in particular she went to this house on the first day of May to borrow and she asked for various things and they said they didn't have it. And she was so chagrined on her way out she picked up a handful of earth off their farm and she went with it. She was determined she was going to have something.

HUGH MACKINNON: I only seen one thing... Donald John MacMullen's Bonnie L., you know the horse, he was stretched out behind the barn and Donald John came after my father and of course I had to go. And they were having confessions in the house—there was a lot of old women there—and he told Donald John, "Wait till some of them leave the house till I get down with the horse." "Ah, you needn't, she's dead." Well, my father went down, he went around the horse two or three times, he looked at him—the horse jumped up to his feet, start eating hay. For two days he wouldn't move. And old Archie MacInnes the same thing, when I went with my grandmother. But she went on her knees and I don't know what she was saying. The third time...

HELEN: Did she have silver in a dish?

HUGH: Yeah. The third time the horse...

MALCOLM: Water out of a running brook and some silver...

*Malcolm Campbell today (left) and (below) at his family farm at Woodbine when that place was an active farm community. Pictured with Malcolm are his uncle Peter Campbell, his mother Jessie, John Archie MacInnes and Malcolm's sister Helen (Mrs. Helen Howatt). The horse's name was Lynn and the dog was Pal.*

*A Céilidh at Malcolm Campbell's*

HUGH: The third time the horse jumped up to his feet. The third time she went on her knees, Jesus, the horse jumped up. But he didn't thank the old lady.

HELEN: No, no, no.

MALCOLM: You weren't supposed to thank them. That would spoil it.

HUGH: But I believe it's all fake.

HELEN: They maintained in those days it was a Godgiven gift. Everybody didn't have it.

MALCOLM: Now you know there were people in our community if they looked out at your horse or your cow and said that was a fine animal, would say, "Well, God bless him." That was to ward off the curse in case he had the evil eye and didn't know it. Otherwise the next day the animal would be sick.

HELEN: And with your children as well.

HUGH: But just the same, I went over to John Hayes' and the three-year old heifer was dead stretched out in the field. I said, "Jesus, John, take a walk"—and I went and got my jack-knife and I went to the ear. The heifer jumped up. For Jesus' sake I took half of the ear off him with the knife. "Thank God, thank God you were here to cure her." "Cure her nothing," I says. Be Jesus when she was an old cow you could see her ear split. But my grandmother done that to Archie's horse. And Mrs. MacAskill, Malcolm. Old Mrs. MacAskill. John Alex' horse in Salmon River. I went on a Sunday for a string and went back to the camp and tied the string on the knee kind of tight. In the morning the string was down and look the knee was all right. Now what are you going to do about that? But on your life with these fingers [the forefingers and thumbs] you tied the string. You wouldn't use any of the other fingers. The horse's knee was way out—okay in the morning. But where did it all go? I don't know.

MALCOLM: It's just like a lot of the fish on the fishing ground. When the people stop fishing there's no fish there. I heard this now in 1937. They used to fish off Port Hood Island and Henry Island. And there was an awful lot of fish, everybody was fishing. And the reason somebody told me that there's no fish is there's nobody fishing, there's no bait on the grounds. So why were the fish going to congregate there? Then the few that were fishing were going there and they weren't getting the fish they were supposed to get. It's the same with other things, like seeing things, like forerunners.

HUGH: I'd like to see my own forerunner. I'd get the hell out of there right away.

MALCOLM: But it might take years. There used to be a theory if you saw this forerunner early in the morning it was going to take a long time but if you saw it late in the evening it was going to happen very soon.

HUGH: Old MacLean on this day was haymaking, raking near the door and she seen this ball of light coming, fell right at the door, right alongside of him, and she started to cry. He said, "Don't cry. You may be ahead of me." It took twenty years, Malcolm. He died ahead of her yes. But it was a forerunner. It dropped right near the man's toe.

SADIE CAMPBELL: They used to claim it was coming from the grave.

HUGH: It's only a ball of light, you know. A big ball of light.

SADIE: With a tail.

MALCOLM: This light would go in the direction of the graveyard or come from that direction and stop at this man's house. One ball of light and a bit of tail on it.

SADIE: Once it drops on the ground it lights up the whole building on the outside.

MALCOLM: It's an eerie light. You know it's not a natural thing. I have seen one in a house. My sister was with me. We were coming past this house. It was about midnight I guess. It was in wintertime. We had a horse and sleigh. And this was a house where after nine o'clock you'd never see light, they'd gone to bed. We stopped at the brook to water the mare. I looked up at the house and just joking with her, I said to my sister, "This old lady"—her name was Ann—"she must have bridge club or something tonight. The house is all lit up." It was a strange thing because we passed there hundreds of times and they never kept a light.

HELEN: The house was lighted upstairs and down.

*Left: Malcolm and Sadie Campbell. Right: Malcolm at eight or nine.*

MALCOLM: Oh, every window. And you could see, when we were passing—there were barns between us, barns at the road, and when we got past it and were about to turn up our own road, I looked back at the house again and we could still see it. But you could tell that it was an eerie light.

HELEN: And you couldn't see anybody moving in the house. Not a shadow in a window.

MALCOLM: A very short time after that the old lady died and it came a snowstorm. She had a son away and a daughter and they waked the body for four or five nights—maybe they were a whole week, waked the body. And that was a very unusual thing because it was two nights usually . . . and there were lights on every night, all this time. People congregating at the wake. The house was lighted up every night.

HUGH: How long did Margaret Campbell take?

HELEN: Well, you saw the forerunner of her funeral in 1925, June of 1925 and what year did she die?

MALCOLM: She died in 'thirty-three.

HELEN: The forerunner wasn't a light. He saw a horse and wagon coming out of a driveway.

HUGH: The horse and wagon. I didn't know who's funeral, remember. I was as near to it as you are. Right there at Angus MacLean's. And I said to her, "For God's sake, don't say anything. Somebody's going to die at Angus MacLean's."

HELEN: We were coming from a party. It was a Saturday night. We left the dance at twelve o'clock. People were very particular then about finishing up their parties at midnight. And we came up the road and at the end of this driveway he said, "Do you see anything?"

HUGH: I saw the horse and wagon, the funeral procession coming out. I knew everything. I could have put my hand just like that. But I was trying to show her. I knew the horses. And when she did die, these were the horses.

*A Céilidh at Malcolm Campbell's*

HELEN: He counted them when he saw the forerunner and when the procession came out through that driveway my brother counted them too—and said to my mother, "There's the funeral that Hughie saw." But that girl didn't belong in that house at all. That was the strangest part of it. And she was at that party the same as we were and went to Massachusetts and died there eight years afterward.

MALCOLM: And she was brought home and buried from her father's house.

HUGH: Everything is funny. We went into Dan Peter's and he was saying the rosary, Dan Hayes and I. When I went on my knees, right at the door, well hell started upstairs, upon my soul. The noise and shifting and everything. I followed right through and we had a cup of tea and I asked Dan Hayes, "Did you hear it?" "Hear what," he says. "Well," I said, "you were right along side of me." I was in the house when that man was dead, mister, when they were taking him down—and that was the noise. How many years was that?

HELEN: A good many.

*Hugh MacKinnon.*

MALCOLM: A forerunner can be when you see a living person too. A stranger was going to come. And you'd see a forerunner of a stranger. It might have no connection with death at all. I remember Uncle Peter seeing one home. He saw this woman going around the barn. And I don't know how many years afterward this girl came to teach school and she was boarding at our place and she and I were out throwing the ball over the barn, you know, and he saw her running and he remembered that.

SADIE: What about seeing John Campbell?

MALCOLM: Yes. And the man was living and lived for many years. He was a neighbor of ours and my uncle was working over at the barn. He was fixing the barn door. I was with him. I was about nine I guess. Nine or ten. And about three o'clock in the afternoon—mother was in the house alone—and we saw this neighbor of ours going in on the front door. He only lived up the road I suppose five or seven minutes walk. And while my uncle was taking off his shingling apron, I went in the house—ran over to the house, looked into the living room, kitchen—there was no sign of the man and I called to mother. She was upstairs running a sewing machine. Oh she got kind of cross with me, said this man's not here at all. So my uncle came in and he asked me where this man was. "He's not here." "I saw him. He must be here." So he got after me for telling lies. He called her and she came downstairs. And they had an old belief if you saw a man like that, that he was dead. He had dropped dead. Well they sent me over to the house. To see. You talk about anybody being scared. I went and into the kitchen and just sit down long enough to see the old fellow there in his usual place smoking his pipe. They figured I came for something and didn't want to ask for it. So I took off for home boy as fast as ever I could. I told them. They hardly believed me, that he was all right. But that man lived. I often heard my grandmother saying if you *wished* yourself in such and such a place—it was an awful bad thing to wish that I was here or there—because sometimes people had done that and something had happened to them.

And there is another thing: there is nobody very sure about this business of time. Something might have happened a hundred years ago and you're going to run into it today or tomorrow. You can't tell about this business of time whether it's going to stop still for somebody, somebody gets killed here or there and you're going to see this. Maybe that was a re-occurrence of a time when he did come to the house and did come in.

# Mary Ann Beaton Makes Country Cheese

*Mary Ann Beaton of Mabou Coal Mines.*

They don't make so much of it now as they used to. Years ago pretty near every family made so much cheese. There was some sale for it but the price then was very small. But it would help to buy their groceries, I guess. And butter too. They could sell the butter. Cheese just keeps. The older it gets the better it is. Just keep it in a cool place. It'll stand six months. Around November they'd make their cheese for the winter. It was my mother-in-law taught me. My mother made so much but my mother-in-law used to make quite a bit of it. She lived here with us for twelve years or so after we were married. Her name was Sarah Beaton. I try to have six or seven cakes put away for the winter—we call it cakes—just a round block of cheese. We used to have quite a few cows—used to have ten. Years ago they'd have as high as twelve. Right now we have six. My husband and the boys milk them. Then you have to separate the milk—separate the cream from the milk. You make butter with the cream and then you have the skim milk. And you take the skim milk and you put it to one side in a plastic pail or whatever you have large enough to put it in to save it for your cheese. The way it is, you save your cream. Every day you get half a gallon in the morning and another half gallon in the evening—and you save your cream until you have six or seven gallons and then you make your churn. And you save your skim milk. There's quite a bit

of skim milk—perhaps in two days you have enough to make a cheese. It takes about fourteen gallons of skim milk to make an eight-pound cheese. It doesn't have to be all skim milk. I put some sweet milk in with it, you know. Sweet milk is the whole milk that hasn't been separated.

*Apparently the milk changes slightly throughout the seasons. Mrs. Beaton told us that when you're used to it you'll know how much of each to add. She told us that it never turns out the same, not once.*

You take fourteen gallons of skim milk and you let it get kind of sour. You let it sit about a day, two days—you let it sit in its container in an outhouse or in a milkhouse if you have a milkhouse. Not exactly a cool place but on a hot day it gets

*Left: Heating up a tub of soured skim milk. Below: As the curds form she takes them up in a sieve and puts them into a metal bowl to stand. She places a colander in the sink. Then with her hand supporting the curds she gently transfers them to the colander and leaves them to drain.*

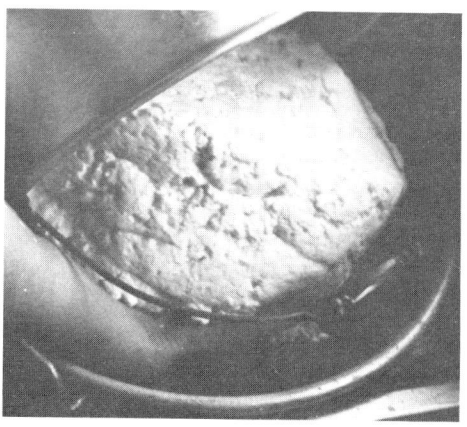

34  *Mary Ann Beaton Makes Country Cheese*

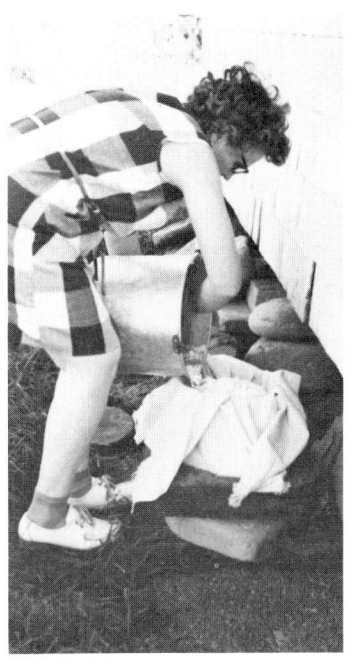

sour faster. When it's cold it takes perhaps a couple of days before it'll get sour. Then you take it in and put it in a tub on the stove and you warm it up—just lukewarm. And you stir it.

*While she stirred, she kept a finger in the milk to test the heat. When it seemed to be getting too hot she moved the tub over on the stove. She didn't want to scald the milk or let it boil. The heat started to separate the curds and the whey.*

Then I always put a little rennet in it. [Rennet is the inner lining of the fourth stomach of calves and other ruminants. Dried extract of this lining is used to curdle milk.] I believe years back they used to make their own rennet. We buy it at the store. The local co-op has it. You put about a tablespoon or two in. Without rennet it doesn't work as well. I've tried it. Rennet seems to make the whey and more curds and gathers it up better, I find. When it's warm you put your rennet in and you keep stirring it and that makes your curds and brings it all together.

*She gathered the curds and took them from the tub with a wire strainer, letting the whey drain back into the tub before putting the curds into a metal bucket. Then she put a metal strainer, a colander, into the sink and dumped the curds in to drain further. She said that years ago they would hang the curds in a cloth and press the sides to help get the whey out. She doesn't collect the whey or make any use of it.*

I find the best way is to put it in the strainer and let it sit there perhaps two or three hours. Then all the whey runs out of it.

*To test it, she pressed a little on top after half an hour to see how much whey would rise. Sometimes she turns the curds over in the colander. The longer it drains the better. If you put it in the press with a lot of whey in it, when you take it out of the press the cake will crack.*

Sometimes it takes longer than others. You know by the feel of it. You let the whey drain out and then it's pretty dry. You can feel it with your hands, if the curds are soft or kind of dry. And then it's easier to salt and put in the press.

You just put, say, a half a cup of salt on a gallon or a gallon and a half of curds—and that'll make about an eight-pound cheese. You shake the salt on and you mix it all up, sort of like when you're washing butter. You just squeeze the salt all through the curds, you know, with your hands. Then you add a little more and you squeeze it all through the curds. And you add a little more salt until you think you have enough—about half a cup I would say. Some like it saltier. [She used fine fish salt, breaking the curds up very small.] Then you'll put it in what we call the press and you'll put a weight on it and you'll leave it there for a day and a night. Then the next day you take it out and you have your cake of cheese.

*Mrs. Beaton has her cheese press set up at the side of an*

*Mary Ann holding a finished cheese.*

outbuilding. It consists of a level stone on which she places a bucket or pot with the bottom removed. This is the mold. She put a flour-bag cloth into the mold with the bottom spread flat and the cloth coming up and over the sides. Into the cloth she poured the fine, salted curds, pressing the curds down evenly with her knuckles. Then she gathered the edges of the cloth up over the top of the curds. She had a wood top cut small enough to fit down into the mold, and she placed this on top. Then she added two bricks and another piece of wood so that the whole thing came up almost to the height of the sill of the building. Then she slipped a long board under the sill and down on the mold, the board sitting there pretty much level with the sill. Then she placed two heavy stones on the far end of the board. The pressure drives down on the curds, forming them into a cake of cheese and squeezing out the rest of the whey, which runs out the bottom of the mold. Mr. Beaton told us this is far better than a screw press, which is only as tight as you screw it down. The sort of press the Beatons use gives the same amount of pressure even as the whey goes out and the curds get more and more compact. After twenty-four hours they will put the cake of cheese in a cool place. If there are no flies around, it is just as well to leave it bare. It can be eaten right away but the longer you wait the better. The older the cheese gets the more the sour taste will wear off and it gets a better flavor. Mr. Beaton said that cheese can spoil if it's kept too warm. But he added that "after a while it will turn green. Perhaps in one or two months. Sometimes it never turns green. And sometimes you'll think it's spoiled when it's green but that's when it's really getting good."

# Lee Cremo and Scottish Fiddling

*When we talked with Lee Cremo he had been back a few days from The Old Time Fiddler Contest in Shelburne, Ontario. He placed fourth out of 132 fiddlers. We wanted to know, among other things, how Lee Cremo, a Micmac Indian, became a great Scottish fiddler.*

I was born December 30, 1938, at Barrahead. When I was about three or four we moved to Eskasoni. I went to school there as far as fifteen years of age. Then I quit school on account of my father had a stroke.

The question I get asked the most is how did I become a Scottish fiddler, and the answer is I got started with my father. All his life he was a fiddler. He started when he was five. He was forty-nine or fifty when he had the stroke. So the fiddle was there, nobody was using it. I never played the fiddle till my father had the stroke. I played the guitar. But I knew all his tunes. We were living in the same house, every time he takes the fiddle I hear the tune. After a while, I'm playing by ear.

I don't know how my father got started on the fiddle. I

*Mary Ann Beaton Makes Country Cheese*

think Father Soniay, something like that, gave him a lot of boost. When he was a kid, living up there at Barrahead. Chapel Island they call it today. Father Soniay was doing parish work there, and Father MacLellan took over when Soniay left. And he knew a lot of Scotch music. He got sheets and books from Scotland. So he taught my father. He didn't teach him notes but he taught him tunes.

My father built the name Cremo, not really me. He played all over the island and Nova Scotia. He used to have a basket and he sold tickets. Put the tickets in the basket and he'd give you a tune. He'd do that at every house. So everybody knew him. He'd play right in the house. Every child knew him. Sometimes he'd get to a house and stay overnight; the mother and father would go out and he'd stay and keep house for them. So the children knew him, even the dogs knew him. I used to go with him sometimes. He'd know the names of the dogs. He'd never make a mistake on the name of a dog so he must have known people real well.

I don't think I'd want to play door to door the way my father did. The only way it would pay for me is that I would get a lot of practice. Some people today they still say your father was way better than you. I have to admit he did a lot of practice. If you walk all over Richmond County, every house, play ten to fifteen tunes at each one—that's a lot of practicing. One month one place, another month another place. So I have to admit if you play ten thousand tunes in two weeks there must be good in there somewhere.

Another fellow who taught me, gave me a lot of boost too, that's Prosper, Wilfred Prosper. He was a next door neighbor in Eskasoni when I was up there. A *really* good boost. I'd go up to his place in the evening and wouldn't come out of there till nine, ten the next morning. Play all night. Me and Prosper, he was along side of me. We had two fiddles and what I didn't know he'd teach me, and what he didn't know I'd teach him. He taught me a lot of things. I don't *know* if I taught him a lot of things. But I tried anyway. I have to shake his hand, he gave me a lot of boost.

So my father taught me a lot and Wilfred taught me a lot, and I learned a lot listening to Buddy MacMasters—a hard man to beat. I think he's from Judique. There's another fellow who's good—made a lot of tunes—Dan R. MacDonald. You can get a lot of tunes from him. I'm not saying I'm depending on them, but I catch on their tunes. I don't try to copy anybody. The things that come to my head I play. I play them the way I think. I could be making hundreds of thousands of mistakes in one tune but that's the way I feel. It's just

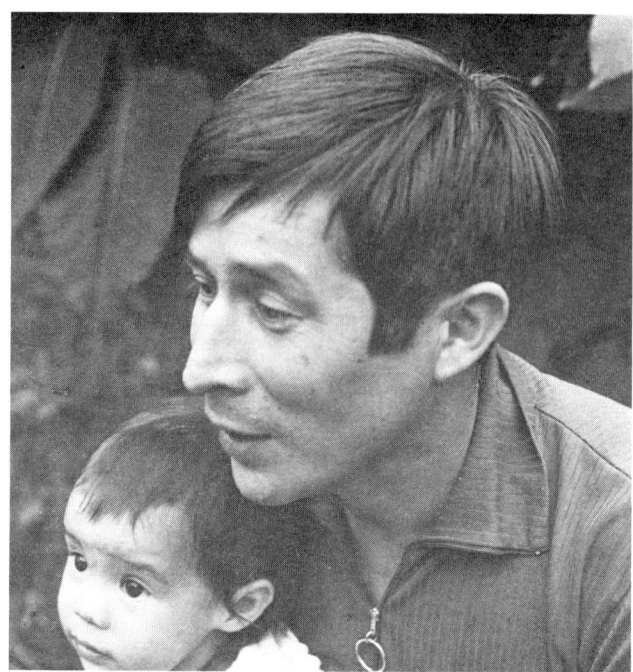

*Lee with his father.*

the way you feel the way you play. This is my style. The only thing I don't play too much is slow airs. I don't think I'm qualified. That's for a concert fiddler. I'd just make a mess out of it.

Cape Breton Fiddling is really quite hard, perhaps harder than any other. I would say it's coming from the bow, the bow thing—it's not the fingers but the bow—it's more difficult than anything. Like—how can I say it? You shiver that bow at the end, try to get that dadada-dum. That's the hardest thing. You have to judge if you're da-dadadum, if you put seven you're out of time. It has to be five or six, in between. But some of them have eight beats, they have triple, double and triple beats. That's why it's hard to play this kind of music. You have to hear a lot. It's like a language. If you hear a strange language it's pretty hard for you, but after a while if you stay with them you speak it. It's the same with Scottish music. It's hard. You'll never learn in one year. You have to be almost born with it. Or surrounded like where I lived. It's all Scottish. Everywhere I go I hear the tunes.

And there's a music you could call Micmac music. They don't use any kind of instrument. They just take a little piece of stick and they tap on the bottom of their sole. There's good rhythm to it. That's why I think today when I play a reel, a Scottish reel, I make it a little faster. I think it's the Micmac rhythm. Indian music you can step-dance to real good. You have to use both of your feet in the same way. If one foot is delaying the other you are losing your timing on the music. Same goes for step-dancing.

Now, when I make a tune I never try to use Scottish or Micmac tunes—I think what comes is a different thing all together. I've had different styles. I'd take it a little slower but they didn't seem to go for that. I'd put it a little faster. Another time I put it really tremendous fast and nobody could go for that. This speed I have now—I think it's the speed, not the fiddling—it's the tempo of the tunes they go for. You can mix them with the older people and the younger people. They seem to love it. We get a full house for dances, a good clap at concerts. The audience gets excited. They shout for tunes. I like that. When you're on the stage sometimes you've got a blank mind, really. You don't know what you're going to play. Then somebody hollers and that gives you a lot of boost.

You know, I'm a carpenter. I went to school for it at Eskasoni. Right now I'm a full-time fiddler, but I'll be a carpenter again. There's only so much time a fiddler has. A good fiddler you'll find between twenty-one and fifty-five years of age. That's when a man makes his sweetest music. That's how I see it. After that your bow arm's gone and your fingers are getting numb. So you start losing.

It's not that the spirit isn't there. I got a lot of spirit. If the world was like this I'd be going till about two hundred, playing till two hundred. I'll still have music up there in my head. But I won't be able to produce what I want. The reflexes will be slower. The timing, I'll lose the timing. The only thing I'll be able to do is listen.

# Deux Contes Merveilleux pour les Enfants

*by Sophie Deveau*

## Le Conte du P'tit Coq P'is d'la P'tite Poulette

C'était un p'tit coq p'is une p'tite poulette. I'vivint ensemble dans un p'tit hangar, sous les arbres dans les champs. Mais là, l'hiver s'en v'nait p'is il allait faire frette. Une journée le p'tit coq dit à la p'tite poulette, "J'crois que j'devrions nous faire chacun une maison. Nous viendrions nous visiter pareil, mais nous aurions chacun notre affaire."

"Ah! mais," a'dit, "tatbein!"

I'dit, "Moâ, j'va'faire la mienne de pièce su' pièce, avec des rouleux d'boâ." I'fut dans l'boâ, i'coupit du boâ rond, ôtit l'écorce p'is i'fit une belle p'tite maison.

P'is la p'tite poulette a'dit, "Moâ, j'va's pas faire la mienne de même." A'dit, "J'va's faire la mienne d'épingles et d'aiguilles, en laissant les pointes en l'air." A'fut au magasin, achetit ses aiguilles p'is ses épingles. Quand le soleil se levit, ça brillait, c'était joli.

Toujours, une bonne journée, i'v'là un gros t'ours. Ah! pour l'amour! I'fut su'l p'tit coq en premier. I'dit, "Ouvre-moâ ta porte ou bi'n don' j'va's t'manger!"

## The Story of the Little Rooster and the Little Hen

There was a little rooster and a little hen. They were living together in a little shed, under trees in the fields. But now winter was coming and it will be cold. One day the little rooster said to the little hen, "I think we should each make a house. We could visit anyway, but we could have our own life."

"Oh!" she said, "Maybe!"

"As for myself, I'm going to make mine a log house." He went in the woods. He cut some logs, took off the bark, and he made a beautiful little house.

And the little hen said, "I'm not going to make mine like that. I'm going to make mine from needles and pins, sharp ends up." She went to the store, bought some needles and some pins (and built her house). When the sun rose, that was shining and pretty!

Then, one fine day, a big bear came. Oh! for the love of...! He went to the little rooster's first. He said, "Open your door or I'll eat you!"

"No, no!" he said, "I won't open my door."

He said, "Open your door or I'll pull it down, and I'll eat you."

"No, no," he said, "I won't open my door."

"Oh!" he said, "if you don't want to open your door, I will go up on your house, I'll make 'caca' and 'pipi,' a lot of noise, and I'll pull it down and I'll eat you."

Oh! for the love of...! The little rooster was very upset. While the bear was climbing up, he went to warn the little hen. "There's a big bear at my house!"

He got inside just in time. The big bear came! "Open your door!"

But she thought of the needles and pins. She said, "No, I won't open my door!"

He said, "Open your door or I'll climb up on your house, I'll pull it down, I'll break it, then I'll eat you."

But as he was going up on the house, he was stuck and scratched and went wild. All those needles and pins with sharp ends up hurting him. He told them, "Come pick me up!"

"No, you wanted to eat us, we won't pick you up!"

He tore himself all up, and by and by he pulled out his insides. He went to the woods. They found him, a couple of days after that, dead. He had lost all his blood!

*Sophie Deveau of Cheticamp.*

"Non, non," i'dit, "j't'ouvrirai pas ma porte."

I'dit, "Ouvre-moâ ta porte parce que j'te defoncerai p'is j'te mangerai!"

"Non, non!" i'dit, "j't'ouvrirai pas ma porte."

"Ah! bi'n, si tu veux pas m'ouvrir ta porte, j'va's monter su' ta maison, p'is j'ferai du caca, du pipi, p'is du bruit, p'is j'te défoncerai, p'is j'te mangerai!"

Ah! pour l'amour! Il était manière de mal, le p'tit coq. Le temps qu'i'montait, i'partit, s'en fut avertir la p'tite poulette, "Y'a un gros 't'ours che' nous!"

I'rentre mais tout'suite v'la l'gros 't'ours, "Ouvre-moâ ta porte!"

Ielle a'pensit: les épingles p'is les aiguilles: ça pique! A'dit, "Non, j'ouvre pas ma porte!"

I'dit, "Ouvre-moâ ta porte parce que j'va's monter su' ta maison, j'te briserai, j'te défoncerai, p'is j'te mangerai."

A mesure qu'i'montait su' la maison, ça piquait, ça grafignait, ça l'tannait, ça y faisait mal toutes les aiguilles, les épingles, la tête en l'air. I'leu' disait, "V'nez m'charcher!"

"Non, t'as voulu nous manger, on va pas t'chercher!"

I'savait toute déchiré, à force, à force, s'est arraché le dedans. I's'en fut dans l'boâ. P'is i'l' trouvirent après ça un' couple de jours après, mort: il avait toute perdu son sang!

*Deux Contes Merveilleux pour les Enfants*

## Le Conte du P'tit Garçon d'Beurre

C'était un homme et une femme, étiont seuls, p'is i'l'aviont pas d'enfant. P'is l'homme il allait travailler dans l'boâ, c'était ein bûcheron. P'is c'était un peu loin d'la maison. Une journée i' dit à sa femme, "Si j'avais un p'tit garçon pour v'nir me porter à dîner, j'aurais pas besoin d'm'en r'v'nir."

"Bi'n," a'dit, "j'avons une pleine tinette de beurre. J'crois que j'pourrions t'en faire un avec du beurre, faire un p'tit garçon avec du beurre."

Ah! bi'n l'souère, l'homme l'était content. P'is i' dit, "D'main tu l'enverras m'porter à dîner."

Sa femme prit l'beurre, p'is alle l'travaille, le brasse, p'is a'fit un beau p'tit garçon. P'is a'fut au magasin, lui achetit un bel habit, une belle ch'mise, des bas, des souliers: i'était beau!

P'is alle a preparé à dîner, p'is le p'tit garçon s'en fut l'porter à son père. Mais a y'avait donné une feuille de chou parce qu'a'dit, "Si i'fait soleil ça va fondre, le beurre, tu mettras ça su' ta tête."

Dans son chemin, le p'tit garçon i'rencontre un gros boeuf. Lui, i'vu le p'tit chou. Ça lui fit envie. Emporte la feuille de chou, p'is mange, mange toute le p'tit garçon d'beurre. Ah! i's'trouvait bi'n arrangé dans l'ventre du boeuf!

Quand l'homme eu assez faim i'r'tourne à la maison. I'dit, "As-tu pas envoyé le p'tit garçon m'porter à dîner?"

A'dit, "Oui."

Mais i'l'avait pas vu. I'partit avec la hache, p'is i'l'charche. I'passe devant Blanchet, le boeuf s'appelait Blanchet. Ça huchait, "Ma mère chu' dans l'cul à Blanchet!"

L'homme le tuit. Mais pas de p'tit garçon. I'jette les tripes dans l'champ. Là i'passit un vieux corbeau. Un corbeau i'z'appelliont ça une vieille picotte. Ça huchait, "Ma mère, la vieille picotte m'a emporté!"

La vieille picotte laisse tomber les tripes. Ça tombit su' un poteau d'bouchure, p'is ça fit un p'tit trou. P'is le p'tit garçon sortit, mais i'l'était dans un état!

L'homme l'amène à la rivière, le lave avec d'l'eau frette parce qu'avec d'l'eau chaude i'fondrait.

P'is i'furent au magasin i'acheter d'autres vêtements. P'is l'homme dit, "Astheure, dorénavant tu l'enverras p'u pour m'porter à dîner. I'va rester à la maison!"

## The Story of the Little Butter Boy

There was a man and a woman. They were alone. They didn't have a child. And the man was working in the woods. He was a woodcutter. And he worked a bit far from the house. One day he said to his wife, "If I had a little boy to bring me my lunch, I would not need to come back."

"Well," she said, "I have a full jar of butter. I think I could make you one from butter, make a little butter boy."

Oh! well, at the evening the man was satisfied. He said, "Tomorrow you'll send him to bring me my lunch."

His wife took the butter, and she worked it, stirred it, and she made a beautiful little boy. Then she went to the store, bought him a beautiful suit, a beautiful shirt, some socks, some shoes: he was beautiful!

Then she prepared the lunch, and the little boy went off to bring it to his father. But she had given him a cabbage leaf. She said, "If it is sunny, the butter will melt. But you'll put this on your head."

On his way, the little boy met a big bull. He saw the little cabbage. He felt like eating it. He took the cabbage leaf and ate it, ate all the little butter boy. Oh! he was trapped in the bull's belly.

When the man felt hungry enough, he returned home. He said, "Didn't you send the little boy to bring me my lunch?"

She said, "Yes."

But he had not seen him. He went with his axe. And he looked for him. When he passed by Blanchet—the bull was called Blanchet—there was shouting, "Mother, I'm in Blanchet's arse!"

The man killed it. But there was no little boy. He threw the guts away in the field. An old crow happened to be passing by. They used to call a crow an old *picotte*. And there was shouting, "Mother, the old *picotte* took me!"

The old crow let the guts go. They fell on a fencepost and that made a little hole. Then the little boy came out, but he was a mess.

The man took him to the river, washed him with cold water because hot water would have melted him.

They went to the store to buy some other clothes. Then the man said, "From now on, you'll never send him again to bring me my lunch. He will stay home!"

*Deux Contes Merveilleux pour les Enfants*

# Tius Tutty and Handpick Mining

I'm ninety-three. I was born the fifth of August, 1880. A mile from Louisbourg. Lorraine. They call it Lorraine Road, you know. That's between Lorraine and Louisbourg. My father fished. That was it. Fish and, well, catch rabbits in the winter, whatever you could in the fall. Tough goin' sometimes. Yes, I can remember right back to three years old. Old fashioned woodstove, an old Waterloo—big oven on it, you know, low and a neck coming up from the stove and a big round oven on top. Most all softwood there, wasn't very much hardwood. I'd say I'd be about ten years old the first time I went fishing. I went with two old men. And they made a little hardwood board, about that wide, you know? And a little like a shingling axe. And every fish I'd catch I'd have to cut a piece off of the tail. Well they took them and cleaned them and salted them and dried them and sent them to Halifax, and in the fall when the returns come back I had $12.39 when we settled. For my summer's work. Pretty good, wasn't it? And I used to be so terrible seasick. Oh, my. But, no, I wouldn't quit. It was all right when there was a good breeze on, but when it was calm, the heavy roll—especially off Louisbourg there. We moved to Louisbourg after my father was drowned. Ten years old I was fishing. Codfish, haddock, stuff like that.

Then I went to sea. I was eleven years old. On an old schooner. I was cook. Went from Louisbourg to Halifax to Yarmouth to Bridgewater, Liverpool—carrying coal, carrying coal.

Then when I was fourteen I went into the mines. My mother and all the rest of the family, they'd after moved to the coal mine—so I came to the coal mine. At Bridgeport. Gone and forgotten long ago. Between Glace Bay and Dominion. I worked four years there and I worked six months up in Dominion. The mine was down then, she was only what they called the narrow works, only worked in the winter, see? And the rest of the mine it'd be down. Well, the first job I did was tend the rapper. Instead of using wires and signal wires like they use today in the mine, used to use a thing with a hammer. You pull on this and there was a plate and this thing would go down on the plate and give the raps. So many raps for a smash or whatever was on. Say there was a smash on, boxes off of the road—then if the mine knocked off they'd give you six raps from the pit bottom, bottom of the shaft—and you'd give six raps to the next fellow, and he'd give it—messages. There was no telephone then. And then I went driving after that. That's a horse and boxes about as long as from here to the wall. Then I left there and went to Dominion, worked up there—six months or eight months—and I left there and I come down to Caledonia Mine. And that's where I finished up at. A long time. Around fifty years, I guess. And that's the first mine there was ever a telephone put in. I was tending what they call the landing, putting on the full boxes and taking off the empty ones, off of the main haulage, see? And when that was done I shipped them the east side of Caledonia, that was going under the ocean—and there was a telephone on that landing. They didn't think a telephone would work underground, you know. But it did.

Most of the time, you know, I worked at the coal face, mining coal. We done handpick and load it with the pan shovel. You had to dig her down. You have her up pretty near as high as them curtains there. You'd lay on your side, like this, put a little soft coal, minings, under your shoulder—and you'd get in so far. Course when you'd get it opening out you'd be in on your knees. Then you'd get in so far you'd have to get down on your side, see? You're underneath the wall of coal. Picking away, picking away. You didn't brace that wall. Not with the handpicks. But with the machine they did. Put what they call a sprag. You'd go in round about five feet I guess, just as far as you could reach in. Then you'd back out, bore and shoot—blow it all up. That was in rooms. In pillars you had to sprag your coal. If you are mining out what they call pillar work, well there's a room out on both sides of you.

*Tius Tutty of Glace Bay (left) as a young miner and (right) when this story was told.*

*Handpick miners opening a mine in Port Morien in 1880.*

This is a pillar. You'd have to sprag that when you'd be in under that. In case there'd be any loose coal on the face would fall. Sprag was made of wood. You mined on a bench you know—left a bench of coal about so high. You mined on that. You'd dig a hole in that and put your sprag in and a wedge in over it, see?

You had a handpick and a pan shovel and an auger for boring your hole for shooting it—had a little thing called a breast auger. You put that up to make a little hole first. Then you'd take a bar they called the stand bar—you'd drive that in the hole. Then you had a thread bar—and you put your augers onto that. Then you turn it. You'd bore it and then you'd fill it up with powder, shoot it. Shoot it yourself. You didn't have to call a shotfire—not then, when they had the handpick like that. Shooting your own coal, yeah. You had all loose powder then, see? And you had a stick about that long and it had like a piece of pipe on it—call that a caster—powder was in a can. You take it up on your arm like that and pour the powder in there. Put it in, you know, shoot it in—put it in with your stemmer they called it, piece of copper on the end of it—you'd push it back and then you'd stem it up—then you'd put what they called a needle. There was copper on the end of the needle, copper so that it wouldn't make a spark—and you'd run that in underneath, under your powder. When you had it all stemmed up you pulled the needle out and at that time you used what they called squibs—powder done up in paper, you know? You'd open up the end of it and tear a little piece off and you'd stick that in the hole. It would go right in the hole where you pulled the needle out. And you'd light it—with your lamp. Then you'd take off. You'd duck down. There was always an opening you could run to, because they had places for air to travel, you know? You'd sing out, "Fire!" There'd be only two men in the place anyhow. Only two men working together. You had a pair in another room and another pair in another room and on like that. You wait a few moments after that goes off in case there'd be some coal loose that'd fall and then after the smoke would drive out you'd go up and start loading your coal. Just shovel it, load it up, with a pan shovel. Any coal hanging, you take her down and load her in boxes.

A driver—fellow with a horse—would haul the coal. Bring in an empty and he'd take the full one out. They'd go to the pit bottom, rope haulage. They'd put them on the haulage there. They call it a grab. Then it was hoist to the surface. I drove for a while. There was a stable in the mine, and a stableman. Used to send the hay down, all that. Stableman used to clean them and look after them and harness them. All you had to do was go in and take them out, down to the landing or wherever you worked. They had shafts with a kind of bow on it, and a queer thing like a shackle on the end. Then a bolt like an eyebolt is fit on the box—and you'd put that shackle over that and you'd put a bolt down through it. When he didn't have a box on the driver held the shafts up and drove his horse along, cause they'd be dragging. You generally stood in the box, you know, when you were driving. That's the empty box. And when you were coming back to the landing you were on the front of the box—drive the horse. They used to load the manure and shift it to the surface. They had a place outside of the bankhead, they called it, they used to dump it over there. Oh, Lord, quite a lot. Oh, yes. And different ones died down there. Got killed, too. There was horses got killed. Runaway boxes. Now there was a driver he wasn't killed but he got hurt pretty bad—he never got over it. He was going up what they call a headway. And a fellow that was working in this headway—had a box and had no sprag, only had something under the wheels. And when they started chucking the coal in, before they got about half full she took off. The driver was going up this headway and the box come down and hit the horse. Killed the horse and broke the driver, pretty bad. He was in the box.

We had a little lamp something like a teapot hooked in your cap. A little spout on it. And a wick in it, seal oil. Yes, I had my light go out in the mine. Different times. Dark? Well you couldn't be any darker. You'd just try to get a light. With the old oil lamp they carried matches, and the next thing they got was the closed light—it had a plug and a kind of a lip come out on both sides of it and a plug in it. That's the way it was locked. And if you got in the dark with that you'd have to

walk as far as from here up to darn near where my son is living up there, to the landing to get a light. And you'd be going along like this, and rubbing your foot against the rail—unless the driver come in. Well then you'd send your lamps out with the driver. If you just made a move with them, they'd go out. They were not good. But the last light they got, there was no trouble to light that—there'd be something like your battery. But the old oil lamp, yes, that was open flame. But there never was an explosion caused through that. But there was an explosion in Caledonia, about four years before I started. It was eight men killed. A pumpsman was looking after the water—water pumps to pump it into a sump and then a big pump would pump it to the surface—and the pump was froze and he lit some waste and it was burning and it seems that the smoke from it got back into a dead end, blind end—and of course when it was reported that there was trouble down below to the manager—his name was Johnson—he went down and instead of going around where the pump was he opened a slide, a little trap slide in the stoppings and stuck his open light in and when he did she went up. Eight men killed. They found his lamp—used to carry it with their finger through the hook—and they found the lamp, his finger still in the hook.

Oh, I've had a lot of accidents. There's no questions about it. If there was something to get I got it. I remember I wasn't feeling too good, my eyes bothered me—lost the sight of my eye since—in the coal mine. So I went to Sydney to work in the fire station for the coal company there, at the piers. You may remember when the building was there, just between the steel plant and the piers. I was there about six years I guess. All nightshift, all backshift too. I used to have to put the water aboard the ships, you know, when they'd come in. The pipes run out on the pier for water. And you hook on your hose and put it aboard the ship, fill up her tank. So this time I went out—it was New Year's Eve—I forget the name of the boat now, coal company boat—put the hose aboard of her, give her water. So I said, "When you're through, pull the hose ashore will you?" So they pulled the boat off from the wharf. And let the hose drop overboard, see? And where the slack used to come down from the chutes, it froze icicles on it. And I got a hold and was pulling about like that and I lost my balance and over I goes overboard. And there was ice all around, and those piers are about forty feet high—and look that was low tide and twice that high up. I couldn't see nothing else but the ice. There was weights that come down from the chutes at the pier. And I tried with my gloves on but I couldn't stick. So I took my glove off—bit it off—and I put my hand on the weight. And I did the same with the other

*Tius Tutty seated among other young miners. Standing in the second row, left to right, are Jim Wadden, Peter Jobes and Tim Wadden. The shift has just finished and they have changed to street clothes. The men in the front row, left to right, are (seated) Tius Tutty, Fred Wadden, Bill MacKenzie, (standing) F. K. Wadden. Off to the left is Allie MacKenzie, and behind him Tom Wadden.*

*Allie MacKenzie will go on to become one of Canada's finest football and baseball players. His picture will hang in the Hall of Fame, Halifax. And Allie will die in a gas attack in the First World War, at thirty years of age. But when this photograph was taken, Allie was nine years old and he had already worked three months as a Trapper Boy in Caledonia Colliery.*

*We asked Gordon MacGregor to give us an idea of just how young some of these boys were when they entered the mines, and Gordon said: "In those days, if the head of the household died—there was no such thing as a widow's allowance. No such thing as relief. That widow was depending on what her neighbors would give her. It fell on the shoulders of the oldest boy to go to work. And many of them, many of them went to work as young as nine years old. My cousin Peter had to go to work. He was so young that when he'd start early in the morning in the winter, between their house and the mine there was a cemetery. And he was so young and so many ghost stories told in those days, he was scared to walk by the graveyard in the dark. And his mother used to have to take him by the hand to get past the graveyard, to go to work. He was that young."*

Tius Tutty and Handpick Mining

one. Steel weights. My two hands. I'll bet you I was there all of a half hour or more, sticking to the steel weights. I sung out a hundred times. Fellow by the name of Billy MacPhee, Second Engineer, happened to come out of the engine room and he heard me. The boat was off oh quite a distance—so they started the winches up and pulled her in and put the gangplank out and come ashore and one fellow come down—he slid down on a wire rope—he put the rope under my arms and they pulled me up. Of course my fingers were sore after, stuck right in frost, kind of burned me. They give me about that much rum. And they said, "Okay you little bugger, take it off for home." I lived only a short ways away. I started up the hill but my legs got stiff—kind of froze.

And I'll tell you how I lost the sight of my eye. We were boring a hole, working at the coal face then—and the drill wasn't working. This was a power drill and there's a hole through those drills for blowing air in there for to blow the dust, the borings out—and it was sticking. It was only a brand new drill and the hole wasn't open enough to blow the air. We used to have to pull it back like that for to clear it. And a piece of stuff from the drill—whether it was piece of shell off the drill or whether it was a piece of cement—hit me in the eye. And the shotfire was waiting for us to finish up to shoot the coal—at that time we had shotfires—the shotfire had to help my buddy finish boring and shoot the coal down, finish the box. I had to go and lay down. My eye was paining boy like blazes. Well then after I got up and washed it seemed to ease up and it didn't bother me too much. Boy I got up the next morning it pained terrible. So my wife was living then—and it was a great remedy in them days to keep down inflammation to put on cold tea leaves. You might have heard tell of it. Put the tea leaves on the eye and that kind of keeps the pain down. It got a little better so I went to Dr. MacLennan in Sydney. He couldn't find nothing but the sight was split—whatever was in there penetrated right through, split the sight.

And I had this hand smashed. I was working at the coal face alone that day; my buddy wasn't out so I was alone—so the manager came in, said the face wasn't very good, pretty shaky. I said the overman told me the place was all right. He said, "Your opinion's as good as the overman's." He said, "How many boxes you got?" and I said, "Two." He said, "There's a pair of men going to sweep the colliery—I'll give you a shift with your two boxes, go up and sweep. You can bugger around after that." Pretty good fellow. So anyhow, you laid the road out—and I had this hand on the rail like that, the gauge—you know what a gauge is on a railroad, an arm goes across like that. And I was pushing the rail out on this side and down come a timber loose in the way. I said to one of the fellows, "This timber's loose, come knock it out." He knocked the timber out. And the roof just looked as good as that. And I had my hand on the rail. And down come this little pot—they call it a pot—it's thick in the middle and thin on the edge—right through my hand. That's how I got that. But I was very fortunate in a way. Cause I had that skull fracture too. A fall of coal. I don't know yet how I got the skull fracture. We were trying to get a crosscut for a measuring for the opening, you know? There were two pair of us in this pillar. So I said, "You fellows go and have a bite to eat, have a lunch, and I'll make the box." And I was loading away and walked around the box to the other side, and a big piece of the roof come down. That's all I remember.

And when they took me to the surface the doctor claimed that I couldn't live to get to the hospital. I was bleeding that much. St. Joseph was just built a short time. Old Dr. MacKean was there at the time. And the nurses was trying to get my clothes off—a nurse told me this after—he said, "Take your time, you'll soon be able to get the clothes off easily." Never thought I'd recover. They had a horse ambulance at the time, no car. And I lost quite a lot of blood. And there was a fellow used to be a kind of a watchman around the colliery there—Angus MacAulay—and he went up in the ambulance with this man. And every time he'd see me afterwards he'd say, "My God I can't believe it's you." I got over it. I was pretty near six months in the hospital. The doctor told my wife, "Well if he does work it will be a very light job."

Well I went back to the coal face again. Yes, sir, that's as true as I'm sitting in this chair. And the manager said to me, "Look I don't think I should let you go." I said, "Look, Mr. MacDonald, I got to make a living and there's no other place to go." I said, "I'm not a coward. If I die down there well I'll die down there." And then shortly after, before I was pensioned off, I got my knee ripped open. I was on ventilation work that time—putting up what's called a brattish, to carry the air to the face where the men are working. I went to pull this piece of coal down and a fellow got to picking and pulled this same piece of coal—down on my knee—boy right to the bone. And I guess no more than about six months after that, didn't I get my ankle broken? Still, I'm going to try to make the hundred. I took care of myself when I was young. I worked hard. But I never abused myself through drink or anything. I took a little you know. Always be home and get in bed. But, yes, a lot of accidents. Maybe I should have kept fishing. I don't know now how I'm living. I really don't.

# The "Pluck Me": Life and Death of the Company Store

BILLY PITTMAN: When the mines first opened around the 1800s, the companies decided to build stores that supplied groceries, meats, dry goods—most everything the employees wanted. But the trouble with the stores was that when you were hired on you were given a check number, a brass check number—and you could get credit on that number at the store. And many's the man that when payday would come he wouldn't have any pay because his earnings would be taken up by his family in the store.

THOMAS DAYE: I remember we used to call it a bobtail paysheet.

GORDON MACGREGOR: I worked in the office, on the payroll. The clerks would bring over the deductions for the week. Say you used up twenty-six dollars worth. They'd sing out to me the check number and name and twenty-six dollars. You may have only made twenty-six—so they would take the whole works and you'd draw a bobtail. Nearly everybody drew money—but I knew, week in, week out fellows who never drew a red cent. But you didn't *have* to deal in the company store. To my mother there was a kind of blight, in a way, for everybody to deal there. She had a fear of it. Lots of women did. Because once they got a grip on you—like this Buchanan fellow I told you about, standing there with his bobtail and saying, "They plucked me"—he had nowhere else to go.

DANNY "DANCER" MACDONALD: But what you got at the company store was quality and quantity. A private merchant might cut a few ounces off, but working there in the company store it was our own flesh and blood—daughters and sons of miners. If there were any breaks you got it. And everything they had was first class. Clothes, furniture, grub was the best of everything. But we're better to have it out of our way, because it created a way of life that wasn't good. You know, there were men that died and still were owing to that store.

ARCHIE MACINTYRE: You could go in and buy until—until it reached a stage regardless the father was sick, when you went to the company store they had what you call you've drawn up your lot, and if you didn't have enough in to cover for that pound of butter you didn't get it. And there were other disadvantages. They had what was called the Provincial Workers Association, organized in Springhill in 1882. It was a no-strike union. So about 1907 the United Mine Workers entered Cape Breton and they started to organize. The P.W.A. was recognized by the company and the government. They took a vote, and the U.M.W. carried the majority. The P.W.A. said no—and the result was happened there was a

Top left: Archie MacIntyre.
Above: Billy Pittman.
Left: Gordon MacGregor.

strike. It became a strike between two unions instead of for rights and wages. And there in our early life we saw that instead of being an advantage and a godsend to the people, the company houses and the company stores were instruments the company could use to browbeat the miners into the union of the company's choice. Then in 1925 the men were threatened with a 37½ percent reduction in wage. When the strike came on the company cut them off. There were donations coming in from U.M.W. and others. Local bakers would donate some bread. They could not sell it anyway. The way the rations worked, each area like Caledonia, New Aberdeen, Glace Bay—they had stations set up and you'd be notified a certain day in the week to go down. And you went down with an ordinary potato bag. And you'd probably get a little bit of stew meat, and some potatoes.

BILLY PITTMAN: Dry codfish, don't forget that. And molasses out of the punchion.

THOMAS DAYE: It was often referred to as carrying the bag.

ARCHIE MACINTYRE: The violence broke out at Waterford. A fellow named Davis was shot. For years we had a holiday,

Davis Day, June 11. He was shot when rioting started, after pickets tried to stop officials from running the plant. And that led to the end of the company stores.

DANNY "DANCER" MACDONALD: They were burnt to the ground, every one of them. I helped to do it. I'll tell you how it came about. Desperation, mostly. It wasn't vandalistic, understand, as desperation. As the strike got more desperate we started to withdraw our maintenance men. It's always the policy of mine workers to leave our maintenance men on, to see the mines are not flooded. Well our electricity for this town, Dominion, was supplied by the Dominion Coal Company's plants here. The alternate one was at Karney Lake in New Waterford. Well, everything was in darkness. The hospitals had their own generators. And the company was determined to open that plant at Karney Lake. They called in their officials to do it. And they took as protection for those men the coal company watchmen. Men that had no experience as horsemen, less experience with a shooting iron. They armed them and they put them on the horses that we took out of the pit. Men were angry. You can understand the mind of a man when he's looking at some children in front of him crying for some grub that he's not able to give them. We got word that five strikers were killed. Turned out one *was* killed. We didn't wait. I had a gun. There's no doubt in my mind that our intention was to kill every one of them. But before we got over there the men there blew up and rushed the plant. They rushed these fellows on horseback. All them fellows had was a chamber full of bullets. They wasted them. They backed them up to the plant where the men were working. They yelled they were out of ammunition. Well, Jesus, that was an admission, and the crowd got next to them and they got the goddamndest hammering they ever got. But Waterford is a Catholic district, and a priest there had a wonderful influence. He jumped up and pleaded with them not to hurt these men. They took them and put them all in jail, for protection. Well we were going over—we knew they were in jail—it was our intention to kill every one of them. The authorities knew this parade was coming over and they knew the priest wouldn't have any influence with us. It wasn't religion. It was the force of mob rule. And just as we got in, the train with them was pulling out. But we stayed there. We went in and wrecked the plant.

The first raid on the company stores took place that night in Waterford, at dark. That was a private place. The company didn't own it. The mayor, the vice president of the union at one time, he said for Jesus sake, boys, if you're going in, there are a lot of wooden buildings, be careful of fire—or Waterford is finished. Without electricity there was nothing to pump with. So we went in and cleaned her. In the meantime we had three big stores at Number Two mine, stocked to the top. And them fellows said by Jesus what are we doing here. It took us three nights to clean them stores out. The third night—and not exactly cleaned—they put the match to it. Then they went to the general store in Glace Bay. That store supplied all the stores. Cleaned that out and burnt it. Then Number Eleven. Then burnt them all.

GORDON MACGREGOR: I can remember just how it happened. Everybody knew, you see, that the stores were to be raided. I was living in Number Six. There used to be a train ran from Donkin—I always call it Number Six, little bitty town—to Glace Bay on Saturday nights. The train had just come in. I heard a great big store window—bang, and that was that. And for a small village like that—there were I'd say about five hundred people there. Some would take the whole family with them. And there were some blackened their face. Some put masks on. The company knew it was coming—they had been warned. And previous to the raid the manager and the assistant manager they took the shoes, say a pair of brown shoes—they'd take a size seven brown shoe and perhaps put it in with a black eight; so people went and grabbed

*Danny "Dancer" MacDonald and his son.*

The *"Pluck Me": Life and Death of the Company Store* 49

the shoes and ran with the box. Next morning everybody's going around—"Have you got a brown seven?"—trying to get the right shoes.

BILLY PITTMAN: There was a lot of humor. There used to be a big hoist to hoist up furniture. And a fellow came in there half drunk and put a bureau on his back and walked out through the door. He fell thirty feet. If he'd've been sober he'd've broke his neck but he didn't get hurt.

GORDON MACGREGOR: There was one big fellow coming out with a roll of linoleum on his back, calling out: "Make way for a hungry man."

DANNY "DANCER" MACDONALD: The company never tried to re-establish company stores after that. Never made a try. Now here's a peculiar thing. Do you know it took women a long time to get acquainted to go to stores with money. They were lost. When we went back to work we were paid cash, and we shopped where we wanted. Cash, but also so much on that back bill that you still owed the company store. They made sure their records weren't burnt.

# The Eyestone

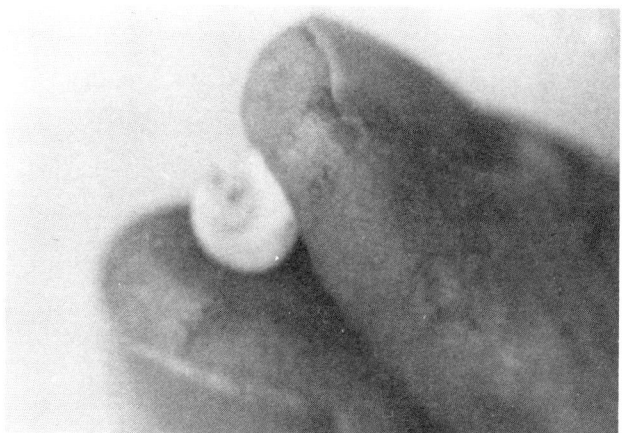

We have now seen two eyestones in Cape Breton—an item so rare and so long out of use it seems no longer to be remembered in Scotland, the place from which both of these eyestones came. John Tom Urquhart of Skir Dhu first told us of the eyestone. Later, we met John A. Wilkie of Sugar Loaf. He showed us his eyestone and told a story almost identical to the story John Tom had told.

The eyestone was not originally found in Scotland. They seem all to have come there from the Far East. They are the color of flesh and about the size of half a pea. And they are said to be the tip of a conch shell. The eyestone is alive, and has to eat—and both men keep theirs in about an inch and a half of sugar (John Tom uses white sugar; John A. uses brown). John Tom sometimes feeds his a little rum, and he changes the sugar every two or three years. When the first Highland settlers came to Cape Breton, they brought the eyestone with them. It was used extensively here, and passed along from father to son.

John Tom said that the eyestone would be used to get a splinter out of a man's eye. Years ago, when it was common

*John Tom Urquhart of Skir Dhu holding an eyestone in his hand.*

50   The *"Pluck Me"*: *Life and Death of the Company Store*

*John A. Wilkie standing with a shingle-maker near his home at Sugar Loaf. It is his eyestone held in the picture opposite.*

for men to work with chisels and hammers and sledges, men often caught a speck of steel in the eye. John A. said that the eyestone could retrieve other things as well. He said, "I was sawing wood at Bay St. Lawrence. I got sawdust in my eye, and in the evening it got to be sore—it got so bad the other eye was getting sore. And they said to me, 'You better go to where the eyestone is tonight.' I went and they put me to bed with it. Put it in my eye. And you couldn't notice it. The size of it, you'd think it would bother you—but it didn't. I woke up and my eyes were clear. I was twenty-two or twenty-four years old."

When there is someone to be helped, the eyestone is taken out of sugar and carefully cleaned. John A. said that down North it would be put in a weak vinegar solution. Both eyestones we've seen have a tiny dot—the center of a perfect whorl—and when in vinegar two or three bubbles would come out that hole. Then it would be put in the afflicted eye. The patient must sit still or lie down while the eyestone does its work. This is simply so that it will not be lost. This is also the reason you go to the eyestone and it rarely travels. In the eye, the eyestone would move round and round the eyeball, searching for the speck. When it came out it would have the speck, and the eye would be clear—and the eyestone would be returned to the sugar.

"Years ago," said John A., "there was a man who wanted to say just how awful a certain woman was, so he said of her she was so mean she wouldn't feed the eyestone."

# Rita and Rory Murphy Remember Moonshining Days

RORY MURPHY: I was born right here in Reserve. My people before me made moonshine. It was never legal. An uncle of mine taught me. He didn't have to teach me. I was just with him every day and I learned it. Simple. Half the people who make it today make it for their own use, only make a couple quarts at a time. I was making it by the gallon. I was eleven years old when I first made it. My old man was just after dying then. So we were only getting like the fellow says sixty dollars a month for eight of us home. So ma was nine. So I was making a few dollars on it then.

Good? I hope to tell you it was good. You ask if it's true you can poison yourself. How are you going to poison yourself? It's only sugar and water and yeast. That's all it is. There's nothing in it that'd hurt you. Same as eating a bite to eat in a house—no difference. Of course, it's all according to the people who make it. You have to give credit to the Murphys of Reserve. I guess they're about the best at it—right down to the point they drink their own stuff. What you call bad moonshine comes from people who are greedy. And they'll doctor it up and water it to make more to make more money. You see, in a gallon jar you get about seven quart beer bottles. And they're not satisfied, they want to make it to ten or twelve.

You'd have to have good water. You make it out of

molasses. Sometimes you make it out of sugar. You set it with sugar and water and yeast and you leave it brew for two weeks. And it's sweet, and then it turns kind of a sour taste when it's brewed out like—like it's flat. It's ready for running then. It's only the steam you get off it. You take it to your still and you build a fire and you boil the steam through the coil—comes out there on the bottom—and it comes out clear just like the water in the tap. And you'd run that right off perhaps twenty-five or thirty gallons of it. Then you put it back in again, back into the still. Run it over again. Then you take the first four gallons off it—and that's all you take. And it's ready to drink. The rest you just throw out. That's four gallons off of fifty but we've had as high as thirty-five to forty barrels at one time. We'd always have a bunch of barrels set, four gallons would come off each barrel. When you're making shine for your customers, you've got to run it every two weeks, or every week, trying to keep up. I had enough customers for it all.

RITA: And they're just crying for it. Especially the old-timers.

RORY: Jeez, they're after me all the time to make it. Fellows that work in the pit. Jeez, get us a good gallon for Christmas, get us a good gallon for vacation time. But I quit it altogether. I'm fifty-one. And I worked all my life in the pit. Handled stone, bored stone all my life in the pit. The first time I was arrested I was fifteen years old. It was on a Christmas Eve morning and the Mounties walked in on top of us, me and a first cousin of mine—the two of us were the same age. We were right at the still and she was going full blast when he got us. It was six o'clock in the morning. They followed us through the snow. They knew I was making it. It was the idea of catching me, that was all. And a lot of times I was caught I was squealed on.

RITA: But I mean he never got rich over it. He never could put money in the bank. We had a lot of kids, too. We had nine. Did it help raising the kids? No. I think it hurt more than it helped because he was in jail more than he was out during the time when they were small. And it was hard there because in those days you were only getting four dollars relief from the county.

RORY: But you never met a better bunch than the Mounties. It was not the Mounties' fault. He had a job to do and the squealers on his back all the time.

RITA: I've seen them come here on a Christmas Day. They didn't have a search warrant but I let them look through the house. They wanted to look at Rory's boots. They had taken plaster casts of boots that were around a still. They tore the house upside down. But they damn well put it back together again. Just wanted to see if he was in on this. Which he wasn't.

The last time he was caught it was with a polaroid camera. He went out to the woods to run off—he just had one barrel left in the woods. And it was there, what Rory, three weeks or more?

RORY: I knew they had the place caught, you know?

RITA: So it was on a Sunday and Rory said, "I think I'll go out and bump a barrel." Then, "No," he said, "I don't think I better." Well he changed his mind and made it up three or four times. At last he left. It was about ten o'clock in the morning and he said, "Expect me back around two." Well, if Rory ever went to the woods and said Rita I'll be back a certain time, you can bet your sweet dollar that's the time he'll come back. He could time from the time he left home till he ran a pot or two pots and came home—and you can have his supper on the table waiting for him. Anyhow, I saw this car coming in the yard around two o'clock and it was an unmarked car. But he opened the door and I just looked at the boot and knew it was a Mountie—and then I saw Rory falling out of the car, paralyzed drunk. He said he was caught. The Mountie let him sit down at the still and get drunk. And took him in and showed all the pictures from the time Rory went in, set the still up, getting the wood—all pictures of him.

Now out of the years we've been married, I guess Rory did about seven years out of that. Now that's combined.

RORY: I did three months the first time.

RITA: He did nine months. Came out and went back. Did eighteen months. Came out and went back. Did fifteen months. Went back and did another eight—and there I'd be with another baby ready to have one. And like for what they gave him for making moonshine for a living for the kids—you go and rob a bank today and you wouldn't serve half as much time. But given half a chance he'd go back to it today. It's in your blood. His father. His grandfather before him. Probably his great-grandfather before him, who came from Ireland. It's down through the years and it's just Murphy's moonshine.

RORY: You know what, I was proud to be a moonshiner, boy. At least no one told me what to do. If the kids were all grown up and I didn't have any worries on my shoulders—yes, I'd go back at it and go back at it tomorrow. Just that I like making it, that's all. It's not what I'd make off it, but I'd just like making it. I mean, it's a good life. You're sitting by a nice brook there, you've got a still going, you've got a drink when you feel like it. Have a little bite to eat and enjoy yourself.

RITA: It wasn't easy. And it wasn't the life of luxury, that's for sure. It was hard. It was hard on the kids. At the time they were only small. There's a lot in it, a lot that I can't explain, really. The wife of a moonshiner. If I had to do it all over again, I think I'd do it. You meet a lot of people—awful lot of people—and you get to know your Royal Canadian Mounted Police very well. There were good times. Though we didn't abuse it. Only for moonshine in those days I don't know where we'd be at because all my kids were small. I had five babies ranging from crib to just walking age. And we weren't eating the best—but we were living.

But there's an awful lot of worry to it. And it's hard work. Don't ever kid yourself that making moonshine is easy because it isn't. It's hard. Yes, I played a part. I used to go to the woods. And there's many a gallon I carried across the Glace Bay highway in a baby carriage. There was a lot of traffic up and down this road and a lot of knocks on the doors. And you never get any rest when you're making it and selling it. But I'd never allow it to be drunk in the house. And then you're always on your toes. You're watching the windows and you're going to the door, wondering if a Mountie's going to come in the yard or not.

But you're always sure of a loaf of bread on your table if you always have a drink of shine around. Never go hungry. I mean you wouldn't have steak or any of these luxuries but you were always sure to have beans, bread or whatever. You were never down without anything in the house to eat. Because you were always waiting for someone to come and buy a bottle and you were sure before that night was out that you wouldn't go to bed hungry—you have something to eat before you'd go to bed. The neighbors were good. The people who came to buy, they all knew Rory. We even had professionals coming to the house, buying. But that was not as weekly as the coal miners would. We trusted them all—except for the exception. We never made any money though. We never held a bank book or had a new car, new home or anything—it was just a struggle...that was all. I suppose if I had to do it over again—I'd do it. I'm older today...but to look back on it, if I had my day over, sure I would.

RORY: As far as my making moonshine, I only did it to make a living off it. I didn't do it to make money off it. Put a bite to eat on the table and clothes for school on the kids' back—that's all I made out of her.

# Waltes: An Ancient Micmac Game

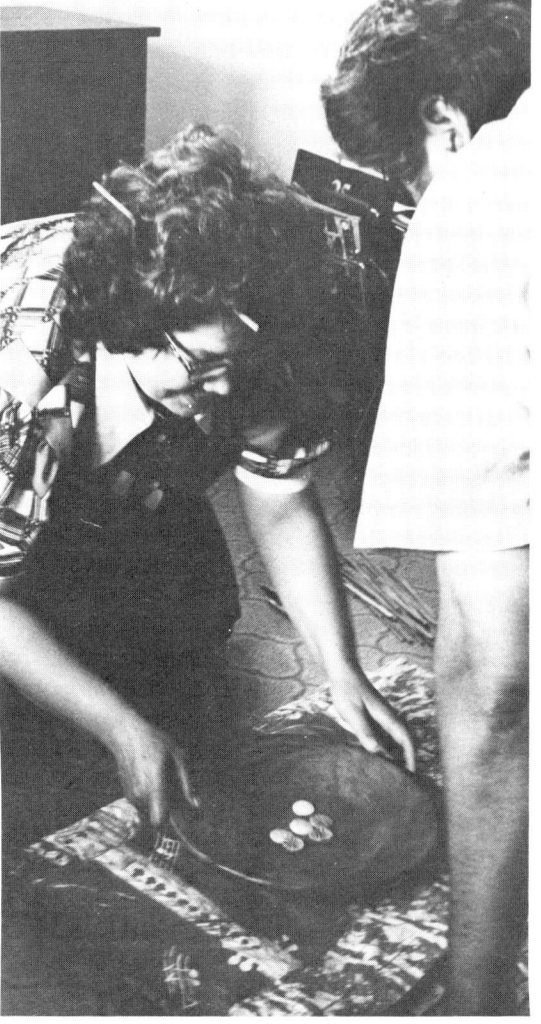

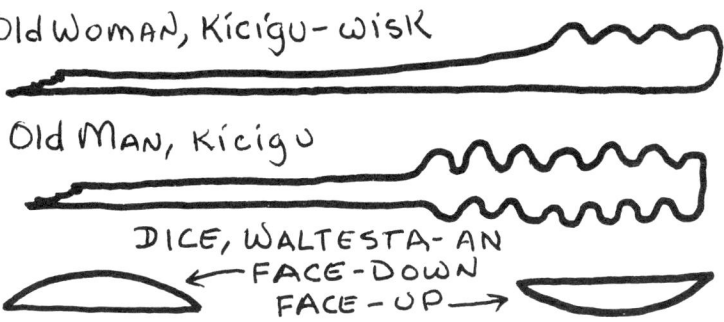

Waltes is a beautiful, vigorous, ancient Micmac game. It has remained with the Micmacs despite the many other changes in their lives. It is now linked primarily with Christian pre-Lenten activities and is played especially on Pancake Night—Shrove Tuesday—the night before Ash Wednesday. Years ago the old people would play Monday through Tuesday midnight—non-stop—simply changing partners as they played. Mrs. Elizabeth McEwan, Kate McEwan, Mr. and Mrs. Wallace Bernard, and Mr. and Mrs. Charlie Herney—all of Membertou—took time to teach the game. There are words used here to approximate the *sound* of Micmac; they should not be considered the correct spelling of these words.

Waltes sets are rare. They include one Old Man, three Old Women and three times seventeen Sticks. They say three times seventeen instead of fifty-one, because it takes three sticks to make one point. There is a bowl (or plate, *waltestan-i*), a hardwood bowl with a flat bottom and gently upcurving sides. It is made from a burl, a queer lump that forms on the trunk or branch of a tree. A burl does not seem to have a regular grain and can thus take a terrific pounding without cracking—and that is exactly the right property for the bowl used in Waltes. There is a hole about three-eighths of an inch in diameter in the bottom center, said to be an air hole to help the dice jump, and said also to be found only in the bowls in Nova Scotia. The dice are known as Indian Dice, *waltesta-an*. Traditionally they were made from the flat side of the caribou shinbone, but in later years it was the moose, then the cow. From the shinbone one-and-a-half-inch squares were cut. Then with a file they were rounded to about one-and-a-quarter-inches square, flat on the face and softly rounded at the sides. A design was scratched into the face.

A soft blanket is folded to about two-and-a-half-feet square and placed on the floor. The blanket takes up a lot of the noise of slamming the bowl down, and protects the player's fingers. The bowl with the dice in it is set in the center of the blanket, and two players sit or kneel on the floor across from one another. Two people can play, or four people as partners (two play the first part, dividing sticks till one gets the Old Man; the other two play to the end). Even when only two play, it is good to have one or two others there to manage the sticks for counting, because the game often moves very fast and having to stop to move a stick or take it back destroys the rhythm of play.

In the beginning, no one has wood. The Old Man, the Old Women and all the sticks are in one general pile off to the side (perhaps in the hands of an observer). The opponents face one another. They simply agree as to who will go first. The game we saw began with all six dice face-down in the bowl. We watched, among others, Tillie and Charlie Herney play a game. We'll use their names here in describing an example game.

Tillie takes the bowl in the fingers of both hands, holding near the edge, raises the bowl a few inches and slams it down solidly. Even with the blanket the bowl makes quite a rap on the floor. The dice leap in the bowl and settle. If she gets all but one face-up or all but one face-down, she gets one point. One point is three sticks from the general pile. The observer will place three sticks at Tillie's side. Because she got a point she gets to lift and slam the bowl again. If she again gets all but one face-up or all but one face-down (either possibility) she wins again—and she receives two points, six sticks from the general pile—that is, one point (three sticks) for the win, and one point (three sticks) for winning twice in a row. Now she has nine sticks in her pile and she gets another turn. If she again gets one face-up or one face-down she again wins—and each time she receives two points (six sticks), one point for the win, one point for it being a consecutive win. Let's say this time she does not get a winning throw (perhaps it is four dice up and two down). Now it is Charlie's turn.

Charlie takes the bowl in his hands, raises and slams it down. He gets three up and three down. Nothing. Tillie raises and slams. Two up and four down. Nothing. Charlie raises and slams. Five up and one down. He wins one point, three sticks from the general pile. He begins a pile at his side. He gets another turn. He raises and slams. All the dice fall face-up. This is a win, called *e-tkum-woway*. It is worth five points and Charlie receives one of the Old Women (*kicigu-wisk*). (The Old Woman is worth five points but she is also worth sixteen sticks—five groups of three sticks which makes the five points, plus one stick. This will be important in later counting.)

All right. Now Tillie has nine sticks (three points) in her pile. Charlie has three sticks and an Old Woman. It is still Charlie's turn. He raises and slams. All the dice fall face-up. *E-tkum-woway* again. He receives an Old Woman for making *e-tkum-woway* and another Old Woman for getting *e-tkum-woway* twice in a row. Two *e-tkum-woway* is called *Gwed-a-bal-ud-kwi-mu*, Sinking the Loon—and it is worth a total of fifteen points: five for the first *e-tkum-woway*, five for the second and five for having *e-tkum-woway* twice in a row. (There are only three Old Women. You have to work your way up to the Old Man. If, earlier, Tillie had won one Old Woman, Charlie would have won two Old Women and the Old Man. If two Old Women were gone—won by Tillie or Charlie earlier—he would have received one Old Woman, the Old Man and "four times four sticks"—that is, sixteen sticks (five points plus one stick). If three Old Women were gone, he would get the Old Man and "four times four sticks two times.")

Charlie slams again. All but one face-up—another win. He gets one point, three sticks. He raises and slams. Four up and two down. Nothing. Tillie, nothing. Charlie, nothing. Tillie gets one down and five up: one point. She slams again, nothing. Charlie slams, nothing. Tillie, nothing. Charlie slams and gets one up and five down: one point. He raises and slams: one down and five up—two points. He raises and slams: one down and five up—two points *and e-tkum-woway* for having three consecutive wins of one up or one down. If there is still an Old Woman in the general pile, he receives her. If not, he gets her equal in points: five points, fifteen sticks.

Getting *e-tkum-woway* in this manner is called "patching." Even though the Old Man is still in the general pile and all the Old Women were gone, Charlie would have received sticks and not the Old Man. You can patch for the Old Women but you cannot patch for the Old Man. He can only be taken by making all face-up or all face-down. Charlie raises and slams. Nothing. Tillie raises and slams. All dice face-up. *E-tkum-woway*. And since the Old Women are gone—they go first—she receives the Old Man.

It is winning the Old Man that ends the first part of Waltes. But it often happens that all the sticks and Old Women have been won, and no one yet has the Old Man. In this case the first part of play continues. Perhaps Charlie gets one face-up. He is entitled to one point, three sticks. To show this, Charlie (or whoever is handling his score) makes a second pile beside his first. The second pile uses a kind of notation. Here, it is *understood* that one point equals three sticks—but only one stick is put out to indicate that score. So Charlie got all but one face-up and there are no sticks left in the general pile—one of his sticks begins a second pile, indicating one point or three sticks. He slams again. All but one face-down. Two more sticks move from his first pile to his second, indicating two points (six sticks)—one point for the win, one point for twice in a row. Sticks go into a second pile and sometimes into even a third pile—until one player gets all face-up or face-down and wins the Old Man. The new pile formed while trying to get the Old Man is known as "collecting firewood for the Old Man." Players often rise to their knees for this part, heads together, and the play moves very fast.

Charlie now has three sticks of firewood in his second pile. Tillie slams, one face-up. Instead of forming a second pile, one of Charlie's sticks is returned to his first pile. Tillie slams, one face-down. Two sticks of Charlie's are returned to his first pile. Tillie slams, nothing. Charlie, nothing. Tillie, one face-down. Now that Charlie has no firewood, Tillie puts out one of her sticks to begin a second pile. She slams, nothing. Charlie slams, one face-up. Tillie takes her stick back. Charlie slams, one face-up, puts out two sticks. And so it continues trying to gather firewood, until one of them gets *e-tkum-woway* and wins the Old Man.

The Old Man must be paid for and all debts must be paid. First, whoever wins the Old Man receives beside the Old Man a payment of five points from the other player. If Tillie had won the Old Man, Charlie could pay her with fifteen sticks from his first pile to her first pile. If he had an Old Woman he could have given her that. If he was the one with a second pile and it contained five points, he could have returned those five points to his own first pile and the debt he owed Tillie for the Old Man would be considered

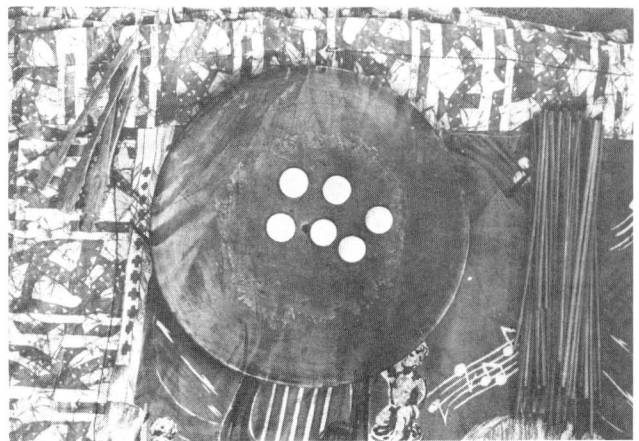

paid. This is because whoever holds a second pile holds an evidence of debt the other player owes to him; it is a debt to be paid at a rate of three sticks for every one in the second pile. After the Old Man is paid for, whoever has the second pile is entitled to full payment. If Tillie had a second pile then Charlie would have to pay her for it from his first pile—three sticks for every one in her second pile. If he cannot pay up, the game is over and he has lost. If he *can* pay, and if he is left with more than three sticks—the game continues.

They play as they did when collecting firewood for the Old Man. The difference is that the Old Man is gone. They are both trying to build a second pile, collecting points and therefore evidence of debt the other player owes. Perhaps Tillie gets one face-up and puts a stick in her second pile. Then Charlie gets one face-down and Tillie has to return that stick to her first pile. Charlie slams again, *e-tkum-woway*, all face-up. The Old Women and the Old Man are gone. So Charlie puts a single stick from his first pile up into his hair. It is equal to the five points of *e-tkum-woway*, and it will remain there defiantly until Tillie either knocks it off by winning *e-tkum-woway* herself, or is called upon by Charlie to pay for it. The call for payment—*a-bunkit-woway*—can happen any time one player figures he has gathered more debt than the other can pay for. Debts are paid, and if both still have a minimum of four sticks the game continues. If one player is wiped out the game is over. But if one player, after paying all his debts, is left with one, two or three sticks—he gets to dance.

Dancing is an extraordinary element of this game wherein a player who has lost almost everything is yet entitled to a final chance to win. They say you have a chance to dance. The word is *ela' lagwet*, and it also means drifting, as over water. Pauline Bernard explained that by dance was meant some sort of act such as would happen if, say, her sister sat across the room and she, Mrs. Bernard, should dance across to her. The players continue exactly as before, but now the one who is dancing must make a certain number of points before the one who is not dancing makes even one point. If the dancer has ended up with one stick, he has to "dance" seven points (that is, get seven before his opponent gets one). If two sticks, he has to dance six. If three sticks, five points.

Let's say after *a-bunkit-woway* Tillie is left with two sticks. She has to dance six points before Charlie makes even one point. When a person goes dancing, the play begins with the dancer setting up the dice. She can shake them in her hands and cast them in the bowl up to three times. If any of the casts results in one or more points, play begins with that cast. She would count that point (or points if *e-tkum-woway*) toward the six points she must dance, raise the bowl and slam it. If after three casts by hand she failed to make a point, she can place the dice in the bowl any way she chooses, raise the bowl and slam it. Often, during the playing of Waltes, the players will slam and then wave a hand over the dice before they settle, giving them air and encouraging them to come down in a scoring combination. During this part of the game, only the dancer can wave the hand. Also, all face-up or face-down, *e-tkum-woway*, counts as three points (not five) when you are dancing. Tillie can win by making any combination of six points before Charlie makes one point.

Here is a simple example of how debts might be paid. Remember, Tillie paid for *e-tkum-woway* (the stick in Charlie's hair) with an Old Woman (worth five points, but also worth sixteen sticks). Had she instead paid with sticks it would have cost her only fifteen sticks, the equal of the five points she owed. Then, let's say Charlie had ten sticks (ten points) in his second pile, and called for *a-bunkit-woway*—payment. Tillie, if she had it, may have paid thus: an Old Woman plus two sticks to make six points (sixteen sticks plus two sticks equals eighteen sticks or six points). To this she could add twelve sticks, making a total of the ten points.

In Waltes there is no final score, except that one player has everything and the other has nothing. There are some people with real skill at it, who can slam the bowl with such control they can get point-making combinations several times in a row. They wave their hands, giving the dice air, and they talk to the dice. In old times it was never played without stakes; today gambling at Waltes would be very rare. Some sources believe that the Old Women and the Old Man fit together into a kind of arrow, and that the bowl itself was important in Micmac legend as a kind of ark or boat for a journey. One source speaks of *waltesigaan buoinwe*, referring to its use in magic and foretelling the future. We can play the game—but it is clear that it contains meanings probably no one alive can relate to us—a game that includes the Loon, the act of Sinking the Loon, and dancing, drifting over water.

# Reitach: A Scottish Engagement Rite

A Reiteach is said to be an espousal, held before the bans of marriage are proclaimed and sometimes considered as important as the wedding feast itself. But that is a later definition. If a man happened to be out by the road, cutting away small spruce and hardwood, clearing the area—and if you asked his wife what he was up to, she might tell you in Gaelic, "Tha e trang ag obair reiteach" ("he's busy working at clearing"). And that's what a Reiteach was. Joe MacNeil told us, "I guess it comes from the word like settling things, clearing out obstacles, trees and stumps, making the ground tillable". It was a formal way of asking for a young girl's hand, clearing the ground as to would there be a marriage, who would perform the ceremony and where, probably questions of dowry, where the couple would live—making certain that everyone involved was satisfied with the arrangements. It was very important in the preservation of family and community. Today such a practice is all but forgotten, and the last Reiteach on Cape Breton seems to have been that when Sandy Kenny Morrison of Wreck Cove brought his cousin Alex J. Morrison to speak for him, asking for the hand of Rhoda MacDonald of Skir Dhu—in 1923.

Over the years what must have been a very rich tradition gradually wore away until only the barest outlines of Reiteach were left. It must have been at one time quite a performance. It was for some reason never held on a Friday. The bridegroom-to-be and an older friend, someone respected in the community, would come to the home of the girl he hoped to have for a bride. The father would usually know why they had come, but nothing would be said outright. Instead, they would pretend they had come to buy a cow or a horse or a boat—and everything they said would have a double meaning. If it was a boat they were claiming they wanted to buy, they would ask such a question as, Is she broad in the beam? Eventually they would get down to talking about the real purpose of the visit, and when the older friend had finished speaking well of the bridegroom-to-be and asking for a certain girl's hand, the father would then go through the formality of first offering his other daughters. Sometimes, in fact, the offer was quite serious, as he perhaps wanted to marry off a particular daughter and would actually refuse to give up the girl the young man had come for.

Malcolm Angus MacLeod of Birch Plain remembered

*The wedding of Rhoda MacDonald of Skir Dhu to Sandy Kenny Morrison of Wreck Cove in 1923. This wedding is said to be the product of the last formal Reitach on Cape Breton Island.*

having seen only one Reiteach. He said the table was prepared for a little feast, and everyone except the young girl herself sat at the table. Her chair was left empty at the table. And the young man who wished to marry her had brought an older man to speak for him, and this older man described the future groom's qualities and love for the girl and asked for her hand. And when all other arrangements were made, as the final act of agreement, the young girl came to the table and sat—and strong drink was available, and the feast was served.

Sometimes a Reiteach would not come out at all as planned. Tommy Peggy MacDonald of Breton Cove told us the following story of a man who was to be married and some time after the Reiteach the girl jilted him. But the young men of the neighborhood were determined to have a wedding, as well as the fine party that would certainly follow. So they concocted a scheme to take him another night and ask for the hand of a girl he had never met—and here in Gaelic and then English is the story, and a hint of the happy life that followed.

Moran bhliadhnaichean air ais bha 'n cleachdadh anns an dùthaich seo, 'nuair a bha gille agus nighean a' falbh cuideachd ùine, bha iad a' deanamh rèiteach ri parantan na h-ighinn mus pòsadh iad. Aon uair thachair gu robh reiteach gu bhith air a dheanamh air a Chladach-a-Tuath ann a sheo, 's bha h-uile dad air a chur air doigh eadar an gille agus an nighean; bha iad, mar a chanadh iad anns an t-seann tide, air na "pairings" a cheannach—an t-aodach a bha iad a' dol a chur oirre 'nuair a bhiodh iad a pòsadh. Ach mus tainig tide na rèiteach dh'fhàg an nighean an gille agus chuir i cùl ris. 'S bha h-uile dad aigesan deiseil son a phòsaidh, 's bha h-uile dad aicese deiseil son a' phòsaidh. Ach bha cuid mhór dha na gillean oga bha 's an dùthaich, a bha 'n aon aois ris a' ghille bha dol a phòsadh, bha iad a' faicinn gu robh iad gu bhith mach as banais. 'S bha iad gle dhèonach gu faigheadh iad banais, 's rinn iad suas eadar iad fhein gu feuchadh iad ri nighean fhaighinn dha'n ghille a phòsadh e.

Sin mar a thachair. Chaidh coig no sianar aca aon oidhche 's fhuair iad cuideachd 's fhuair iad botul de dh' uisge beatha, 's chaidh iad a choimhead air nighean araid a bha 's an duthaich. Cha robh innte ach nighean og; cha robh i ach mu thimchioll air naoi bliadhna deug a dh'aois. Fhuair iad cuideachd co-dhiubh 's chaidh iad suas gu aite na h-ighinn leis a' bhotul uisge beatha, no 's docha gu robh dhà dhiubh aca. Fhuair iad na parantan an darna taobh 's thug iad dhaibh drama no dhà de dh'uisge beatha, 's dh'innis iad an turas air

*Thomas A. MacDonald.*

an robh iad. Bha iad a' coimhead airson lamh na h-ighinn òig a bha 's an dachaidh, leis gun do chuir an nighean cùl ris. Chuir iad seo mu choinneamh nam pàrantan. Dh'fhaighnich iad dhaibh am biodh iad deonach an nighean an duine seo a phòsadh. 'S bha iad gle leagte air gum pòsadh an nighean e. Ach an nighean bhochd, cha chreid mi gu robh i air an duine fhaicinn riamh. Cha robh eòlas 's am bith aice air. Thug i oirre gu ceann eile an taighe 's thoisich i caoineadh, 's dhiùlt i tighinn a mach mu choinneamh an duine bha iad a' coimhead son gum posadh i e.

Ach co-dhiubh, 'nuair a bha iad ùine muigh as an taigh, rinn na pàrantan suipeir mhor, 's bha h-uile duine 'na suidhe timchioll air a' bhòrd, 's chan fhaigheadh iad air an nighean a thoirt a mach chon na suipearach. Ach bha na pàrantan, bha iad gle dhèonach gum pòsadh an nighean an gille bha seo, 's chaidh là a' phòsaidh a chur air doigh. Mu dheireadh 's mu dheòidh thainig an nighean gu gnothaichean fhaicinn anns an aona doigh 's an robh a pàrantan 'gam faicinn. Na balaich òga thainig a dheanamh na reiteach, chuir iad an gille òg suas ris a' ghnothach cuideachd, gum pòsadh e an nighean seo. Thainig am posadh dheth, 's bha banais mhòr aca, 's dh'obraich a h-uile dad gle math.

Bha mu chuairt air ochdnar de chlann aca as deidh a' phosaidh sin. Agus tha cuimhna agamsa air am boireannach sin a chluinntinn anns an dachaidh anns an deach mise thogail. Bha frolaig sniomh aig na boireannaich, 's bha iad a bruidhinn air a h-uile dad a thachair anns na bliadhnaichean air ais, 's bha i 'g innse dha na boireannaich an stòiridh a bha seo mu dheidhinn a' phòsaidh aicese 's cho fada 's a bha i 'n aghaidh an duine seo phòsadh. Ach thionndaidh i ris na boireannaich eile 's thuirt i, "Bheil fhios agaibh gu robh ochdnar chlann agam, 's cha do leig mi le duine aca cadal eadar mi fhein agus an duine agam as deidh a h-uile dad a bha sin."

In a lot of cases, it might be the first time the groom had ever seen the prospective wife—and in a lot of instances it wasn't a very happy episode for the girl, but it turned out quite happily after that for most of them. I know of one particular case—I wasn't there but I knew the people involved—it happened the girl had never seen the man brought before her this particular night for the Reiteach. This man had got the marriage garb to marry another woman, and she had jilted him. It was the custom then the man bought the apparel for his wife to be married in along with his own. I don't know whether this woman returned the clothes or did she get married in it to another fellow. Anyway, she jilted this man. But the young fellows wanted to have the wedding, by hook or by crook. There was one fellow just full of devilment. They were fishing, and they used to have shacks down at the shore—fish and stay there all night—and this one night they were trying to figure out how they were going to get a wedding. This man said they'd take the man to his sister. They got a bottle or two of whiskey, I don't know how many of them went. I doubt the girl had ever seen the man because he was quite a bit older, and she lived six miles away. But the idea there was he was more or less a little more prominent citizen of the community and the parents were quite willing to look at the matter in that light. The girl was taken by surprise and she cried her heart out that night. But I heard of her relating the story years after to the women at a carding and spinning frolic, and she said in the final analysis—she was talking in Gaelic, of course—after all the discontent of that first night, they had eight children together, and she said, "Do you know that I never let one of them sleep one night between my husband and myself."

# Chandeleur: An Acadian Feast

MARGUERITE GALLANT, *La Pointe:* And something else they used to celebrate which they don't now is something they called the Chandeleur, when they bless the candles. Oh, it used to be a great feast. You should have seen what they called "la cane de la Chandeleur"—it was a big staff—oh, it must have been about eight feet. And it had a crook in it. And the man that carried that cane was in full dress, and in the olden time they had shoes—they used to call them little red-topped boots—it had a sort of heart design. It would be handmade, the red top. It was beautiful, more like chamois. He had on an evening coat, a split-tailed coat and everything. And a lovely handmade shirt. Oh, I remember the beautiful linen they used to weave on the loom. And there was a song we'd sing: "Nous sommes les gens de la Chandeleur/Si vous-voulez nous donner de quoi/Si vous fournissez vous y viendrez/Si vous fournissez pas vous viendra pas." There were all kinds of songs and dances. It was a kind of an Indian song and a kind of Russian dance: first they'd go and tap their feet, and after their knee down and their backside down on the ground. And the man there would have his cane all decorated with ribbons and lace, and there would be eyes you'd put the ribbon through and make a bow knot. And the Chandeleur—they used to have two or three carts, and every house they went maybe one would give a chicken, one give a great big chunk of meat, maybe somebody would give a whole lot of flour and raisins and lard and what have you. And then they'd take that to the lower end of the island there, to a big house. And they'd cook it there. And as long as there was food there, they'd eat and drink and dance.

JOE DELANEY, *St. Joseph du Moine:* Take the Chandeleur my brother and I were playing down there at Marcellin Charlo Doucet's at Ruisseau du Lac in about 1934. That was one of the last ones in the district. We were playing violin. We started at three in the afternoon and we finished the next day at eleven-thirty in the morning. At that time nobody'd hire you. What they used to do, about four times during the night they'd pass the hat, taking up a collection for the fiddlers. We were on the kitchen table playing—and all you had was a

*Joe Delaney.*

*Marguerite Gallant.*

break for supper and a break for lunch and a break for breakfast—and then somebody'd be after you, "Come on let's go. Let's get the music going." Well, you didn't want to refuse. Well anyway, they took us up four collections during the night and between the two of us it amounted to fourteen dollars and forty cents. So it gave us seven dollars and twenty cents for having played for about nineteen hours you might as well say. There was no money at the time. But all the treats and the hospitality—you know, the friendship that reigned—look, you would have played for nothing. I mean, you saw that everybody was so satisfied. Because—let's take it from when the dance first opened—three—there were no teenagers there—all parents, fathers and mothers, elderlies—and the way it started off is with a French Four. There'd be two men and two women. It was a fast tune, and they would be around sixty years of age—and it was something pretty to look at, to see those two men and those two women working away. They'd step for a while standing one opposite the other—the four on the floor—then all of a sudden they'd start going around accompanying the music—and then they'd stop again and drive her again at stepping. You'd get the four best ones on the floor and look, everybody'd be looking at them. And to play for them was a pleasure, you enjoyed so much to see them dance—especially at that age. And the other one—they used to call them in French "Une Huit"—"An Eight"—something similar to the square sets they dance today but there's a difference. And the ones that could dance those Eights—they'd get almost the best there—four couples. Well, listen here. Boy, everybody did their part so well, and they were stepping away also. It was something beautiful to look at. They don't have anything today like that. No banquet to compare or wedding festivities to compare to what that had. This was a community spirit, a community festival—this thing. And everybody pitched in. Everybody wanted to make sure that it went over good. It's too bad, too bad, that it did come to an end.

MARGUERITE GALLANT: The festival of Chandeleur used to start before the second of February, because Lent would generally begin there. Not always, but when it did they'd make sure that Lent wasn't going to bother them—they had to plan their holidays. For a week they wouldn't do anything else, they wouldn't go to the woods—generally they would be all through with chopping wood, hauling it and sawing it. They'd go fishing for smelts and they'd go hunting for seals—oh, it was great sport in the olden times. Now the people are too lazy. And now they have to be paid no matter what it is. They used to work work work like slaves for nothing. Now to work for nothing is no pleasure for anybody. They would work two or three for one man, two or three for another man, until all the work was done. Then, Chandeleur.

JOE DELANEY: The first thing you had to do you had to go and visit somebody if they'd be willing to give their house for the Chandeleur. By giving the house that didn't mean they were only going to use the kitchen and the front room. In St. Joseph du Moine alone there were fifty-five families and a lot of people home at that time. When you gave your house for the population it was going to serve, well the upstairs was just as busy as the downstairs. There'd by ten or twelve in one room and fifteen in another—and they'd be talking and drinking and having a great time. So the first thing was to get someone to donate his house—and you had a hard time because it's not everyone who wanted to give his house. You generally went to the biggest houses. Then on the last of January and on the first of February—generally on the first of February—the younger men would get together. They'd use sleighs for hauling wood and they'd have an open box on it. And in there they'd have a tub for meat and containers for flour, sugar, salt, potatoes, carrots and everything. There'd be about three sleighs covering the district and they'd go to

*Chandeleur: An Acadian Feast* **61**

every house and everybody would go in and they had what they called "la cane de la Chandeleur." That was your leader. Well this cane was all decorated with ribbons up on top. And the people were expecting you because they knew you were gathering the grub to be cooked the night before and the morning of the Chandeleur. And you had a dance that they called "L'Escaouette"—the leader up front with his cane and you were dancing in a circle going around in the kitchen (each with his hands on the shoulders of the one in front, beating time)—and when it came to the chorus of the song, then you'd start stepping away.

*L'Escaouette*

C'est monsieur l'marie et madam' marie' (bis)
C'est monsieur, madam' maries (bis)
Qu'ont pas encor soupe. (bis)
Un p'tit moulin sur la riviere,
Un p'tit moulin pour passer l'eau.
Le feu sur la montain, boy run, boy run,
Le feu sur la montain, boy run away.
J'ai vu le loup, le r'nard, le lièvre,
J'ai vu la grand' cite sauter,
J'ai foule ma couvert', couvert', vert', vert'.
J'ai foule ma couvert', couverte aux pieds.
Aouenne, aouenne, guenille,
Ah! rescou' ta guenille,
Aouenne, aouenne, aouenne, nippaillon!
Ah! rescou' tes brillons.
Tibounich, nabet, nabette!
Tibounich, naba!

It's Mr. the groom and Mrs. the bride (twice)
It's Mr. and Mrs. the newly wed (twice)
Who haven't had supper yet. (twice)
A little mill on the river,
A little mill to pass over the water.
Fire on the mountain, boy run, boy run,
Fire on the mountain, boy run away.
I've seen the wolf, the fox, the hare,
I've seen the grand city leap,
I've tramped over my quilt, my quilt, quilt, quilt
I've tramped over my quilt, my quilt.
Aouenne, aouenne, raggedy dress,
He! mend your raggedy dress,
Aouenne, aouenne, aouenne, little one!
He! mend your brillons
Tibounich, nabet, nabette!
Tibounich, naba!

Then once the song was over the people'd give us the food—whatever they wanted to donate—you accepted everything. And once you had everything gathered you finished off by thanking the people with a song: "En vous r'merciont mes gens d'honneur d'avoir fournis pour La Chandeleur. Un jour viendra Dieu vous l'rendra. Alleluia." "We thank you very much folks for having contributed to the Chandeleur. One day will come, God will bless you. Halleluia." In every house it was the same ceremony. And every time your sleigh was loaded you'd take it up to the house. And the next move was to get the ladies of the district—about ten or twelve of them—to assist the woman of the house—for peeling potatoes, peeling turnips and all that. Some ladies would take home a pot of meat. There wasn't enough room to cook everything at one house.

Just to give you an idea—February second—we got into there at three in the afternoon down at Marcellin Doucet's. That was one of the last ones in the district done in the old way. My brother Arthur and I were playing the violin. Those were the hungry thirties, mister, and times were hard. We left with each our fiddle, and for our cases we had a white pillow case. We landed there at three o'clock. They were waiting for us to get the dance going. So we played till about five-thirty and then we stopped for supper. It would only be for the parents—the head of the households. The teenagers would be arriving about seven to dance. As it was they were serving seventy-five to 110 people. And you didn't stop playing the violin for the whole of the supper. We were the first table to eat. And listen here, at that time, when you went to a place like that, and once you entered the dining room and saw that table—well listen here that would make your eyes open mister twice as big as what they were. It was the Depression, and let me tell you that tables loaded with food the way these Chandeleur were presented—to see the food that was on there! Well they'd take off the potatoes and the meat, parsnips, carrots, chow, turnips and all the rest and then they'd come on with the pastry: pies, cookies, cakes, donuts—homemade donuts—well listen here were you ever full! Quarter to seven then get started back on the violin. Till about eleven, eleven-thirty. Then there was another big lunch: meat sandwiches and sweets of all kinds but the meat sandwiches were the ones you'd go for. Why? Because at a party like that—at that time you didn't talk about going to the liquor store. Everybody knew that this Chandeleur was coming. Everybody would get a gallon of molasses, you know, and make his own home brew. Molasses, yeast cake and water—that would only take you about a week to get a five-gallon keg. Others made their beer in December and they distilled it for moonshine. And some thoughtful residents had made some homemade wine for the ladies: beet wine, blueberry wine and another they used to call "chaspareille" which had a good kick in it. Mister, all the stuff to drink!

This big lunch and you'd stop for an hour and get right back at it. Round twelve-thirty the dance would continue. They were dancing in two rooms—one set in one room and one set in the other—and drive 'er MacIver. This went on till five-thirty, but about one o'clock some of the elderlies would start leaving—but some of them were going home to get a few hours sleep in order to get back there about half-past-six in the morning. We played till half-past-five and then stopped for breakfast. And after having been on home brew and moonshine for almost sixteen hours—just because we had come there to play you were offered more treats—well sometimes you had to refuse because we had been asked to play and you had to watch out not to pass out. Anyway for breakfast you didn't care for sweets, eh? You weren't too fussy about pastry and preserves. You wanted something salty. And what did they have on the menu—potatoes and pickled mackerel. Well does that ever hit the spot. And now the old timers who had gone home were coming back because they were saying to themselves, "At home we might get preserves." And after breakfast again the dance would go on till about eleven-thirty—then everybody would head for home.

MARGUERITE GALLANT: You know that Chandeleur I believe was an Indian holiday. I kind of think so. The song they used to sing: "Aouenne, aouenne"—it was supposed to be an Indian song. You know here in Cheticamp there was an awful lot of Indians when they first came. Living on the beach here. And there was some kind of village over there on the island. When you plow you find—well, yes, I found some arrowheads in my garden—but where the camps were you find oyster shells, a foot or more of oyster shells—they would plow through that. Then the French people came and the Jersey people—they used to celebrate that. They called it the Chandeleur—that's because it's the second of February—that's the day the blessed candles used to be blessed. And they *are* blessed, if you have faith. They are used if there's a big storm, a big southeast. Whether it does good or bad, it's faith. Some do it still. You get the candles from the church. You light these candles whenever you're sick, when you're going to be prepared for death. I have faith in those things; I think that's what they're blessed for. If you have no faith you're not fit to live. That is the best way to express myself.

*Mrs. Willy Deveau.*

And at the feast of Pentecost and Holy Saturday they bless the holy water. You know they use it for baptism and they use it for sacramental work. And then the other holy water is blessed for the land and the sea. You know, when I make my garden I'm going to spray a whole lot of holy water in it.

MRS. WILLIAM D. DEVEAU, *Belle Marche:* They are blessing the candles yet but we go and get them from the priest. In those days they used to make candles. Not everybody, but whoever did would make some for the neighborhood. Like an old lady who was right by where we were living. She used to make candles. She had molds, you know, and she used to melt tallow—it wasn't bee's wax then. They would take the candles to the church to be blessed on the second of February. We used to have a lot of confidence in them—more than the young people—when it was thundering, lightning and things like that—well we used to light the candles for God to preserve us. It was better than cursing, eh? And the holy water—we used to go around the house and make a cross on all the windows. Well, the old people had faith in that. But listen, if you have no faith in it, it's no use to do it. Well, I *do* have faith in it but I don't do it. I pray. Say if I was scared, I'd pray. Maybe I would light a candle if I was scared. It depends on how scared you are.

JOE DELANEY: And in those days also people would go to the church in the morning to get their throats blessed. The priest at the altar had two candles—the candles of St. Blaize—and they were crossed and caught together. There would be one on each side of your throat. The candle would be straight coming at you and then it was turned up on each side of your throat. And these candles were lit. And a lot of people wouldn't miss mass that morning—to get their throat blessed. They also blessed the candles that morning and everybody was given two. It was a yearly event.

# Oidhche Na Calluinn

*Roderick MacLeod of Wreck Cove, the last man to wear the dried sheepskin on the North Shore.*

There are a good many men today on Cape Breton who remember going out on a frosty winter evening to celebrate Oidhche Na Calluinn. They would set out in a small group or if there was a lot of territory to cover perhaps there would be two groups, one at each end of the district—and each group would have a leader who would take them door to door. Sometimes they would go on sleighs and bells would be ringing, and on stormy nights they would be on snowshoes. The occupants of each house would see their lanterns and hear them but they would not open the door. For they would hear strange sounds and see from the window a strange, strange sight.

The leader of the band would be wrapped in a dried sheepskin pulled up around his head. He would be running with another man running behind him, beating on the skin and sending up a horrible rattling sound as they circled the house three times in the direction of the sun. Then they would come to the door and the leader would yell out the

"Duan Na Calluinn." When he came to the last lines the door would be opened and the people would give something—perhaps potatoes or mutton or beef, and it would go in a bag brought to handle the goods.

Finally, they would all go to one house. It was usually a home where the people were less fortunate than their neighbors. Perhaps the father had died or was ill and it did not look as though there would be much of a holiday season in this house. They would get pots boiling and take food from the bag and cook up a terrific feast. And there would be singing and perhaps a story, and the tables would be pushed aside and a fiddler would set the whole room to dancing. And a wonderful time would be had in this house where only hours before it did not look like such a fine time could possibly be had. And it would be the wee hours and a sharp frost for the merrimakers to take off again for home, leaving behind what was left of the food—often a supply for a long, long time.

*Duan Na Calluinn* mar a thuair sinn e bho Scalpach bliadhnachan air ais

Thàinig mis' an seo air tùs
A dh'ùrachadh dhuibh na Calluinn;
Cha ruiginn a leas siud innseadh,
Bha i ann bho linn mo sheanar.
Théid mi deiseil air an fhàrdaich
'S teàrnaidh mi aig an dorus.
Craicionn Caluinn 'na mo phòcaid,
'S maith an ceò a thig bho'n fhear ud;
Chan eil duine chuireas r'a shròin e
Nach bi e ri bheò dheth fallain.
Gheibh fear an tighe 'na làimh e
Gus a cheann a chur 's an teallach.
Théid e deiseil air na pàisdean,
Ach gu h-àraid gheibh a' bhean e.
Gheibh a' bhean e, 's i as fhiach e . . .
Làmh riarachaidh na Calluinn.
Leis an tart a th'air an dùthaich
Chan eil dùil againn ri drama.
Aon rud beag a tha mi diùltadh,
Rùileagan a' bhuntàta charraich.
Cha ghabh sinn an t-aran gun an t-im
'S cha ghabh sinn an t-im gun an t-aran.
Gabhaidh sinn an càise leis féin
'S cia air éisd a bhitheamaid falamh
'S ma tha e againn r'a fhaotainn
Ma dh'fhaodas na cùm maill' oirnn.
'S fosgail an dorus 's leig a stigh sinn.

*The Calluinn Rhyme* as we got it from Scalpay (Harris) years ago

I came here first of all,
To renew for you the Calluinn;
I need not tell you that
It was there from the time of my grandfather.
I'll go sunwise round the house
And I'll descend at the door.
The Calluinn skin in my pocket,
And good will be the smoke coming from it;
There's no one who will hold it to his nose
But won't be healthy all his life.
The man of the house will get it in his hands
To put its head in the fireplace.
He'll go sunwise round the children,
But over and above, the woman of the house
will get it, The woman of the house will
get it, and she well deserves it . . .
The hand that dispenses the Calluinn.
Because of the drought in the countryside
We don't expect a drink.
One small thing that I refuse—
The tiny scabby potatoes.
We'll not take the bread without the butter,
And we'll not take the butter without the bread.
We'll take the cheese on its own
And how then could we be empty-handed
And if it's there for us to get it
If you may, do not detain us.
Open the door and let us in.

As far as we have been able to discover, these marvellous rites were last carried out on Cape Breton about forty years ago—and they had retained many aspects of the ancient pagan ritual carried out among the Celts before recorded time. In the Highlands it was a bullskin, not a sheepskin, the horns and the hooves still attached. He ran around the house sunwise—*deiseil*—because the ancient Celts oriented all things according to the direction of the path of the sun, and to have gone contrary to this would have been considered unlucky. According to Carmichael's *Carmina Gadelica*, the line "descending at the door" refers to the time when the old Highland houses were built of local stone, with very thick walls. The thatch was attached not quite to the very outside of the wall, leaving a ledge for men to stand on when thatching. The bullman would presumably run sunwise around this ledge, because projecting from the wall would be a series of stones from the ground to the ledge, usually near the door.

Carmichael adds that there were two skins, the one worn, the other carried in the pocket, a very small piece—and thus line seven of the poem.

John Gregorson Campbell in his book *Witchcraft and Second Sight in the Highlands and Islands of Scotland* (1902) describes the disorderliness of the Calluin ritual and adds another aspect we have so far been unable to explain—another poem, presumably recited prior to the Duan Na Calluin. It went: "The New Year of the yellow bag of hide,/Strike the skin (upon the wall),/An old wife in the graveyard/An old wife in the corner;/Another old wife beside the fire,/A pointed stick in her two eyes,/A pointed stick in her stomach,/Let me in, open this." This is quite far from the Calluinn as practiced on Cape Breton—but much of its old form did survive here long after it had deteriorated in the Hebrides. Today, in Scotland, on the eleventh of January, Hogmanay (the old date of New Year) what is left of the Calluinn is a children's festival. They go door to door and recite a poem and receive a treat. On Cape Breton the ritual survived more in its old form because of changes that gave it a new lease on life. Specifically, it was infused with the spirit of giving traditionally associated with Christmas. In fact, while the people of the North River district continued to go out on the last night of the year, the people of the North Shore only a few miles away practiced Oidhche Na Calluinn on Christmas Eve.

# Dan Murdoch Morrison Makes an Axe Handle

Making a good axe handle begins months in advance when you select just the right tree to cut and make splits. Ash, maple and yellow birch seem to make the best handles. Dan Murdoch used a dry split of maple with a good, straight grain.

Remove the bark and expose the sapwood of the split. This will be the back of the handle. Take a piece of lathe you know to be straight and draw lines top to bottom along the center of the sapwood and heartwood (1). It's a good idea to dig out a little gouge in the chopping block to help hold the split while you work.

You begin by holding one of the drawn lines facing you, chopping away at one of the rough sides. It is a small-scale job of hewing. You don't try to hack your way down from the top. Instead, start low on the handle, cutting in every few inches, scoring your way up (2). Then cut back down, starting from the last score, each stroke a little bit longer and heavier, driving one chip into the next and forming one long piece that falls off at the bottom (3). Look down from the top to see that the side is straight. Dan Murdoch's was. If yours is not straight, do it again, this time scoring much less deeply. Then turn the split and cut the other side in the same way.

*1*  *2*  *3*

Take your working axe handle, place it against the side of the split and trace its shape (4). Be sure to leave enough space at the top for the eye (the part that goes up through the eye of the axe head). Dan Murdoch worked with this tracing faced away from himself, but you might prefer seeing it while you work. Cut into the heartwood the shape that you've drawn, using the same hewing method—but this time do not finish the cut right to the bottom. Instead, work toward the center of the handle, into the curve at the back. Cut halfway down, leave the chip, turn the handle over and cut to the center—a sort of moon of wood chip falling off (5). Then Dan Murdoch turned the handle over, still working at the heartwood but this time with the traced lines facing him, cutting away right to the line.

Draw a new straight line top to bottom at the center of the heartwood and of the sapwood, in other words along the front and back of the handle. Instead of cutting them away, use these as your guides as you begin rounding the handle to fit the hand. Remember, you want to keep the sides of the axe handle flat, the edges of the sides gently rounding toward the center of the heartwood and sapwood. And as you work, never complete a shaving from top to bottom. Always work toward the center, turn and work toward the center—thus you will complete each shaving smoothly and controlled (6).

*4*  *5*  *6*

7

Now shape the grip, using your working handle as a model. Cut toward the center (7). Even here there should be no abrupt angle. The rightness of your handle will be its feel in your hand. The groove of the grip is made with many small cuts. These are extended toward the center. Then you cut from the center into the groove, and remove the shaving whole.

When you shape the eye to fit the eye of an axe head, it is best to work from the top. You want a straight cut. If you put the handle eye-down on the block and try to shape it, the tendency is to cut in and wedge it. It is better to stand the handle eye-up, place the blade where you want to cut and tap the new handle down on the block, working the blade in.

You now have not a split but a rough handle (8).

Now go to a workbench with a block of wood nailed to support the handle while you work. Pressing the eye of the handle against the block of wood, plane the sides flat and smooth (9). Turn the handle sapwood-up. Keep the eye wedged against the woodblock but raise the grip end in your left hand. Plane with your right. You want to keep the sides flat and curve the edges in *toward* the center of the heartwood. Take nice long strokes about three-fourths the length of the handle. Turn the handle around and over, the grip end wedged and the heartwood up. Use a small plane working in the edges where the hand will go. Note the drawing. You are planing the shaded areas. You see a line forming, a long soft S curve. Flatten the sides once again with the big plane, gradually narrow at the edges with the small plane.

8

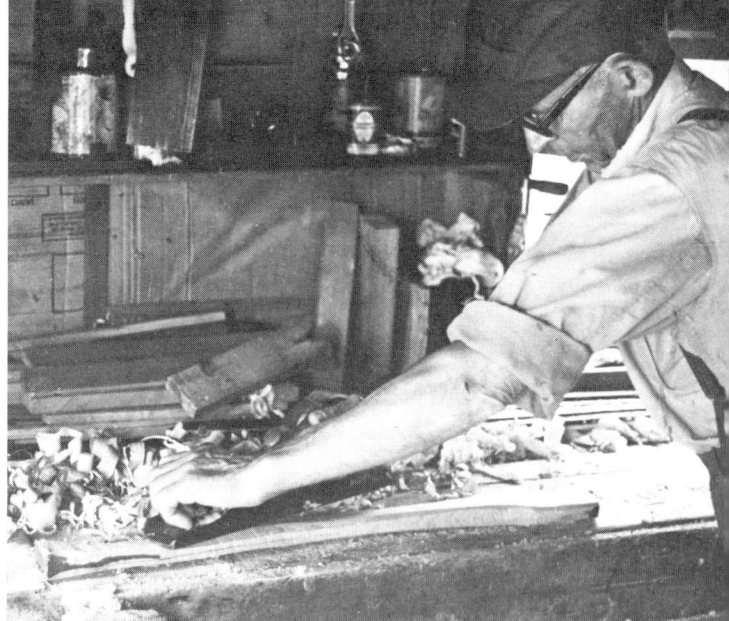
9

Dan Murdoch Morrison Makes an Axe Handle

Put the handle in a vice (10) and use a spoke shaver (a tiny draw blade). Work as you did with your axe, except that now everything is more refined. Work toward the center, turn the blade and work away completing the shaving. Now square off the top of the eye with a saw and plane the edges of the eye to fit the eye of an axe head.

Set the handle upright in one-quarter inch of oil (Dan Murdoch used Tibbetts "Boiled Oil"). This softens and swells the wood at the grip end to prevent cracks and chipping.

The handle is almost finished. Sand it with medium flint paper, by hand and with a block of wood with the paper wrapped around, always turning the handle side to side as you sand. Then take a small piece of broken window glass and use the edge of it as a plane (11), drawing it toward yourself and pushing away (see the drawing). Do not let the tips of the glass touch and gouge the wood. The edge should be flat to the wood, and the shavings will be soft and fine. Buff with fine paper.

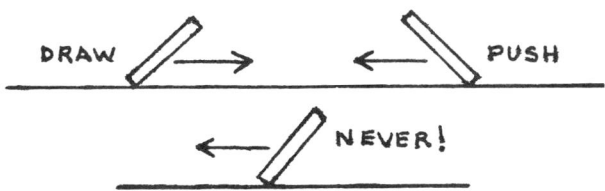

Now draw a line down the center of the top of the eye (see drawing). Some people say you should not cut the wedge slot until you've fit the handle up into the axe head. This way, if the handle is not straight you can correct the degree it is off by the angle from center you place your wedge slot. This is really only a problem with store-bought handles. You've made this one and you've been careful to keep it straight, so

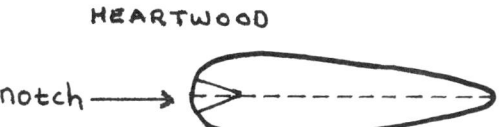

10

11

*12*

you know it is safe to slot it now. Draw the line and cut a notch to receive your sawblade. Put the handle in a vice (12). Use a hard point saw to get the slot started, then a rip saw to open the slot to receive the hardwood wedge. Saw down about two inches on one side, turn the handle and saw until the slot comes down two inches on both sides.

And there you have a strong, light, well-made axe handle.

# How I Learned to Smoke
*by John J. Matheson, 95*

My grandfather, when he died, was 105. And when his wife, my grandmother, died, she was 102. And I remember the night he died. Very fine. My cousin, this night he came to visit grandfather and grandmother. The old fellow says, "I wish you'd take me out of bed for a while. It would do me good." So they got him up and took him out of bed and set him on a chair. "Ah," he says, "that's enough. I'll be tired enough. Take me back to bed." And not as long as you were out to the machine, and back again—that would be the time he passed away.

He taught me to smoke. I was—I don't know—four or five. He was using tobacco. But he had no sight. And he couldn't make a smoke right. And it was Macdonald's Twist. There was a way of cutting it up in small pieces and putting it in a pipe. He couldn't do it. He said to me, "Did you ever use tobacco?" I said, "Yes." He said, "Did you ever make a smoke?" "Yeah," I said, "I made more than one." He said, "Tomorrow you come down with me." He gave me some matches, and the pipe. He said, "There's the pipe. I hate for you to take it from me. It's a good pipe." "Ah," I said, "I wouldn't spoil it."

I cleaned it out to make it free. I said, "I want to put them in good so it will be a good smoke." I cut them up small. And I rolled them and rolled them. I got it pretty good in the pipe. He wanted to know before he'd take it if it was all right. But the only way I could tell that was for me to try it. I'd have to light it and pull it to see if it was going good. But that's all I wanted, you know, smoke. In the kitchen, the stove was just like that, and he was pretty near the stove, in a chair. And I used to sit down, at his feet, on the floor. And when I'd get the pipe going I could smoke it till he was good and ready. I did that for I don't know how many years.

So that's the way I learned to make it, and to smoke. I was probably five. And I've been smoking for the last ninety years. I never quit.

# Remembering St. Paul's Island

St. Paul's Island is the northernmost tip of Cape Breton Island, thirteen miles northeast of Cape North in Cabot Strait. J. S. Erskine writes "The island is three-and-a-quarter miles long, a mile wide, and is strategically placed to be the greatest possible danger to shipping entering the St. Lawrence. Warm eddies from the Gulf Stream at times come so near the island that flying fish are seen in Atlantic Cove, the tail of the Labrador Current also swings past, and the St. Lawrence River, now warmer, now colder than the Atlantic, flows to it from the northwest. So fogs are frequent, winds violent and lasting, and currents uncertain. Waves and ice have gnawed at the island shores, until now the cliffs rise to an average of thirty feet."

It became known as the "Graveyard of the Gulf." There is no one who knows how many shipwrecked bodies are buried there today, or how many more lives were lost at sea around her. In the spring, parties used to go out from northern Cape Breton to bury the dead. Fires would be seen in the winter, but there was no way to reach those brief survivors and give aid. Then the wreck of the Jessie (from which Jessie's Cove on the southwest gets its name) made the need for some sort of lifesaving station horribly clear. Most of the crew and passengers got ashore after she wrecked at St. Paul's, January 1, 1825. They lived on for over ten weeks, and then died of starvation. A diary kept during those weeks told the story. Still, it was 1832 before Humane Establishments were put on the island—the governments of New Brunswick and Nova Scotia, unknown to one another, sent small crews and provisions to live on the island. In 1837, the British Government erected two lighthouses, one at each end, and in 1838 a station was built at Atlantic Cove. Today, there are few people stationed on St. Paul's, and they all live at the northeast. But it was not so long ago, that there was quite a community there: a wireless station, families at each of the lighthouses, a family at the fog alarm, a

*A view of St. Paul's Island, looking across the Tittle (called The Tickle on the map).*

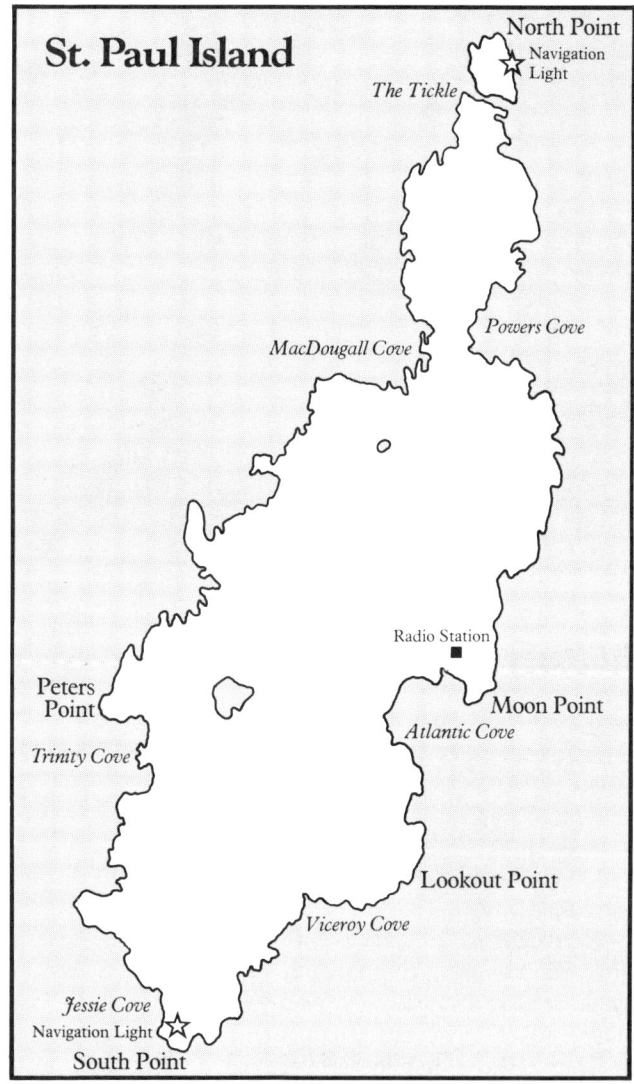

*Jack Nicholson.*

*lifesaving crew, a number of assistants and a governor to oversee the whole operation. At Christmas time there would be such an exchange of presents it took the whole day just to open them all.*

*Here are some memories of people who lived out there fifty to seventy years ago.*

JACK NICHOLSON: I was born here in Baddeck in 1885. And I first went out to St. Paul's Island 1911. That first time I was out with those fellows building a fog whistle, a new one, on the northeast. They used to call it The Tittle. Then I went back and I went with the lifesaving crew. And I was out a fall and a winter and part of a summer, 1912. I made thirty-two dollars a month and found. The winter's not too bad, not too bad at all—but you're shut in. You can't get out. It gets pretty rough, very rough. You weren't allowed outside on a windy day. The wind was bad and there were particles of ice flying—that was where I was first. It was worse the other place, the northeast. They had to have a rope between the kitchen door and the lighthouse. And I had to hold onto that to get to the lightkeeper. But we were young. It was an adventure. We liked it all right.

In the spring, this time, we went after seals, on the north side. We got four hundred seals that spring. We had a sheath knife in our belt, and a club—and when you'd see a seal you'd club him cross the nose and sell him. That's the way we done that. We'd pelt them right there. We had an old Newfoundlander, he was a sealman—he used to go sealing on the schooners. And he showed us how to sculp them and leave the fat right on the hide. We'd clip them in the tow. We'd lace a rope through the eyes. Well, if they were heavy or big, four would be a load to haul on the ice, you know. It was slippery, of course, the fur was slippery, and that's the way we used to get them into the land. You had to go way out on the ice. You'd have to go out and get among the seal—they were thick, thousands of them. Once we got on an ice floe and were drifting, but they got us off. The boss saw us and got a boat out to us. I think I had five pelts on a drag that time.

Then you'd take the pelts and put them ashore. Put them up on the cliffs, here and there and everywhere. Then when the ice would go, in the spring, we took the surf-boat around and picked them all up. It was a big boat, something like a lifeboat, but the oars were sixteen feet long. There was no talk of motor boats them days—just muscles. There was four or five of us on the oars. The boss was in the stern steering. He was a good one. John M. Campbell. There was just a lightkeeper and a cook for crew. We didn't even have a wireless. We had a cable running to Cape North. And the ice came in and broke it. We were out trying to fix it but we never could. That was the year the Titanic was lost, and we never heard for over a month. In the evenings we'd read novels and tell lies. Play cards. And we ate well. The food was perfect. Fresh cod any time you want. Lobsters. Once I got the cook to cook flippers. We had a fussy cook you know. I said to the boss one day, I'd like to try a flipper. He said, Well you can go up and ask the cook but I wouldn't. Me and the cook was pretty good friends. I went in and I said—her name was Mrs. MacMillan—Would you mind cooking a flipper for me? What are they like, she says? Smell? Aw, I don't think, I says. All right, she says, I'll try them, and God help you, she says, if they're smelly. After half an hour or so a fellow says go on up now and see what she's like. Jeez, I went in she was lying on the lounge with an apron over her head. I says, How're you getting on? You fly the hell out of here, you and your darn flippers. But we had the flippers. I liked the flippers. They were good.

KATE REDMOND: People used to tell stories of people who died on St. Paul's. You see, if you died there you had to wait until summertime to be buried. And there were stories—I don't know if my older sister made them up—that there were money-hunters and they'd dig them up and take the rings off people's hands. There was a funny thing happened when I was very young. I had a younger sister, Marie. She was a very beautiful child. She had golden hair and the most beautiful

*Remembering St. Paul's Island* 73

eyes you ever saw. She looked like an angel. We all sort of worshipped her. Some people told my mother she would never raise her, she was too beautiful. Anyway, she did live. But anyway I remember this night. The night, the moon would shine, you could see the pictures on the wall in the bedroom. It seemed like a brighter moon than we get here [on Cape Breton Island itself]. And we were in this great big bedroom. My older sister, Caroline, she slept in one corner. My bed was over in the other corner. And I had my sister Marie with me. And during the night, I felt like there was something in bed with us. And my sister Marie was on the inside, next to the wall. And this thing pushed against Marie and I got over to the edge of the bed and pulled Marie over by me and it kept pressing. And I put my foot down and it was like a hairy leg. And I'd look around the room and I could see the sky and the pictures on the wall. And I'd whisper Caroline, Caroline—and every time I would say anything this thing would press harder. I was scared to get out of bed, this thing would jump and catch me. But I was wide awake. And I could hear him breathing. Queer heavy low breathing. So anyway I put through the night. When I heard mama moving down in the kitchen I beat it downstairs. I told mama. And she moved my bed. Oh, she said, I think you were just imagining. But years afterward, I asked her why she moved it if she didn't believe. Well, she said, There were bad things happened there. And who knows but what some spirit was earthbound. That was my only experience. But it was so real that I can feel it, feel the shinbone. The hair on whatever it was legs.

On Sunday afternoon—you see there was no minister out there—in the summertime a student minister would come out—mama used to have Sunday school, Sunday afternoon. She'd invite all the people on the island. And they'd read the Bible and sing. We had an old fashioned organ. This afternoon after Sunday school we were all sitting around, and the wind sort of opened the front door. It was a beautiful afternoon. And there was the most beautiful music you ever heard. Just like a choir, the voices came in. And we all looked around. There was no radio or anything then, you know. And mama said, Oh, I've heard that often. Mama used to go for a walk, just in the woods around, and oftentimes she heard music.

I was three or four when I went out to St. Paul's. I can remember traveling by the *Harlaw*. A big steamer, she's been gone a long, long time. [The *Harlaw* was wrecked near St. Paul's April 7, 1911—first battered in a storm then crushed in the floes.] They'd anchor offshore and the lifeboats would come out to meet you. We were sort of between the gover-

*Kate Redmond.*

nor's house and the lighthouse, and we had this big old fog alarm. The fog would come in very, very suddenly. Sometimes you'd go to bed at night the moon would be shining. You'd get up an hour later fogged in. They'd have to hustle down and until they got the steam up they'd have to pull the alarm on by hand. And as long as there was fog that had to be going. There was no weather forecast. It was very desolate. The winter was cold. But it was really a glorious world, a world of make-believe for us kids. It was beautiful when the sun came up over the ice. I have seen scenes from the Arctic that remind me very much. White ice for miles. And then the seals used to come in. The men would go sealing. That wasn't very nice, to see blood on the ice. And they used to pull a boat with them, just in case the ice would open up. It made excitement for them. And we used to eat the flippers. I don't suppose I'd eat them today but I thought they were great. My father when it was iced in would build furniture. Mama kept everybody busy. She'd be hooking mats. The boys from the lifesaving crew weren't fed very well. She'd have them up and she got them all hooking and she'd put a big feed on for them. I can remember one time she made a mattress and she got a bunch of them combing horsehair for that. They were nice boys. And they were lonesome.

One story that amused me. There was this old cow down at the governor's mansion and oh she'd been giving milk for years and years and years without having a calf—and she was as tough—you know, there wasn't too good a pasture. So the time came to cut Daisy's head off. The boys butchered her and fixed her all up. And one of the boys put a brand on her. He said, I'll know this old carcass if I meet her in Hell. And they shipped the cow away to the meat processing place. Anyway, the last boat that came in that fall with supplies for the winter—didn't that old carcass come back to the island for the boys to eat that winter? Two of the boys cried.

SARAH GWINN: I had a baby born out there with no doctor. My husband brought the things I needed. I had lifted a trunk and it was quite heavy. I knew I wasn't the same. I was seven months pregnant. There was a storm. The lightkeeper's wife and her husband must have been an hour and a half before they got to our place. She was very nervous. There was nothing she could do for me at all. I said, "You go sit out in the hall till I call you." Dr. Munro sent a message to press down on the lower part of my stomach, so I did. Then I just took two bad pains and the baby came. The telegram was on the chair. Wilson brought me up a spool of coarse thread. I twisted it. The telegram said to tie an inch and a half from the mother and an inch and a half from the baby and cut both places, so I did. Then it said to knead my stomach down. I gave it three hard pushes and the afterbirth came. After that came I was frightened of hemorrhaging. I called Mrs. MacLennan. She just took a blanket and rolled the baby right up in it. The doctor wouldn't let me nurse it. Kept putting a little warm water in her mouth, Mrs. MacLennan did. But she washed the baby, which she wasn't supposed to do. Didn't do any harm though. It was twenty-four hours before Dr. Munro got there. He made little jackets out of cotton cloth and he'd stick them in warm olive oil and rolled her up in it. We kept her on top of the warming closet in a little shoebox. She was about ten inches and she didn't weigh quite four pounds. But with the help of the Lord she lived, and she's married down here and she has three daughters married. But I lost a little boy out there. He was only five months when he was born. He's buried alongside an old captain's grave, just a little piece from the southwest light. Wilson always looked after the captain's grave. He kept a cross made for it.

WILSON GWINN: Dr. Munro made quite a few trips out there for us. When that baby was born he came out and there was a storm on. The government steamer took him out, the *Stanley,* and they wouldn't put a boat off at the island at the south side. And me and the wireless operator offered to put our boat out, and that kind of nettled the captain. He came along to the other side of the island, landed the doctor there. And when the doctor was through and called the ship she was anchored in Bay St. Lawrence. He was left out there seven days in December. The weather shifted northerly and the *Stanley* had to go on to Sydney. And I didn't like the look of fifty dollars a day. That was what they charged then, but Dr. Munro didn't charge that much. You know, it never occurred to us to worry about being so far from a doctor. The children never got sick. If you could get by there for six months you'd never get a cold on St. Paul's Island. Unless somebody came from the mainland to bring it.

SARAH GWINN: Once Wilson went ashore, for the mail I think. He left in the morning. He intended to come back that evening. It started to blow hard. So he wired a message out from Dingwall that he couldn't. Well that's the only really time that ever I was scared. I was frightened if I'd fall asleep, that I wouldn't get up. You had to go out every four hours to wind this light. I set the alarm. Oh, it wasn't nearly as far as from here to the road at all. But it was just the ocean on one side and a grove of woods on the other. I didn't mind going to the light, but it was coming back. I just thought if an old boat came ashore... I got in the house and locked the door. I thought, Well, it will go four hours. I fell asleep anyway. And I woke up just in time I was supposed to go out. But it was real dark. I said, No. I didn't go out. And the light kept

*Sarah and Wilson Gwinn and two daughters on St. Paul's Island.*

a-going for over five hours. It was bright when I went out. Otherwise, I wasn't scared. I've come from the wireless station home in pitchdark. The only thing I was scared of was some kind of bird—Mother Carey's Chickens. They fly right up in your face almost. You only see them at night. If you put your hand near them the smell was something awful. They'd bore down in a hole in the ground. [The bird Mrs. Gwinn refers to is Leach's Petrel, a bird noted as a problem for keepers of island lighthouses. It lives most of its life at sea but comes ashore to breed in colonies, burrowing up to three feet in the ground. There is a 1930 record of a breeding colony on Ciboux Island, Victoria County, and a 1954 report of a small colony on a peninsula near Louisbourg. John Erskine wrote: "The boys at the Southwest Light found the nests by their smell, and the chicks defended themselves by spitting a reddish fluid... These curious seabirds hatch out their eggs in seven weeks. They then feed the chicks on oil, one feed at midnight so that the chicks may take three months to grow to flying size." Because of this quite a few are often frozen in their burrows.]

WILSON GWINN: Oh, St. Paul's is a nice spot. But when you spend as much time as we did—a year and a half at the lifesaving station, a year and a half at the wireless, and then ten years at the Southwest Light—when you come off of it, it's just that much time of your life you might as well not have lived. There was nothing. No excitement, no nothing. Just a blank. I figured once, I think I got thirteen cents an hour for the time I put in with the light and like of that. Twenty-four hours a day. Eighty dollars a month at first. Then ninety-five was the highest. And you paid for everything but the kerosene you burned in the lamp. You'd send in a monthly report—oil consumed, weather report—and if you put an extra gallon they came back quick where was it. I went out with nothing and I came back with nothing. But it wasn't awful lonesome out there. I never found it lonesome. And the time just flies by.

SARAH GWINN: Looking back, I enjoyed myself so much, if I was young I'd go back again. It's a beautiful spot, St. Paul's. There were times in winter I'd get lonely but I'd never get lonely in the summertime—because of the Newfoundland fishermen. In the evening we'd have high as sixteen to supper. I've seen seven or eight Newfoundlanders in a single day each with a nice great big fresh halibut. I used to bottle it and have it for a whole year out there. It was a good life. I was only married a little over a year when we went out there. I never had any regrets.

# How Leather Was Sewn

"Now this wax, this is stuff that's very poor. It's too old to begin with. I remember my grandfather used to make this stuff. Used to make it from rosin and pine tar and I know he used to put a little grease in it. He had this one little ladle, he used to boil it in that. And when he had it all ready mixed up he'd just dump it in a pan of water. Cold water. Then he'd take it in his hand and was working it and working it until he'd get it right. Rosin and tar and a little grease. That would be cow fat or sheep fat. I imagine you can buy rosin in any drug store. Violin places are using it yet anyways."

Then Donald Garrett took the ladle to the stove and put it into the firebox, right into the wood coals. The mixture melted, soon began to smoke, and then boiled. He'd take it out, stir it and put it back. Boiling down, the stuff began to thicken. He said that sometimes it has to be boiled three times

*Donald Garrett MacDonald.*

*Stirring a mixture of rosin, tar and fat in a ladle.*

*Top: The mixture goes into the firebox at the stove. Above: After it's chilled on water the wax is made pliable again by working it in the hands.*

to get the right consistency. Then, the stuff smoking furiously, he took the ladle to the sink and dumped the contents into a pan of cold water. It spread on the surface of the water and immediately became hard. It was like a sheet of thin plastic. He took it and cracked it up in his hands. The warmth of his hands made it pliable again. "If it wasn't hard enough, my grandfather'd put it back and put in a little more rosin, and if it was too hard you'd put a little extra pine tar. You just have to try it." He put the wax on a small piece of leather to give it backing, and brought up the sides to make it comfortable to hold and to run along the threads.

"Well, I'll bet it's been forty-five years since I didn't make that. My grandfather made it. I was always with him whatever he'd be doing. I remember he used to let us take some for gum. It was good. Then he'd want to stop us, so he'd put the wax on a piece of leather and lift the dog's tail and pretend to rub it on the dog's behind. It was the only way to stop us from taking it for gum."

Making a good piece of wax is the first step in sewing leather. You want to end up with a sewing thread made of a number of plies of shoemaker's thread twisted together and thoroughly waxed, the ends tapering to a needle-like point, and (if available) a pig bristle added at each end. You buy a ball of shoemaker's thread and wind off about four feet. To break it properly, take it between your thumbs and forefingers and turn it against the twist of the thread, opening the separate strands and weakening the thread at that place. Take a tight hold at both sides of this opened place—Donald

Garrett wraps the thread around his little fingers so it won't slip—and in one quick pull snap the thread. This will break and fray the ends, so they will later taper. Do this to two more threads, each four feet long. (This will make a finished sewing thread of three-ply, which is good for most work. Heavier work might take five-ply. It would depend, also, on the weight of thread you use. Donald Garrett's was Number fifteen.) Take the ends of three lengths and put them together, each a little bit back from the next, so as to taper the point and keep it from becoming blunt. Hold the three

*How Leather Was Sewn* 77

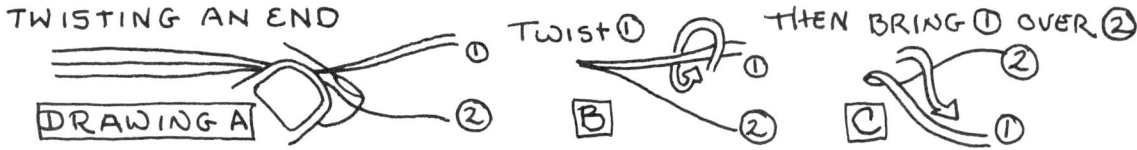

lengths back about 3 inches from the end between the left thumb and forefinger and separate the threads so that two are together and one is alone (see Drawing A). Holding the lengths gripped tightly in the left hand, thoroughly wax the two strands and the single strand. Look at Drawings B and C. Twist strand no. 1 *away* from yourself, between the right thumb and forefinger. Then, keeping the twist in it, bring it toward yourself over 2 and grip it tightly between the little finger and the ring finger of the left hand. This holds the twist in 1. Now take strand no. 2, twist it away from yourself between the right thumb and forefinger, then bring it toward yourself over strand no. 1, placing it between the little finger and ring finger and taking up 1 to be twisted again. Keep doing this, one after the other, adding wax now and then—and because of the way you tore off the lengths, the thread will come down to a firm hair tip, quite good for sewing. Wax the end some more. Now do the same to the other end of the three strands. Run your fingers the length of the three strands to get them even. Then separate to one strand and two strands, wax and twist the other end.

Now you want to put a twist along the 4 feet of thread. Donald Garrett wrapped one end of the strands a couple turns around an awl and stuck the tool in the couch. He held the other end across his knee and used the flat of his hand pushing away from himself over the strands, putting a twist in it. Now and then he would run thumb and forefinger the length of the strand toward the awl, running the turns up the length of it. When he had a good even twist the whole length of it, he took the end from over his knee and put it *back of that knee,* drawing his leg up to grip it there. Then he took the other end off the awl and held it so the turns would not come out. Caught at the back of his knee and wrapped once around that knee and then held high (see the photograph), the strand was firm enough to run the wax back and forth along it, heavily waxing. The natural color of the shoemaker's thread disappeared under the very dark brown of the wax. When half the length was waxed he shifted knees, turning the thread so the well-waxed end was gripped back of the knee and once around it, and the unwaxed portion was held aloft for waxing. The wax actually fills in the thread and makes it stiff. To take the stickiness out of it, Donald Garrett ran it through his hair. He said that it leaves nothing in your hair.

With this waxed thread alone you could do your sewing, but Peter Kerr of Cape North told us that years ago, "when

*Making three-ply thread.*

*Putting a twist in the thread.*

*Left to right: Waxing the thread; running the thread through the hair to remove stickiness.*

we killed the pig late in the fall we always took the bristles for to have to sew. You took the bristles before you scalded it for to clean it. If you scalded them it took the good out of them. And then you'd take that bristle and split it down to an inch and a half you'd leave for sewing with. Then you'd put your thread end in the split." It had to be an older pig, something very difficult to find today. You put the very tip of your thread well into the split, close the split and roll the entire bristle away from you, winding the thread on six or seven turns along the split (see Drawing E). Hold the bristle as you did the threads in Drawing A. Let the bristle be no. 1 and the waxed thread no. 2. And twist each in turn exactly as you did the separated strands of the thread. Keep doing this till you come to the portion of the thread where it begins to be its full thickness (after about five or six twists and exchanges)—and it is stout enough to open the thread with the awl, back about ½ inch from your last twist (Drawing F). Put the pig bristle through this opening and *gently* draw it through. Always be extremely careful of the bristle when sewing—it is just to get through the awl holes easily. Once through, grip the thread itself to pull. Wax all but the end of the bristle. Put a pig bristle on the other end, and sew.

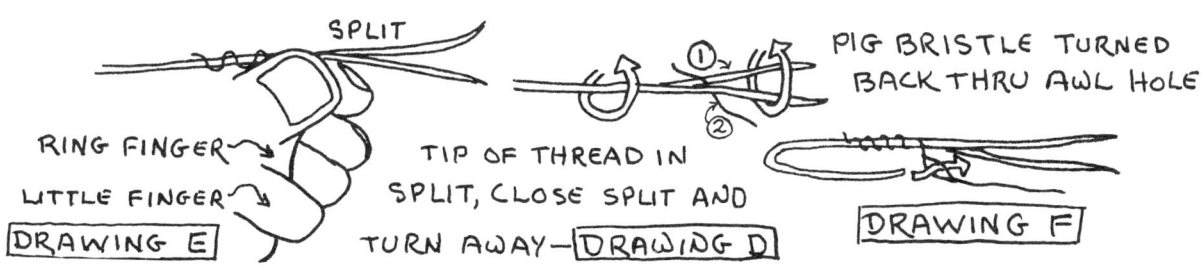

*How Leather Was Sewn*

We offer below instructions for making a pair of larrigans. It requires a single basic sewing stitch. It's a good idea to make equally spaced marks where your awl will go through. A wheel of a clock or some such tool will do this neatly, but Donald Garrett told us that an experienced person would never bother with this. Put the material to be sewn in some sort of clamp. One like Peter Kerr is pictured with would be ideal, but very careful use of a vice (probably with some padding) should do the trick. You most likely will not be working with pig bristles, and thus the following is your method of sewing to get both ends of the thread through the same awl hole.

Make a hole through both pieces of leather with a straight awl and put the waxed thread through to the center of its length. Now follow the sequence of Drawing G. Make a second awl hole and put end A through about 6 to 8 inches (2). Wax end B and twist the very hair tip of it onto end A, back a couple of inches (3). Twist toward yourself. Pull end A back through the awl hole until you can get hold of end B (4). Separate the ends and take A in one hand and B in the other and *start* to pull them through. BUT don't pull them quite all the way. First put end B through the loop of A (6). You could also put A through B's loop—but just one will do the trick. Now, when you finish pulling the stitch tight, you will have formed a knot and buried it in the leather—a knot that will keep the stitch snug and prevent it from ripping.

In case you have to sew with two shorter pieces of waxed thread (perhaps perfectly good scraps each a couple feet long), start out at the place where you intend to make your second awl hole. Using the twisting-on method, draw both ends through the awl hole until about an inch of each is left. Back up and make the first awl hole and take both ends through as you did the single thread. Take end A through B's loop and end B through A's loop. Go once again through the second awl hole, and continue on.

*Pete Kerr with sewing clamp.*

# A Pair of Larrigans

Larrigans were once a popular form of footgear on Cape Breton Island. Made of well-oiled leather, they stood up well in wet or dry weather, were excellent on snowshoes, but were slippery as the devil on wet snow or ice. There was more than one Maritime firm producing larrigans, but Cape Bretoners usually preferred to make their own. It depends on what part of the island you are from, just what the word larrigan means. Down at Cape North a larrigan would have a tongue and lace up the front; a stovepipe legging would be called a moccasin. On the North Shore it would be exactly opposite. We'll use larrigan here to mean a moccasin bottom with a stovepipe legging having a single lace through belt-like loops to draw the top closed above the calf. We chose that not only because it is a simpler shoe to make, but because we think the origin of the word larrigan is in the Gaelic word *luirgeann* (or *luirigeann*) meaning legging or shin. *Luirgneach* means sheepshanked, but larrigans were always made of cowhide for the moccasin, the leggings of calfskin. Nowadays the toughest part about making larrigans will be finding that calfskin.

The pattern is only for general help. You'll know how much you need for the heel only after the instep (top) is sewed to the bottom and you can put your foot in—so cut it extra large at the heel. Look at the cross-section, front view. It will give you an idea of how much leather you will need at the sides. Notice how the bottom comes up and around, and how the instep (the piece covering the top of the foot) fits and is joined with the bottom. We have seen a last carved by Donald Garrett MacDonald's grandfather, Phillip D., used just for the shaping of the toe of a larrigan. It was good for both left and right, as the final shaping took place when the larrigan was worn. Wet leather would be drawn up tight around the last and tacked in place to dry. It would hold the form. Then the bottom could be slipped on a foot and the size of the instep determined. But many people we talked to said that a good job can be done by simply tacking the instep to a piece of leather cut for the bottom—a stitch or two at A and B and C. The bottoms, of course, will bulge, being longer and wider. You will take bigger stitches out of the instep—$\frac{2}{8}$ inch long in the step, $\frac{3}{8}$ inch long in the bottom. As you draw each stitch tight you will be crimping the bottom and bring it up and round. It will look as it does in the photo of toe stitching. The vertical lines were not made by the stitches; a dull piece of metal has been rubbed into the center of each crimp, to help it gather smoothly and even. Sew from toe center to side (B to A, then B to C). Draw each stitch good and tight, and don't forget to come through the loop to seal each stitch and to keep it from ripping.

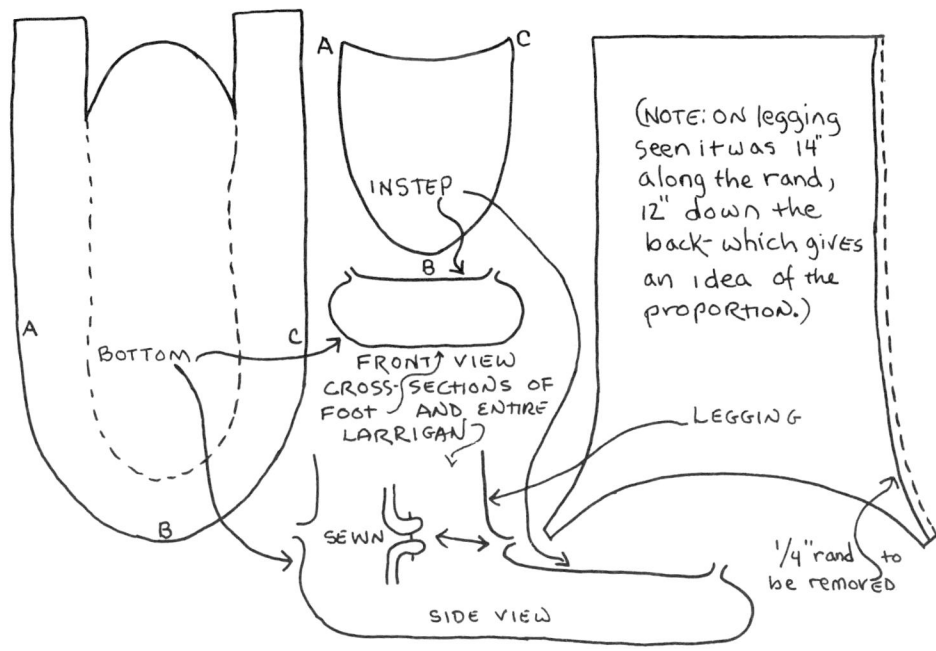

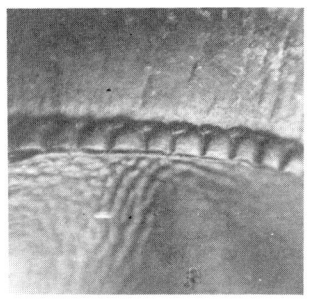
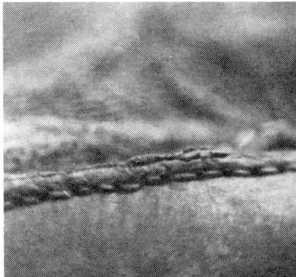
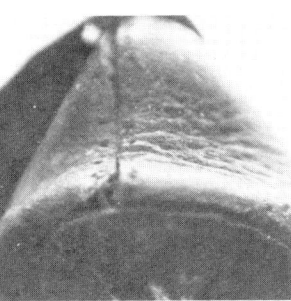
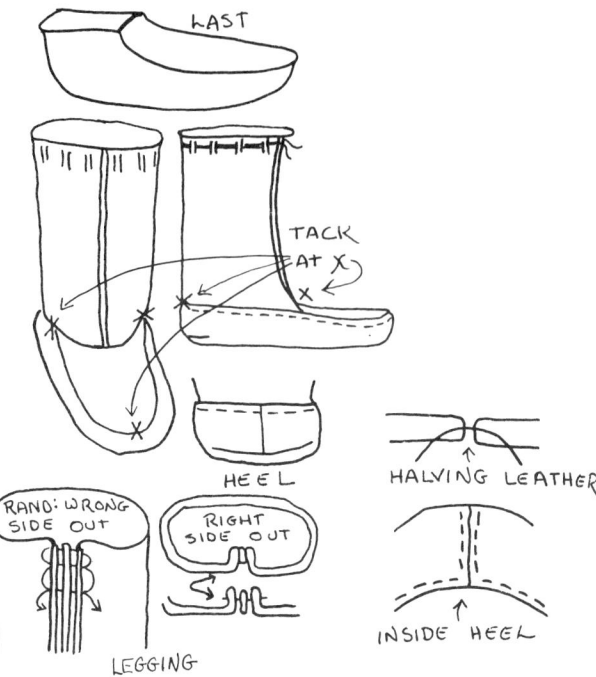

*Above: Toe. Above right: Legging sewn to bottom. Right: Heel.*

Once the toe is finished, slip your foot in (wearing as many pairs of socks as you think you'll want), and determine where to cut the round at the heel and how long the flaps should be to meet end to end at the center of the back of the heel. Disregard the awl holes you see in the photo of the finished heel. You do not want your stitches to come all the way through, not if you expect your feet to stay dry. Sew the heel from the inside, and only halve the leather as shown in the drawing. This will require a very crooked awl. Sew the bottom first, then up the back. Finish off by going back through your next-to-last stitch a second time. Then take a string and run it along the opening of the finished moccasin. Measure it and you'll know how wide to cut the leather for the bottom portion of the legging (D to E). How high they go is up to you. Tying just below the knee is good. Wrap the calfskin around your calf and determine the curve at the instep. As shown in the pattern, when you cut the legging, trim off a strip the full length and about ¼ inch wide. This is your rand (some people call it the cord). Turn the legging wrong side out and place the rand as shown in the drawing and sew from top to bottom. Trim the rand flush and turn the legging right side out. Tack the legging front and back and perhaps also once on each side—and sew it on one side at a time, front to back. You take the same size bit (the same size stitch) out of both pieces of leather—and thus you will end up with the even stitching in the photograph. Cut belt-like loops about 1½ inches apart and ½ inch down from the top, around the legging. Put a lace of leather ³⁄₁₆ inch wide through the loops and tie it as you would a shoelace. And finally, to be larrigans they must be waterproof. Every man you'll meet has a formula. Here is a practical one from Tommy Peggy Mac-Donald. Mix beef tallow, kerosene to penetrate, and linseed oil. Heat it up and apply with a small mop. Three applications and you can stand in water.

# Joe MacNeil Tells a Wonderful Story

*Gaelic was the first language of most of the older generation of the Scots of Cape Breton. Whether or not the language will survive here is still a question, and there is some evidence of younger people willing to see to it that in their own lives it will be a living thing. If it does survive, Joe Neil MacNeil will be regarded as a man who not only refused to turn his back on the language but who also kept alive much of the traditional material that belongs to it. While it can be argued that there is something of the quality of a bearer of tradition in nearly everyone in this book, Joe Neil stands out. He is a corridor through which tradition passes unaltered from the distant past into our own present. It is an exhibition of incredible obedience to not impose yourself upon the tale, and it is an equally incredible demonstration of social responsibility to both bear the tales for the community and to share them willingly.*

*We offer this extraordinary story, of course, in both Gaelic and English. It was transcribed and translated by John Shaw of Kingsville, who has devoted the better part of the last fifteen years to the Gaelic language and its traditional materials. That this story has been saved is an achievement for both men, and a gift to us.*

I used to tell a lot of stories, but then after a time, when you'd get out around where people weren't so interested in that line, you more or less give up the telling of stories. And then you wouldn't be so good at it, once you give it up. For a long time you didn't have much confidence in yourself. I don't have so many as I did. You forget them. Giving them up for a while you don't remember certain parts. It puts you astray. There were no listeners. You need both sides. There has to be a side that produces the sound and there has to be an ear to hear it, otherwise it doesn't register.

I don't know why I tell stories. Some people tell stories, well, from just hearing them and I guess you like to follow along those lines. If the stories appeal to you I imagine that you'd like to be able to tell stories as well. If you like people telling you stories you'll eventually get to learning them and tell them. I always liked to hear stories. In my time you'd hear lots of stories. Folklore was so common. There were old maids traveling in the country years ago and they were wonderful, wonderful entertainers. They had stories and songs. They would go visiting, and of course they were going to entertain you if you went to their homes. Some of the women were terrific there. They were gifted. Some families had both the boys and the girls as they grew up—both sides were good at telling stories.

To be a story, it had to be fairly long. Too short would not be appealing to us. We wanted a story to have quite a little bit to it. A short story, we didn't think there was quite enough in it for us. And it wouldn't make any difference how long the stories were, I'd be learning them as they'd be telling them and when they were through I knew them, every word.

## Iain mac an Iasgair Mhóir

Bha fear ann ris an abradh iad an t-ias-gair mór agus tha e coltach gu robh e ùine ri iasgachadh 's gu robh e 'na iasgair math. Thàinig an sin ceiltinn air an iasg agus cha robh iad ri'm faotainn idir. Bha a h-uile rud gu math gann. Ach lath' dha 'nuair a bha e amach ag iasgach thàinig maighdean-mhara neo creutair mór anuas as a' chuan ri taobh a' bhàta agus dh'fhoighneachd i dha an robh e a' faighinn iasg an diugh. O, thuirt e nach robh. A nisd bha seòrsa de dh'eagal aige ro chreutairean mar sin—gu robh droch-chumhachd aca—agus bha e glé choma dhi. Ach co-dhiubh, dh' fhoighneachd i dha gu dé an duais a nisd a bheireadh e dhi-se nan cuireadh i gu leòr de dh'iasg fo na lin aige. O, thuirt e nach robh duais aige-san a bheireadh e do dhuine sam bith airson sian. Agus dh' fhoighneachd i dha an robh sian aige 'na ainm fhéin. O, thuirt e rithe nach robh sian aige-san ach seann-làir agus seannghalla agus seann-bhean: gura h-e sin a bh' ann a bh'aigesan ris an t-saoghal uile.

"Matà," ors' ise, "nan tugadh tu dhomhsa gealltanas air do cheud mhac 'nuair a bhios e seachd bliadhna a dh'aois, cuiridh mi iasg gu leòr gu d' lìn a h-uile latha."

"Bu duilich dhomhsa," ors' esan, "sin a dheanamh. Mar a thuirt mi cheana," ors' esan, "tha mi fhìn agus mo bhean sean le chéile agus cha'n eil dùine idir theaghlaich againn."

"Coma leat," ors' ise, "ma bheir thu do ghealltanas dhomhsa."

A nisd aid tàilleabh gu robh eagal aige roimpe, thuirt e rith' gu'n toireadh e a ghealltanas dhi. Agus chuir i gràineannain de dh'fhùdar neo de shìol air choireiginn 'na làimh anns an dealachadh agus thuirt i ris, "Seo," ors' ise, "gabh cùram dheth sin. Agus 'nuair a theid thu dhachaidh," ors' ise, "cuiridh tu trì ghràineannain dhe sin anns a' bhiadh a bhios a' bhean a' gabhail. Agus cuiridh tu," ors' ise, "trì ghràineannain dhe anns an t-sìol a bhios tu a' toirt dha'n làiridh. Agus cuiridh tu trì ghràineannain dheth anns a' bhiadh a bhios tu 'toirt dha'n ghallaidh. Agus theid mi'n urras," ors' ise, "mun tig trì bliadhna a dh' ùine gu'm bi atharrachadh air an dachaidh agad seach mar a th'oirre an diugh."

Co-dhiubh, thainig esan dhachaidh agus fhuair e iasg gu leòr aig an fheasgar a bha 'sin. Ach ged a bha e a' faighinn an éisg bha seòrsa de dh'eagal air ro na cùisean a bh'ann. Ach co-dhiubh, mar a thuirt an té ris, thàinig e fior gu leòr: mun d' thàinig na trì bliadhna a dh'ùine bha trì searraich mhòra, bhriagha, dhubh' aig an t-seannlàir, agus bha trì cuileinean briagha, reamhar' aig a' ghallaidh. Agus bha triùir mhac aig bean an Iasgair Mhóir.

Ach co-dhiubh bha an ùine a dol seachad agus thàinig e gu

## Iain, the Big Fisherman's Son

There was once a man called the Big Fisherman, and it seems that he had worked at fishing for some time and was a good fisherman. Fish became so scarce then that none were to be found, and everything was scarce for him. But one day as he was out fishing a sea-maiden or some other creature came up out of the ocean beside the boat and enquired if he were catching fish that day. He replied that he was not. Now the fisherman was afraid in a way, of creatures of that kind—perhaps that they had evil powers—and was very indifferent toward her. But she asked him what reward he would give her if she were to drive a good share of fish into his nets, and he answered that he did not have a reward to give to anyone for anything. She asked him then if he had anything to his name and he told her that all he possessed in the entire world was an old mare, an old she-dog and an old wife.

"Well," she said, "if you promise me your first son when he is seven years of age, I'll put plenty of fish in your nets every day."

"That would be difficult for me to do," he said. "As I told you already, my wife and I are both old and we have had no offspring at all."

"Don't be concerned with that," she said, "if you give me your promise."

Now because he was afraid of her, the Big Fisherman agreed to give her his promise, so as she left him she put grains of powder or some kind of seed into his hand and said to him, "Here. Take care of this and when you reach home put three grains into the food that your wife eats. Put three grains in the oats that you give to the mare, and three grains into the food that you give the she-dog. And I'll wager," she said, "before three years have passed that there will be a change in your house from the way it is today."

Anyway, the Big Fisherman went home, and he had caught plenty of fish that evening. But even though he was catching fish again he was still somehow fearful concerning the state of things. In any event what the mermaid had told him came true: Before the three years had passed the mare had given birth to three big, fine black foals, and the she-dog had three fine, fat pups. And the Big Fisherman's wife had three sons.

Time passed and the end of the seven years arrived. The

ionnsaidh nan seachd bliadhna a dh'ùine. Ach chaidh an t-Iasgair Mór amach a dh'iasgach mar a b'àbhaist ach cha d'thug e leis a mhac. Agus 'nuair a bha e amuigh ag iasgach thàinig a' mhaighdean-mhara an àirde ri taobh a' bhàta 's chuir i fàilt' air.

"Cha d'thug thu do mhac an seo idir," ors' ise.

"O," ors' esan, "cha do chuimhnich mi air."

"An dà," ors' ise, "bheir mi dhuit seachd bliadhna eile a dh'ùine. Ach feuch," ors' ise, "nach dean thu diochuimhn' air."

Agus co-dhiubh, bha an gnothach a' dol air 'n aghaidh gu math fad seachd bliadhna, agus an ceann seachd bliadhna chaidh an t-Iasgair Mór amach. Mar a b'àbhaist cha d'thug e leis a mhac. Thàinig a mhaighdean-mhara an àirde ri taobh a' bhàta agus chuir i fàilt' air.

"O," ors' ise, "cha d'thug thu do mhac an seo an diugh na's motha."

"Cha d'thug," ors' esan. "Cha do chuimhnich mi air a thoirt ann, ged a b'e seo an latha."

"An dà," ors' ise, "faodaidh tu tilleadh dhachaidh. Ach," ors' ise, "an ceann ceithir bliadhna bho'n diugh feumaidh tu," ors' ise, "do mhac thoirt an seo neo mura toir," ors' ise, "cha'n ann dhuit a's fheàrr."

Ach co-dhuibh dh'fhalbh an t-Iasgair Mór dhachaidh 's bha e a' faighinn an éisg mar a b'àbhaist. Ach cha robh an ùine fada a' dol seachad agus bha ceann nan ceithir bliadhna gu bhi ann. Agus bha fios aig a bhean mar a dh'inns' e dhi mu dheidhinn mar a bha cùisean co-dhiubh, ach thug an gille an aire gu robh coltas car mi-thoilichte air 'athair—nach robh e idir cho tioliichte's a b'àbhaist dha a bhi—agus dh'fhoighneachd e dh'a athair gu dé a nisd bha a' cur trioblaid air.

"O," ors' esan, "cha'n eil," ors' esan, "sian a dh'innsinn dhuitsa."

"'S có dha," ors' esan, "a dh'innseas sibh e mur 'n innis sibh dhomhs' e?"

"O," ors' esan, "coma leat dhe sin."

"An da," ors esan, "tha mi'n dùil gu feum sinn fhaotainn amach bhuaibh gu dé 'tha 'cur dragh oirbh."

"Agus co-dhiubh dh'inns e dha mar a bha agus rinn an gille gàire.

"O," ors' esan, "na cuireadh sin cùram sam bith oirbh. Falbhaidh mis'," ors' esan, "agus theid mi cho fada air falbh bho'n chuan agus nach bi cùram gu bean creutair sam bith a bhuineas dha'n chuan dhomh."

Agus co-dhiubh thug Iain—'se Iain a b'ainm do mhac an Iasgair Mhóir—leis biadh agus thog e rithe a' falbh air ceann an fhortain. Agus fada neo goirid gu'n deachaidh e air a shiubhal, thàinig e gu àite agus bha trì chreutairean ann a' sin,

Big Fisherman went out fishing as usual, but he did not take his son. But when he was out fishing the sea-maiden rose up beside his boat and greeted him.

"You did not bring your son here at all," she said.

"Oh," said the Big Fisherman, "I did not remember to."

"Well," she said, "I'll give you seven more years' time, but watch that you don't forget again."

Things went well for seven years, and at the end of those seven years the Big Fisherman went out. As usual he did not take his son with him. The sea-maiden came up beside the boat and greeted him.

"Oh," she said, "you didn't bring your son here today either."

"No, I did not," he replied. "I did not remember to bring him here, though this is the day."

"Well," she said, "you may return home now, but four years from today you must bring your son here or you will be no better for it."

In any case the Big Fisherman went home and continued catching fish as usual, but the time was not long in passing and soon the end of the four years was about to arrive. His wife knew how things stood already from what he had told her, but the lad noticed that his father was looking displeased—that he was not at all as happy as he used to be—and he asked his father what was troubling him now.

"Oh," said his father, "It's nothing I'd tell you about."

"To whom would you tell it if not to me?"

"Oh," said his father, "don't concern yourself with that."

"Well," said the lad, "I expect we must find out from you what is bothering you."

So the father told him how things were and the lad began to laugh.

"Oh," he said, "don't let that worry you in any way. I'll set out," he said, "and I'll go so far away from the ocean that there will be no cause to fear that any ocean-creature will touch me."

So Iain—as the Big Fisherman's son was called—took along some food and set out to seek his fortune. Long or short as his journey was, he reached a place where there were three

agus iad ri conas 'us ri cath mu dheidhinn biadh a bh'aca. Agus gu dé bha an sin ach an Cù Ciar agus an Dobhran Donn agus an t-Seabhag Chrom, Liath. Ghabh e suas far na robh iad agus dh'fhoighneachd e dhaibh gu dé bha 'dol air 'n aghaidh ann a' seo, agus thug iad dha ri thuigsinn nach b'urrainn dhaibhsan biadh a ghabhail gus an riaraicheadh cuideiginn dhaibh e. Agus thoisich esan air riarachadh a' bhidh, agus thug e roinn dhe' n bhiadh a bha 'sin dha'n Dobhran Donn agus thuirt esan, "Gheobh thusa biadh air muir 's air tìr agus fo'n uisge, agus bheir mi dhuit-sa an roinn a tha seo." Agus thionndaidh e ris an t-Seabhaig Chrom, Liath agus thuirt e, "Gheobh thusa biadh air talamh agus gu h-àrd os do chionn, agus bheir mi dhuits' an dà roinn a tha 'seo. Agus," ors' esan, "cha'n eil aig a' Chu Chiar bhochd ach na theid a shineadh dha, agus tha mi a' toirt dha-san trì roinnean." Agus sin mar a bh'ann.

O, bha an cù fuathasach taingeil mar a chaidh an gnothach a lionadh agus thuirt e, "Ma bhios feum agad air lùthas mo chasansa gu bràch foghnaidh dhuit cuimhneachadh ormsa agus thig mi 'gad chuideachadh."

"Agus mise," ors' an t-Seabhag Chrom Liath, "mar an ceudna. Ma bhios feum agad air lùthas mo sgéithe agus air spionnadh mo spuir, smaointichidh tu ormsa agus thig mi."

"Tha mis'," ors' an Dobhran Donn, "air an dòigh cheudna. Ma bhios feum agad air mo luas 's air mo neart-sa, air uachdar an talmhainn neo fo'n uisge, foghnaidh dhuit smaointinn orm agus thig mi."

Co-dhiubh dh' fhalbh Iain air a thurus agus fada neo goirid an t-astar gu'n deachaidh e thàinig e gu àite rìgh. 'Nuair a chaidh e suas gu àit a rìgh chuir e fàilt' air a rìgh agus chuir an rìgh fàilt air. Dh' fhoighneachd e dha co esan agus thuirt e gura h-esan duin' og a bha 'coimhead airson cosnadh. O, bha an rìgh fuathasach toilichte gu'n d' thàinig a leithid a dh' ionnsaidh an taighe.

"An dà," ors' esan, "'s e do leithid a bha 'dhìth orm, ma ni thu buachailleachd," ors' esan. "Tha feum agam air buachaille. Agus," ors' esan, "tha do thuarasdal a' dol a bhi," ors' esan, "agus do bhiadh a réir mar a bhleogh'neas an crodh."

O, thuirt Iain gu robh sin ceart gu leòr agus chaidh e gu tàmh an oidhche sin.

Dh'fhalbh e anns a' mhadainn leis a' chrodh, ach bha an t-aite cho lom agus cho truagh cha robh ann ach air éigin a chumadh beò an crodh agus 'nuair a thill e am feasgar 's a thàinig a'bhanarach 's a bhleoghain i an crodh cha robh aca ach fior-bheagan de bhainne. Cha d'fhuair esan ach rud beag de bhrochan air an fheasgar a bha 'sin—biadh glé ghann—agus thuirt e ris fhéin, "Cha fhreagair seo dhomhsa. Ma tha mis' a'dol a dheanamh cosnadh neo buannachd air an obair

beasts quarrelling and battling over some food that they had. And who was there but the Dusky Hound, the Dun Otter and the Grey Hooked Hawk. He went up to them and asked them what was going on here, and they made him understand that they could not eat their food until someone had divided it for them.

The lad began dividing up the food, and he gave a share of the food to the Dun Otter saying, "You can find food on land and sea, and under the water, so I'll give you this share." Then he turned to the Grey Hooked Hawk with these words: "You can find food on the ground and high up above you, so I'll give you the two shares I have here. But," he said, "the poor Dusky Hound can only get what's extended to him, so I'll give him three shares." And so it was.

The hound was awfully thankful for the way in which that task had been performed and he said, "If you should ever need the quickness of my feet it will be enough to remember me and I will come to your aid."

The Grey Hooked Hawk said likewise, "If you should need the swiftness of my wings or the strength of my talons, think of me and I will come."

"I'm of the same mind," said the Dun Otter. "If you should need my speed or my strength, on land or under water, it will suffice to think of me and I will come."

So Iain continued on his journey, and after covering a long distance or a short one, he came to a king's residence. As he approached the royal residence he greeted the king, and the king greeted him likewise. The king asked him who he was and he replied that he was a young man seeking employment. Well, the king was extremely pleased that this sort had come to the house.

"Indeed," he said, "you're just the sort of person I wanted, as long as you herd cows. I need a cowherd, and your wages and your food will depend on how the cows milk." Iain said that that was fair enough and he went off to retire for the night. In the morning he started out with the cattle, but the place was so sadly bare that what little there was would hardly keep the cattle alive. When he returned that evening and the milkmaid came to milk the cows they only gave a very small amount of milk, so that evening all he got was a small bit of porridge—very little food indeed—and he said to himself, "This won't suit me. If I'm going to make any gain or profit from this work I must take the cattle to a place where they'll find better grazing than they have now, or they won't survive."

The next day he took off with the cattle. He set out with them and continued on his way until he reached a big garden. A big fence had been built there, but he opened a gate and let

'tha 'seo feumaidh mi 'n crodh a thoirt gu àite 'sa faigh iad criomadh na's fheàrr na th'aca, neo cha bhi iad beò."

Agus thog e rithe air la'r-na-mhàireach leis a' chrodh. Dh' fhalbh e leo' agus chum a air 'astar gus na ràinig e gàrradh mór. Bha callaid mhór air a togail suas ann a' sin. Ach dh'fhosgail e cachaileith agus leig e astaigh an crodh dha'n lios a bha 'sin. Neo-ar-thaing nach d'fhuair an crodh gu leòr de chriomadh ann a' sin! Cha mhór nach robh iad fodha gu'n sùilean anns a' chuid a b'fheàrr de dh'fheur. A nisd bha claidheamh mór aig Iain Mac an Iasgair Mhóir—thug e leis sin bho'n dachaidh—agus tha e coltach gu robh an claidheamh 'bha 'sin sònraichte. Ach cha robh e ach gle bheag de dh' ùine 'na shìneadh a null 'an iomall na h-innis a' leigeil 'analach 'nuair a dh'fhairich e crithe air an talamh agus thug e sùil agus bha fuamhaire mór, oillteil a' tighinn ann a' sin agus ghabh e a null agus thòisich e air togail a' chruidh agus a' breith orra air earball agus 'gam caitheamh air a ghualainn. Cha robh e ach 'gan caitheamh cho aotrom 's a chaitheadh tu rodan. Dh'éirich esan 'na sheasamh agus dh'eubh e dha, "Fàg, fàg," ors' esan, "an aona-mhart aig mo mhàthair."

"'S e," ors' esan, "droch-chomhairle a chuir an seo leo' thu ma bha cùram agad dhaibh. Thig a nall an seo," ors' esan, "agus bheir leat i."

Ach co-dhiubh ghabh esan a null air a shocair agus fhuair e 'chothram agus thug e sràc air an fhuamhaire leis a' chlaidheamh agus bha trì chinn air an fhuamhaire 's chuir e dhe fear dhe na cinn neo ma dh' fhaoidte a dhà.

"Am bàs os do chionn," ors' esan, "gu de t'éirig?"

"Cha mhór 's cha bheag," ors' esan, am fuamhaire, "ach fàg mo bheatha agus 's leat m'each briagh, dubh agus deis'-armachd a fhreagras air aon sam bith a chuireas air i. Agus sin agad m'éirig."

"Bidh sin agam agus do bheatha," ors' esan, agus chuir e crìoch air an fhuamhaire. Dh' fhan e ann an sin gu feasgar anmoch agus dh'fhalbh e 'n uair sin 's shaodaich e'n crodh air n-ais gu àit' a' rìgh. Ach 'nuair a ràinig an crodh air n-ais am feasgar sin cha robh iad gann de bhainne. Bha na cumain a bh'aca air an lionadh mu'n do sguir a' bhanarach a bhleoghain a' chruidh, agus neo-ar-thainig nach d'fhuair esan deagh-shuipeir an oidhche sin. Fhuair e pailteas ri ithe dhe'n chuid a b'fheàrr de bhiadh agus chaidh e gu tàmh.

Ach co-dhiubh lean e air buachailleachd a' chruidh agus chaidh e na b'fhaide air 'n aghaidh leis a' chordh gu àite a bha e a' smaointinn a bhitheadh na b'fheàrr agus dh' fhosgail e a' chachaileith agus chaidh e astaigh dha'n innis a bha 'sin agus O, bha an crodh ann an àite neònach an sin leis na bh'ann. Bha feur suas dha na cliathaichean aca agus thòisich iad air criomadh ann a' sin. Cha robh iad cus de dh'ùine ann 'nuair a

the cattle into that garden, and didn't the cattle find plenty of good grazing there! They were nearly up to their eyes in the best of grass. Now Iain, son of the Big Fisherman, had a great sword which he had brought with him from his home, and it seems that that sword was particularly good. But he had not been stretched out over on the edge of the pasture catching his breath for long before he felt the earth tremble. He looked up and there was a big, terrible giant coming. The giant went over and he started lifting the cattle; catching them by the tail and throwing them over his shoulder. He threw them around as lightly as you would throw a rat.

Iain rose to his feet and he called to him, "Spare, spare my mother's only milch-cow."

"You were ill-advised to bring your cattle here at all if you were concerned for them. Come over here and take her away."

Iain walked over in a leisurely manner, and when he saw his chance he took a stroke at the giant with his sword. There were three heads on the giant, and he took off one of those heads, or perhaps two.

"Death is above you," he said, "What is your ransom?"

"Neither large nor small," said the giant, "but spare my life and my fine black horse is yours along with a suit of armor which will fit anyone who puts it on. That is my ransom."

'I'll take that and your life too," and he dispatched the giant.

He remained there until the late afternoon and then he departed, driving the cattle to the king's residence. But that evening when the cattle returned they weren't short on milk. All their milking pails were filled before the milkmaid stopped milking, and Iain certainly had a good supper that night. He got plenty to eat of the best of food, and then he went to rest.

Anyway, he continued to herd the cattle, and he went on further with them to a place he thought would be better. He opened the gate and went inside to the pasture and [he and]

chual' e fuaim uamhasach agus thàinig crith' air an talamh agus thug e sùil 's bha fuamhaire mór, eagalach e' tighinn. Ma bha a' cheud fhear a' coimhead gàbhaidh, doirbh agus oillteil, seo fear a bha coltas truaighe buileach air le 'mheudachd agus le 'ghràindead, agus thòisich e air caitheamh a' chruidh air a dhruim mar nach bitheadh aig' ach sopan. Dh'eubh an t-òganach dha, "Stad, stad," ors' esan, "fàg an aona-mhart aig mo mhàthair."

"An dà," ors' esan, "nam biodh cùram agadsa dhaibh, cha bhitheadh tu astaigh an seo leo'. Thig," ors' esan, "agus bheir leat i ma tha."

Ghabh e suas air a shocair ach fhuair e cothram 's thug e sràc leis a' chlaidheamh air an fhuamhaire agus tha mi cinnteach gu'n d'thug e leis a' bhuill' a bh'ann a dhà dhe na cinn agus thuit am fuamhaire.

"Am bàs os do chionn," ors' esan, "gu de t'eirig?"

"Cha bheag sin," ors' esan, "each briagh buidhe agus deis'-armachd ridire air dath buidhe agus freagraidh i air aon sam bith a chuireas air i. Agus," ors' esan, "tha iad thall anns an stàbull."

"'S eadh," ors' esan, "bidh sin agam agus do bheatha." Agus chuir e crìoch air an fhuamhaire.

Dh'fhàg e 'n crodh gus na robh i glé anmoch agus shaodaich e 'n uair sin air n-ais iad agus b'fheudar dhaibh air an fheasgar a bha 'sin tuilleadh de chumain a dheanamh. Cha robh cumain gu leòr aca a chumadh am bainne ud uile. Bha an rìgh cho gàbhaidh toilichte as a' ghnothach a bh'ann, cha robh fios aige gu dé bheireadh e ris mar a bha cùisean a' dol. Agus chaidh cùram uamhasach a ghabhail do dh'Iain an oidhche 'bha 'seo.

Agus co-dhiubh dh'fhalbh esan mar a b'àbhaist leis a' chrodh ach cha robh e riaraichte idir gu fuirgheadh e air n-ais; 's ann a rachadh e gu àite a b'fheàrr, agus chum e air 'n aghaidh an turus seo. Ràinig e àit' agus dh'fhosgail e cachaileith 's chuir e astaigh an crodh. Agus sin agad far an robh am feur dh'a riribh:bha am feur suas gu faisg air mullach an droma. Ach cha robh a fada astaigh anns a' mhachaire a bha 'sin 'nuair a chual' e fuaim a bha gàbhaidh agus nochd fuamhaire mór. 'S ma bha càch eagalach 'nan coltas agus 'nan cumadh is as a h-uile sian, sin am fear a b' oillteil dhiubh gu buileach. Thòisich e air tilgeadh a' chruidh air a dhruim 's cha robh iad cho trom ris na sopan fhéin a bhi 'gan togail 's 'breith orr' air earball 's 'gan sadadh suas air a ghuaillean. Dh'eubh Iain, "Stad! stad!" ors' esan, "fàg an aona-mhart aig mo mhàthair."

"A," ors' esan, "a dhaor-shlaightir! 'S tus'," ors' esan, "a bha an seo 's a mharbh mo dhithisd bhràithrean-sa."

"Cha robh mis' an seo," ors' esan, "riamh gus an diugh."

the cattle were in an extraordinary place for all that was there: the grass came up to their sides and they began grazing there.

They had not been there for long when they heard a terrible sound and the earth began to tremble. He looked and there was a big dreadful giant approaching. If the first one looked wild and dangerous and terrible, this one looked altogether evil in size and ugliness, and he began tossing the cattle on his back as if he were only handling wisps of straw.

The youth called to him, "Stop! Stop! Spare my mother's only milking cow."

"Well," said the giant, "if you had been at all concerned for them, you would not be in here with them. Come over and take her with you then."

He walked up in a leisurely manner and when he saw his chance he took a stroke at the giant with his sword, and with that blow I'm sure he took off two of the [giant's] heads and the giant fell.

"Death is above you," he said. "What is your ransom?"

"No small thing," said the giant. "A fine yellow horse and a knight's suit of armor yellow in color, which will fit anyone who puts it on. And," he said, "they are over in the stable."

"Very well," said the lad, "I'll take that and your life, too." And he finished the giant.

He left the cattle until it was very late and drove them back. That evening they had to make more milk-pails because they did not have enough to hold all the milk. The king was so extremely pleased with the whole affair that he did not know what to say to him about how things had progressed. A great fuss was made over Iain that night.

Anyway Iain left as usual with the cattle, but he was not at all satisfied with staying back; he was going to a better place, so he continued onward this time. He arrived at a place, opened a gate and drove in the cattle. That's where there really was grass: it almost came to the tops of their backs! But he had not been inside that flat meadow for long when he heard a fearful noise and a great giant appeared. And if the others were dreadful in appearance and form and in every other way, that one was the most terrible of all. He began throwing the cattle on his back and they were no heavier for him to lift and catch by the tail and throw on his shoulder than wisps of straw.

Iain cried, "Stop! Stop! Spare my mother's only milking-cow."

"O, you arrant rogue!" said the giant. "You're the one who was here and killed my two brothers."

"I've never been here before," he answered, "until today."

"Ma tha," ors' esan, "thig's bheir leat am mart sin. Nam bitheadh cùram agad dhaibh bha thu air an cumail as a' seo."

Ach dh'fhalbh e a null air a shocair 's fhuair e 'n cothram. Tharraing e sràc 's chuir e a dhà dhe na cinn bhàrr an fhuamhaire agus thuit am fuamhaire gu làr.

"Am bàs os do chionn," ors' esan, "gu de t'éirig?"

"Cha bheag sin, matà. Thà," ors' esan, "each briagh, geal agus is coingeis leis a bhi air talamh neo as an iarmailt a' falbh. Agus tha deise ridire," ors' esan, "air dath geal agus freagraidh i air aon sam bith a chuireas air i. Agus sin agad," ors' esan, "m'éirig agus tha e thall anns an stàbull."

"Bidh sin agam," ors' esan, "agus do bheatha." Agus chuir e as dha'n fhuamhaire, agus am feasgar thill e dhachaidh leis a' chrodh. Cha robh de shoithichean aca air a' rioghachd a chumadh na bha de bhainne aig a' chrodh am feasgar 'bha 'sin—bha iad ann an àite 'sa robh an criomadh cho beairteach buileach.

Ach co-dhiubh dh'fhalbh e leis a' chrodh—tha mi cinnteach gur ann air la'r-namhàireach thog e rith'—agus bha e 'fàs cho sanntach, bha e 'dol na b'fhaide air 'n aghaidh agus ràinig e àite an lath' 'bha 'seo agus 'nuair a dh'fhosgail e a' cha-chaileith 's a leig e astaigh an crodh dha 'n àite 'bha 'sin cha'n fhac' e riamh a leithid de dh'àite airson spréidh a bheathachadh. Ach cha robh e fad' an sin 'nuair a chual' e fuaim a bha neònach, agus nochd cailleach oillteil astaigh. Cha deachaidh i 'n comhair a' chruidh idir ach ghabh i far an robh e a throd ris agus thuirt i, "'S tus' am fear a mharbh mo thriùir mhac," ors' ise.

"Cha robh mis' an seo riamh gus an diugh," ors' esan.

Agus thòisich iad air cath 's b'e sin an cath a bha fiadhaich. Ach mu dheireadh fhuair e a chothram agus thilg e ise air a druim air an talamh agus bhrist e a druim agus bhrisd e a gàirden os a cionn.

"Am bàs os do chionn a nisd," ors' esan, "gu de t'éirig?"

"Cha bheag sin," ors' ise. "Tha ciste de dh'òr agus ciste de dh'airgiod agus ciste làn de sheudan luachmhor fo'n starsach aig bonn a' bhothain."

"Bidh sin agam," ors' esan, "agus do bheatha." Agus chuir e crìoch air a' chaillich, agus thill e air n-ais.

Co-dhiubh bha e 'falbh, air a bhi a' dol leis a' chrodh agus 'gam buachailleachd ach thainig e dhachaidh feasgar agus an aite an gnothach a bhi cho aighearach mar bu tric' leis a bhi 'nuair a thilleadh e, thachair a' bhanarach ris agus bha i 'sileadh nan deur.

"Gu dé," ors' Iain, "tha ceàrr air an fheasgar 'tha 'seo gu bheil a h-uile sian a' coimhead cho mi-shunndach, cho trominntinneach?"

"O," ors' ise, "tha aig nighean a' righ ri dhol a dh'ionn-

"Come over here, then," he said, "and take this cow. If you had cared about them you would have kept them out of here."

He walked over at his leisure and he saw his chance. He gave a stroke and took two of the heads off the giant and the giant fell to the ground.

"Death is above you," said he. "What is your ransom?"

"No small thing," he replied. "A fine, white horse, and it makes no difference to him whether he travels on the earth or in the sky. And a knight's suit of armor, white in color, which fits anyone who puts it on. There you have my ransom and it's over in the stable."

"I'll have that and your life as well." And he slew the giant and returned home that evening with the cattle. There were not enough containers in the entire kingdom to hold all the milk that the cows gave that evening, for they had been in a place where the grazing was altogether so rich.

In any case he set out with the cattle—I'm certain that he took off on the next day—and he was growing so greedy that he kept going on farther. That day he reached another place, and when he opened the gate and let the cattle in, he had never before seen a place that was equal to it for feeding cattle. But he had not been there long when he heard an extraordinary noise and a horrible old hag appeared inside. She did not approach the cattle at all, but came in his direction meaning to contend with him and she said, "You're the one who killed my three sons."

"I was never here before," he said, "until today."

And they began battling and that was indeed a fierce struggle. But at last he got a chance and threw her on her back on the ground and broke her back and broke her arms above her.

"Death is above you," he said. "What is your ransom?"

"No small thing," she said. "There is a chest of gold, and a chest of silver and one filled with precious jewels under the threshold at the foot of the hut."

"I'll have that and your life too," said he. So he finished off the old hag and went back.

He continued going off with the cattle and herding them, but he came home one night and instead of things being so cheerful as they usually were when he returned, the milkmaid met him and she was shedding tears.

"What is so wrong this evening," said Iain, "that everything looks so cheerless and melancholy?"

"Oh," she said, "the king's daughter must go to the loch

saidh an loch, agus béist a' tighinn as an loch," ors' ise. "A h-uile bliadhna tha a' bhéist ud a' tighinn as an loch agus tha té dhe na h-igheannan a th' anns a' rioghachd aice ri fhaighinn gus a h-ithe. Agus 's e an doigh a bh'aca mu dheireadh anns a' rioghachd a bhi a' tilgeadh chrann—taghadh chrann—feuch có té dhe na h-igheannan a dh'fheumadh falbh, agus 's ann air air nighean a' rìgh a thuit na cruinn air an turus seo. Feumaidh an nighean falbh," ors' ise, "agus suidhe shuas aig ceann àrd an loch' air leac agus a bhi ann a' sin gus an tig a' bhéist."

"Cha'n fhaoidte a bhi," ors' esan, "gu bheil iad a' dol a leigeadh leis a' bhéist nighean an rìgh a thoirt leis. A bheil idir," ors' esan, "aon ann a shàbhaileas nighean an rìgh?"

"O," ors' ise, "cha'n fhaod a h-aon a dhol ann ach tha 'n gaisgeach a's fheàrr 's a's motha a th'anns an duthaich a' dol a dh'fheuchainn ri a sàbhaladh."

Co-dhiubh bha ise 'na suidhe shios air leac 's bha 'n gaisgeach am falach air eagal 's gu faiceadh a' bhéist e 's nach tigeadh i 'n àirde. Thug ise sùil agus chunnaic i ridire a' tighinn air each dubh agus bha e 'tighinn anuas as an iarmailt cho luath 's a dh'fhalbhadh e air talamh agus anuas a bha e. Stad e air a' chladach ri 'taobh. Leum e anuas bhàrr na diollaid' agus chaidh e a null a sheanachas rithe agus dh'fhoighneachd e dhi gu dé chuir an seo i agus dh'inns' i dha mar a bha cùisean.

"Agus a bheil idir," ors' esan, "a h-aon ann a dh'fheuchas ri d' shàbhaladh?"

Thuirt i gu robh an gaisgeach a b'fheàrr a bh'anns an dùthaich, gu robh e ann ach gu robh e 'm falach gus an tigeadh a' bhéist. Thuirt e gu fuirgheadh esan airson cuideachadh a thoirt dhi—airson a sàbhaladh—'s gu rachadh e eadar i 's a' bhéist.

"O," ors' ise, "cha'n fhaod thu a bhi ann a' seo. Ma chi a'bhéist thu ann a' seo," ors' ise, "cha tig i idir."

"Ma tha," ors' esan, "thig mise sios 'nam shìneadh air a'chladach ri d' thaoibh far nach fhaic i mi agus leagaidh mi mo cheann air do ghlùin. Agus ma chaidleas mise mun tig a' bhéist a' tighinn an àirde, ma dh'fhàilnicheas ort mo dhùsgadh ann an dòigh seach dòigh," ors' esan, "am bior crom a tha seo, cuiridh tu sin suas 'an cuinnlean mo shròineadh agus dùisgidh sin mi."

Ach co-dhiubh an ceann greis de dh'ùine 's esan 'na shuain fhada thainig a' bhéist a bha 'seo agus tri chinn oirre. Bha i 'coimhead gu math grànnd' 's thàinig i 'n àirde. Agus thòisich ise air fheuchainn ri esan a dhùsgadh 's ged a bhiodh i 'g éigheach dha 's 'ga chrathadh cha dùisgeadh esan ach smaointich i air a' bhior chrom a bha 'seo agus chuir i seo suas ann an cuinnlean a shroìneadh agus leum esan air a bhonnaibh agus tharraing e'n claidheamh. Agus b'e sin an claid-

where a monstrous beast will come out of the loch [to meet her]. Every year the monster emerges from the loch and gets one of the girls in the kingdom to eat. Finally it has become our custom in the kingdom to cast lots to see which one of the girls must go, and this time it fell to the king's daughter. She must go," she said, "and sit on a flat rock at the upper end of the loch and remain there until the monster comes."

"It cannot be," said Iain, "that they'll let the monster take away the king's daughter! Is there anyone at all who can save her?"

"Oh," she answered, "none may go there, but the best and greatest warrior in the country is going to try to save her."

Anyway, the princess was sitting down on the flat rock and the warrior had concealed himself for fear that the monster would see him and would not emerge. She looked up and saw a knight approaching, on a black horse, coming right out of the sky. The horse was travelling as fast in the sky as he would travel on the ground, and down he came. He came to a halt beside her on the shore. The knight leapt down from the saddle and went over to talk with her. He asked her what had brought her here and she told him how things were.

"And is there anyone at all," said he, "who will try to save you?"

She said that the best warrior in the country was there hiding until the monster came. The knight said he would stay to help her—to save her—and that he would go between her and the monster.

"Oh," she said, "you can't remain here. If the monster sees you here it will never come."

"Then I will stretch myself out," said he, "on the shore beside you where it won't see me and I'll lay my head on your knee. And if I fall asleep before the monster emerges and you fail to waken me by trying one thing after another, put this curved stick into my nostril and that will waken me."

After a length of time, when the knight was in a long slumber, the three-headed monster arrived. It came up, looking very ugly, and she began trying to wake up the knight. But though she called to him and shook him he would not awake. But she thought about the curved stick, so she put it up his nostril and he leapt to his feet and drew his sword. That was some sword indeed, and he advanced.

Well, they had an extraordinary battle and they engaged in a terrible struggle until at last he severed one of the heads from the monster and down it fled. He walked up toward the top of the shore, leapt on the back of his horse, and whether it

heamh a bh'ann dh'a rìribh agus ghabh e amach. O, bha cath aca 'bha neònach agus chuir iad cath a bha oillteil ach mu dheireadh gheàrr e fear dhe na cinn dhe'n bhéist agus sios a ghabh i. Choisich esan suas a dh'ionnsaidh bàrr a' chladaich agus leum e air druim an eich agus co-dhiubh 's e an t-athar a thog e neo'n talamh a shluig e cha robh an còrr sealladh aice dheth. Ach co-dhiubh, an ceann a gheàrr e bhàrr na béist', bha e air a chur air gad agus dh'fhàgadh sin aice. Dh'éirich an gaisgeach a bha 'm falach agus thog e rithe suas gu taigh a' rìgh agus ceann na béisteadh aige air a' ghad agus cha'n fhaodadh nighean a' rìgh guth a radha nach b'e seo an duine a rinn an gnìomh, agus ràinig iad shuas. O, bha an naidheachd mun cuairt ach cha robh ise riaraichte ris a' ghnothach co-dhiubh.

Dh'fheumadh i falbh air la'r-na-mhàireach agus air an fheasgar bha i 'na suidhe air an leac agus tha mi cinnteach gu robh i gu math tùrsach. Ach bha beagan de dhòchas aice gu faodadh an ridire tighinn mar a thàinig e air an fheasgar roimhe sin. Agus bha an gaisgeach duineil a bha 'ga geard, bha e 'm falach 'n cùl tom neo an àiteiginn am falach co-dhiubh. Thug i sùil 's chunnaic i each briagh, buidhe a' tighinn agus bha e 'falbh na bu luaithe anns an iarmailt na dh'fhalbhadh each air talamh. Thàinig e anuas 's bha mar-caiche air a dhruim: ridire àlainn agus deise bhriagh, bhuidhe m'a thimcheall agus leum e anuas bhàrr druim an eich agus chaidh e far an robh i. Dh'fhoighneachd e dhi gu dé a b'aobhar dhi bhi ann a' sin. O, dh'inns' i dha mar a bha cùisean agus thuirt e gu'n geardadh esan i.

"O," ors' ise, "cha'n fhaod thu fuireach an seo. Ma theid t'-fhaicinn cha tig a' bhéist."

"O," ors' esan, 'theid mi sios 'nam shìneadh air a' chladach ri d' thaoibh far nach teid m'fhaicinn agus cuiridh mi mo cheann air do ghlùin agus ma chaidleas mi," ors' esan, "dùis-gidh tu mi 'nuair a thig a' bhéist. Ach cha'n eil ach aon dòigh a theid mise dhùsgadh. Ma thòisicheas tu air mo chrathadh 's air éigheachd dhomh 's mura duisg e mi," ors' esan, "geàr-raidh thu bàrr beag bharr mo lùdaig' agus dùisgidh sin mi."

Co-dhiubh 'nuair a nochd a' bhéist an àirde bha dà cheann oirre fhathasd. Nochd i 'n àirde 's bha i 'tighinn astaigh gu tìr 's thòisich ise ris a' ridire a dhùsgadh ach cha ghabhadh e dùsgadh. Ach smaointich i air an rud a thuirt e rith' agus gheàrr i 'm bàrr beag bhàrr na lùdaig' aig' agus leum e 'na sheasamh. Tharraing e 'n claidheamh agus amach a ghabh e an coinneamh na béist' ach ma bha cath ann am feasgar roimhe sin aig ridire an eich dhuibh 's ann a bha an cath aig an fhear seo. Agus bha cath ann a' sin a bha fuilteach gus an robh a' ghrian a' dol fodha ach gheàrr e 'n ceann bhàrr na béist' agus sios a ghabh i 's cha robh a nisd oirr' ach an aona-cheann. Co-dhiubh ghabh esan air druim an eich 's cha robh an còrr

was the heavens that raised him or the earth that swallowed him, he vanished from her sight. He had put the head he cut from the beast on a withe and that was left with her.

The warrior who had been hiding arose then and took off toward the king's house with the monster's head on the withe, but the king's daughter could not say a word to the effect that he was not the man who had performed the deed when they arrived there. Well, the news went around, but she was not at all satisfied with that affair.

The princess had to go again the next day, and that evening she was sitting on the rock, very sorrowful I'm sure. But she had the faint hope that the knight might come as he had the evening before. The manly warrior who was guarding her was hiding behind a hillock, or hiding somewhere anyway. She looked up and saw a fine, yellow horse approaching, travelling more swiftly in the sky than he could on the earth. He descended and there was a rider on his back: a splendid knight encased in a fine, yellow suit of armor, and he leapt down from the horse's back and went over to her. He asked her what was her reason for being there. Well, she told him how things were and he said that he would guard her.

"Oh," she said, "you can't stay here. If you are seen the monster won't come."

"I'll stretch myself out," he said, "on the shore beside you where I won't be seen and I'll put my head on your knee and if I should fall asleep," he said, "you can wake me when the monster comes. But there is only one means by which I can be awakened. If you begin shaking me and calling to me, and it does not waken me, cut the tip from the end of my little finger and that will waken me."

Anyway, then the monster appeared, rising up—it still had two of its heads. It appeared, rising and coming in to land and she began to waken the knight, but he could not be aroused. But she thought of what he had said to her, so she cut off the tip of his little finger and he leapt to his feet. He drew his sword and out he rushed to meet the monster.

But if the knight with the black horse had had a battle the evening before, this one really had a struggle on his hands. They fought a bloody battle until sunset, but he cut a head from the monster and down it fled with only one head. So the knight mounted the horse, and whether it was the heavens that raised him or the earth that swallowed him she did not have another glimpse of him and did not know where he had

sealladh aice-se dheth; co-dhiubh 's e an t-athar a thog e neo an talamh a shluig e cha robh fhios cà'n deach e. Dh'fhalbh e co-dhiubh. Agus bha an gad air an robh a' cheud cheann, bha 'n ceann eil' air a chur air còmhla ris agus bha sin aice. Thog i fhéin agus an gaisgeach a bha 'm falach orra dhachaidh agus bha na cinn aige-san air a' ghad agus ràinig e shuas—neo-arthaing nach robh e bòsdail an oidche sin! Bha i gus a bhi air a sàbhaladh co-dhiubh ach bha aice ri dhol air feasgar eile sios.

Co-dhiubh dh'fhalbh i air an fheasgar sin agus bha esan am falach mar a b'àbhaist an cùl tom neo 'n àite choireiginn agus tha mi cinnteach gu robh seòrsa de dh'eagal air ma chunnaic e a' bhéist a thàinig co-dhiubh. Ach bha ise ann an deagh-dhòchas air an fheasgar seo gu'n tigeadh cuideachadh agus ann an ceann tiotadh thug i sùil agus chunnaic i each geal a' tighinn anuas as na h-iarmailtean agus ridire geal air a dhruim 's deise bhriagh, gheal air. Agus dh'fhalbhadh an t-each sin, tha mi 'n dùil, na bu luaithe gu h-àrd 'san iarmailt na dh'fhalbhadh e air talamh. Leum am marcaiche anuas agus chaidh e far an robh i agus O, mar a b'àbhaist, dh'inns' i a sgeul agus thuirt esan gu geardadh esan—gu rachadh esan an coinneamh na béist' agus thuirt i nach fhaodadh e fuireach an seo. Thuirt e gu rachadh e 'na shìneadh ri 'taoibh air a' chladach far nach rachadh 'fhaicinn agus chaidh e sios. Leag e 'cheann air a glùinn.

"Ma chaidleas mise," ors' esan, "cha'n eil ach aon dòigh air mo dhùsgadh. 'S e sin;" ors' esan, "mu mheudachd lann an sgadain a ghearradh a mullach mo chinn, eadar craiceann agus feòl, agus dùisgidh sin mi."

Co-dhiubh 'nuair a nochd a' bhéisd dh'fheuch ise a h-uile dòigh air a dhùsgadh ach cho robh dòigh air. Ach smaointich i air an rud a thuirt e rith' agus gheàrr i rud beag a mullach a chinn 's leum esan 'na sheasamh. Tharraing e 'n claidheamh 's ghabh e amach an coinneamh na béist'. Agus 's ann an sin a bha 'n cath fuilteach, oillteil nach robh riamh a leithid, tha mi cinnteach, ann eadar ridir' agus béist, neo rud eile. Ach gu math ro dhol fodha na gréineadh gheàrr e 'n ceann bhàrr na béist' agus sios a ghabh i dha'n ghrunnd. Co-dhiubh bha nighean a' rìgh air a teasraigeadh a nisd agus chuir esan an ceann air a' ghad còmhla ri càch agus leum esan 'na dhiollaid, 's an athshealladh cha robh sgeul air. Co-dhiubh 's e an t-athar a thog e neo an talamh a shluig e, cha robh an còrr sealladh air. Ach suas a ghabh iad gu taigh a' rìgh agus, O, bha 'n gaisgeach seo ag iarraidh a nisd bainis a chur air bhonn gun dàil. Ach thuirt ise nach biodh i deònach air a' leithid sin idir gus am faighte amach co 'n gaisgeach a thàinig 's a shàbhail ise, agus thuirt i gu robh comharra aice fhéin air, agus gu'n aithnicheadh i e, agus a thoirt a h-uile duine a bh'anns a' rìoghachd far an robh i. O, thuirt an rìgh nach deante bainis

gone. He just vanished. As for the withe where the first head was, the second head was strung there alongside it and she had them there.

She and the warrior who had been hiding set out for home. He had the heads on the withe when he arrived there and wasn't he boastful that night! She was about to be saved anyway, but she still had to go down one more evening.

So she departed that [next] evening and the warrior was hiding as usual behind a knoll or somewhere and I'm certain that he was at least somewhat frightened at seeing the monster that approached them. But this evening she had high hopes that help would arrive. And after a short time she looked up and saw a white horse descending from the skies and a white knight on its back wearing a fine white suit of armor. That horse could travel more swiftly, I expect, high up in the heavens than he could travel on the ground. The rider jumped down and went over to her. She told him her story as usual and he said that he would guard her—would confront the monster and she said he could not stay there, but he told her that he would stretch himself out on the shore beside her where he would not be seen. So he let himself down and laid his head on her knee.

"If I fall asleep," he said, "there is but one way to waken me. It is this: to cut a piece of skin and flesh about the size of a herring's scale from the top of my head. That will awaken me."

When the monster appeared she tried every means of waking him, but there seemed to be no way to do it. But she thought then of what he had said to her so she cut a small piece from the top of his head and he leapt to his feet. He drew his sword and rushed out to face the monster.

That battle was indeed a horrible, bloody one whose kind had never before been waged by a knight against a monster or, I'm certain, against anything else. But well before sunset he cut the head from the monster and down it went to the bottom. In any case the princess had been saved now, so he put the head on the withe along with the others, jumped into the saddle and the next time she looked there was not a trace of him. Whether it was the heavens that raised him or the earth that swallowed him, he was no more to be seen.

So the others went up to the king's residence, and by this time the other warrior was all for having a wedding arranged without delay. But the princess said that she would not at all be willing to take part in that sort of thing until it was found out who the warrior was who had come and saved her, and that she had a means of identifying him so that she could recognize him, and that all the men in the kingdom were to be brought to her. Well, the king said that a wedding, a wedding

an dràsd', neo bainis mhor agus féisd, ach gu feumte dàil a dheanamh.

Agus chaidh fios a chur mun cuairt air feadh na rìoghachd uile iad a chruinneachadh agus bha aig a h-uile h-aon dhiubh ri dhol seachad fo chomhar na h-ighinn. Agus cha b'e seo am fear; cha b'e am fear seo agus bha iad air tighinn uile—thàinig a h-uile h-aon a bh'anns a' rìoghachd is chaidh iad uile seachad. Ach cha d'thàinig am fear a dh'aithnicheadh is' an comharradh air. Bha an gnothach gu math truagh gu'n deachaidh a h-uile h-aon dhiubh seachad. Dh'fhoighneachd i,

"An deach iad uile seachad?"

Thuirt iad rith' gu'n deachaidh, ach am buachaille. Chaidh òrdugh a thoirt 'sa mhionaid am buachaille a thighinn. Thàinig am buachaille. Thug e a leisgeul: thuirt e nach b'urrainn dhasan tighinn idir; nach robh e glan gu leòr 's gu'm biodh fàileadh as a thaobh a bhi timcheall air buachailleachd na sprèidh; gu'm biodh fàileadh làidir bhàrr a chòmhdaich agus nach tigeadh e idir. O, thuirt iad gu'n gabhte a leisgeul, gu'n rachadh a leisgeul a ghabhail airson sin a dheanamh ach nach rachadh a leisgeul a ghabhail airson tighinn fo chomhair a' rìgh agus gun a cheann-aodach a thoirt dheth. Agus chaidh iarraidh air an currac a bha m'a cheann a thoirt dheth. Dh'fhoighneachd ise dha c'arson a bha 'n currac m'a cheann. Thuirt e gu robh lot air mullach a chinn agus gur e sin a b'aobhar dha-san a bhi a' cosg a- churraic. Thuirt i ris an currac 'thoirt dhe agus 'nuair a thug e dhe an currac chaidh a choimhead air agus bha an lot beag a bha 'seo air mullach a' chinn aige. Sgaoill i a nèapaicin-pòc' agus ann an oisinn na neàpaiceadh thug i amach am pios a bha 'seo de chraiceann 's de dh'fehòil 's de ghruaig. Chuir i seo 'na àite fhéin 's fhreagair e ann agus cha'n aithnicheadh tu le coimhead air gu'n deachaidh a ghluasad riamh.

"Ach c'arson," ors' ise, "a tha cuaran air do làimh?"

"Tha," ors' esan, "far a bheil bàrr mo lùdaig' 'gam dhìth."

"Bheir dhiot," ors' ise, "an cuaran, ma tha."

Thugadh an cuaran bhàrr na làimh' aige agus sgaoil i amach a neapaicin-phòca 's anns an oisinn eile thog i amach pios a bh'ann a' sin agus chaidh am pios sin a chur air bàrr na lùdaig' aige agus cha'n aithnicheadh duine gu'n deachaidh e riamh a ghluasad dheth leis mar a fhreagair e.

"Seo agad," ors' ise, "an ridire a shàbhail mise bho'n bhéist."

Am fear eile, bha e 'g éigheach 's a' dol mun cuairt 's 'g éigheach pears' eaglais fhaighinn, ach chaidh breith air an fhear eile 's a chur air falbh 's tha mi cinnteach gu'n deachaidh a chur air eilean neo air ait' iomallach air choireiginn. Agus chaidh cur mu dheidhinn féisde mhòr agus bainis a dheanamh. 'S 'nuair a chaidh an gnothach 'bha 'seo a chur air saod with a big banquet, would not be performed right away, and that these must be postponed.

Word was circulated throughout the whole kindgom for the men to gather, and every one of them had to go before the princess. It wasn't this one, nor that one and soon they had all come—every man in the kingdom had come and passed before her, but the man had not come whose signs she could recognize. When every one of them had passed by it was a sad state of affairs indeed, and she asked, "Have they all passed by?"

They told her that they had, except for the cowherd. An order was immediately given for the cowherd to come. The cowherd arrived and excused himself; he said that he had not been able to come at all, for he was not clean enough and he stank from being about herding the cattle and there was a strong stench from his clothing so that he didn't want to come at all. Oh, they said that he would be excused for having done that, but he would not be excused for coming before the king without removing his head-gear. So he was asked to take off the cap that he wore on his head.

The princess asked why the cap was on his head, and he replied that there was a wound on the top of his head and that was the reason why he wore the cap. She told him to remove the cap and when he did they examined him and the little wound was there on top of his head. She spread out her handkerchief and out of its corner she took the piece of skin and flesh and hair. When she put it back in its proper place it fitted so that you would not know from looking at it that it had ever been removed.

"But why," she said, "are you wearing a fingerstall on your hand?"

"That's where the tip of my little finger is missing."

"Then take off the fingerstall," she said.

The fingerstall was removed from his hand and she spread out her handkerchief and from the other corner she took out the piece that was there. That piece was put on the end of his little finger and it fitted so well that no one would know that it had ever been removed.

"Here you have the knight," she said, "who saved me from the monster."

The other warrior was going around and shouting, calling for a clergyman to be fetched, but he was caught and sent away, and I'm sure he was sent to an island or some other remote place.

It was decided to have a big feast and a wedding, and when that was getting underway the cowherd fled; he took off up to the loft where there were things that he had obtained, I'm theich am buachaille; thog e rith' 's ghabh e suas a dh'ionnsaidh na lobhtadh agus bha gnothaichean ann a' sin a fhuair e, tha mi cinnteach, bho mhàthair nam fuamhairichean agus chuir e e-fhéin ann an éideadh gu math grinn agus thàinig e anuas. Bha e 'n deaghaidh a cheann a chireadh 's bha cìr aige 's 'nuair a chìreadh e a cheann leath' bhiodh a ghruaig air dath an òir. Agus tha mi 'creidsinn nach fhaca an rìgh riamh a leithid de dhuine eireachdail 'na rìoghachd fhéin neo ann an rìoghachd sam bith a shiubhail e oirre. 'S chaidh a' bhainis a chur air 'n àghaidh agus féasda mhór a dheanamh.

Beagan uine as a dheoghaidh sin bha Iain Mac an Iasgair Mhóir agus a bhean, nighean a' rìgh, bha iad a' coiseachd sios taobh na tràghad, gu b'e de a chuir ann iad, agus thainig béist mhór anuas as a' chuain. Thachair gura h-esan a b'fhaisg' air a' chladach agus shluig a' bhéist leath' e. Bha a' bhean og gu math duilich 's gu math bronach. Cha robh fios aice gu dé dheanadh i agus chaidh i gu seannduine—fear-comhairleadh fìor-ghlic a bh'anns a' cheàrnaidh—feuch am faigheadh i amach bhuaithe-san gu dé ghabhadh deanamh. Dh'innis' i mar a thachair agus thuirt e nach fhaigheadh i cothram ma dh'fhaoidte air 'fhaighinn ach air aon dòigh, nan oibricheadh sin: a dh'fhaighinn a h-uile seòrsa flùr by bhriagha 's a b'eireachdail a b'urrainn dhi fhaotainn, agus tha mi cinnteach seudan eile còmhla ris a' sin, agus an toir' sios a dh'ionnsaidh a' chladaich agus an sgaoileadh 'nan sreathan gu h-àrd air an tràigh. Agus 'nuair a thigeadh a' bhéist an àirde 's i ag iarraidh pàirt dhe'n eireachdas a bha 'sin, a chantail rith' gu faodadh i 'm faighinn uile nan sealladh i dhi-se na bha os cionn a' chrios neo os cionn na cruachainnidh aig a companach. Agus ma dh'fhaoidte, thuirt esan, gu rachadh aige fhéin air tighinn as a' sin.

Seo an rud a rinn i. Bha i shios air a' chladach a' cur nam flùran 's nan nithean a bha 'seo ann an òrdugh agus thàinig a' bhéist anuas gu iomall na tràghad agus dh'fhoighneachd i an tugadh i dhi pàirt dhe na flùran agus dhe'n eireachdas 'bha 'sin. O, thuirt i gu'n tugadh i dhi uil' iad nan sealladh i dhi na bha os cionn na cruachainn a companach agus 'nuair a rinn i sin fhuair esan tighinn gu tir. Agus cha robh aig a' bhéist ach na gnothaichean a bh'ann a thoirt leath' neo 'm fàgail.

Ach co-dhiubh bha iad a' coiseachd sios taobh na tràghad agus bha iad cho tiolichte le chéile mar a thachair agus gu dé thachair ach gura h-ise 'bha amach air an taoibh a b'fhaisge a dh'iomall na tràghad agus thàinig a' bhéist anuas agus chaidh ise a shluigsinn leatha. Bha esan na bu mhiosa dheth na bha e riamh an uair sin, agus b'fheudar dha falbh a dh'fhaicinn duine seòlta air choireiginn feuch gu dé ghabhadh deanamh. Chaidh e far an robh duine fìor-fhiosrach anns a' cheàrn agus dh'inns' e dha mar a thachair.

"An dà," ors' esan, "cha'n eil an gnothach furasd' idir. Ma

certain, from the mother of the giants, so he clothed himself in his quite elegant apparel and came back down. He had combed his hair and he had a [special] comb: when he combed his hair with it his hair was the color of gold. I believe the king had never before seen such a handsome man in his own kingdom or in any other that he had traversed. So the wedding was performed and a great feast was given.

A short time after that Iain, Son of the Big Fisherman, and his wife, the king's daughter, were walking down along the beach, whatever had brought them there, and a great monster came up out of the ocean. It happened that he, Iain, was closest to the shore, and the monster swallowed him and took him away.

The young wife was very grieved and sorrowful. She did not know what to do, so she went to an old man—a truly wise counselor in that region—to see if she could learn from him what could be done. She told him what had happened and he said that she might not have a chance to get him back except by one means, if that would work: by collecting all kinds of the finest and prettiest flowers that she could find, and other ornaments along with them, I'm sure, and taking them down to the shore and spreading them in rows high up on the beach. And when the beast came, asking for a share of that finery, she was to tell it that it could have them all if it would show her what was above the belt or above the hip of its companion. And maybe, he said, he would be able to escape from there.

That is what she did. She was down on the shore putting the flowers and the other things in order and the monster came up to the edge of the beach and asked her whether she would give it part of the flowers and the finery that was there. Oh, she said she would give it all of them if it would show her what was above the hip of its companion. And when it did that, Iain managed to reach land. All that the monster could do was to take or leave the things.

*John Shaw, collector and translator, with storyteller Joe MacNeil.*

Joe MacNeil Tells a Wonderful Story

dh'fhaoidte," ors' esan, "gu'n gabhadh e deanamh. Ach cha'n eil ann ach ma dh'fhaoidte. Chaidh thusa ghealltainn dha'n mhaighdean-mhara agus a reir na fàidheadaireachd chaidh do ghealltainn dha'n mhaighdean-mhara agus dh'fheumte an gealltainn sin a chomhlìonadh. Cha'n eil ach aon dòigh," ors' esan, "air an gabh e seachnadh: 's e nam faigheadh tu anam na béisteadh agus cur as dhi."

"'S gu dé mar a ghabhas sin faotainn?"

"An dà," ors' esan, "cha'n eil sin furasda. Tha reithe fiadhaich gu h-àrd air mullach Beinn Sheilg, agus tha lach' 'am broinn a' reithe, agus tha'n t-ubh 'am broinn na lach' agus 's ann am broinn an ubh a tha anam na béist'. Agus gun sin fhaighinn," ors' esan, "cha'n fhaigh thu cuibhteas i gu bràch. Ach ma gheobh thu an t-ubh," ors' esan, "cuir an t-ubh air leac air oir a' chladaich agus do chas air a mhuin, agus bi a' leagadh chudthrom air an ubh. Anus 'nuair a thig a' bheist an airde 's a dh'éigheas i dhuit, 'Fàg m'anam, fàg m'anam,' can 'cha'n fhàg mura leig thu dhoms' fhaicinn na bheil os cionn a' chrios dhe'n bhana-chompanach.' Agus 'nuair a gheobh thu do bhana-chompanach cuibhteas a' bheist spleuchdaidh tu an t-ubh agus bidh tu an uair sin sàbhailte."

Ach co-dhiubh dh'fhalbh esan dha'n bheinn ach cha mhór am feum a dheanadh sin dha. Bha an reithe fiadhaich cho luath 's 'nuair a biodh esan air an darna beinn bhiodh am beathach fiadhaich air a' bheinn eile. Ach smaointich e an seo nam biodh an Cù Ciar aige gu robh e luath gu leòr airson a bhi a' breith air a reithe. Agus cha bu luaith' a smaointich e air a' chù na thàinig an Cù Ciar agus ghabh e as deoghaidh a' reithe agus cha robh e fada gus na rug e air. Cha bu luaith' a rug e air a' reithe na amach as a bheul a thainig an lach' agus thog i rithe. Bha e a nisd na bu mhiosa dhe na b'àbhaist, ach smaointich e nam biodh an t-Seabhag Chrom, liath an seo gu'm beireadh i air a' lach'. Smaointich e oirr' 's thainig i agus as deoghaidh na lach' a thug i agus cha robh i glé fhada gus an d'fhuair i a h-ìnean a chur an sàs anns a' lach'. Ach ma fhuair, bha iad cho faisg air oir an loch anns an am agus dh'fhalbh an t-ubh as a' lach' agus sios a ghabh e dha'n uisge agus thug e grunnd a' loch' air. Bha Iain Mac an Iasgair Mhóir cho dona dhe 's a bha e roimhe. Ach smaointich e an sin nam biodh an Dòbhran Donn an seo gu faigheadh an Dòbhran Donn an t-ubh dha-san. Thàinig an Dòbhran Donn agus dh'fhoighneachd e dha,

"Gu dé," ors' esan, "an cuideachadh bu mhath leat fhaighinn bhuamsa."

"Bu mhath," ors' esan, "gu faigheadh tu an t-ubh ann an grunnd a' loch."

Sios a ghabh an Dòbhran Donn agus cha robh e glé fhada gus an robh e 'am bàrr an uisge agus an t-ubh 'na bheul.

Anyway they were walking down along the beach, both of them so pleased with what had occurred, and what happened but that she was out on the side closest to the edge of the beach and the beast came again and she was swallowed by it. Iain was worse off then than ever, and he had to go and see some clever man to see what could be done. He went to a truly knowledgeable man in the region and told him what had happened.

"Well," he said, "that is no easy matter. Perhaps it could be done, but only perhaps. You were promised to the sea-maiden, according to my divinations you were promised to her, and that promise must be fulfilled. There is only one means by which it can be avoided: if you should get the monster's soul and do away with it."

"How can that be obtained?"

"Well," he said, "that is not easy. There is a wild ram high up on the summit of Ben Sheilg, and there is a wild duck in the ram's belly, and the egg is in the wild duck's belly and inside the egg is the monster's soul. And unless you get that," he said, "you'll never get her free. But if you get the egg, put it on a flat rock at the edge of the shore with your foot resting on top of it, and apply your weight on the egg. And when the monster rises up and calls to you, 'Spare my soul, spare my soul,' say, 'I will not, unless you let me see what is above the belt of your female companion.' And when you get her clear of the beast you can tramp on the egg and then you will be safe."

So he departed for the mountain, but doing so was not much use to him. The wild ram was so fast that when Iain was on one mountain that wild animal would be on another. But he thought to himself then, if only he had the Dusky Hound he would be swift enough to catch the ram. No sooner had he thought of the Hound than the Dusky Hound arrived. It took off after the ram and it was not long until it caught it. No sooner had it caught the ram than out of its mouth came the wild duck, and it took off.

Now Iain was worse off than he used to be, but he thought if only the Grey Hooked Hawk were here, that she could catch the wild duck. He thought of her and she came to him. Off after the wild duck she went, and it was not very long before she managed to fix her talons on the wild duck. But though she did, by then they were so close to the edge of the loch that when the egg went out of the wild duck, down into the water it went and straight to the bottom of the loch.

Iain, son of the Big Fisherman, was as badly off as before, but he thought then, if the Dun Otter were there that it would find the egg for him. The Dun Otter came to him and asked him, "What help do you wish to have from me?"

"I would like," he said, "for you to get the egg at the bottom

Ghlac Iain Mac an Iasgair Mhóir an t-ubh agus chuir e 'n t-ubh air leac agus a chas air a mhuin. Thòisich e air leigeil cudthrom air an ubh agus dh'éirich a' bhéist an oir a' chuain agus thuirt i,

"Fàg m'anam, fàg m'anam."

"Cha'n fhàg," ors' esan, "gus an leig thu dhomh fhaicinn na bheil os cionn a' chrios dhe'n bhana-chompanach."

"Ni mi sin," ors' ise, agus leig i anuas na bha os cionn a' chrios dhe'n bhanachompanach agus amach a thug ise à beul na béisteadh. Bha i air oir na tràghad agus mu'n d'fhuair a' bhéist gluasad dh'a h-ionnsaidh spleuchd esan an t-ubh f'a chois agus thuit i 'na closaich sios marbh do ghrunnd a' loch'.

Thill iad an uair sin dhachaidh gu taigh a' rìgh agus bha gnothaichean gu math aighearach, toilichte. Ach co-dhiubh thuirt an rìgh gu robh esan air fàs cho sean a nisd airson a bhi a' gabhail curam dhe na gnothaichean 's a' siubhal mun cuairt air feadh na rìoghachd, agus thuirt e ri Iain Mac an Iasgair Mhóir,

"'S fheàrr dhuit," ors' esan, "thu fhéin a ghabhail curam a null a nisd dhe'n rìoghachd air fad. Tha mise a' dol a dh'fhuireach 'nam thàmh ann a' seo gun an còrr 'ga dheanamh."

Bha sin ceart gu leòr, agus 'nuair a fhuair e na gnothaichean air an suidheachadh chuir Iain fios dhachaidh air 'athair agus air a mhàthair airson iad fhéin a dh'fhuireach còmhla riu' air a' rìoghachd agus chuir e fios air a dhithisd bhràithrean. Agus 'nuair a thàinig iad sin chuir e iad 'nam fear-riaghlaidh: fear dhiubh air ceann an ear na rìoghachd agus fear air ceann an iar na rìoghachd.

Agus sin agaibh an sgeulachd mar a fhuair mise i air Mac an Iasgair Mhóir.

of the loch." Down went the Dun Otter and it was not long before it was on the surface with the egg in its mouth. Iain, Son of the Big Fisherman, caught the egg. He put the egg on a flat rock and rested his foot on top of it. He began applying weight on the egg and the beast arose at the edge of the ocean and said, "Spare my soul, spare my soul."

"I will not," he said, "until you let me see what is above the belt of your woman companion."

"I'll do that," said the monster, so it let up what was above the belt of its female companion and out she went from the monster's mouth. She was on the edge of the beach and before the monster had a chance to move toward her, Iain flattened the egg under his foot and the beast fell down a dead carcass to the bottom of the loch.

They returned then to the king's house and things were very happy and cheerful. Anyway the king said that he had grown too old to be taking care of various matters and travelling around throughout the kingdom, and he said to Iain, the Big Fisherman's Son, "You yourself had better take care of the entire kingdom from now on. I'm going to stay in retirement here without doing anything more."

That was all right, and when Iain had settled his affairs he sent home for his father and mother to stay with them in the kingdom, and he sent for his two brothers. And when they arrived there he appointed them governors: one over the eastern end of the kingdom and the other over the western end.

And there you have the story, as I heard it, of the Big Fisherman's Son.

# This Was Swordfishing

*told by Jack Ingraham*

Swordfish *come* to the surface. They're not up all the time. They come up and they what you call "fin." You see their fins out of the water. And a lot, they get under the water; they don't show their fins at all—but you can see them from a high mast. You could see down quite a piece, you know. And you'd see some that you could get round close enough to get a shot at them. You'd get them that way, stick them under the water. You'd have a wheel on the mast. Come a rough wind you had to get down out of it, get off the mast and steer below. You wanted pretty good weather for swordfishing. There'd be two or three up the mast, watching the water. Everybody watching to see who could see one. Some were better than

*Above: Jack Ingraham. Right: Percy Dixon through a hoop on the spar, watching for swordfish. In fine weather the boat could be steered from here. The second hoop is for a second man to look out for fish. Below right: The sticker waiting in his stand, an iron frame out on the tip of the bowsprit. (G. M. Somerville)*

others. The sun off the water—some people it used to hurt their eyes. It never hurt mine, but it used to hurt some—burn up their mouth and everything. The sticker wouldn't be out there all the time. If there was swordfish being struck, a good sign of them—he would stay out there. Sometimes he'd get one before the fellow on the mast would see it. There was never any bait used. Just looking. And they might be under and you could run around for hours and not see one. You'd just be in a place where you thought they *should* be. But you'd probably be there hours and not see a thing. All coming up at the same time pretty near. Just a matter of an hour or two would mean the day. If you were somewhere else you mightn't be there at all. And you could be where there was thousands of fish and not have the luck to run into one. Everybody else getting fish in the boat and you could do what you like you could not see a fish. The right place and the right time. They were kind of hard to get, once you look at it. You go a long time sometimes and not get any. Then probably you get a few good days, get more than your share sometimes.

*This Was Swordfishing* 97

Then some more times one fellow would have all of them. And then a lot of times you see them and couldn't get them. That was the worst of the lot. They'd run before you could get close enough. The sound of the boat. If you had rattles in the boat, the shafts were rattling—you wouldn't get near a swordfish. They didn't mind the engine, they didn't mind the exhaust—but some kind of vibration in the water, that will scare a fish. And another thing that will scare them was a shadow. You had to be careful going on to them. If the sun—you know, fishing in the evening—if the fish is out and you cross on the inside of him, when the shadow of the mast was on him whoosh he was just gone like lightning.

Queerest fishing it was, you know. But we enjoyed it. You went after the fish. If you were fishing you went after anything that was fish. It was great sport in a way. It was fishing but it was more of a holiday. Everybody went at it. It was quite a trip, you know. As good as a vacation. And you could go anywhere. And the boats came down from everywhere. Right from Digby, right around down Nova Scotia and all down the shore. And they'd all get down here [Neil's Harbour] at one time. They wouldn't fish all the time down here.

*Left: A swordfish is struck. Below (left to right): The drowned swordfish tied alongside a dory; hoisting a swordfish aboard the vessel; a schooner-type swordfishing vessel. (G. M. Somerville)*

98   This Was Swordfishing

They'd fish at Louisburg, Scatari. Then probably they'd be in Glace Bay, depending on where the fish were. Later in the season the fish come down this way—the whole works would be down here. I've seen five hundred in Dingwall, that was strange boats. They started coming down here around the 1930s and it was pretty near 1950 when they quit that. The swordfishing continued, but then they got different boats, bigger boats, and they went on the Banks and they got catching them with trawls. Here we kept doing it all on the darts, you know, the spears. Everybody caught them that way, schooners and all.

There was not too much taking swordfish here until the 1920s. Ingonish was the first place they started. They had bigger boats in Ingonish. I know the first fellow was a Dunphy. He was telling me one time he went and caught some swordfish kind of late in the season. The swordfish was inshore, up around Smokey there—and he salted them and sent them to the States. Salted them. That's the only time I hear tell of that. Get about twelve dollars a barrel he told me. John Dunphy. He's dead now, old John. A lot had to do with the market, you know. Somebody to buy them. They were buying swordfish first up in the States, and when the fleet started moving—when they found out there was swordfish down this way—a lot of the buyers had somebody to buy from down here. Some company went to work and went into the swordfish business and put on boats to go where the fleet was at and collect the fish. The rum-running days were over and they had lots of those rum-running boats—just the thing for it, you know. They'd go in the harbor and bring a load of ice and take the fish and ice them aboard and when they'd get a load they'd go to Boston with them. And another one would take their place.

There wasn't much swordfish when I started. Wasn't looking for swordfish at all, catching codfish, handlining—we would see an odd swordfish pass by. So we started to get a pole aboard and see could we get one. That's how it was. I don't know if there wasn't many fish or people weren't so good at it and didn't understand it. We got a few like that. Sometimes we didn't have a rig or anything—just down in the bow of the boat. Then after a while they started putting stands on the little boats. Get a few. They weren't worth a great lot. Nothing was in them days. And everybody hunted in close to the shore, right in. A mile, two miles out from the shore—and that was about where they thought all the swordfish was. Somebody would stick some and everybody would hang around and by and by somebody else would stick some—there would be some fish there all right.

But around Glace Bay, in the rum-running days, the rum-runners were out about six miles, you know? Anchored there. They had to be out three miles then, so they stayed out

*This Was Swordfishing*

The bronze dart was commonly called the lily iron. One end of the warp (100 to 125 fathom of rope) went through the dart. Most fishermen were never satisfied with the shape of the purchased dart, so they'd hammer more bend in the tail. The iron at the end of the sixteen to eighteen-foot pole would be greased and slipped into the dart. It was meant to come out easily. The dart was actually held in place by the warp drawn back and snug, tucked into the becket near the rear of the pole. From the becket the warp was usually tied in a slip knot at a rung of the iron stand where the sticker (the harpooner) stood (also called the chair, it was about twelve feet out over the bow), and tied again in another slip knot before the fore rigging of the vessel. The rest of the warp was coiled in a dish on deck, the end tied to a keg. The pole itself had a separate bib line tied securely to the stand. Whether stuck or thrown, the iron comes back, leaving the dart in the fish. If stuck, the sticker often pulls the tuck from the becket. Otherwise, when the fish takes off it frees the tuck and the series of slip knots, taking warp from the dish. The keg is thrown over as a buoy. Then a man was put out in a dory to pull on the rope, turning the dart crosswise and dragging the fish backward, forcing water into the gills to drown him.

Most fishermen who have been out in a dory trying to drown a swordfish, know something of the sword as a weapon. Once struck, they are liable to come through the dory. We heard of one that went through the big boat—two inches planking plus six inches hardwood. Bob Fitzgerald of Dingwall told us: "The kind of fight they put up depended on where they were hit. If they happened to be hit in the head or any vital spot, you know, they would not last too long. If you got close enough and drove that harpoon right down through them, sometimes go right through on the other side and clinch, turn crosswise—that would damage their insides and they wouldn't last so long. But the ordinary, if you struck them back close to their tail or in the fleshy part, they'd put up a good fight, half hour sometimes an hour. Of course, I have seen real devils, you know—two or three hours. They get down on the bottom there and just keep going, fast as they could, and you haul them back trying to drown them, if they'll come back they'll come back so far and then they'll take off again. Some of them will come to the top of the water and jump, and I've had two or three of them come and ram the boat. Yes, indeed, I was the dory when they came through the dory right to their eyes. I don't know if they turn on the boat or it just happens in the fight. You never know the mind of a fish, if they have such a thing. I've seen one that I figure he was trying to kill me. He didn't jump at the boat, he jumped at me and came right in across the side of the boat and rolled down on the side of the boat and then rolled back off into the water again. The next time he came through it, right to his eyes. Then I was off Neil's Harbour and I was drowning a fellow and he came through me. And I've had two fish that stuck in the bottom on me. Sometimes you strike them in the side of the head they go crazy, you know? This fellow went crazy and dove down sixty to seventy fathom of water. You know he's stuck when you pull up over him and that's it, not a sound nor a kick out of him. And you come up solid and you can't move him so you know he's dead. Up to their eyes."

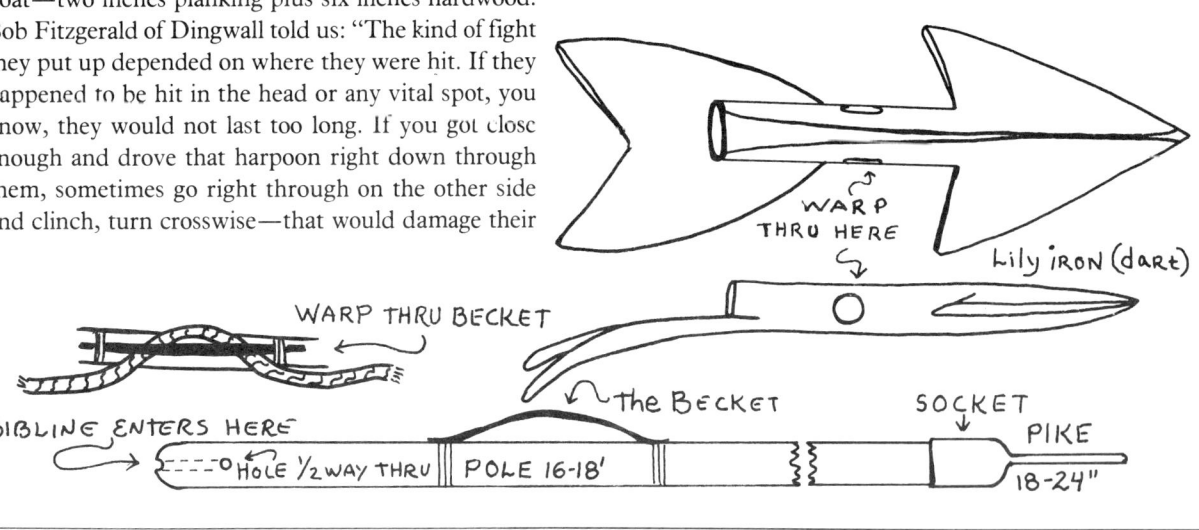

*100*    This Was Swordfishing

six—they anchored and stayed there till they got rid of their load. And some of those fellows out more for rum-running than anything else, they used to get some swordfish. They got more swordfish than anybody else did. Sometimes they did pretty good at that. So after that the swordfish fleets started going out looking for them further off.

The Newfoundland boats were coming over already. They fished Glace Bay. Not very big boats, sail boats, they'd have eight-horsepower engine in them—and to go off very far they couldn't do it in a day. Where the swordfish turned up to be plentier was what they called The Edge, on the edge of the Bank. The edge of the ground. The continental shelf. You go off the water wouldn't be very deep. From the shore off the bottom was pretty level; it just deepened a little. Thirty to forty fathom. You went off and by and by you started going seventy fathom. When you go so much further than that you go right over and there would be over a hundred. That was the edge of the ground. That would be thirty miles offshore. Some of the Newfoundland fellows started going off thirty miles—they'd just about go and come in the day. But some of them started to go off and stay off all night—and they'd get all day. Come in, they'd have two days fishing. And all big ones they'd get off there. Five hundred to seven hundred pounds, that'd be a big one. It's a pretty good fish when they average three hundred pounds. We didn't have the boats in Neil's Harbour for that but afterwards we got some. Then the Nova Scotia fellows—western fellows we used to call them—they came down and they only had small boats. They were lobster fishing up in their own towns. But after a while they started getting bigger boats. Two car engines in them. They could go off pretty quick, you know. Ten miles an hour. They could get off on the edge a pretty good day there.

When the ban came on [banned because of mercury content], pretty near everybody that fished went swordfishing here at Neil's Harbour. There's no boats now; it's all lobster boats. There was about nine swordfishing boats there in Neil's Harbour. Took quite a bunch of men, you know—three and four in every boat. There was nine just there alone, and there was hundreds used to come there. And they banned it, and no more of that. It kind of got bad on the end of it. They got scarce. They started fishing them offshore is what probably caused that. They cleaned up the schools or broke them up before they had a chance to come inshore.

*Bob Fitzgerald beside a catch.*

And I think that was it. They started fishing on the banks, you know, up around Sable Island and all the banks up there, up on Georges and everywhere. Even went onto the Grand Banks swordfishing. They took big, big fish. Some of those fellows had been at it from the time they could walk pretty near, and they kept getting bigger boats, bigger boats—and they found out more about the swordfish—they found out they were down on the Grand Banks.

# John Joseph LeBlanc Shears Sheep

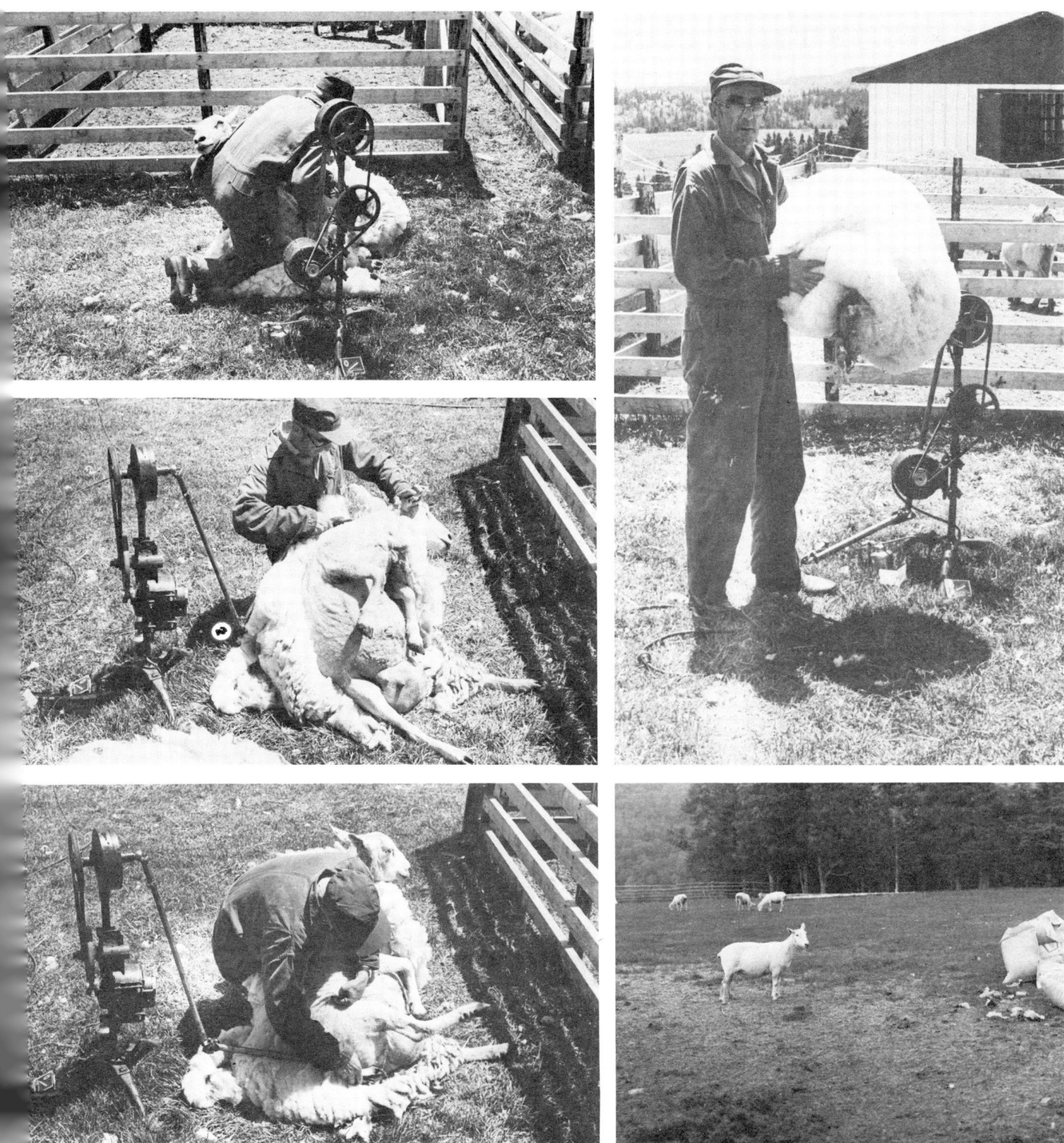

John Joseph LeBlanc Shears Sheep

# Remembering Rum Running Days

SAMUEL HARDY, *North Sydney:* You could be out there and it didn't make any difference—the cutters could be coming right on you for weeks—it didn't make any difference to you. You were there because you had a load of rum to unload and there was nobody was going to come onto you when the cutter was there. That's for sure. You were the mother ship—the schooners. You would be outside the territorial limit and that cutter could lay on your ship a month if it wanted—there's nobody go aboard you while the cutter was there. Cause they knew the cutter was a revenue boat. Say you were in a big vessel, you might go a hundred miles out of your way; then, after dark, come back. Of course you know there wasn't too much power then. It was all sail. You had to get weather. That's what takes time. You might plan on it's going to be nice tonight—by the time you get there it'll come up dirty weather and you'll have to heave off and jog the sea again. And when it came up you could manage a boat again, you came back as close to land as you could get. You'd come back as far as the limits.

Most of the mother ships would go to Demerara [British Guiana, now Guyana, South America]—and then they'd go from there off the States. And the smaller boats would know you were coming. You'd have that made up before you'd go out at it. And you'd know what kind of an order they wanted. You'd have an order for so many cases of whiskey, so many kegs of rum, so many cases of brandy, gin, wine—whatever it might be. You'd have to have Demerara rum if you were going to work around Cape Breton. St. Pierre rum was no good around Cape Breton, and rum was no good above New York. No, no, no, you'd starve to death up there before you'd sell ten kegs of rum. You see, up there you had to have malt, whiskey and malt—the malt they'd make their whiskey.

My first time to Rum Row [out beyond the limits], I was about eighteen. We went up to Saint John, New Brunswick, for a load of whiskey and took it up to New York. The schooner we were on—they didn't go in the harbor. All these small boats would come out. They'd come at night and pick you up. You didn't know who was coming but you did know that you were expecting a boat. It could be police but they wouldn't very likely come aboard a rum runner—sometimes if they thought they could get away with it—but aw, no, you'd know who was coming. They'd come alongside of you;

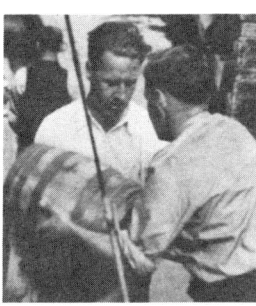

*Above: Samuel Hardy. Top right: Milton MacKenzie. Above right: A keg of rum seized by the RCMP.*

they'd ask the vessel's name. They might not know the man exactly but they'd know his name, whoever was in charge of the vessel. And they'd have an order, probably, from ashore. You'd load her up and she'd go on her way. I thought it was a good job. Well, there wasn't too much work to it, you know. You weren't skipper of the vessel and you wouldn't know where it was going. You were only just passing it out to them. You didn't *want* to know. You just wanted to get back to land, to get in for a week or so. Go on the slip and get cleaned off and painted and come out again. Then coming out you'd see the cutters. You'd have to fool around, have to get clear of them, after dark. You wouldn't want them to see some boat come alongside of you. Fool around, go around somewhere else, fool around—the cutter didn't know where in the hell they were going to. Come dark and the mother would sneak up alongside of you. They'd know where you'd be.

I got about thirty-five dollars a month the first time I went rum running. It's just like you signed up on one of these boats going across the Gulf [of St. Lawrence] carrying cargo—

same thing, except you couldn't come in the harbor. And you were glad to get a job. Men came out of soup kitchens onto them boats. Do anything. There was nothing for people to do. There was no work for them ashore. The fishing wasn't worth anything. The man that was fishing them big Lunenburg vessels, night and day and tearing and dragging—and you're at it all night long—you were damn lucky with a good fellow if you made three hundred dollars that season. For your own share, for the whole season. You had to work at something didn't you? And those schooners would be like coasting, see?

After I got into it a while I decided to have my own boat. Got somebody to go good for you, buy an old vessel or something—set up on a small scale and decided to get along the best I could. The last one I had was my own. At first, the bigger schooners—the Lunenburg fishermen—you'd charter them. You'd charter them for to go south. You'd keep them all the summer—big Lunenburger, a three-mast schooner maybe. A trip to Demerara was a good trip if you struck good weather. You had to have the weather. You get out there, strike bad weather, get the sails broken, torn to pieces, you know—then you would get calm, you'd be drifting around days in the vessel. You strike a good time, Halifax to Demerara, you'd go it in sixteen to seventeen days. And no trouble to buy the rum there. All they want is the money. It

*Below: The schooner* Liberty *and a "standard coaster" transferring cargo. Bottom: A speedboat of the type that brought rum inside the limit and raced it to shore.*

was just a business. Some people tell you all this bull about somebody chased me, somebody fired at me and all—a lot of goddamned bull. I was into it for a long time. There weren't too many went up off of New York—1923-24. I never seen any of that. And I was up New York when it was bad. But there was vessels taken like that. A different bunch went aboard, tried to hijack the vessel, you know what I mean. Take her over. They stole the cargo out of a number of ships up there. I had a cousin that was on one. They took the cargo and told them to get the hell off the coast—and they came back to Halifax. But never touched them. Just want the cargo. But oh, they were good days, good times. You know, like every other business, if you watched yourself, what you were doing, you wouldn't get in any trouble.

MILTON MACKENZIE, *Preventive Service:* Samuel Hardy. I've stood by him on Rum Row up in the Gulf—oh, several times—to keep him from landing his stuff, keep the other boats from coming and taking it. I was in the Preventive boats. And any Canadian boat—any boat registered in Canada—must stay outside the twelve-miles limit but any boat registered outside of Canada can stay just outside of three miles—three-mile limit from any headland or coast—if they're carrying liquor or any contraband as far as that goes. Because any coast guard could go aboard, ask for your manifest and search you if you're in territorial water. You can't board a ship on the high seas. They're safe as long as they're outside the limit. But they'd be trying to land it. Speedboats would come out from the shore and run it in—what we call the snapper boats or Cape Island boats. And some of the bigger boats would come right in but we had them pretty well tagged you know. We knew every one of them and they always layed off, layed off. And we lived on the Preventive boats. Be out sometimes ten and twelve days at a time, before we'd come in to re-fuel and get more grub.

You couldn't do anything about them. No, nothing. Just stand by them. Lay off. We knew they were there, see them all the time. Nighttime, you put the searchlights on them. Those big fellows anchored off, they're only warehouses—floating warehouses. And these speedboats—well, we called them speedboats—they run out from land, load and come in, make a landing. Maybe forty to fifty kegs at a time—three hundred cases—whatever. We seized quite a few of them. But a lot would get in. You can't watch it all you know. You'd get two or three different fellows to load that night. You don't know which one to call. There was always a decoy to draw you away. They weren't fools you know. They had tricks. They'd reverse their sidelights. You'd think they were going

*Milton MacKenzie and preventive cutters* Louisbourg *and* Fleur de Lis.

opposite of you. But we had big searchlights. Then they put smokescreens up—come out of their exhaust. They had things to put on the exhaust—old oil and stuff—and one mass of smoke, just fog all around—but we'd find them after. But they'd get clear. It'd all get clear. The big warehouse would be empty and away he'd go.

Oh, it was quite a game, boy. A lot of fun in it. The way the world is today with dope and heroin and all—everyone thinks it was all like that—but it wasn't like that at all. They were all respectable people making a living. Some of those captains were real gentlemen up there. Oh, yes. There was no animosity among us. They were making a living and we had a job. You'd go up alongside, ask them how they were. I threw a newspaper aboard. I wasn't supposed to. I just passed and threw. Those were all good fellows. They weren't bothering anybody. Of course the fellows that took it ashore—well now if they got caught it was their hard luck. If you got clear, good enough. A lot of it got ashore. When we'd be around it just took them longer to land it. The real good fellows landed lots of it, they never opened their mouths. They never said, well, I fooled them yesterday, never told it out. But you get a fellow that lands a couple of bottles, you get "Oh jeez I fooled this Mountie"—them fellows didn't land no liquor. Long as they got clear and landed, good luck to them as long as they didn't blow about it. But if they'd say they fooled us and this and that, that's the time we'd get after them worse than ever.

FERMIN FLEET: This schooner that I was on—the *Tillie*, a three-masted schooner—I never went to Scotland on her but she loaded in Scotland with Scotch whiskey—37,000 cases of whiskey in the hold in wooden boxes, twelve in a case—they were glass bottles in straws at the time. I joined her in Halifax. Ninety dollars a month and twenty a month bonus. We left the eighteenth day of December. We were going to take it to New York. Six days and six nights to Ambrose Channel Lightship. And when we got there an American yacht—a steam yacht—come out and tied up alongside of us. And he had to be up in the docks at New York at six o'clock Christmas Eve. So we loaded. We put 6000 cases aboard of her and it got rough—right there on the open Atlantic, twelve miles out. Captain said, "We can't stay no longer. We're parting lines." So he left and went into New York. And we laid off about fourteen miles. You could just see the land and the lights of the land some nights. Just eating and standing out watch—four on and four off—telling lies and playing cards and having the odd drink. We were waiting for that yacht to come back out. But she got caught and she couldn't get out. She didn't get caught with anything aboard but she got caught with straws or cases—and they held her on a sort of detention. And we waited for her. Two or three weeks and our grub got all out. We couldn't go in the States. Oh, no. The odd time we'd see a four-stacker—so we'd put to sea further. What I mean a four-stacker is a U.S. Coast Guard and they

*106   Remembering Rum Running Days*

burnt coal at that time and you could see their smoke. And when you'd see their smoke you'd get as much headway up as you could and to be on the safe side you'd get out a little further. She'd come maybe take a turn or two around you, and spy at you and all that sort of thing. But leave you alone.

Anyhow, we went back to Halifax. Our grub was gone and all we had was two or three dried codfish and a few turnips, cabbage and a little bit of cornmeal. That's the God's honest truth. Lots of liquor—well, we only got clear of 6000 or 7000 cases in all that time. So we went into Halifax and customs come aboard and sealed her up. Well, what I mean now by sealing her up: They put a big blob of sealing wax—you know, that red wax—you melt it on the hatches—and when it was melted there was a hammer with a crown on it—the Queen's crown like—and he stamped it into that wax with a red ribbon and that red ribbon run right across the hatch, you know, just the same like you tie up a Christmas parcel. It run right across the hatch and another blob of sealing wax and another crown. And if this ribbon was broken while we were in port the ship would be seized. That seal couldn't be broken till you were outside the three-mile limit.

We were in there I guess about a week—grubbed up. Then we came out of Halifax on this bad trip on the thirteenth of February, 1927. That was an unlucky Jesus day to go. We anchored off of George's Bank on the American coast—around one hundred miles from Boston Lightship. It was a fine Saturday. Oh there wasn't enough wind to blow a match out. And this Boston beam trawler come along. I can remember as well as if it was yesterday. Her name was the *Foam*, she was going into Boston. They had a wireless operator so the old man hollered to him, "Have you heard any storm warning?" No, nothing. So he kept going. And he got about a mile from us and he turned around and come back toward us. "We got a storm warning just now. Gale of wind, northeast, and snow. All over the New England coast." Skipper said, "I guess we better heave up" and the Supercargo said, "It may not be much." It was his cargo and his ship. So the skipper said, "We'll hang on then." Well, we hung on so long that by and by we couldn't heave up, couldn't get the anchor up—blowing too hard. And eleven o'clock Sunday morning she parted the chain. Well then we had to get underway, try to get the sails on her, get off the shoals—we were up on the shoals—fourteen fathom of water—George's shoals. A bad spot, oh yes.

We got underway and we deepened the water a fathom an hour, getting off—till twelve o'clock that night we were safe. We had lots of leeway then in case anything happens. We came down toward Cape Sables and she was blowin' all the time. We stayed a couple of days till the wind moderated, and then we came back. We didn't anchor no more but we laid there for maybe a week or so and then it come on April and was thick of fog. We still had the cargo. And food is getting pretty well gone again. So we went back into Halifax and they sealed her up again. And that was the end of that voyage. Ha ha ha ha. Still got it all aboard. So we grubbed up again and we started out again. The next time we only went four or five miles off of Devil's Island. A boat by the name of *Newton Bay* came alongside and took about half the cargo. Then we went back into Halifax and that's where I left her. That was enough for me. They started shooting them off the States, started firing on them. They shot a fellow named Captain Cluett. He was on the *Josephine K*.—shot him at the wheel. I give it up after that.

CAPTAIN JACK WILLIS:   Oh, yes, I'd go right into port. We wouldn't lay off on Rum Row. We went right in New York, East River. We went in and discharged. Forty-five thousand cases at a time. Go in one way and come out the other. Back to St. Pierre and load up and back again. The people that were handling the cargo—discharging—were all picked up before the ship got in. They were drunks, dope fiends and everything. All the scrapings of New York. And they had them into a place and gave them food and stuff until the ship got in—kept them there in a shed. So when the ship was finished discharging, they would take them all back into the van, to the same place, and pay them off twenty or thirty dollars for

*Fermin Fleet (left) and Captain Jack Willis.*

discharging the boats—only take them two or three hours—give them a kick in the rear and away they're gone. Until the ship would come back again. Then two or three days before she arrived they would gather those fellows around again and have them all ready when the ship docked. They would have them down there in the vans.

But the third time we went in we weren't supposed to go in. There was supposed to be a message sent to us to keep away. Somehow there was a mistake made in the message. So we went on in. When we got in off Battery Place, tug boat came out. Said, "Christ, you fellows shouldn't be in here at all. Beat it." Well, by the time they got talking about it, it's too bloody late now to go out. So we go up the Hudson. And we anchored in full view of Sing Sing. We were in trouble. We were supposed to carry on to a place way up the Hudson River. We got a message telling us to drop the anchors and leave her. The revenue cutter is on its way up so get away, get ashore. So we dropped the anchor and everybody got down in the boats. I got back up the ladder again and got myself a couple bottles of whiskey and back down again—and we put her ashore. And there was a big ice house—sawdust and everything in it—but it had been neglected for some time—this is where we went to hide until a bus came for us.

After a while the bus came and we went to the New Yorker—officers and engineers. We left the wireless operator in charge of the crew to wait until the bus came back to pick them up. They were not to wander around, people might see them. But they did wander around and the police came and picked them all up. My brother was in the bunch. We were in the Hotel New Yorker now. We were talking to the old man when this Big Louie came in. He had a grip and plunked it down. "Are you people ready to go back to the ship if everything is all clear?" We said, "Sure." But in the meantime a message came through. It was too late. The revenue cutter was alongside and the ship's under arrest. So he reached in his bag, picks up a roll of money—bag was full of money—rolled up, big rolls—and fired this at the captain. "Take this and head for Montreal." So we all got on the train. The old man paid all our passages, we had all we wanted—and when we got to Halifax the captain and I lived all winter, kept our families, on the money that was left over.

RED DAN SMITH: They were at that rum running on a small scale—it wasn't rum running then but it's the same—when I was small and when I was a kid. People here then were poor, and they were good workers; and they were raising a lot of cattle, more than they would plan to eat, a lot of them. And it was all sailing vessels then and they were going to St. Pierre with them—taking cattle to St. Pierre and getting money for some of them and rum and stuff for others of them. But it was then lawful to get rum in here. It wasn't rum running. And a few years after the government made a law that it would be stopped. But it never stopped—small boats going and getting a load and landing it here. And do you know, it's quite a joke—perhaps it made bad habits for people because they liked to drink—but there was a lot of stealing in it. Stealing. It was hidden, and like everything else they got acquainted with it. And if you were hiding some liquor perhaps there was two or three watching you, from different anchors, where you are hiding it. And when you'd go for it there wouldn't be a bit of it there. Those would go and steal it and hide it for themselves. And where those fellows would be hiding it there would be somebody else watching them. And when they would go back there was none of it there.

I fished in Ingonish in rum running time, and I don't believe I'm stretching it—the same keg would be stolen a dozen times. Yes. The same keg. I'm saying keg. There was kegs and kegs and kegs.

My own relatives. My second cousin, he was good at that work. He was to St. Pierre. He was a good seaman. The boat was the *Joseph Patrick*. Went over to St. Pierre—this would be around 1926 or 7—they came back to this side and I don't know. There was a lot of crooked work done around the vessels then. He got in on thick fog and put her ashore down on Plaster Point coming on morning. In July. Fellows from there had nets out and when they went out, here was the boat ashore with the stuff in her. Took it all ashore out of her to the woods here, scattered it here and there through the day.

I was staying at Big Grapplen, in a shanty. We went across to the nets all right—thick, thick of fog. And here it was the *Joseph Patrick*, not a thing aboard her and her rolling on the bottom there. Everything out of her. Well, we knew very well what happened. The tide was right and we put the little motorboat on her and we towed her off and once we got her off to deep water she was all right. We put a fellow aboard of

*Red Dan Smith.*

her and he took her over to North Gut and put her on the beach there, so they wouldn't have to pump her out. The owners that had the rum was over in Sydney. They came over to North Shore with cars but they didn't find a thing. They raised Cain. They found out that I was around the boat. They went back to Sydney. They were going to send a captain to come and get her. And when they were away we seized her. Put the yellow sticker on her and the watchman—and when they came back with a captain they couldn't go aboard of her. We had taken her there and we wanted to get paid for salvaging her. Well the next thing we knew we got a letter from a lawyer—piracy. One of the worst crimes you can be at. Piracy. To appear in court in Sydney for piracy. The time came and we went to Sydney and there was nobody appeared against us. So, we got sixty dollars a man there, for salvage.

ALEX GOLDMAN: The first time I ever went out to make a landing I was fifteen years old. They asked me if I would go out overnight, ten dollars a night. We went out—we had seven touring cars all with the back seats out and the curtains up. They gave me a Nash to drive, of which I was very proud—and of course the seat was out to make room for the ten-gallon kegs of rum. And the very first landing we made was somewhere near Irish Cove on the Bras d'Or Lakes. I was a big boy then. I was the same size I am now. Strong. So I was anxious to get right to work—to lift those ten-gallon kegs out of the dory. The big boat of course couldn't come that close to shore. We'd go into the water to our knees and above our knees—you had on rubber boots. One would take a ten-gallon keg, put it on his shoulder and walk with it. The next would take a ten-gallon keg, put on his shoulder, walk ashore with it. I took a ten-gallon keg, put it on my shoulder, and I tipped over. Right in the water. They had a great laugh over that. Must have been eight or ten of us. Most of them would carry it right in front against their chest. This is after midnight.

And we'd stay at this, finally get the boat unloaded. We had to take the kegs across a sort of sandbar to the lagoon and load it into another rowboat and take it up onto the farm and hide it into a cache. We had a horse to put them in the cache, right in the middle of the woods—about eight-by-ten-by-six-feet-deep hole. This would be filled with kegs of rum then covered with tree branches. This was an arrangement they'd made with a farmer. And any time any of this would be sold—say someone, one of the bootleggers, whoever around town wanted two or three or five kegs of rum we'd go out there and pick up the order and deliver. The cache is the warehouse, as it were.

*Alex Goldman.*

SOL GREEN: I was a so-called bootlegger. That's what they called them in those days. As far as I was concerned I had a respectable business. I had a hotel here in Sydney. The Victoria. I went down there in 1921 or '22. I started bootlegging in '22. I could get it through a vendor. He could get it from Halifax. But he could only get a half a case at a time. Half a case of rum or whiskey. And that wasn't daily. That was a quota. It wasn't enough but it was a help in putting out, if you had a reputation for having good liquor. Then in '23 the rum runner started coming. We were buying from people who'd bring it in. We'd buy rum in ten-gallon kegs and scotch was in twelve bottles to a case. I'd just serve it by the drink or serve it by the bottle. No bar there. Bring it to you. You'd sit at a table. Oh, yes, it was open enough. The law didn't want to stop it no more than we did. They'd come up and every now and again you'd pay a fine—and that was it. They never cleaned you out. If you were convicted a Second Offence, well it meant a thirty-day jail term. It was up to the inspector himself whether he wanted to put a Second on you. They didn't want to jail us.

ALEX: They could keep on getting you and calling it a First Offence. Oh, yes. To put a Second on you—very rarely. They'd have to hate you. I had more than one First Offence. Oh, yes. How many? Who can remember? It was practically

*Remembering Rum Running Days* **109**

wide open, yes. But it was up to yourself whether you wanted to serve them, a stranger—he could be an informer that might have informed on someone else or someone you didn't want in there—you just tell them you didn't have it, that's all. Make some excuse and try to do it the nicest way you could. We never had any trouble. We had a certain clientele would go down there. We had a nice Glace Bay trade. Until the time they started to put the dog to us. That'd be around '27 I guess. We had three inspectors in town that time. They were out to get what revenue they could for the city. McConnell was mayor at that time.

SOL GREEN: What came in, we used to have to water it down.

ALEX: I remember this day we opened up a ten-gallon keg and boiled I don't know how many gallons of water and put it into one of these big boilers and mixed the water and the rum—and then bottled it.

SOL: That's right. It wouldn't lose its strength as much with boiled water as it would with cold water.

ALEX: This was hot water.

SOL: That's the idea. Then let it cool and it would still hold its strength. You'd lose a lot of strength with cold water. You'd mix it for a certain strength. The rum that was coming off Rum Row was I think thirty overproof. Actually thirty-two. That was fairly strong. If you got it down to proof you had a good strong drink. I'd mix it a little better than a third.

ALEX: Two parts rum to one part water.

SOL: You cork them yourselves. As far as rum was concerned, it came in kegs. You had your own corks and your own bottles. But other liquors came bottled from wherever it was manufactured. We were selling rum for a quarter a drink and thirty-five cents for scotch. Only thing was scarce was beer but we were getting fifty cents for a pint of beer. That's when we could get it. We stored it friends' places, here and there. Oh, yes, we lost some. Anybody that was in business lost some. A party you'd trust. You would have the wrong person. It'd just disappear. You had no comeback. When you went to get it it wasn't there, as far as they were concerned. But getting liquor? No, never had any trouble getting it.

Every now and again there was what you'd call a [Temperance] revival. Just lay low for a while till everything would

*Sol Green.*

quiet down, then you'd start all over. They'd push up the police and the inspectors that they weren't doing their work and so on. And they'd get a little busier for a week or two, get a few more convictions. Headlines in the paper. Gradually it would die down again. Churches. You'd never get it from the Catholic Church. Always the Protestant Church. I belonged to a Temperance Union. They called it the I.O.G.T. The International Order of Good Templars. We used to meet every week. And you'd take a pledge that you weren't going to take a drink. I had to take a new pledge every week.

DUNCAN CAMPBELL, *RCMP Retired:* I didn't work on the boats, the cutters. I was with the land force. We'd patrol the shorelines in a car. We usually went out about nine or ten o'clock in the evening till about four in the morning. Sometimes we were lucky and other times we weren't so lucky. Once in a while we would have information there was going to be a landing made. A schooner would come into some cove and they would take the rum ashore in dories. I remember one particular seizure, we had good information. Well the first night we went out they didn't come in; and the second night—that would be a couple of days before Christmas, 1936. We saw the schooner come in and there were men there brought the kegs of rum ashore in dories. And they were pretty cute, too. They came up a little brook. There'd be four or five fellows and each one would have a keg of rum and they'd walk up the brook in their fishing boots, so that they

*Remembering Rum Running Days*

didn't leave any tracks. And in the side of the embankment there was a wooden door, and it led into a cave in the side of the embankment—and there'd be one fellow inside taking the keg and piling it away. That went on for over an hour I suppose. And they never left any tracks. We were very close to them. It was about two o'clock in the morning and we had on a big buffalo robe—they don't have them now.

And when the job was finished we went down and declared ourselves. We arrested two of them. There was 375 five-gallon kegs in there. Tony MacKinnon and Sgt. Churchill went back to North Sydney to arrange for a truck or one of the RCMP cutters to come and take the rum back. They took the two prisoners. And the boat arrived about six in the morning—and oh my God it was a cold night. We had to watch it all this time. It was taken to the customs warehouse in North Sydney. It was left there till the case was disposed of in the courts. And after the court proceedings were all over we would be instructed to destroy that liquor.

No, it wasn't all destroyed. But I never knew any of the RCMP fellows being dishonest with it—selling it to others. In the wintertime we would make hot toddies. When we were ordered to destroy it, we would knock out the top and spill it out into the sewer. In the customs warehouse. I used to think that was so foolish. They could give it to an old person's home

*Duncan Campbell.*

or something like that. Because it was good rum—it was 130 proof at least. It was the very best. You could take quite a few drinks and it never made you sick. That time it was 375 kegs and it all went into the sewer.

They've tried to hijack the stuff stored at the customs warehouse, but they weren't successful. But when they learned we were spilling it into the sewer, I've heard stories afterward that they were down collecting it with cans and pails where it was running out into the sea.

I didn't like liquor work. I didn't mind patrolling the coast at night or being in on a rum seizure where kegs were being landed; but searching houses and beds and looking for floor hides—I never cared for that at all. I just wasn't suited for that kind of work. And the penalty—you could find them with a tablespoon full of rum and the minimum penalty was 100 dollars. You can be plastered drunk today and driving a car and the fine is about the same. Many of the bootleggers in those days they could not make a living in any other way. They be cripples or a widow woman or something like that. Life was pretty hard in those years.

WILLIAM FRASER, *Inspector RCMP Retired:* I remember searching for liquor one time and we couldn't find it anywhere, and I was leaving the place and I heard a pig in the pig pen. And I went over to have a look—I actually went over to look at the pig—there was another constable with me. And the pig was running around the pig pen and he slipped—and when he slipped he pushed the dirt aside and here was the shiny head of a spike, under about an inch of dirt in the pig pen. Aw, I said, this is it. So we got some boards, penned the pig up against the wall in a small area, tore up the floor and we found the cache of rum. That happened north of Smokey. I remember one time we searched a house and searched and searched and searched and finally we were leaving and coming outside, I looked at the floor, the step you see, and it looked odd. I got down and looked at it and I saw a little pinhole. I found a darning needle and I pressed it down into this hole—the whole thing flew up. There was a spring, the board came right up—and that was the cache of rum. Another place we were searching the water tap was where the rum came out. You turn the hot water tap and rum would come out of a big tank in the wall. They had some good caches; they were ingenious, really. Then lots of times you'd come along at night and you'd stop a car and there'd be a keg in the trunk or in the backseat.

There was a bootlegger in every community. Sold it out of his home, out of his barn, out of his field. Everywhere.

Just as soon as we found one hide they made a better one. And there was no stigma to being a bootlegger and handling contraband rum. Everybody did it. There was nothing morally wrong. The liquor stores came in '31, '32—but it continued long after that, because it was cheap. It was a dollar and a half for a quart where it was three dollars in the store. And it was much better liquor, eh? It was thicker and it was stronger. But once in a while they used to get some sour rum as they called it and the people'd be cross for a little while and they'd go to the liquor store—but they would come back to the bootlegger again. And you'd lay in wait, watch a place, watch a fellow coming out with a bottle and try to grab him—and they'd throw it and break it, you know, if they had a keg they'd push it out of the car and speed away. It was great fun those days, chasing cars. Two or three well-known rum runners on Cape Breton drove around in big cars for those days while we were saddled with Fords and Chevs. But we did very well.

In those days we charged them with selling under the Liquor Act if we had any evidence whatsoever and we charged them with possession under the Customs Act. We always charged them with dual prosecution, and the second offence under the provincial statute was always three months and the second offence under the federal statute was a fine of 500 dollars and six months or in lieu of the 500 dollars another six months. So it was pretty stiff. If you caught them they fought very hard. They had good lawyers because they had the means of getting good lawyers. But then coming along 1938-39 we started to use the provisions of the Conspiracy sections ["conspiracy to defraud the revenue"] and that was the end of it. The war came right on that. As a matter of fact during the first month of the war we were deep into a conspiracy trial where there were fifty-seven charged, all in the one big conspiracy. The investigation went on for a couple of years and we were tying everything together.

We suspected rum was being hauled from Canso to Isle Madame. I got a telephone call and they said it was a small swordfishing boat, a green boat—and I went to Petit-de-Grat and Arichat and West Arichat and D'Escousse—looked at all the boats, who had been out the night before, tried to get some information. And there were five or six boats tied up at Arichat and I went to jump down off the wharf onto this boat and to support myself my hand went down and touched the gunwale. And my goodness when I brought my hand back up it was white paint. Wet. All above the waterline the boat had been green and just painted that day. I got a fellow and questioned him and he admitted that he had hauled a load of rum that night. The guy knew I had him. There was marks on the floor where kegs had ben standing. I made a seizure, got some of the rum, and he was in the conspiracy. I seized the boat from him and he went to jail—and I eventually burned the boat. Oh, yeah. Smashed the engine up with an axe and sledge hammer, threw a five-gallon can of gasoline into her and threw a match at it. Right near the customs house in Arichat. That was common. Sure.

We practically eliminated them before the war but I think it really was the war starting in 1939 that really put the rum running out of business. The men who were on the ships then went to the navy. Our patrol boats—our seagoing RCMP—all went into the navy or the air force. There was nobody left, really—everybody was too busy. There was nobody left to bring rum in from the Barbados or British Guiana or from St. Pierre. I would never be so brash as to say we had it stopped. Oh, no.

The last big seizure of rum on Cape Breton—I made it

*Bill Fraser.*

*Top left: The schooner* Nellie J. Banks *seized by the patrol boat* Ulna *on June 16, 1938. Left: Men on the truck are unloading kegs from that seizure. Above: An RCMP officer dumping rum down the drain in the customs house.*

myself—was on New Year's Day, 1939. And that seizure was from a bunch of hijackers. We knew there was a cache of rum over around St. Esprit. Couldn't find it. Finally the hijackers found it. They knew how to locate it. It was about ten feet under the top of the sand, a big cache built up with logs. Hijackers from New Waterford. They found the cache and started transporting it to the mining towns to sell it. I think we got 150 kegs and they all went to jail for it. I think we seized five cars. We eventually caught them all, once or twice. We had a rum runner down north—it took a long time but we finally got him. They'd make a mistake, take too many chances. I think they were just greedy, you know, wanted to make as much money as they could. But it's a funny thing: I don't think many of them ever ended up with money, from rum. And everywhere it was the same: St. Peters, Ingonish, Cheticamp—there was rum everywhere. Everywhere. There was no question about that.

# How to Make Spruce Beer

You've got to make it from the black spruce. You know, there's three spruce trees—black, red and white. Take it any time at all, as long as it's black—but be sure and get somebody that understands the different colors of the spruce trees. And you take your limbs—the needles are still on—and you boil them. You'd have to have a pot—perhaps a six-quart pot—to boil your spruce in. But keep that pot for nothing else only boil the spruce because there'll be more or less balsam form around the pot, you see? And every time you use it just wash it, get the balsam all off. You'd be surprised what balsam comes out of the spruce limbs. Don't use too much spruce because if you make it too sprucey it's not good. Just enough to taste the spruce off it. I'll tell you, you'll have to make a couple of batches before you will get the taste that you'd want. I just go by guess. Boil them, and then you strain that water through an old piece of clean white cotton, say an old pillowcase—something like that as long as it's nice and clean. Cheesecloth is too open and a needle might go through and you wouldn't want to find a needle in your spruce beer. You strain your water that you boil your spruce in into a crock or a plastic bucket. And you put your molasses in—two pints of molasses to eight quarts of water. That will make eight forty-ounce bottles. And you just put a little yeast into it—not very much yeast. Not a whole envelope. You'd make two batches with a baker's envelope of dried yeast.

When you see it coming to the top, the froth coming to the top—then you take it and strain it in your bottles. Have your funnel with a piece of cotton over the top so there'd be no dirt or dust or anything. That's two strains. And that's that. The yeast is all mixed up with the water by this time. You'll see ingredients settle to the bottom and you'll wonder where it comes from because it's been strained—you'll wonder where it comes from. There was a time I used to use the cork corks. You know what a cork is. Well, you'd have to tie those down. Otherwise when your beer'd begin to work it'd pop off. But with the bottles that I get now there's just round corks on them that you just screw on the top. Fill your bottle three inches or more from the top. It makes a good drink, especially in the summer when you have it in the fridge and it's good and cold. You learn to like it.

*Mrs. Williams and everyone else we spoke to insisted that you have to use only the black spruce, but apparently the red spruce can be used with equal success. And this is especially good news when you realize that the red and black spruce interbreed, adding to the difficulties of telling one from the other. Also, brown sugar, honey and maple syrup can be used instead of molasses. The spruce beer Mrs. Williams makes is a mild, delicious and refreshing drink. Years ago the old people would make a more powerful spruce beer. Where Mrs. Williams boils the spruce in a small quantity of water—just to get the taste off it—people used to use a large pot to be sure that all the water used was brewed with the spruce limbs (usually the last six inches or so of the limb). The stronger drink depended on adding more molasses and yeast to the concoction. The final step was heat. The tightly corked bottles could be warmed behind the stove or if you had reason to hide it (or really wanted to drive the head to it) you could bury it in horse manure. A good many bottles can be expected to explode in the manure. The old people used this more powerful brew more as a tonic than a beverage, taking only a little at a time. They claimed that it was good for your health and, in fact, spruce beer is a noted cure for scurvy.*

*Mrs. Lillian Williams.*

# Willy Petrie: A Man Who Finds Water

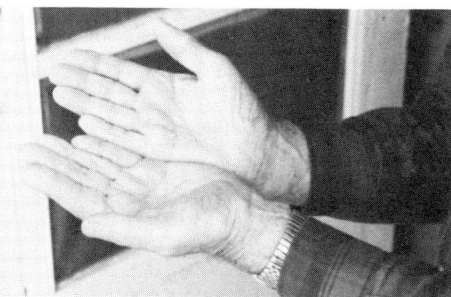
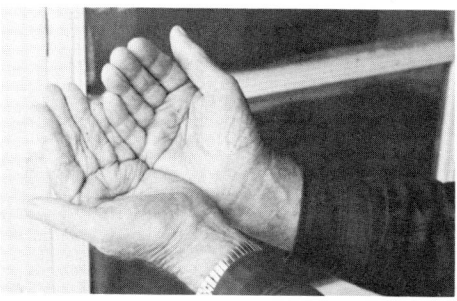

*Willy Petrie shows how he holds his hands when gripping the forked stick. His hands (right) reveal creases that seem to connect across the two hands. This is said to be a sign of a person with the ability to find water.*

Yes, I can find water. Any place I go. Oh, yes. I heard tell of it years ago, so I just tried it, see how it would work. Went to a spring, cold spring you know, and tried it out. I saw it was working then, so I started in trying it. Oh, I been I suppose now forty years since I knew about that. I was surprised. I can't hold it. I can brace my two feet, I can't hold it at all. It'll twist, keep on twisting, I can't stop it. Keep on turning on the end. You just put the prongs across your hands this way. And if it's gonna go it'll go down, you can't hold it. I don't have to move my hand, and it'll twist turn right in my hand. If I've got one anyways big or something, jeez, if I tried to hold it it'd tear me to pieces, the strain on me, the terrible strain on me in trying to hold it. It effects my whole body when I try to hold it. It won't cut me, but a small stick will break. It'll twist right off. I can hold it in my hand but it will twist right off. And I can find the depth of the water too. If it was fifty feet—say that the edge of the seam was here. Well, I've got to keep on going out, going out and perhaps it was fifty feet, well then I'd go past it and then I'll come on in and just the minute I get the depth it'll jump. Well, now, if it was twenty feet it'd be the same thing. And if it was only six. I've got to keep coming, keep coming, and it won't move till I end up at the depth of it—it'll just twist. Then all you have to do is measure from the seam to where I'm standing at—and that'll give you the depth. That's where you'll strike the water. I can't tell the amount of water. Only thing, when you strike the water you'd have to dig down further, the same as when you're digging a well. The idea there is, when you've got your seam you dig so the water is coming in all right around it.

You can use alder or poplar, apple crutch or hazel. I just use the alder, the alder is the handiest for to get to. Sometimes you go some places, an old farm or some place, you get an apple crutch. Apple and chestnut tree I guess is all. There's only five or six kinds of wood that'll work. Take spruce or fir or birch or maple—it wouldn't work at all. I'll just tell you what it is. Back in the Bible, in the Old

Testament, where Jacob put the rods in the tubs for to turn the animals in the different colors—rings you know—animals he took from his father-in-law—well, it's some of the wood he used. It's way over in the Old Testament, way over in Genesis: "And Jacob took him rods of green poplar, and of the hazel and chestnut tree; and pilled white strakes in them, and made the white appear which *was* in the rods." That's where he went to work and took those rods and took all the good cattle away. See, the ones that wasn't fattened he wouldn't put the rods to, only the good ones. Today you see all the cattle and animals with the rings and different colors—well that's supposed to be what happened there from that. You've seen those horses and things with rings round and different colors and shapes and everything—well they claim that that's what it was, see? But it only seems that this wood that he used now—that could be all wood relations—the different kinds of rods that he put in. The others don't seem to be any good. Why wouldn't spruce or fir or beech or birch be all right? Why not that bark? That's Genesis thirty, verse thirty-six. But I didn't know about that before I found out I could find water. It was afterwards I saw that. I don't know what you'd call it. Some say about my hand, across your hand. Supposed to be that line when you double your hand up. [See photographs of Willy's hands.] Now yours, you see, parts. I've got them together—one seam right into the other—it joins. Yours'll go clear of it. Mine joins right together, both hands right across when I put my hands together. It might be my hand, but I could use my fingers. I can do it with the stick in my fingers just the same as across my hand.

*Willy cut into the end of his alder stick and put in a coin. He said that the stick was no longer good for finding water, but that now it could find money—it could locate any metal stuck in the end of it.*

I remember one time we were trying for money. Well I put the money in the end of it, it would go to my pocket. I said, There's no money in my pocket. I don't know why it's going to my pocket. So, it was no good anyway. It wouldn't work. Well, you remember them small little five-cent pieces? Well now right down in one corner of my pocket there was one of them. I

*Standing at a place where he knew there was water, Willy said he would hold the stick as tightly as he could and try to prevent it from pointing down toward the water. His hands didn't move but his stick turned downward all the same.*

*Willy Petrie: A Man Who Finds Water*

didn't know that was down there. But that's what was doing it. When I took that out, that was okay.

Now I'll tell you something: If I got lost in the woods—there are seams like in the ground, perhaps about a foot wide or something. There's a dot of gold into it, a pick of silver—dust, dust you'd say, a dust of gold, a dust of silver and a dust of copper mixed all up through it. And the seams run right through the earth. All right now. You wouldn't be bothering with the gold, you wouldn't have that in your pocket. But if I had two dollars worth of silver, I'd have to take one quarter out of her—or a five cent piece—and fire the rest away. Otherwise it would not go to the seam, it would go to my pocket. But if I had some coppers too, well I could put a copper in the end and the silver in my pocket wouldn't make any difference—copper wouldn't effect or bother the silver—but I'd have to chuck away the other coppers. You'd split the end of the alder and put in the copper. Then you'd find the seam. You'd have to hunt. You may have quite a bit for to find one. You might have to travel quite a bit across. Once I'd find a seam I'd be okay. I could come onto it just the same as you were coming out of the woods with a compass. Every one comes to the ocean. And there's something else: If you get lost in the woods, get on a deer trail. Well, all right, doesn't make any difference what way you go on a deer trail, it'll take you to a brook. Once you've got the brook you're okay. Follow the brook down because it'll come to the ocean. Every deer trail crosses a brook and every brook comes to the ocean. Finding money is the same thing. You can't find just anything. You can find whatever's in the

*Here the stick is notched and a coin has been inserted. Now the stick is said to be of no use in finding water, but it will locate the kind of metal stuck in the end.*

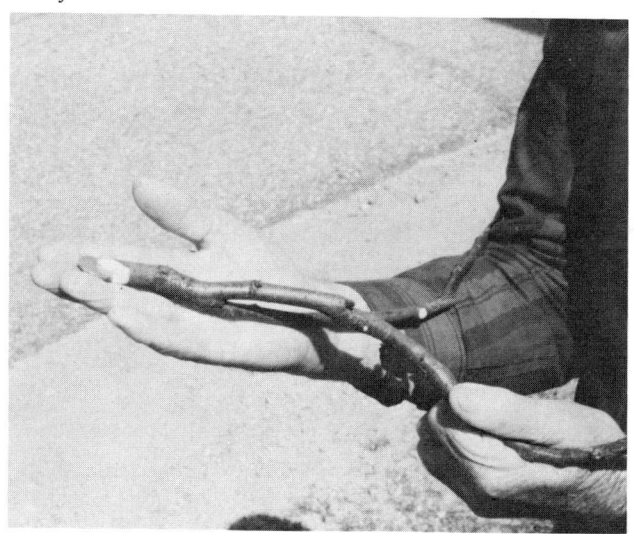

ground. Oil. It'd work for oil. Coal or slate, you know. Slate rock, you've got to have one piece into the stick. Or silver. Whatever's down there draws the other one down.

When I started finding water, forty years ago, everyone was carrying water. Neil's Harbour is no good because of the solid cliff. When you dig down wherever you go it's all a cliff. The only way to get a well is bore it. Every well that's here has been bored. There's only an odd one that struck a place. Even twenty-five years ago there was a spring down there and everyone just carried water. We carried it too. We lived up on the hill. And we carried it to pretty near October one time. When the rains came you would fill up with rainwater. In the wintertime, in the fall of the year, any water would be all right. But now if you're into a vessel, you go get spring water and put it in a barrel—it'll rot right in no time. You want to go get surface water and put it in a barrel. The water'll get bad and then get good again. It'll purify after. But spring water'll just rot. I don't know why. You want surface water and take that into your vessel, don't go to a spring. Spring water's all right for just a few days or something like that—but go get a jar and leave it in a boat for a while, you got to fire it away. Will last three or four days or so, and will start getting bad.

No, my father couldn't do it, couldn't find water. Not one in the family. And I never met anyone who could do it. I don't know what it is. I wouldn't know what to say how I got it. It must be electricity or something that's in your body that must be doing it. I don't know what you would call it. It's just got to be. I happen to be born like it, I guess that's what happened. It has to be. Just something the same as music or anything like that. You've got to be born to play the fiddle or any kind of music. It's got to be in you before you can do it. I never had any trouble with it, and it never failed me. And I found lots and lots of water.

*Willy Petrie: A Man Who Finds Water* **117**

# In the North River Lumber Woods

*In 1923, with nothing but the double-bit axe and the crosscut saw, seven hundred men from all around Cape Breton and beyond cut 45,000 cords of pulpwood. They cut it, landed it by the river, came back in the spring and blasted the frozen piles and drove that wood along the brooks and branches of the North River, till it gathered at the boom at the Murray Road.* Willie Petrie told us: "I always knew there was work there, from when I was so high. They were working there before I was born, I suppose. We had to travel then. We used to walk from Cape North right up to North River, stay at Murray there, at the boarding house. Sometimes you'd go on the Aspy. Then next day walk back into the woods. Sometimes you'd get in with the tote team, but it would be just as easy to walk as to get on one of them. There'd be a bunch of us travelling at a time. Half a dozen or like that. You didn't bring no saw or axe. They had it all when you got in there."

JOHNNY MURPHY, *Cutter and Scaler:* By golly that was awful slavery. We got a dollar seventy-five a cord, for cutting this pulp four foot long. Most of it carried further

*A group of men working for the North River Lumber Company at Murray in 1905.*

than the length of this house, piling it. It isn't like today. Today they pile it where they cut it and they cut it eight feet long and they get seven dollars a cord and they have those powersaws—we had crosscuts. You talk about cutting eight and nine cords with a powersaw. My brother and I cut as high as seven cords with a crosscut, piled it and carried it out in a day. Then on the drive, driving it into Murray down through the woods—you left camp at five o'clock in the morning and you'd be in half-past seven at night. Five and six feet of snow and that cold water all day. I was fifteen the first year, and it was eleven o'clock when we got down that night to Oregon Road. And we had only one meal that day. That was the Oxford Paper Company. I was a cutter in the woods, and I scaled the wood the others'd cut, and kept the time. And kept what they called the wangan. The wangan box is where they kept the tobacco, shoelaces, boots and sox and underwear and stuff like that, you know. Come up from the depot. Scaler had to keep track of that, and sell. And then that come off your pay at the end of the month. Something like the company store.

Great time? Great time all right. I loaded sleds there nine feet on the level and the big blocks'd be in the bottom, and I had the load of two sleds there one winter—I was getting forty-eight dollars a month and board. And the teamster was giving me ten cents a cord because it was hard to get loaders and you'd have to put that up out of that hole up on the snow while he was to the landing. Then when he'd come back you'd load those sleighs. You'd be digging the wood back out of the snow because it was cut in the summer—yes, would be right on the ground. Put her over your head. I enjoyed it all right. I used to wish to see fire start one end of Cape Breton and burn her flat to the other end. If they called them the good old days I don't know what in the hell they were thinking about. Now, man alive, you been up Big Interval, up the head of the Margaree River. Must be about twelve miles from here. Well that's the way we used to go in there, and we figured when we were up there we were halfway in to Camp seven. And it was nothing to walk there in a day. I seen a fellow come in there. He was a lath-layer, was his trade. And a lath-layer holds the nails in his mouth. And where he holds the nails in his mouth—I can see that man yet—he got poisoned or something—he had no nose. And all he'd come in there for was to rip those fellows playing poker. He cut enough wood to pay his board, and that's all he cut. And they played poker every night. And Sunday they played all day. And he made a lot more than any of us that was working out there.

But there was good order. The boss walked the length of the camp, just holler five minutes to nine boys. And at nine o'clock you could hear a pin fall. The only time you'd see trouble—say that Saturday was raining, or Friday and Saturday—they never worked on Sunday. Three days in a row idle, a bunch of men like that—they'd get irritable or something. You could figure they'd get in an argument over something. But not too much. And the cook was lord and master of the cookroom. When he said go, you went.

*Below: A sleighload of cordwood. Right: Johnny Murphy.*

*Left: John Joseph Gillis today. Top: Gillis in white cook's clothes with a crowd at Camp 23. Above: Gordon Harvey, Manager (left); George Hamm, Bookkeeper; Bill Ross; Harry Saxton, stockroom.*

The cook showed you your place at the table, and you kept that place. If you took another fellow's place, well he just picked you up by the collar. And he'd just tell you once. And nobody spoke at the table. Positively nobody spoke. Supposing there was no bread on a plate—or if the cookee didn't notice there was no meat—you just tapped the plate with your knife or fork. A cook that would allow talking, he wasn't a good cook. The crosser the cook the better he was. And, oh, they had dandy cooks.

JOHN JOSEPH GILLIS, *Cook:* If they did talk at the tables, the foreman either stopped them or I walked out. Really the important man for the working man was the fella that filled his stomach. And I knew some cooks there that was as cross as hell. But they were good and everybody put up with them. What's the good of having a nice fella if you get raw biscuit? When you went in there you had to be the boss. There was no talk at the table. Absolute silence. Well, the reason for that was, everybody start talking and the fellows watching the tables—cookees as they called them—wasn't watching what was in the dishes. When everything was quiet they paid strict attention to their work. And another thing, you had to get them in there on time in the morning. If you didn't, some of them were coming in all morning. You just couldn't run the place. Wake them 5:30, half hour before breakfast. I was up at four. Beans—oatmeal and beans—the standard morning breakfast. And hot biscuit. And donuts. And I'd make a cup of tea for sixty, sometimes seventy-five men at one time. I've made as high as 120 on river drives. You fed them four times a day on river drives. For breakfast: applesauce, prunes, stuff like that. No such a thing as oranges or bananas. Apples came as dried apples in fifty-pound boxes. Pared and dried. Most of them carried lunch outside. Pack lunch. Usually cold meats, different kinds of sweets. Some of them would prefer to take beans to the woods. They made their own tea. They took enough—if they wanted to eat three or four times a day, well that was up to them. Dinner was generally roast beef, roast pork, mostly corned beef in the summertime. Came in in barrels and barrels. Once in a while they'd try to get in a feed of fresh beef but there were no facilities to keep it. They grew a lot of their own pork too. Probably each camp would have eight or ten pigs. And they kept farms for vegetables.

I liked it. If I was to have my life to live over I'd go there again. There was all kinds of entertainment. They played cards, they sang, danced, they had violin, bagpipes—there was all kinds of it. On Sundays perhaps twenty-five or thirty

*Left: Frank J. D. Barnjum, promoter (left), his housekeeper Bella Matheson, Sarah MacDonald who ran the boarding house, and woodsworker John J. Matheson. Middle: Duncan Morrison. Right: Malcolm MacLeod.*

of my bunch would be visiting other camps and we'd get twenty-five or thirty from other camps visiting their friends. They could raise hell till nine or nine-thirty. Then after that everything was quietness. When the boss said bunktime, they all went to bed.

GEORGE HAMM, *Bookkeeper:* Barnjum was the one that formed the North River Lumber Company. He was pure and simple a promoter, looking around for something to promote. And he played with this thing for quite a long time. He had a sawmill there and he shipped some pulpwood in the summer. The North River operation was small, probably wouldn't be more than thirty or forty men. The first mill burnt. Sometimes those accidents happen a lot. They happen with a little push and they happen accidently. In those days, two to three cents on a dollar and you could discharge bankrupt. There were three or four men in with Barnjum, and they had the lease for 625,000 acres. He was the front man. I don't know the exact amount but I'd say the lease paid a rent of perhaps $25,000. It wasn't much money with the amount of land controlled. I don't think there was too much made there anyhow, until Barnjum sold to the Oxford Paper Company. He sold for a million and a half. The Oxford Paper Company came to Murray in 1916. I worked there nine years—1923 to 1931. Nineteen-twenty-three was the biggest year they cut while I was there. They cut 45,000 cords of wood—seven hundred men in there. I think one year before that they cut 58,000 cords. Then it got smaller—25 to 35,000. Today they're cutting more than they were then, because they've got machines to do the work of a hundred men. The machine just goes into the woods and snips it off like a pair of scissors, whole tree—strips it down, cuts it in eight-foot sections and piles it on itself—and once it gets eight to ten cords it comes out and loads it on a truck. There's only three or four men involved.

But in 1923 it was 45,000 cords. And the next year they drove her down the river. It was a whole year's operation. They got it to the boom and it was taken to the mill and the slasher saw cut the four feet to two. The bark was taken off in the rossing mill. According to the lease, the wood was supposed to be manufactured before it left the country. And that's what covered the letter of the lease. You know, this wood was manufactured, that the bark was taken off. It was very near the borderline but they got away with it. They loaded the wood on chutes like you load coal. They never stowed the wood in the boats; they just run it. When it came

*Above: The mill at the Murray road with an enormous pile of wood to the rear, the conveyor to the ships running off to the right, and the boarding house among the white buildings to the left. Right: Splash dam on one of the brooks feeding into the North River.*

to the deckload they boarded the stanchions right up almost solid and the wood just poured right in. They used to just what they called trim it just like coal. And all the wood from Cape Breton went to Portland, Maine. Oxford stopped here because of the depression, the thirties. And part of the trouble was union. They used to ship it in through Portland. There was a strike there. So they just closed the pier, let it rot.

At the mill the average pay was two and a half a day for a ten-hour day. The tote team, the drivers, they got from forty to forty-five dollars a month. The cooks got ninety a month. The foreman got a hundred. The blacksmiths were eighty-five I believe. But the rest of it was practically all on piecework. They cut rough wood—to cut and pile on what they called yards—they got two and a half a cord. The yard was right near where the wood is. The landing is where you take the wood to the riverbank previous to the drive. They worked four to a crew, and the company supplied a teamster. Two men cut in the woods and the other two piled in the yards and sawed the wood up—and between the woods and the yard the teamster hauled the wood in long lengths. Then it would have to be wintertime when the snow was on to get from the yard to the landing. Then when the spring break came they drove it down the river.

MALCOLM MACLEOD: For the driving, you piled them alongside the brooks maybe twenty, twenty-five feet high, three or four tiers on each side, maybe more than that—and then you know they had splash dams on it, just for to back up the water; and they used to fill the brook up with wood and open the dam and splash that out; then close the dam up again and fill the brook up again—be getting it into the main river. They used to start around the last of March. Ah, a good pastime. I wish we had it back. Yeah. It wasn't bad work. You worked all night and all day. You used to get twenty-five days out of the drive. It would come down the North River, under the North River bridge, and then float away down to the boom. Well the boom would hold it there. The first boom had two logs and it was the one that broke. The wood was in the river and a freshet came, and the snow was melting, and rain—it took the old boom away. Kept on going. They lost a lot of it.

GEORGE HAMM: They lost 11,000 cords.

MALCOLM: But they saved some of it.

DUNCAN MORRISON: They'd pay five dollars a cord to throw it back in the boom. And where the boom broke, the tide was running out—and a lot of it ran behind the beach there and they got a boom behind it there so it wouldn't get out.

JOHN J. MATHESON: It went around the cove to Jersey Cove—that's at the end of the beach going up to the ferry. Well it started to tangle up in the cove there. And they used to do a lot of fishing in that cove, especially eels. And ever since that stick went in the cove—no eels.

MALCOLM: Some of it, by gosh, went to Newfoundland. It went all over creation. And they picked a lot of it around the island here. They got some of it at Mira.

Oh, the last of it they were paying pretty good, $3.75 a cord. Pretty dry the first years, twenty-five dollars a month. One buck a day. Then twenty-seven, thirty. It was going up. Ah, it was a nice outfit. Too bad that it didn't last. And too bad that we're getting old, that we ain't out there now, loading pulp and taking it to the river with horses. A good racket.

# A Pair of Stock Skates

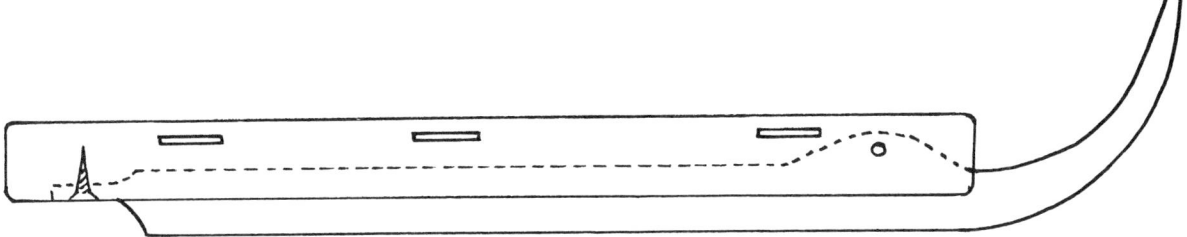

Stock skates were the first kind of ice skates used on Cape Breton. Some people call them block skates. They were followed by the spring skates which clipped onto the shoe, fiercely gripping the heel and often ripping it off. And these were followed by the full shoe and hockey skates we know today. But it was the stock skates people used here years ago when the winters seemed frostier and the scholars around the island could be seen skating to and from school. Alex Matheson took his skates to school, and dried them by the stove. He was born in 1898, at a place called Big Hill. He's been a blacksmith since 1919, and one of the few whose forge (at South Haven) still sees fire. Recently, he made a pair of stock skates from a bar of quarter-inch by one-inch Swedish steel (children's skates long ago were often made from an old

*"The most of the tools are made right here. All the chisels are made, the punches are made. You'd buy an anvil and a blower, a vice and dies, press drill . . . but all the tongs, I made them all here. Everybody did. . . . You get a bar of tool steel—you buy that—and make whatever kind of tool you want."* ALEX MATHESON

*Pounding flat the red hot end of a bar of steel, making the blade.*

*Punching a screw hole to fix the blade to the block.*

rasp), a quarter-inch rod of iron, some wire, two screws and two blocks of ash. He used no mold or pattern beyond a simple tracing to be certain the blocks would be both longer and considerably narrower than the feet of the man who would use them. He worked with only the memory of a finished pair of skates, and a knowledge of what happens to certain metals when they are heated and struck.

To start a fire, he made a little space in the spent coal at the opening of the forge and put in a handful of shavings. He lit the shavings and turned the blast on gently. The air comes up from below and is sucked up the chimney. He built the coal up at the sides to create a good draft, and let the green coal—the soft coal—burn till he had red coals. Some of the days he worked were bitter cold and oddly there was no heat from the forge. When it is right, the chimney sucks up all the gas and smoke, and most of the heat.

He took the bar of steel and put an end in the fire and left it there. The fire was kept small, just enough to heat up the section to be worked. He took the bar out bright red on the end and put it on edge on top of the anvil and with the ball peen hammer he beat the very end to ½ inch wide and ⅛ inch thick. This would be the heel of one blade. He put the end to the fire again, set it on the anvil and punched a hole for the screw. It was a job really requiring three hands. Alex did it with one hand holding the hammer, one hand holding the punch, the punch itself pressing the hot steel to the anvil while Alex neatly balanced the rest of the bar across his knee. Once through the metal, he put the end over the hardy hole and worked the punch to the desired size hole.

He next beat the top edge (the edge that will fit up into the wood) to a thin, feather edge. It is not simply a matter of heating and beating. The flattening and drawing out of both sides of the top edge tends to bring the bottom edge arcing around—and the bottom must be flat. So, beginning at the heel, he heated the metal and beat his way toward the toe, working on a few inches each heating. He beat on one side, then the other—and the top edge thinned and the whole bar bent. He put the bar on edge and straightened it out. Then he heated the bar, thinned some more on each side, and straightened it out again. The feathered portion runs straight until just before the upturn at the toe. Here he draws the metal out beyond the feathered edge, to a sort of hump that will go up further into the wood. This hump he heated and punched through. In the photograph, John Angus MacQueen, a blacksmith from Little River, is holding the blade in tongs with the hump just over an ordinary nut. When Alex Matheson punched, the punch went into the nut, making a clean hole. Then Alex heated the blade once more and rounded the front into a half circle over the horn of the anvil.

The blades were sharpened on a grindstone, first squaring the bottom and then grinding the slightest concave groove running down the center the length of the blade.

Alex made the blocks from ash. He roughed out the shape with an axe and then whittled the form he wanted. The blocks of stock skates are like a boat, the blades the keel. The blocks are much narrower than the foot that rides them, and continue to taper to the blade. They are made so that there is the least chance of wood touching the ice. The openings for the straps are 1-by-¼ inch slots, cut 5/16 inch down from the top of the block. He first drilled three holes in from each side with a ¾ inch drill, then chiseled out the slot. He worked from both sides toward the center, and once open he ran a hot bar of metal through the slot. He finished the three slots, then turned the block bottom up in the vice, drew a line down the center, sawed on the line to get started—then chiseled out a slot to receive the feathered edge of the blade. He chipped a space wide enough at the heel to set the screw hole flush with the wood.

There are a number of ways of attaching the blade to the

*Left: Shaping along the length of the blade. Below left: The upturned front of the blade is shaped. Below: Little River blacksmith John Angus MacQueen holds the blade with tongs while Alex Matheson punches a hole in the humped portion of the blade. This is where the front of the blade is fixed to the block. Bottom: Sharpening the blade at the grindstone.*

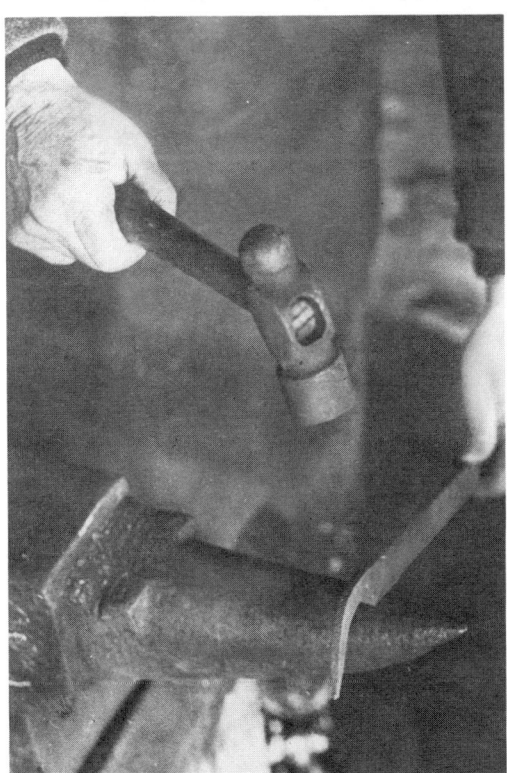

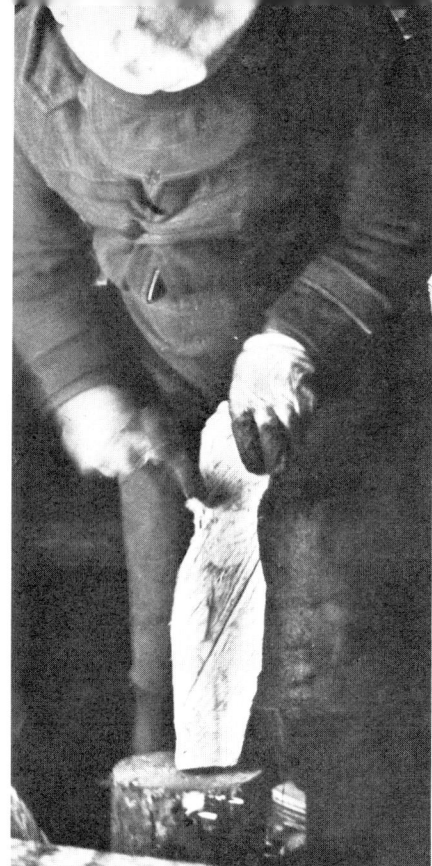  

*Above (left to right): Shaping the block from ash; chiseling out slots for the straps; chiseling out the slot to receive the blade.*
*Below: Making the iron rings to go with leather straps.*

  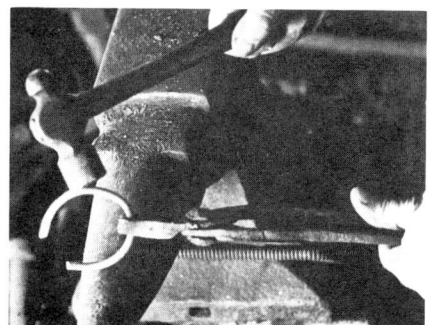

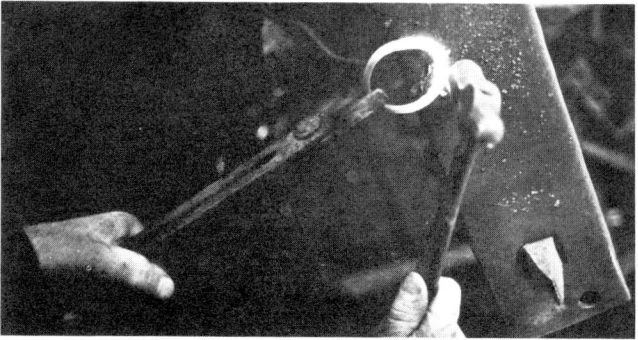 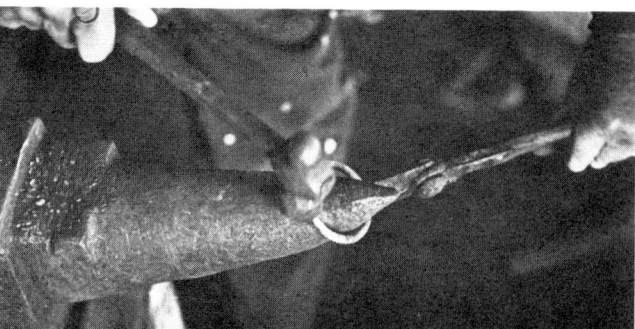

A Pair of Stock Skates

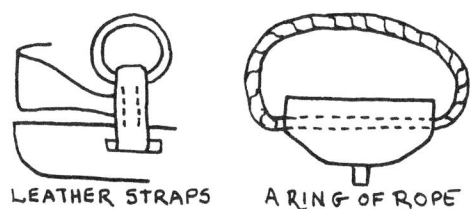

LEATHER STRAPS   A RING OF ROPE

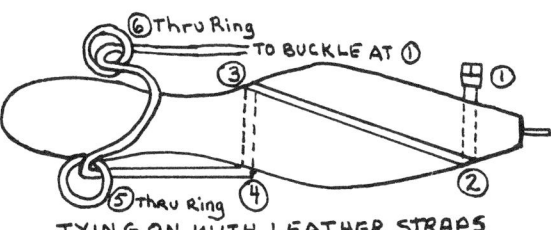

TYING ON WITH LEATHER STRAPS

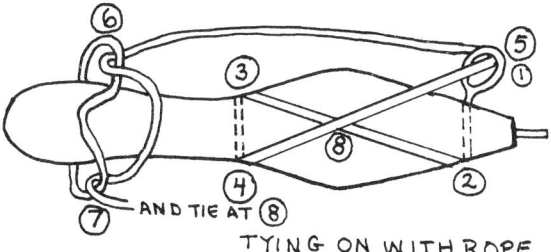

TYING ON WITH ROPE

block. The block could have been drilled through from side to side and a pin driven through the hump on the blade, but Alex felt a tighter job could be had by drilling two tiny holes down from the top, putting a strong wire through the hole in the hump and feeding the ends up through the tiny holes. He gripped the wires in pliers, pulling up and twisting them together, drawing the blade tight. He drove the wires into the wood. Then he put in the screw at the heel.

He made the rings of iron, a coarser material than the steel blades. He cut 7 inches of metal rod with a bolt cutter. Seven inches will give a 2-inch ring. He rounded the hot bar over the horn of the anvil, then he prepared the hot ends. The method is called "scarfing," and it is used to make ends fit without extra thickness at the joining. He heated it once again and put a little Borax or welding compound (flux) at the scarfing and put it back in the fire. He said, "Welding is like bread. Burn it and it's no good. Leave it raw and it won't stick. You have to get accurate heat at both ends. You have to watch your metal. You know it's ready when it's *just* starting to melt." He put it on the anvil, worked the ends together, started with light taps, then heavier ones, welding the ring.

Usually the blacksmith made only the metal parts and it was left to the customer to make his own blocks, and either straps or spliced rings of rope for tying the skates on. Straps usually involved bringing an old pair of reins back to life with neat's-foot oil—then sewing on a buckle and the rings.

# How We Cured Ourselves

*Mary Frickert and her granddaughter, Emily Seymour.*

EMILY SEYMOUR, *Neil's Harbour:* My grandmother, she was ninety-seven when she died, and she nursed everything. There was four years there was no doctor. The nearest doctor was at Baddeck. And she nursed everything. Nursed people that had babies. She brought I don't know how many babies in the world herself, and no doctor, no trained nurse. She never lost a mother. She lost a few babies but she never lost a mother. Her name was Mary Frickert. Granny Frickert. She was one of them that always had things on hand. She was awful smart and she'd go to the stores in town and go to the drugstore and she knew what she wanted. She'd go to the woods and she'd get a bud called Balm o' Gilead—and she'd make ointment of that, she'd boil the buds. Now when they'd kill a pig in the fall she'd take the inside lining without a bit of salt or anything, render that out and she'd put it in a clean jar and she'd make ointment of that. I'll tell you the most thing you used to use for disinfection was carbolic acid. You used that for washing sores, anything. Her mother was a nurse in Newfoundland—not a nurse but, you know—and I guess she learned from her mother. And from that she continued it. It was a gift. It was something that was in herself. She learned from one thing to another. She didn't have any education. It was in my days. It was as far back as I can remember—seventy years anyway. Nineteen-ought-three? Oh yes, she was a nurse before that. My mother was sick for years and she nursed her all through her sickness. And she was right good through to the end and she was right there when people'd be dying. She'd know what to do for them and how to give them drinks. And she'd have things if they couldn't help theirselves—something like a little teapot but no cover—she'd put their soup or drinks or anything in that. She'd know just how to do it. Put the bib to their mouth and feed them slowly. She was awful gentle and kind. Everything was prayer with her. If she went to a bedside where a mother was going to have a baby, the first thing she did was kneel down, ask God to help her and help the mother.

She lived up there, a big yellow house, you might see it going up—on the main road, up on the hill. They'd send for her day and night. When she used to go on maternity cases, well first she used to get five dollars, then she got ten but she never got over. She'd go and she'd stay there ten days. A lot she didn't charge anything for. Such as anybody was sick for a short time, like now say they took sick and was going to die and she went there, no matter how long she stayed she never charged them. She would stay till everything was over. Till everything was all over and cleared away. Perhaps she'd stay for a day or two and help to clean and wash up different people, you know. Oh, she prepared them for the funeral. Yes, she washed them and combed their hair and dressed them and fixed them all up. There was no undertakers or no nothing.

HELEN MARTIN, *Membertou:* I first came to know Bob Paul in 1934 or '35. It was one of the times when I came back from

Children's Hospital in Halifax. I was coming home just for a weekend before this major surgery to have my arm amputated due to bone trouble. I had been in and out of hospitals for fourteen years. My mother told me, "There's a man coming tomorrow. He's going to come and see your arm, see if he can save it. Because you're gonna go back to the hospital and they're going to cut your arm off." Bob Paul did come. He told my mother, "I'm going to get the medicine. Probably I'll be away for quite awhile." So my parents didn't take me back to the hospital. He spent three days in the woods. I don't know how he did it. He was using burnt balsam and something else. And he also mentioned this is the type of medicine that cured scurvy when Jacques Cartier, his men went down with scurvy. It was Indian balsam. Anyway, he brought it over and he asked my mother to bring him a brown paper bag. No cloth. "In the old days they used a piece of birch bark for bandages—we're gonna use the brown paper, it's made of wood." The medicine, it smelled so nice. He put this on the arm. It looked pretty bad. I couldn't lift it. It was nothing there but bone and skin. For three days I couldn't sleep after that medicine was on. I cried and cried and cried. All that night. My mother hit me, for me not to take it off. It hurt so much. He didn't stay. But three days afterwards he came back. And by that time the arm had stopped paining. So he put another medicine on it—the same stuff and wrapped it up in brown paper. Then he came back on the third day again. "It's going to take me twenty-eight days to cure her for her fourteen years in the hospital." I was cured in exactly twenty-eight days. The bone had healed up. And my arm, although it was thin—was better. My mother asked him how much for curing my arm and he said, "Well, four dollars. I just want to get my chewing tobacco." The only thing, when he was making the medicine ready to put on my arm, he told my mother to bless herself and to bless me. He depended on that medicine to cure me. He wore just the plain clothes every other citizen wears.

There were many healers who were considered especially good at just certain cures. Donald Garrett MacDonald told us of a Sandy MacLeod, a man good to cure a toothache. He would write out a verse from the Bible on a sheet of paper. You weren't supposed to read it or even look at it. It would be folded about an inch square, sewn in cloth and affixed to a cord to be worn about the neck. Donald Garrett remembers wearing one of these verses and going without toothache for over two years.

Dan A. MacLeod's mother was a Blood Charmer. She was able to stop the flow of blood. She said she got it from a French doctor when she was young. Like so many cures it could only be passed to a member of the opposite sex; and to work the charm, she had first to be specifically asked to stop the bleeding. Dan A. was making a beam for a bobsleigh, working on the kitchen floor. The axe caught in his clothes and he drove it into his hand above the thumb. His brother hitched the wagon and headed for the doctor in Baddeck; that would be twelve miles round trip. The hand bled terribly. Dan A. said to her, "Mother stop the blood." Then she caught his eye and they looked at one another. She never touched it. And she said something now forgotten. And the bleeding stopped. Jessie MacLeod died in her ninety-sixth year. (John Joseph Gillis, Sydney River, told us that Perry Lewis was a Blood Charmer and the way he worked was to

*Below: Emily Seymour. Bottom: Helen Martin.*

*Above: Mary Smith with Gwennie Pottie. Top right: Dan A. MacLeod. Above right: Jessie MacLeod, a Blood Charmer.*

ask the bleeder's age. And as soon as he was told, the bleeding stopped.)

Gwennie Pottie grew up with Mary Smith and her brother Dan Smith of West Tarbot. Brother and sister were able to work cures. Dan cured toothache. He would say some words, put a hanky over the ear and blow on it three times. Mary Smith cured worms, yellow jaundice and what the old people called gravel—usually referring to stones in the gall bladder, kidney or urinary bladder, usually a difficulty passing urine. For worms it was a kind of prayer that would include the name of the afflicted and end with "in the name of the Father, and of the Son, and of the Holy Ghost. Amen." You had to be very careful about the name. If the child was illegitimate you had to give the father's name. Catherine MacDonald out the Meadow Road told us that Mary Smith cured her of yellow jaundice. She was in the hospital in Baddeck and told not to expect to be out for at least three weeks. Her brother Norman went to Mary Smith, who sent Catherine skim milk to take three times a day. Mrs. Pottie said the old woman would have made a kind of prayer with Catherine's name and breathed three times into the milk. Catherine drank the milk, a little each day—and in three days she was well enough to go home. But she adds that she did not know Norman was going to Mary Smith's. Yet at the time Norman was at the house—

*How We Cured Ourselves*

probably while Mary Smth was alone in her room breathing the prayer into the milk—Catherine began to feel better.

To help someone who had trouble passing urine, Mary Smith would take a piece of homespun yarn the measure of the sufferer's waist. This string would have first been put in stale urine for three days, then dried. A knot was tied on each end of the string and then a knot was put exactly in the middle. Then the string went around the waist with that center knot exactly over the spot where there was pain. Mrs. Pottie said there was a woman with this difficulty in Saskatchewan and Mary Smith was able to help her through the mail. Mary Smith died in 1963, ninety years old. She was herself an arthritic cripple for seventy years.

Several people told us of a cure for asthma. It would work only for someone who is not fully grown. Duncan Morrison said they would blindfold the patient and take him to a tree and bore a hole in that tree at the patient's height and put into that hole a lock of his hair. Then a plug would be driven into that hole. The blindfold was kept on and he was led away so he could never know where that lock of hair was. And when he'd grow up higher than the hole he'd be clear of the asthma. According to Père Anselme Chaisson, in his book about the Cheticamp area, this was among the cures used by the French-Acadians; but apparently the hair had to be taken at the height of the illness and the patient did not have to actually go to the woods: "Prendre la hauteur du malade. Couper un *toron* de ses cheveux. Aller dans le bois, y trouver un arbre caché et y percer a la tarière un trou à la même hauteur que celle du malade; mettre les cheveux dans ce trou. Quand le malade dépasse cette hauteur en grandissant, il guérit." Dan Angus Kerr, whose son was cured of asthma in this way, added that you would want it to be a tree in a gulch, some place you'd be pretty certain no one would come and cut it down. And John William Morrison told us of two young men taken to the woods, both of them sufferers of asthma. They were simply told not to open their eyes. But on the way back home one of the two looked back at the tree that contained a lock of his hair. And when they grew above the hole, the one who had not looked was clear of the asthma, and the man who looked back suffered from it all of his life.

Mary Burns, Baddeck, told us a Seventh Son, a MacLeod, cured a woman of asthma when he told her to get rid of her yellow cat and to wear her husband's dirty sock around her neck. And there are a number of people we talked to who were themselves cured by the Seventh Son, who is said to be able to cure almost anything. It can be a Seventh Daughter as well, and actually it is the Seventh Son of a Seventh Son who has the greatest power. Donald Garrett MacDonald said you could see a Seventh Son of a Seventh Son, or you had to see seven different men, each themselves a Seventh Son. Mike Doyle said the skin along his jaw and at his neck was all eaten away—a kind of skin cancer known as The King's Evil. He had seen a doctor a whole winter without success. He then went to Alex Hines, a Seventh Son in Ingonish, and he had to go only one time. Hines asked for a five-cent piece from Doyle's pocket, and he got a bottle of ordinary well water and dipped the coin in the water and rubbed it on the sore face and neck. Hines returned the coin and told Doyle not to lose it, and he gave him the water to rub on his neck once in a while. In two weeks Doyle was cured. He carried that coin with him to the war in France and back—then lost it. But The King's Evil has never returned. Dan Angus Kerr, North River, said: "Every doctor that I was to see, they were saying it was cancer of the bone. And the only cure was to cut my leg off right at the hip. That was in 1911 or 1912. So I went to the Seventh Son, Neily MacLeod. He was from South Haven. And he dipped five cents in a saucer with a little bit of water and started rubbing my hip there. And he did that three mornings. And after that it broke, the bones started coming out—cracking and coming out. And it wasn't healing. There was a fellow by the name of John MacGregor, came and told my father there was a fellow in Big Baddeck by the name of Hardigan, and he was the Seventh Son *of* the Seventh Son. I was suffering so darn much then, instead of taking me to him

*Donald Garrett MacDonald.*

*Dan Angus Kerr (left) and Mary and Dan MacNeil.*

this John MacGregor went. And this Hardigan sent me a box of ointment. I don't know what it was made of. And I started rubbing that on my hip—and in two months it healed up just the way you see it now. And I never lost my leg."

Donald Garrett MacDonald said that for *heavy fever* you split salt herring and put a piece to the sole of each foot. Mr. and Mrs. MacDonald used this cure on their son when he was twelve or thirteen, and with success. "And when it's there so long, it's cooked the same as if it was cooked on a stove." For *nosebleed*, people would tie a piece of scarlet yarn around their neck and leave it there. This was to prevent nosebleed. Duncan Morrison said a good way to stop one was to put a copper under your tongue. The MacDonalds said to cure *diarrhea* boil milk with a hot iron in it down almost to a powder, then eat it. Donald Garrett said: "You know there was a cure for the evil eye. Say that there was a cow out there and if you had the evil eye and you'd speak about that pretty cow, I'd tell you to put your eye in your arse. There was an old lady in here, she had a cow and a heifer—she always kept them in good shape—and if anybody would speak about how nice they were, that's the first thing she'd say."

Mrs. William D. Deveau of Cheticamp told us: "For a cold, mama would boil some molasses and put a little bit of white liniment or minard's liniment into it, and a little bit of pepper—and she made it like candy. She used to put it on a little dish, let it cool off—but not hard enough to break. It was thick, thick. Then we used to get it with a spoon." Mrs. Deveau told us if you were *hoarse*, you would make a drink of about half a cup milk with raisins mixed in, heated next to boiling; then add one or two teaspoons sugar and drink it hot as you could. "When we would take a *cold* we would get some spruce, wild cherry, balsam—bark of these. You go and get a little tree or the limb of a tree. And we used to strip the bark—cutting *down*. They say if you cut it up the tree, maybe it would upset your stomach. If you cut down, it goes the other way. You can cut them in small portions. And then you had a kettle of boiling water and you poured the water on these barks. Then you put it on the back of the stove. It simmers. And then it comes a nice color, like whiskey. You'd leave that bark at the bottom and as you used the water you put more on. I remember my uncle, every time he had a *fever*, it was *l'herbe à dindon* [turkey grass, yarrow]. He'd make an infusion and steep it and keep it on the back of the stove—and once in a while go and take some." *Headache:* "I've seen people putting white liniment on blue paper—blue paper—and then they used to put the paper right around their forehead. Then put maybe a kerchief over that. *If someone couldn't pass their water,* we used to boil—at least, we used to steep them—bean shells. When you shell beans, dried beans—not boiling them but simmering them—then drink the juice." *Diarrhea:* "Some used to take some pepper and cold water. And some used to dissolve a little bit of flour in water. And they used to drink that. And some used to drink nutmeg, when they had it whole—they used to scrape it and boil it in milk. That was very good. They even used to give that to calves, when they were small, if they had the diarrhea." *Constipation:* "Ah, then it was castor oil and salts and senna leaves. They used to buy those. Nobody was constipated in my time. No sir."

Mary and Dan MacNeil sat one night in Sydney and told

us these cures: For a *cold,* rub goose grease on your chest and then put black wool on top of it. *Sore throat:* black wool with a little kerosene on it, wrapped around the throat before going to sleep. For *measles,* sheep manure tea. This seems to have been a general cure-all all over Cape Breton. Drink a mare's milk, by the spoonful, for *whooping cough.* Goat's milk is said to be good for *tuberculosis.* A cure for *headache* is vinegar on a cloth on the forehead. Also, a speck of saltpeter with a little milk settled the blood and thus relieved headache. Sulphur and molasses was taken in the spring to clear the system, after so much salted food through the winter. (Tommy Peggy MacDonald once told us that when the scholars were walking to school, they would come in all sweaty and stand around the stove—and the heavy odor of sulphur and molasses would come out in the sweat.) *To keep warm,* pepper in the shoes. On a cold night before going to bed they would make a drink of a speck of ginger, molasses, hot water and milk. For *toothache,* fill a bag with coarse salt and put in oven till hot as you can stand—then put against cheek. There were lots of cures for *earache* but Mary said the best is boiled butter, fresh not salted. Dip cotton, cool a bit and put in the ear. They would also use castor oil, even a drop of rum. She said she once stepped on a rusty nail and it started to fester. Her grandmother boiled salted butter and poured it on the foot and put a cloth on. The next day there was no pain and it started to heal. If you had a *sprained ankle,* they'd wrap it in an eel skin.

Mary Barrington told us: "If you ever hurt yourself, like if you hurt your arm and it wasn't broken but it was paining terrible—you couldn't do anything with it and the doctors they all put it in hot water—you take goose grease if you can get it and just grease it like that. And the first thing that'll be blue. Bruised blood comes right to the top of the skin." Use goose grease for a *cold:* one teaspoon with molasses, warm, to cut phlegm and carry the cold through the bowels. Goose grease with dry mustard to make a poultice for *chest cold.* The grease prevents the mustard from burning. Cow manure mixed with linseed meal and made warm will *draw poison* from anything. Dogwood berries are good to take for bad *vomiting.* For *bad stomach,* make tea by steeping the flower and stem. It is bitter. *Worms:* "You'd put one drop of turpentine in a spoonful of sugar. Two drops the second day, till you come to nine drops [the ninth day]. Then you quit. The worms go for the sugar and get the turpentine. That was a sure cure."

Emily Seymour also remembered: "For *colds,* if they had a *chest cold* they'd make a mustard plaster. Dried mustard and flour, cold water. Make a paste. And put it between two cloths, thin cheesecloth. And they'd boil onions and sugar and make a syrup of it and take that for colds. Oh, you'd have to put a little bit of water but not too much—slice the onions up. If you had been *vomiting* for any length of time or your stomach'd be upset, they'd give you lime water. They'd put the lime in a quart bottle—common lime that you buy; loose lime—fill it up with water and let it soak for a while and then drink the water off the lime." Aline and Alex Romard had told us that to get rid of a *boil* anywhere on the body, take nutmeg, bore a hole through and wear it on a string around your neck. Mrs. Seymour had heard of that but said: "Here they'd make plasters out of soap and molasses. They'd put it on the palm of their hand. The green soap. They'd take a knife and smooth it all out—then they'd put molasses in it and make a real ointment. And they'd put it on a piece of cloth with a little hole cut in the cloth, and they'd put that on the boil and draw it out like that.

"Well now if you had a serious cut—and you could have a serious cut—you go to the woods and you pick the fir balsams. On the fir trees, at all times but especially in the spring time of the year and in the summertime—there's a big bubble. Well they sliced them off—they'd take perhaps three or four—as many as they want 'cause certainly you could go every day in the spring and cut new ones—and they'd fill this cut right full of this balsam. Squeeze it out. Then you'd just put the wound together, as close as you could, you know? Even if you couldn't get it together it would heal, and tie it up and leave it for nine days and not open it. And by the time the nine days were up that would be pretty well healed. Never, never get infection. You used cloth bandage. People used to have things washed and sterilized and put away—put it in the oven and make it good and hot. And they'd tear off strips. They'd use old cotton sheets and pillowcases. They'd save everything like that. Never throw away nothing. Everybody had their bundle in their homes."

*Mrs. Willy D. Deveau.*

# Dr. MacPherson, the Cancer Doctor

*told by Mary Barrington*

He's dead and so is she. She took over after he died. And the funny part of it was, she died of cancer. She had cancer of the bladder. That was an inward. [An inward is a cancer that would require surgery to place the poison poultice. Dr. MacPherson wasn't a real doctor and while he did get one or two medical doctors to prescribe analgesics—painkillers—he was never able to find one who would assist him in attacking an internal cancer.] He told me that this was a faith cure that some priest had passed down. I had it. He drew it for me. I'll show you. Thirty-nine years ago. See. See the scar there [on her chest]. You couldn't tell there was anything there. And more than that I had a pain down here [at her side, under her arm]. And I thought that's where the cancer was. He always carried the stethoscope with him. Because he said if you had a cancer that it beat with your heart—that it would beat as your heart beats. The cancer would beat. So that's how he found out where that was. That cancer was there for six years he told me. And do you know where the root travelled? Under my arm. That's where the end of the root was. And he used to say to me, "that damned root won't let go." I was over there with the poison poultice on for nine weeks before it let go. Who knows what it was. Nobody knew that. I knew everything about the treatment only what was in the poison poultice. And the poultice so help me wasn't any bigger than the corner of that card. And you know what the old corn plasters used to look like, the old sticking plaster... It was black, and it was just a little thing like that. He took the lance and like he was going to vaccinate you he made a mark around here [a six-inch circle around the cancer on her chest]. Then he put this black poultice on. Put something over it to hold it there.

I'll tell you now what it looked like when it started to come out. First it sank in. I'll bet you often saw the old-fashioned yeast cakes, the hard ones. About as big as a fifty-cent piece. This whole thing sank in from where he circled. Then when it was dead it started coming out. And it looked—you know the old red jellyfish, the blood suckers that you see in the water—that was what it looked like on the inside. Like a bunch of stuff. And from that there was roots and roots and roots, like thread. You know what the inside of a mackerel looks like—the fine gut in a mackerel—you often saw them. The same color. Just like that. Oh thousands of them. It would come out and they would be on the back. On the back of the poultice. Well, he would dig that every morning and change the poultice. This was the second poultice. He was drawing it then with the yolk of an egg and turpentine.

I saw it and drawed it myself, dear. I came home to Sydney from North Sydney when he started drawing it. He told me if I wanted to I could go home but to be awful careful not to use that arm. In case I break a root. You see those roots are so small and the least thing'll break them off. Then if you broke a root boy, phwoosh—it would go all through you. Now, where they cut a breast off or anything they don't get the whole thing. They're finished. Had to get it all. Every bit. And when you were at Dr. MacPherson he didn't want you to wash your face if you could get along without it, let alone have a bath. You weren't supposed to go near water. Or if there was frost on the window, you mustn't go near it. Oh boy was he strict. He told me afterwards, there's thirty-five different kinds of cancer. He told me that. Some of them are harder I guess to cure. Some of them are a liquid. Some of them are bleeding cancers. He used to sit down and tell me this 'cause I used to tell him queer things, sit down and laugh. But the doctors were the devil. Unless they had somebody of their own, then they would send them over. But the steel company recognized him. They paid that. It was fifty dollars for to draw the cancer. They would also pay your board, two dollars a day.

# Wild Archie Plays the Bones

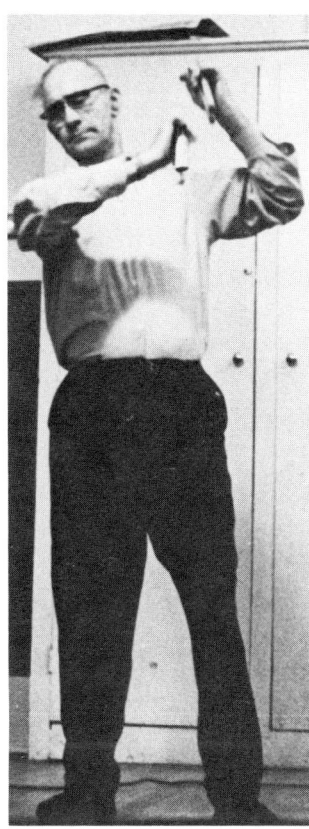   

I never did see anybody playing the bones. I just accidently picked it up myself. I was only about ten years old, in St. Patrick's Home. That's in Halifax. I actually just picked up a couple of sticks and started making noises with them. Then I got a couple for the other hands. And my fingers used to be bulged out and full of sores just from shaking them. So I kept at it. I never heard of anybody playing them. See I was only a kid. I went there when I was seven. St. Patrick's Home. The old chap went overseas and my stepmother went to Halifax and I was picked up here. I was born in Port Malcolm. It's in the Hawkesburys, you know, the Point Tupper side. I was born in 1906. No, I wasn't interested in music. I never was. Even my dad, he was quite a singer but he was never—nothing musical about him. But I found the sticks and I made a little noise and I kept it up.

I went from sticks to bones when I started making a living at it. Hardwood sticks. I used to chip them out of the back of a chair—remember the high-backed chairs with the curve—the wide back. I made a set out of that. That'd give you the curve like's in the bones there. I had them for years and I lost them one night on the train. I had to turn around then and got a couple of rulers. I went to a store and bought a couple of rulers and made four pieces of ruler—made them work. Years ago we had the phonograph, you know. I had some of the fast tunes on. Angus Chisholm or one of the MacLellan's from Margaree or somebody that had recorded out of a studio, you know. When the radio came in I started with the radio. That's all it is is rhythm. Rhythm. Well, that's all I play, you know. Just a rhythm. Body movement and rhythm. The body movement has a lot to do with it. Naturally. You can't just go like that [using only your wrists] all the time—your arms get so tired. You've really got to loosen the whole

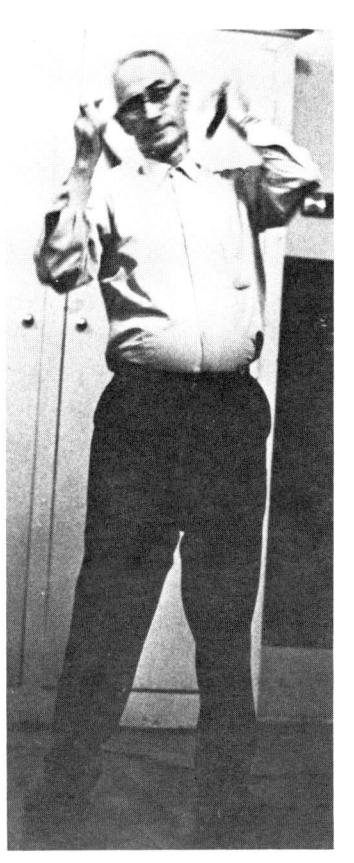

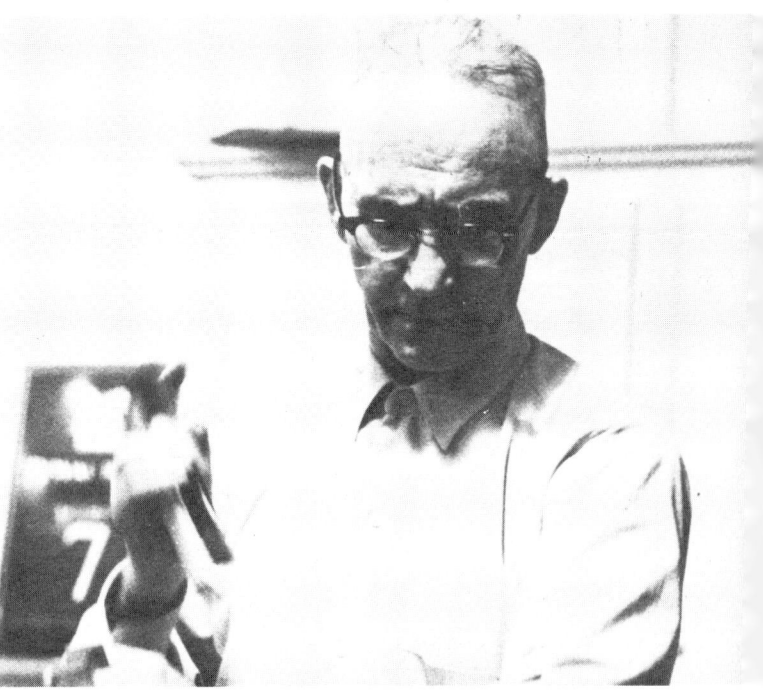

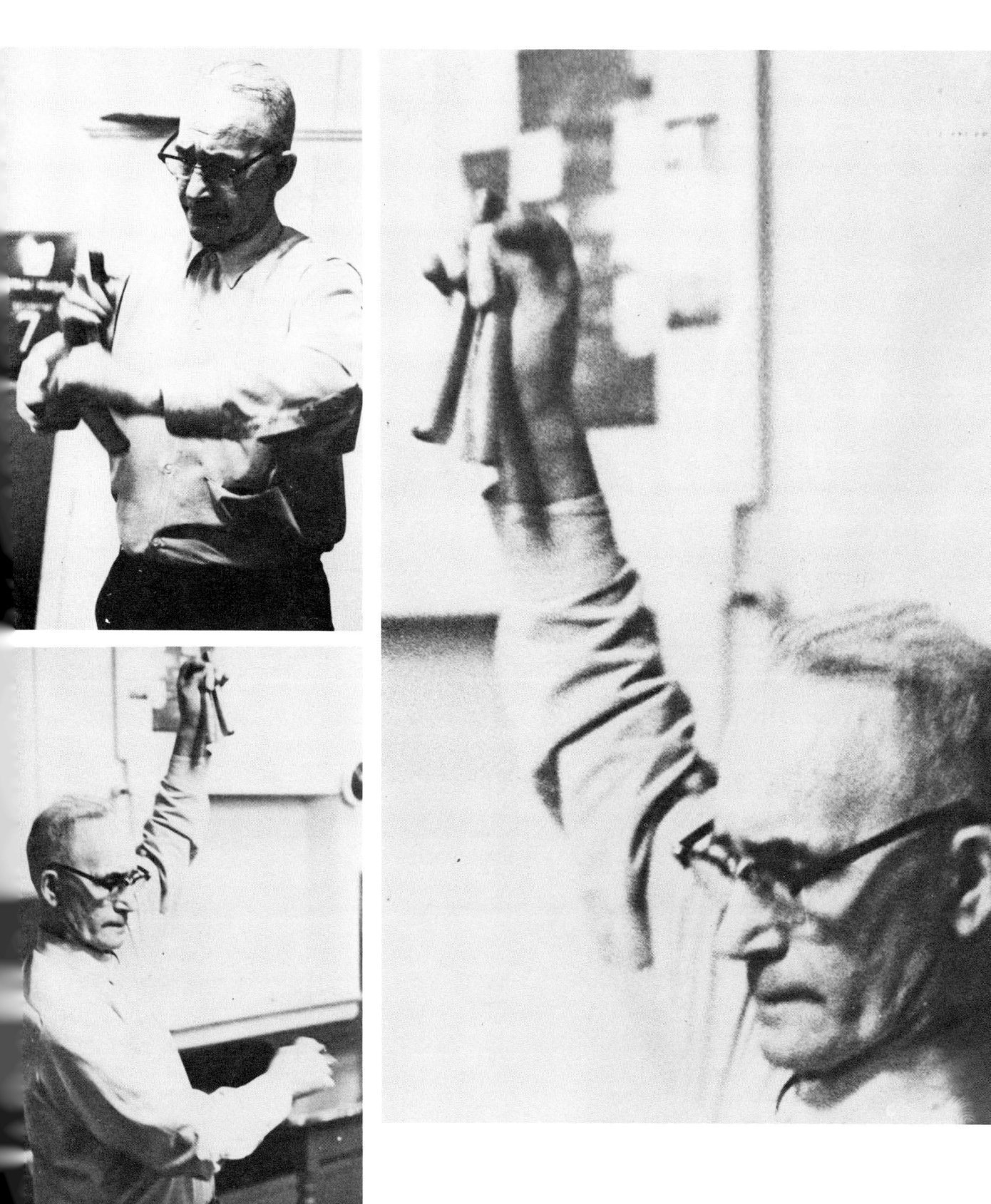

body up. That's the way I do it. Just about the way a boxer moves. Oh, well, I boxed a number of years ago. Well, it's actually practically the same. I never did any training for boxing. The best I ever did was play them. That was as good as any training. Oh, yes, every bone in your body, every muscle in your body's going. Even I was half step-dancing on the stage the other night.

Any bones at all—you hold them with the middle finger, the strong finger. The one next to the index finger, you hold that tight. Then the other bone is right loose. It's only the one bone hits the other. That's what makes the noise. The one bone. See, this one don't move. That's solid. Its the same with both hands. It's your thumb and that's against the bone and your index finger is up over your thumb—it's your thumb that's against the bone, holding it solid—your middle finger is on the front edge of the bone, again holding it solid—so that one bone isn't going to move at all. I don't pull the loose one. No, no. I just shake the wrist. It's only a shake of the wrist. It's awkward at first. Just shake your wrist from side to side, like that. I find very few other people who can do it. It's pretty hard to tell a person how to get the double action. I couldn't teach them because it's in there—it's just the wrist. You lower your fingers down the bone you get a different sound. You move them up and you get a different sound. So that's it.

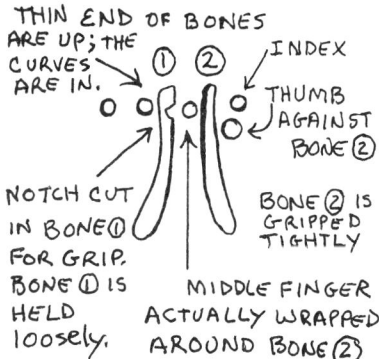

You listen to music and you try and get the same beat. Beyond that, I don't know how I do it. Getting the beat. Now if you keep time with a guitar you've got the beat. Or a mandolin is the nicest thing to keep time with. It's just as good as a violin. I like the violin, yes. I used to play with a lot of violinists. I played with old Sandy MacLean; he's about eighty-eight today. He's out in Inverness. I played with Jack MacQuarry, Gordon MacQuarry. Tina Campbell. I played with Harry Bagnell and the wife years ago. They are from Iona — she was. And Neillie Gillis, the insurance agent. I

*John A. MacLennan.*

went to Halifax in 1956, working all around. And I played the bones. We had a Cape Breton Club in Halifax. Well they have a meeting there the second Wednesday of every month. So we'd all get there and there'd be two or three violin players and step-dancers and I'd be there and we'd put on a little party every second Wednesday of the month.

The police pinned that [the name Wild Archie] on me when I was boxing. I used to box at the Alexander Hall. Used to go training in the police club up there—not where it is now, where it used to be years ago. And my dad was called Wild Archie—so there it is.

# Ellen Googoo Makes a Micmac Basket

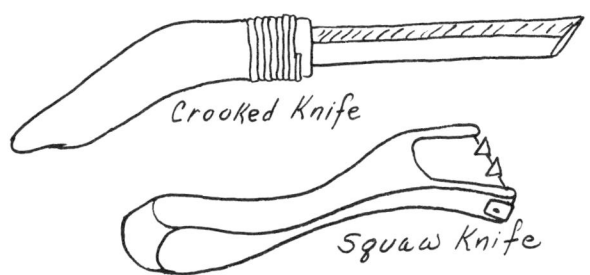

1  *Making large splits with a Crooked Knife.*

Ellen Googoo is a sixty-five-year-old mother of eighteen children (ten of her own and eight foster children). She lives at Whycocomagh where she runs a basket shop. She has been a basketmaker for fifty-eight years. She started working with the Crooked Knife (WAQA'QɨNKN) when she was seven years old, and she has taught her daughter, Barbara, how to make splits and, from those splits, baskets, just as her mother before her taught her.

The Crooked Knife is a very important tool in the making of baskets. Years ago, it was the most popular steel tool used among the Indians building bark canoes. It is made from a flat steel file with one side worked down to a cutting edge. The cutting edge is bevel-form, like a drawknife or chisel, with the back face flat. The tang of the file is usually bent into a slight hook and let into the handle, then secured with sinew lashing. Today, wire lashing is used. Held with the cutting edge toward the user, the handle is made to be grasped fingers-up with the thumb of the holding hand laid along the part of the handle projecting away from the user. It is, in effect, a one-hand drawknife. Mrs. Googoo's blade is curved slightly. It was put into a stove until it was red hot, then hammered into the proper curve and plunged into water. The Crooked Knife is not an easy tool to work with, and although Barbara makes some use of it, it is generally used only by the oldest basketweavers.

The choice of wood to make splits from is very important. The right wood is not easy to find. It must have good straight grain and no knots. Mrs. Googoo makes splits from black and white ash, white maple and birch. Although white maple gives a fine white color it is not the best of wood. Birch is tougher, ash is the toughest. Ash is used for heavy duty creations like hampers, baby baskets and potato baskets. Softwood is used only when making very tiny baskets because it will bend easily without breaking.

The first step is to make from a thin, straight plank of hardwood, splits of the same width and thickness. The plank used was about 3 feet long, 1 inch thick and 2 inches wide. The plank should be thoroughly dampened, and the splits should be kept damp as you keep dividing them. With the Crooked Knife you cut away at the sides of the plank, getting the sides straight and the width even all the way along (1). You work to a width of 1 inch. Then you "splice" the plank at one end to reveal the grain (2). Then take the plank on end

2  *Cutting to show the grain at one end.*

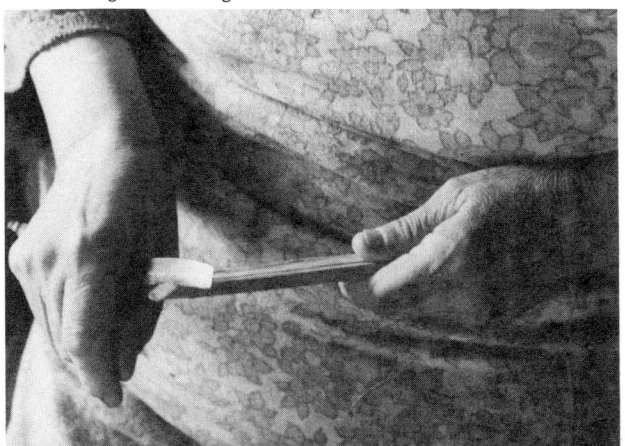

*3   Bending gently so the splits follow the grain.*

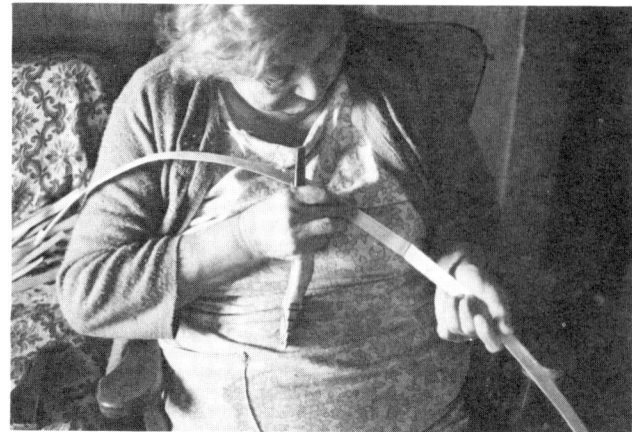

*4   Peeling off thinner splits.*

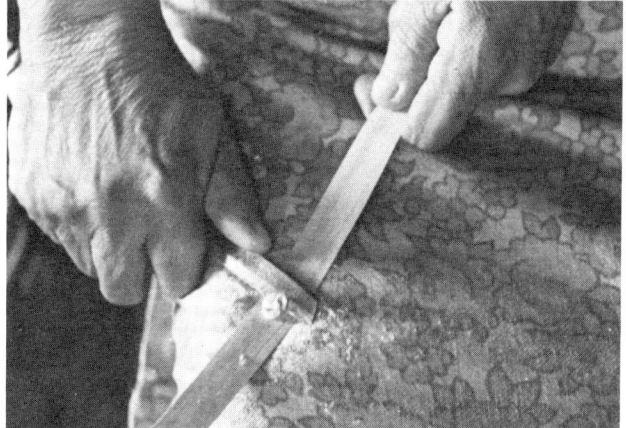

*5   Smoothing the split between the knee and the blade.*

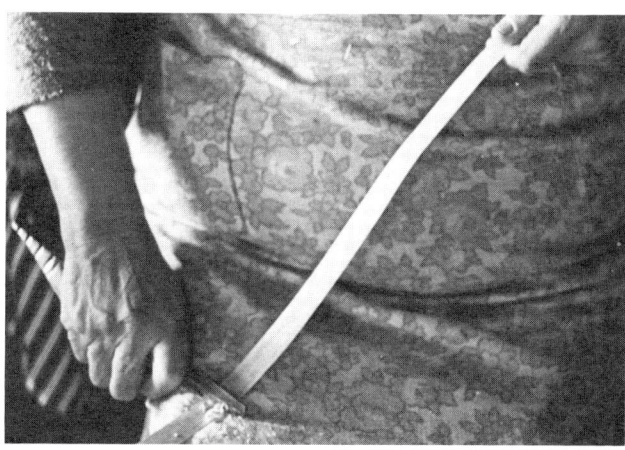

*6*

*7   Smoothing the split between the thumb and the blade.*

and using the Crooked Knife as a probe, work the edge of the blade into the grain. Do not try to take off a split as thin as you will finally want it. It is better to take off a split of several thicknesses, and then to find the line of grain of that split, and then to split it yet again. The actual splitting is slow, careful, not at all a tearing. You are bending the two pieces away from one another (3), and that bending gently pulls them apart so that they will run off along the grain exactly as they started. By the time you have the splits very thin (4), there is no real grain—and so you make a grain. It takes a lot of practice before you can get the thinnest splits, even all the way along. If you try to use splits that are cut only on the grain they will be too thick for anything but bottom splits. You can't make anything delicate with thick splits. For the best work, the splits are not smooth enough. The step of smoothing is known as NULTAQO'QƗN. There are two ways of smoothing

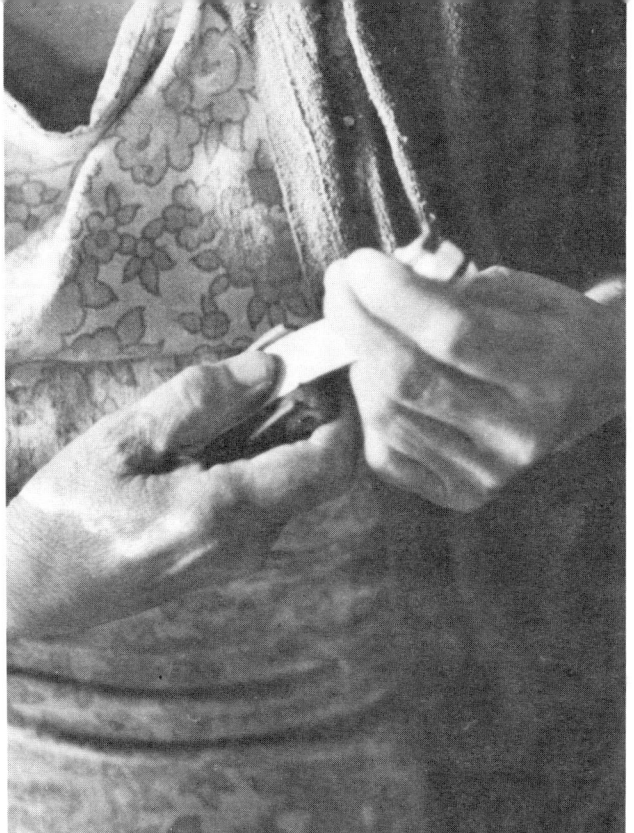 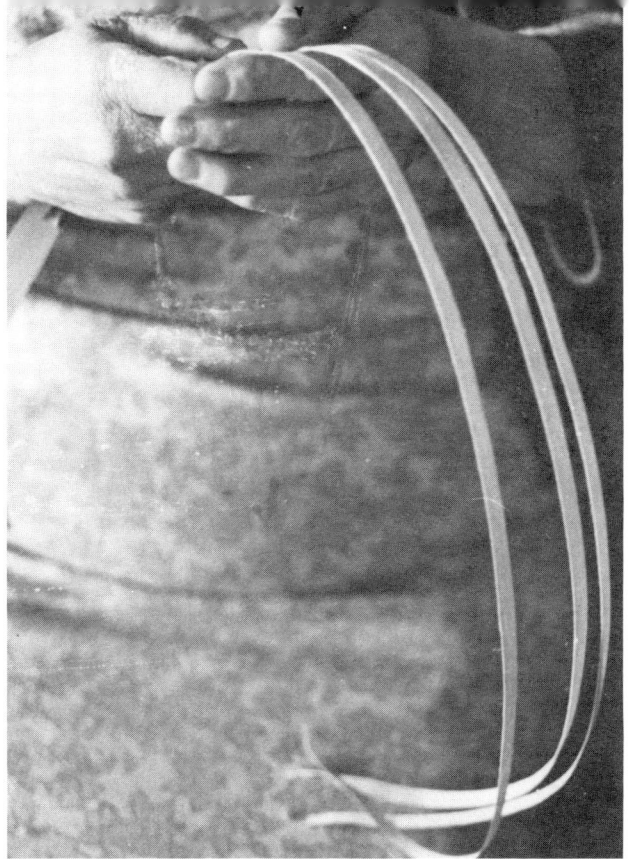

8  9

*Using the Squaw Knife to cut a split into three parts lengthwise. The wider splits are called bottom splits and the narrower are the weaving splits used for the sides.*

and both are used. One way is to trap between the knee and the blade of the Crooked Knife (5), the knife in the right hand—and with the left hand slowly pull the split back (6). The other way, the left hand again pulls the split—but this time it is done in the air with the split tight between the Crooked Knife and the thumb of the hand holding the knife (7). The splits end up smooth as ivory.

One-inch splits are good enough for bottom splits but they are too wide for weaving. Narrow splits are made with a tool called LAPESO'Q+N Squaw Knife. The Squaw Knife is made out of a handle of any kind of hardwood, carved to fit nicely in the hand. Into one end are fitted the points spaced as wide apart as the desired width of the finished splits. These splits are called Weaving Splits. The Indians today make the points out of watch springs, cut to length and sharpened and held in slots in the head of the Squaw Knife by a strip of tin. The knife is held in one hand, points upward. The end of the split is placed over the points and pressed down to push the points through (8). The thumb of the hand holding the knife comes down on the split, pressing into the trough back of the points. Then the free hand pulls the split, dividing it the entire length (9).

At this point you can choose to use the natural color of the wood or to dye the splits. Commercial dyes are used but Mrs. Googoo has used various native dyes, such as boiling the bark of alder to get brown, cherry to get yellow, and hemlock for a red. She sometimes boils both the bark and roots of the tree. The dye is brought to a hard boil, then a bit of split is used to test the color. If it is too dark she adds water, too light she adds more bark and root. She does this right in the kitchen with plenty of cardboard and newspaper on the floor. In summer she often boils her dyes out of doors. In making baskets, Micmac women seem to like certain combinations, such as brown and yellow, or green and white.

Once you have your bottom splits and weaving splits you have done the most difficult thing in basketmaking. The actual weaving is quite simple and allows the basketmaker many choices as to what sort of basket to make. Anyone who actually undertakes a basket will realize very quickly how much latitude there is, and will experiment. The following directions are according to the basket Mrs. Googoo made.

Take six bottom splits and put them on the table, first placing two, then slipping one in from each side, then slipping in two more—fitting them into an over-under pattern (10).

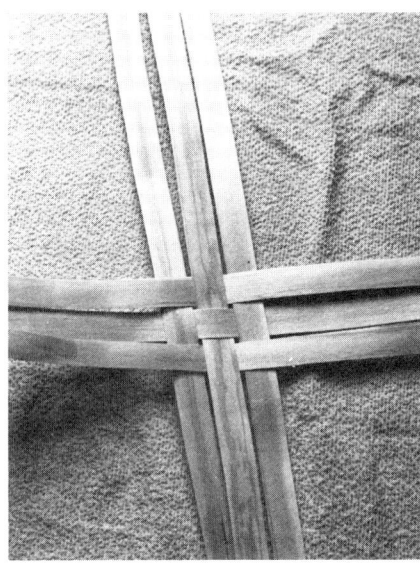  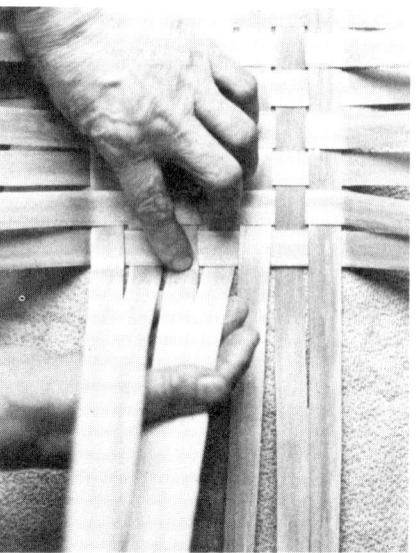 

*10  Piecing together the bottom with the wider splits.*

*11*

*12  Above and above right: Bringing the bottom splits up.*

*13*

This is your weave. Keep equal distances in all directions so the squares thus formed by the weaving will all be the same size (11). Mrs. Googoo used fourteeen bottom splits giving a square bottom and seven splits sticking out from each side. The splits should be kept just damp enough so as not to break when you bend the unwoven portions upright. Stand them upright by placing the finger of one hand at the edge of the woven bottom (12), the other hand reaching under the bottom splits and raising them (13). All around, the sides are eased up. Now the narrower weaving splits are used. You work from the bottom up. Each row is done separately and the weaving split is cut. You do not go round and round. Each row is separate. Always start a row with the weaving split *under* the bottom split—that is, the tip of the weaving split is inside the basket when the row is started (see drawing). The

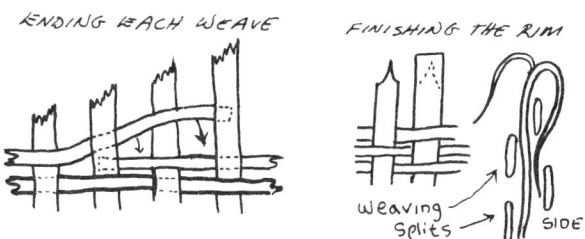

pattern is under one, over one, under one, over one all the way around the basket. When you reach where you began, you continue weaving beyond that point another two bottom splits, doubling that part of the weaving split. The weaving split should end, as it began, under a bottom split. This will hold it snugly (see drawing). With your fingernails, draw the weaving split down all around (14). Then check all the upraised bottom splits to be certain they are equal distance apart. Do this after every row. And remember, you are simply placing the weaving split. Do not pull it tight as this will gradually narrow your basket—unless you want a bottle shape. And unless you want an open shape, do not allow the weaving split to be wound too loosely. As you work up, every other row the weaving split should go behind the bottom splits that, the row before, it went over. This, of course, creates the weave.

Experience will reveal to you many ways of finishing a basket. One way is to cut the bottom splits to a point about 2 inches above the last row. Then bend the cut splits over the top row and tuck them in under the weaving split of the third row from the top. One will bend to the outside, the next to the inside, all the way around (see drawing). Where the point of

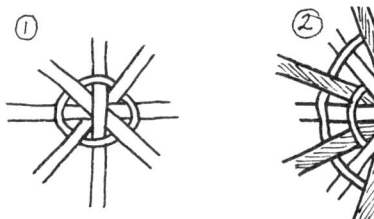

*142   Ellen Googoo Makes a Micmac Basket*

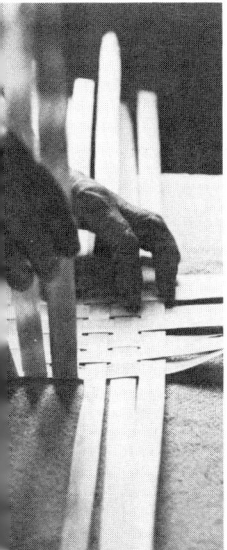 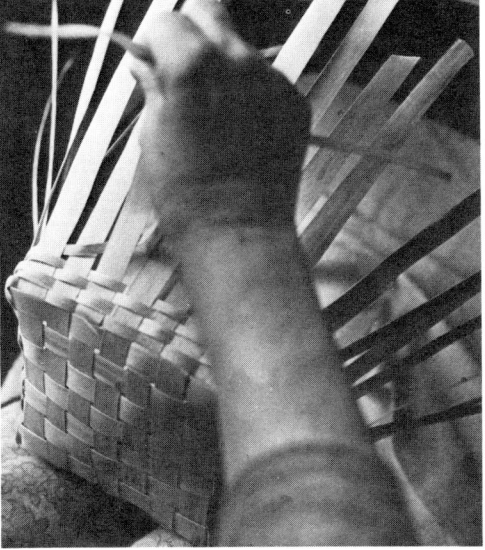

*14  Working with the narrow weaving splits.*

*15  Finishing off a basket by sewing a bundle of Sweet Grass around the top, using a very thin weaving split as the thread.*

the bottom split shows you can simply trim it away. Take a rather thick split (perhaps ⅛ inch) and cut to about ½ inch width, and fit it around the inside of the top of the basket. Sometimes another piece is put around the outside and nails are hammered through against a piece of steel to flatten the nails inside. A much nicer method is to use Sweet Grass on the outside.

This can be done a variety of ways. One way is to trim the bottom splits at the same height all the way around and to fit the thick split around the inside top of the basket. A bunch of Sweet Grass is then put around the outside top and sewn in place with a thin piece of weaving split. You are sewing the thick split and the Sweet Grass together. The sewing goes in between the bottom splits (15). You work all the way around, cross over where you began, and tuck in under the weave inside the finished basket.

Sweet Grass is a delicate sweet-smelling grass found in marsh areas around the edges of lakes and ponds. There is a place near Malagawatch it is so strong you can find it by the odor. But it is not easy to pick, as it is not easy to distinguish it from hay often found in the same place. If the blade you are pulling is hard to get out, it's hay. Sweet Grass will come out easily. Take it root and all, and if it is picked in July it will be strong right through the winter.

*Ellen Googoo with part of her family in 1973.*

*Ellen Googoo Makes a Micmac Basket*

# Hector Carmichael: A Maker of Songs

*Mr. and Mrs. Hector Carmichael, Munroe's Point.*

*Hector Carmichael will be eighty-seven in August [1975]. He probably represents the last of a great Gaelic tradition as practiced on Cape Breton—the local historian as a maker of songs. The songs were sung mostly at parties and millings; especially at millings, the true joy of which we can get only the barest hint today—the joy of a time when the cloth was locally woven and had to be milled, and the singing served both as entertainment and a way of keeping everyone pounding the cloth in rhythm, and everyone knew the true story behind the often exaggerated telling in the song. Old songs were sung and thus kept alive, and new local songs were made to these older tunes, usually retaining the old chorus intact. Sometimes a new song was made on the spot; often one person would make a few verses and another would pick it up and add to it—and because the tune was familiar it was not long before the whole community knew the song.*

The songs I make is making fun of people, you know. Just to make people laugh. I don't write it down, no. I *make* them. I can't write Gaelic, you know. I can read pretty well all the Gaelic but I can't write it. I remember them when I compose them. The first song I composed, a fellow up here had an old horse, you know. Used to drive the children to school with the horse and sleigh in the winter. And the poor horse used to fall down. The horse was so old and not fed too good. Wasn't getting very much oats. Probably after a while he'd get the horse up. The poor old horse was pretty dead, you know. And the song was made that the horse was a wonderful horse. The poor horse was supposed to be one of the best, you know. But I don't think the song is in honor of the horse or in honor of the driver.

---

An t-each ruadh aig Roland Steele  
Gun tug na biastan tachas ann  
'On dh' ith iad dheth an fheoil  
'S cha d'fhàg iad òirleach craicinn air  

O Roland Steele's red horse  
The lice did make him itch  
Since they ate the flesh off him  
They didn't leave an inch of skin on him.  

'S ann mu thoiseach na bliadhn' ùir  
A chaidh e null gu Gearad leis  
Chual' e gun robh e tùrail  
'Son a'bhrùid ecsamanadh.  

'Twas about the first of the New Year  
He went over to Garrett with him  
He heard that he was skilled  
In order to examine the brote.  

'Nuair a rainig e an Cùl,  
Cha d'rinn e fiu is aithneachadh  
Gus an tuirt e ris sa Bheurla  
"Can you treat this animal?"  

When he reached the Cul [rear]  
He didn't even recognize him  
Till he said to him in English,  
"Can you treat this animal?"  

'S ann thuirt Gearad ris gu fiadhaich  
"Cha d' bhiadh thu ceart ro Shamhain e  
Cha deanadh e ach biathadh bhiataidh  
'S tha na biastan damaint' air."  

Then said Garrett to him angrily,  
"You did not feed him properly since before Hallowe'en,  
All he's fit for is raven-bait  
And the lice are Hellish on him."  

"Teich dhachaidh leis gun dàil  
Mas faigh an làir 'san searrach iad  
Na faiceam sa gu siorraidh bràth  
Thu mach air bràigh a bhail' againn.  

"Clear off home with him immediately.  
Before the mare and foal are infested  
And let me never, ever see you again  
Out abroad in our town.  

Ach ma bheir thu e a nùll  
Air cul an t-sabhaill's gum feann thu e  
"Nam faighinn an t-seic' aig airson a ciùrradh  
Dheanainn brògan ùr ma Shamhain dhuit."  

"But if you take him over  
Behind the barn and skin him  
If I could get his hide for tanning,  
I'd make new shoes for you by Hallowe'en."  

Cha'd chuireadh srian am beathach riamh  
Cho ciatach air an rathad ris  
Iomaichidh e leat 'san t-sneachd mar fhiadh  
Ma bhiadhas tu air fodar e.  

Never was rein put on animal  
As comely as he on the highway:  
He will travel with you in the snow like a deer  
If you feed him on fodder.  

Sud far an robh am beathach "Lively"  
A' falbh a'dràibheadh sgoilearan  
Nuair a thuigeadh e commanda  
Cha mhór bhiodh ann air thoiseach air.  

That was indeed the lively fellow  
Driving school children around  
Once he would understand a command  
There would be few ahead of him.  

Se Roland a bha tùrsach  
Nuair a stiuir e dhachaidh leis  
'S cha robh fitheach muigh an Cùl  
Nac d'lean a null do'n chladach e.  

It was Roland who was sad,  
As he guided him homewards  
There wasn't a raven around the Cul  
That did not follow him over to the shore.  

Nuair a rainig e an Cóbh  
Bha e na lon falluis aig  
Thuirt e ri Bessie anns an stòr  
A leoir a thoirt do strabhan dha.  

When he reached the Cove  
He had him in a welter of sweat  
Said he to Bessie in the store  
Give him his fill of straw!

When they used to have weddings long ago they didn't have halls, they used to have the weddings in the houses. And they used to dance and sing songs. I never made up songs about a wedding. That wouldn't be right. And no love songs. Not much love in me, you know. But this one is about two fellows that was butchering a pig.

---

*Oran na Muice* (sung to the air of Tha Buaidh air an Uisge Bheath')

Do chuala sibh na buidsearan
A th'againn as an duthaich seo
'Se Benny is Mac Ghrubhaig
Tha fuireach air taobh shuas deth.

Mu thoiseach na bliadhn' ùire
Bha mhuc a bh'ac ri bhùidsearadh
Bha eoghan 's gunna's fudar aig
'S ann leig e smuid mu cluasan.

Bha Benny ged bu tapaidh e
Nuair rug e air a chas aice
Gun d'thilg i air a tharsainn e
Is thug i casan luath leith?

Bha Benny 'se bh'air botunnan
'S cha robh sin a cordadh ris
'S an car a bh'anns na sroinean ac'
Cha throtadh e gle luath leo!

Bha Eoghan 's bha bròg-shneachd aige
'Se sud a bh'air na casan aig'
Gus na bhuail an t-acras e
Bha e cumail suas ri.

Nuair thug i mach am pastar aisd'
'Sa thug i as an t-sealladh oirr',
Chuir Eoghan fios gu Halifax
Am 'plane' a chuir ga ruaigeadh.

Chuala nigh'n Eoin Mhicheal i
'S chaidh i steach a dh'innse dha
G' robh rudaigin mi-choltach
A bìgeil an taobh shuas dith.

Chunnaic Iain MacNeagail i
'S ged bu duine tuigseach e
Gun d'chuir i moran clisgeadh air
Nuair thug i ruith mun cuairt air.

Thuirt Anna 's i cho bigeanta
"A righ, nam biodh briogais orm
Cha leiginn gin dh'an dithis agaibh
Chuir biodag innt' na luaidhe."

*The Pig Song* (sung to the air "The Virtues of Whiskey")

Did you hear of the butchers
We have in this country
'Tis Benny and MacGruvaig
Who lives up the road from him.

About the first of the New Year
The pig they had for butchering:
Hugh was there with gun and powder
And he fired a volley about her ears.

Benny, though he was plucky
When he caught her foot,
She flung him on his side
And she swiftly took to her heels.

Now Benny was wearing boots
And that wasn't to his liking,
With the twist that was in their toes
He could not trot too fast with them!

Hugh had snow shoes on
That was what was on his feet
Up until he felt hungry
He kept up with her!

When she cleared the pasture
And disappeared from sight
Hugh sent a message to Halifax
To send a plane to chase her.

John Michael's daughter heard it
And went in to tell him,
That there was something unnatural
Squeaking up the road from her.

John Nicholson saw her
And though he was a sensible man
She gave him a great start,
When she took a race around him.

Said Anna very saucily,
"Lord, had I the trousers on,
I wouldn't let either one of you
Put knife or bullet in her!"

*Here is a song that the late Garrett MacDonald of the Meadow Road made about Hector Carmichael. It is called* Eachann agus n "Sparrows" (Hector and the Sparrows), *sung to the air of* "Ho ro, 's toigh leam fhein thu" (Ho ro, you are my darling).

'S tha'n t-each aig Hec' am bliadhna
Gun sian ach g' bheil an deo ann
S'e 'n t-each aig Alexander
An samhla ghabhas a phròbhadh.

Cha dean fodar feum dha
'S de reusd a chumas beo e
Dh'ith na sparrows siol dheth
Tha shabhall am bliadhna beo leo'.

Latha's e 'ga fuadach
Gun tug e suas an Cobh air
Dh'iarraidh ghunna aig sandaidh
'S gun d' sheall iad dha 'n doigh air.

Thuirt Katy ris an uairsin
"Cuir bhuat e 's gun thu eolach,"
'S ann thuirt e, "Tha e 'easy'
Bha J. P. gam' sheoladh."

'Bhurst' e orr' air siaradh
Bha ceud dhiubh ann an comhlan
'S cha deach srad a riamh 'annt
'S bha iongnadh gu leoir air.

Bha Calum Ruadh ag innse
Gum b' iongnadh nach do reoth' e
Ri sealg orr' aig a' bhàthaich
'Se dha dhiubh riamh a leòin e.

Tha shabhall a nis na stiallan
Mar chriathar a h-uile bord dheth
'Se Ron a bha 'ga innse
'S bi'n fhirinn aige 'n comhnaidh.

Now Hector's horse this year
Has hardly got any life in him;
It is Alexander's horse
In comparison which will prove this.

Fodder will not help him
So what on earth will keep him alive,
The sparrows ate the grain off him
The barn, this year, is alive with them.

One day when he was driving them away,
He took off up the Cove
To get Sandy's gun
And they showed him how to use it.

Then Katy said to him
"Put it away, you're not familiar with it."
But he said, "It is easy
J. P. was instructing me."

He blasted them from the side
There was a hundred of them in a group
And not a pellet ever went into them
And he was much amazed.

Red Malcolm was saying
It was a wonder he did not freeze
Sniping at them at the byre.
All he ever wounded were two!

The barn is now in shreds;
Like a sieve is every board in it.
'Twas Ron who told the tale
And he is always so truthful!

Hector Carmichael: A Maker of Songs

# Maisie Morrison Hooks a Rag Rug

*Cutting strips of old cloth to hook into a rug.*

Maisie Morrison of Wreck Cove began to hook rugs when she was about twenty years old. In those days she worked on a large frame her father built, and it was on this frame she made the rug on the page opposite, 6 feet, 7 inches by 2 feet, 11 inches. That was about forty-five years ago. The entire rug is made of burlap. Maisie and her mother pulled the threads from many burlap bags. Maisie dyed the threads orange, green, brown and a kind of soft pink or off-white. Then she twisted strands together five-ply. She sewed two flat 100-pound grain sacks end to end, put them on a frame and hooked. Traditionally, burlap was used only as the backing for a rug, and strips of rag would be the hooking material. Yarn was rarely used. It was considered too precious. Having raised, sheared, washed, carded, spun and dyed the wool—you would want to use it to make warm clothing. The rugs were made from discarded clothing and other worn cloth. Every scrap was saved. Pieces of cloth that had no other worldly use—these would become the lovely rugs they hooked.

To hook a rag rug, you begin by collecting all the old cloth you can and cutting the material into strips—as long a strip as possible, although it is not necessary to sew strips end to end. Thick cloth should be cut to ⅜ inch and hooked in a single

Hooking.

layer. Lighter material should be cut about ½ inch and folded double by the left hand working under the rug, feeding the cloth to the hook. Whether it is used singly or doubled, be certain that in the finished rug the portion of the material that was inside when it was worn, will be the portion that shows. It is the inside of a shirt that has seen much less sun, and the color is thus least faded.

A frame to hold the burlap while it's being hooked is easy to make. We'll use here the measurements taken from Maisie's frame, but none of these measurements is critical. You'll see that there is some size adjustment available in this kind of frame and you can plan your own along these lines. What you want to end up with is a frame that is sturdy but light and capable of being adjusted to keep the burlap backing a flat, tight surface. Maisie's frame was made of pine.

Take two sticks 1 inch by 2 inches by 4 feet long, and chisel out a notch at both ends, something like the notches in drawing 1. Then take four smaller pieces of wood—1 by 2 by 4 inches—and make the same size notches in these and place them as shown in 1. When you nail them in place you end up with two 4-foot sticks, with a slot at either end. When nailing, use a piece of steel to turn the nails back and clinch them. Cut two pieces of heavy wool cloth about 40 inches long and 4 inches wide. Double each piece lengthwise. Now you want a strip of leather. Maisie's brother, Dan Murdoch, cut an old

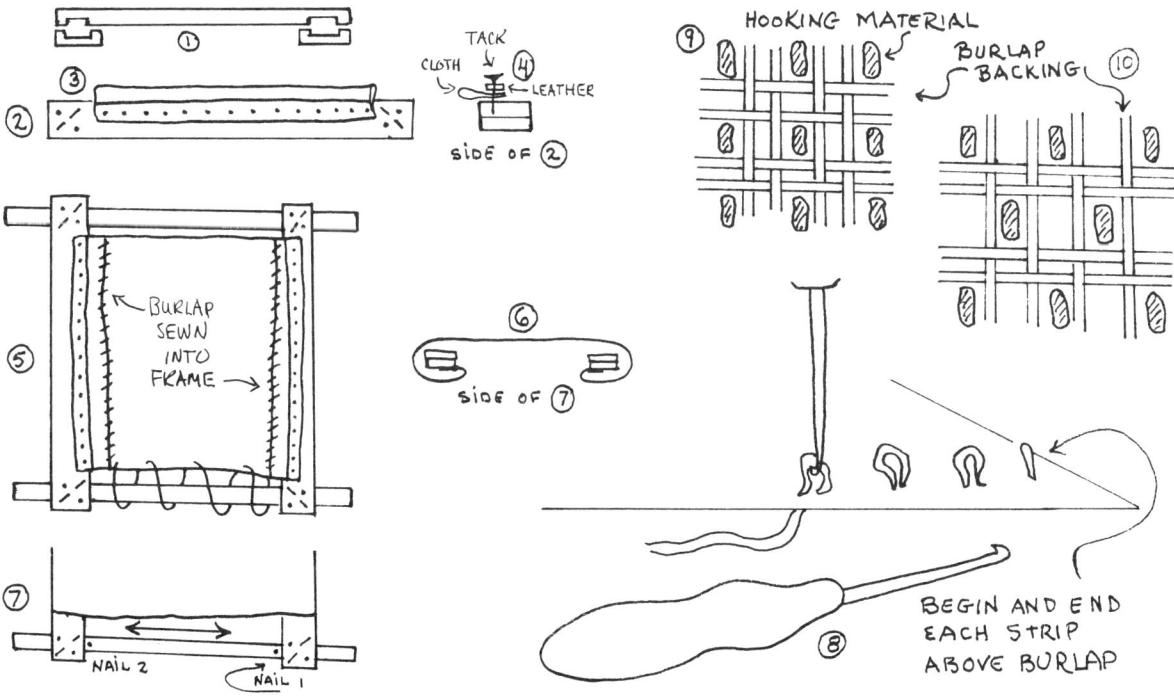

belt into strips 40 inches long and ⅜ inch wide. With the raw edges of the wool joined together, put the cloth along the 4-foot stick and the leather on top of that, running along the raw edges. Tack through the leather and the wool into the wood as shown in 2. Note that the loop of wool cloth should overhang (3 and 4). Do the same to the other 4-foot stick. Take the piece of burlap you intend to hook and sew opposite sides with heavy thread to the overhanging pieces of wool (5). Now turn the sticks away from one another (one or more turns), winding the burlap on the sticks, depending on how large you want your rug (6). Now take two more sticks measuring ½ by 2 inches by 2½ feet and put their ends through the notched openings in the 4-foot sticks apart—get the burlap really taut!—and drive nail 2. Do the same to the other side. Now you may find that your first side is a little loose, so tap a small wedge in between nail 1 and the 4-foot stick. Finally, you take heavy twine—lobster twine is good—and sew the other two sides of the burlap, as shown in 5, to the 2½-foot sticks—drawing the burlap tight and smooth. Now you are ready to hook.

*Reaching into the burlap to hook and pull up the cloth strips.*

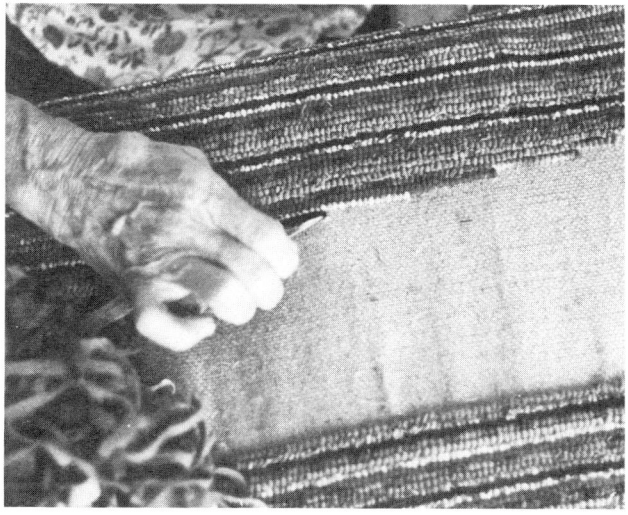

*A closer view showing the loops.*

*A view from below, the left hand holding the cloth and working against the pull from above, keeping each loop the same size.*

*The hooking tool.*

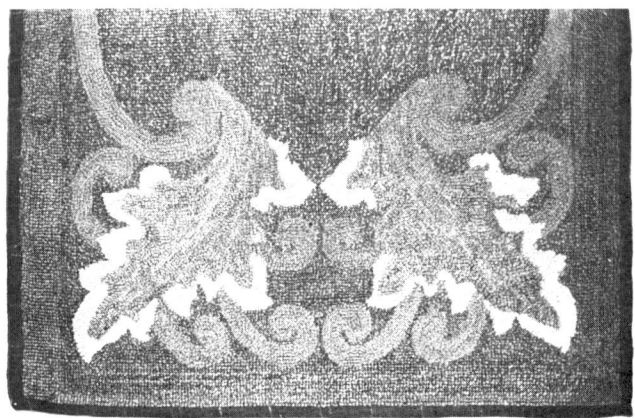

*Examples of Maisie's hooking.*

You can buy a hook, or you can make one as Maisie's father did many years ago. He whittled a lovely hardwood handle. Then he drove a nail into the center of one end. He cut off the head and filed the raw end into a hook.

The principles of hooking burlap or rag strips are essentially the same. You will have to work above and below at the same time. Maisie uses a windowsill and the back of a chair to rest her frame high enough to sit upright and hook comfortably. You can start anywhere, with any color, any part of your pattern or picture. This is not what matters. What does matter is that you maintain the same distance between loops (the same number of burlap strands) in all directions, and that you pull each loop to the same height. You hold the hook in the right hand and poke it down through the burlap. The cloth strip is looped snugly over the index finger and held there by the middle finger and the thumb. This gives you control on the tension of the cloth and maintains the fold in the lighter material. You actually feed the cloth to the hook. This is not easy. You will have to discover your own way of just turning the hook so that it takes a firm hold of the cloth. You raise the hook, drawing a loop of cloth above the surface of the burlap, holding back slightly with your left hand—and this not only helps the hook hold onto the material, it gives you the control to raise the loop only so high, or to draw it back down again if it is too high. Do not release the hook from the loop until the height is just right. Maisie maintains a space of two strands of burlap between every loop (see drawing 9) and keeps straight rows, top to bottom and left to right; some hookers prefer to stagger their rows (10). When doing a form (such as the blocked stars of the large burlap rug),

*Maisie Morrison with her parents and brother Sandy on the porch of the old home at Wreck Cove about seventy-five years ago. There is a hooked rug on the porch.*

Maisie first hooked the outline of each block and then filled in, maintaining the space of two burlap strands in all directions.

There are several ways to finish your rug. Some people baste back about 1½ inches of the burlap edge, then hook through the double thickness. The usual way is to simply finish off with regular rug binding sewed all around. Maisie often turns the burlap under a turn or two and crochets the edges all around with yarn.

# Fishing for Gaspereaux on the Southwest Margaree

*Gerard Chiasson and his son.*

GERARD CHIASSON: I fished gaspereaux with my dad, down at Margaree Forks, from the time I was fifteen. We moved up here eleven years ago and I've been fishing fairly steadily since then. We never did real well down at the Forks because we never had what you'd call a good berth—land that boarded on the river that would suit for a good trap—but some of the land that I purchased here had a fairly good berth. We have been fishing eleven years now and there's only one year that was a failure—so you wouldn't consider that too bad.

My great grandfather, Captain Mose, had a schooner and he used to haul them from Margaree Harbour up to Halifax back in 1885—the market of salt fish to the West Indies has been going a long time, is still going on.

He prepared them same as we do now. There's no change. They're salted as they come from the river—salted round—100 pounds of salt to 200 pounds of fish. They're allowed to sit in that for fourteen days—then they're cured. Then they're re-packed to 200 pounds to each barrel, and they're headed with 100 percent brine. It's used for human consumption [the West Indies]. They tell us that one person may go in and buy only one gaspereaux—they're that poor that all they could afford to buy would be one fish at a time. It's a fish that'll hold well—it can stand two years in a brine pickle—and it won't get rank like mackerel or herring because there's no fat in gaspereaux. That's why it'll hold up. In that warm climate mackerel or herring for that period of time would get rank, would get rusty on top.

My great-grandfather fished them the same way we do now. Same kind of a trap, on the river. But in the late 1800s, early 1900s, each trap would only get fifteen to twenty barrels. My dad tells me each fisherman that was going to fish, he would have the lumber on hand in the wintertime and the cooper would come around and would make the barrels right at the man's place. We order the barrels from outside now, made by a factory. I ordered 400 this year. In those days fifteen to twenty. Probably the big fellows would be getting fifty or one hundred barrels a year—that's all the fish they would get. But there was no market for them for lobster bait in those days. And now they're filleting gaspereaux to replace some of the shortage of herring. They're filleted at big plants here and they're shipped over to Europe in six-pound blocks, frozen—replacing the herring they're not getting there off the coasts.

There were less gaspereaux back then. Yes, my dad would say that. Then there were periods when there were no markets and the fish would get abundance. And then there were periods when they went slack again. And then in the 'thirties and early 'forties they got abundance because of the war and no market in the West Indies. In 1942 there was no market—and the high water in the spring flooded the meadows and

*Mose Mose Chiasson and a gaspereaux dipnet used for bailing out the trap.*

*Above: Two views of Gerard Chiasson's trap, the most elaborate one of the river. Construction is carried out from a flat-bottomed boat anchored above and held out in the river by a man on shore pushing with a pole. The river bottom here is slate, and for each post he must first break the slate with a bar and a mallet, loosening the bar as he works through. Then, feeling under the rushing water, he has to slip the post into the hole just as the bar is removed — or he'll lose the hole and have to start again. Poles brace the posts and are anchored back to the shore.*

156   Fishing for Gaspereaux on the Southwest Margaree

*Opposite page (top right): At Peter Gill's weir, built much closer to shore, men rush along the leads to the mouth of the trap. Opposite (lower right): The trap door is lowered, making a closed rectangular box of the weir. The gaspereaux are taken out of the weir and dumped onto a shoot. Left: From the end of the chute they go up into a truck. Below: Peter Gillis.*

*Fishing for Gaspereaux on the Southwest Margaree*

*At Malcolm MacLennan's weir most of the gaspereaux were being salted and packed in barrels for shipment to the West Indies. The salted fish make a pickle, then are repacked in 100 percent brine.*

when the water dropped, all the hollows, fish got trapped in there and then they died. Couldn't go near the river to swim all summer—the smell was unbelievable. They were that abundant. Every little brook. And then they slackened off in the 'fifties. And in the late 'sixties and early 'seventies we've had a high run again. But this could be that they run in cycles, because the rivers in New Brunswick which fish more than we do have had the same cycles. In the late 'sixties and early 'seventies they've had very, very high catches. In 1974 and '75 we had a couple of days, probably for an hour, hour and a half in the evening—you'd only have the lower gate up six inches off the bottom and you could keep continuously dipping for an hour without closing the gate—they were coming in that heavy.

In 'seventy-three we lost the trap and we fished off the bank for ten days. High water. Lost everything. The ice only left the lake that year the twentieth of May and the twenty-first we had a heavy rain and the ice leaving the lake and it flooded and just cleaned everything completely, any trap that was on the river. And the fish struck the next day. And we had no alternative but to try and we had good fishing for ten days—but it was murder on the arms. You imagine when you're dipping in a trap and you get down to the end, well your gate is there to hold you. But if there's nothing there and you've got half a crate of fish in your net—that terrific pressure on your arms—you had to have a man—a good man—to catch that net. We got two thousand barrels that year. That was good fishing.

The fish are wild this year [1976]. The water is very bright and low. And when they're running in small schools like that they are very wild. When they're running heavy you can't kick them out of your way. You know, they'll just move out a foot and they're right back. When they're running like this year they go out and they don't come back right away. The lobster fishermen tell me where normally they need a depth sounder to see the bottom—ten fathom—this year they can see right to the bottom. So the sea is clear as well. You want a dark water. You want a cloudy day. But I have seen eighty-degree day, sun shining—if it's their nature to move that day, they're going to move.

We find on the first run it's the females—the greybacks—about five to one. And a week and a half later, you'd be

*The Micmac Indians in prehistory used various forms of weir: bushes in the river, posts driven upright close together, even a sort of bag net to collect fish. In recent years they have fished commercially. Stephen Googoo has invented a new trap of steel and wire. No dipnet is used and every fish that comes into the trap is taken. The entire trap-box comes out of the river, dumping the gaspereaux. The men fishing the new-style trap here are John and Joe Prosper.*

getting a higher percentage of males. They go up the river round. They come down—they're right flat. I don't think they take any nourishment while they are there. And a high percentage of what is in them is the spawn. Coming back there's only a small little bit of intestine in there. We see them going back in June. The adults, when they are going down they're not swimming—they're going tail first. They're letting the current carry them. Probably here it's because of the falls. They don't want to go down head first on account of the gills opening in the current—probably one of the reasons why they go down tail first.

The little ones start coming down the river anytime after the fifteenth of July—see them going down right till September, depending on the date they spawned on Lake Ainslie, I suppose. You may have 100 feet, 500 feet, the whole width of the river going down. Then there'll be a break and you'll think there's no more. Then you'll look after a while and there's another school of them. They are about an inch and a half. They look sort of whitish on the top. And they don't go down straight, the small ones. They don't go down tail first or head first—they go down at an angle with the river.

MICHAEL CHARLIE CAMERON: You don't try to fish them with a hook. They won't bite. The only way to get them with a hook is to jig them. People used to use them for fertilizer. Just plow them in with the potatoes, next to the seed. If you put them in with the seed it'd burn the seed—they're that strong. So you put them in the next furrow to the seed. That'd be the use of them those days, except salt a few for the winter. They're just like herring. Everybody put up some them days.

I like them salty. Gaspereaux and two or three potatoes now and you can make a good feed when you're hungry. You split them and gut them and scale them and put them in salt and they make their own pickle. They're good there for the winter. You wash them before you put them in the salt—soak them in water—that draws the blood. Then you salt them and pack them for the winter. Then you take them out and wash them and boil them—a couple of waters. But we don't eat them every day. About once a week. It's like herring. There's plenty bones in them. And they're nice fried. Just roll them in flour or corn meal and fry them pretty crisp. That's fresh. Scales off, gutted and washed good. I had two today. And it was good.

*Michael Charlie Cameron and part of one day's catch.*

# Cleve Townsend of Louisbourg

I remember when I was a boy, any knocks at the door, I wouldn't let anybody go to the door but me. I knew there was nobody there that they could see. I knew the knocks were coming from that world. And I'd always go to the door. And as far as this world was concerned I could say there was no one there. But there was always someone there. From the other world. It would be like to bring a warning about a death close by or something like that. Notice of a death or something like that. I don't think they'd say anything. I'd receive the thoughts from their mind. But I would see them. Yes. I

could see a form, see their face. Oh, yes. Before someone was going to die, very often I'd see a coffin. And sometimes a sleigh of coal would stop at the house of a dead person. Coal would be going, would be traveling somewhere and it would stop at a certain house—that coal is a sure sign of death. In some cases, yes, there were horses. Two loads of coal that stayed down here at the gate, there were horses there, before David and Ida. I turned my back to do something. When I looked around, the horses were gone. But the sleds were there. And the sleighs—there was no snow anywhere—but the sleighs were on top of the snow. I said, "Whoever is gonna pass is gonna pass in the wintertime. And they did. I knew it was this house. One night in a vision, I saw a lot of coal down there on the dump. Oh, lovely coal. I wanted to take it home. And when I started to pick it up—"Leave it alone," someone said from that life. "It's not for you. But watch it." And the coal, the coal that was scattered around took the form of a coffin or a square block of coal. "Watch it. It's going, watch it." And I watched it. It went up the track, went close to a house up there. And I told someone, "Someone is going out of that house—Jim MacDonald is going out of that house." Wasn't long before he was dead. Another time I was down at the shore. It was in a dream—down at the harbor. And there was a couple of colored women there, from that world. And there was someone else. And this someone else said to the colored women, "Here he is. Here he is." The colored woman said, "I don't want him. I'm not after him." And she named the one she wanted to see. Dave, my brother.

When I was a boy I used to take boats out on the harbor, rowing and fishing. I went to the end of the wharf one day—nice day to go fishing—and a little boy came up through the planks of the wharf and warned me. I heard every word. "You go back. You better go back. Or you may never come back this way again as you are." Meaning the physical body would stay in the ocean and harbor. I didn't take any notice of that warning. I went out fishing just the same. And when I was out there, the anchor was quite a good size, heavy anchor—and plenty of rope on it. I'll be damned, I dumped the anchor overboard, I was standing on the rope. I fell overboard and had a heck of a time getting that rope off my ankle. And then I saw him, under the water. "I warned you." Forever after that I never went against them. I saw him again. I don't think he had a name. In our home my father had what you would call a basement; well I would call it a cellar. A grand cellar. Nothing would freeze there. And my uncle, he had nothing. The house was on the ground. He had nowhere to put his apples so he brought them here and put them in our cellar. My sister I think it was said, "Why don't you go down

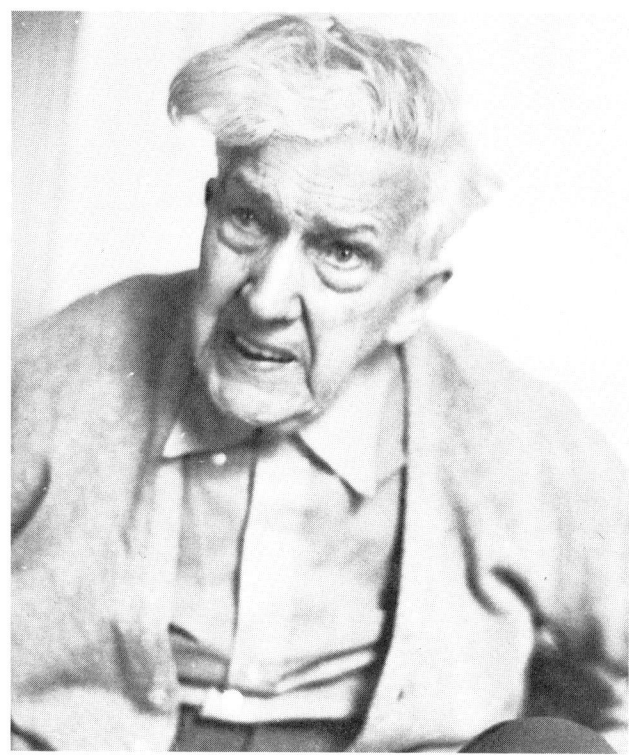

and get us a couple of apples." Steal them, see? "Yes, I will." I went down and got a couple of apples. The boy stood in front of me. "Back." I put the apples back damn quick too. I came up. "Where's the apples?" I said the boy came and told me to put them back and that's where I put them. She said I was crazy. I said, "Maybe, but if you want the apples you go get them yourself." I don't think I saw much of him after that.

Was I ever frightened? I remember I got a little worried that way first time I ever left home, first time I went to Toronto. I was in a restaurant and I was sitting down at a table with another man. He said to me, "Are you a spiritualist?" I said, "No." "Did you ever go to a spiritualist meeting?" "No." "Well, listen, there's an awful lot of people around you, from the other world—that's why I asked you. Will you come with me Saturday night to a spiritualist meeting?" I said, "Yes, if they don't switch off the lights." "They won't switch off the lights." I said, "I'll go." Who was the first one to come to me, was my father. He had passed on years before that. There was a man sitting close to me and he said, "Your father is gone from this world. I'm going to tell you something about him. If I'm wrong you tell me." He said, "I can see where he fell. It looks like a heart attack. I believe he fell over a stove." I said, "Yes, he did." "He fell again here, close by. And the next time he fell he never got up again anymore." I said, "You're right. Every word is right." My father was the first to come. And he used to hear voices from the other side of life. Yes, and his father before him, my grandfather. They weren't healing. They weren't gifted that way. But the other way. My father, he'd go up into the forest, not far, and there was a space there and he'd sit down and talk with his own father, my grandfather and others—other people in that world. *His* people. I never went with him. It seems like he always went alone. I can still speak with my father. Oh,

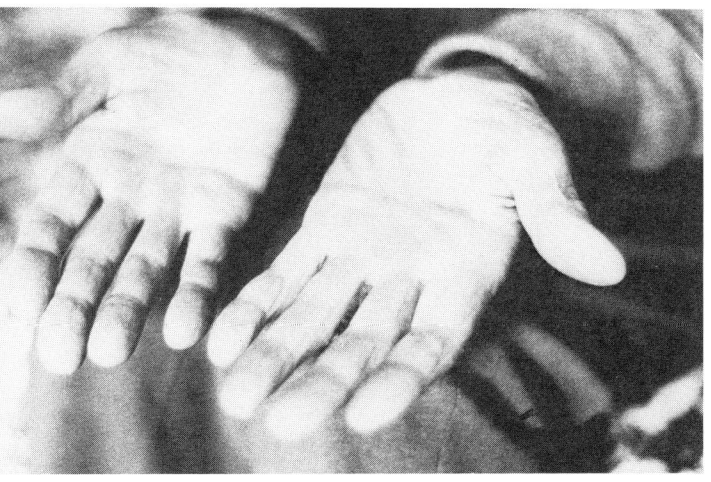

yes. He's a young man now. But he won't come to me that way, I wouldn't know him. He's a young man now. He was sixty-three or sixty-five, something like that when he passed from this life. Grey and a beard. When he comes he comes first with the beard and everything as I knew him. And then after I recognize him, he changes to what he is. The present-day condition. A younger man. My mother the same.

In 1927, long after he had, as they would say, died, my father got me a job. I was out of work for a long while in Detroit. And money was mighty scarce. I did not have enough money to pay for a job. And my father came to me. I think it was around ten o'clock at night. He said, "Cleve, I want you to come down to the employment office. I'll meet you at two o'clock." I said, "My goodness, two o'clock, there'll be a hundred men there looking for jobs. There'll be nothing for me." "At two o'clock," he said. I went down and my father was waiting for me. "Now," he said, "I'm going to tell you what to say when you go in. When you go in there, the man at the desk will be straight ahead when you open the door—the employment agent. You go in and say to him, 'Charlie, have you anything for me today?' But remember, place is full, just whisper to him." Awful time to go looking for anything—two o'clock. But I did it. The employment agent could not answer me. He wrote on a piece of paper: "Go to the manager's office and wait until I come in." I did. After a while he came in there. He said, "Yes, I've got a job for you." I took the job and I made out all right. But it was a job my father got for me, in 1927. And he had died in 1915.

There was an old big towboat, towing barges out of Louisbourg with coal to Halifax. And the captain on the towboat, his name was Harris, Captain Dan Harris. I heard a knock at the door about two o'clock in the morning. This Mrs. Harris heard about me. she said, "Dan may be drowned and the boat may be gone down out in the terrible storm." She said, "Will you try and see if you can see them, see if they're gone?" I said, "Now you just wait a moment and I'll concentrate." I said, "Mrs. Harris, I got them. They're all right so far. But I can see them all working, cutting ice, and the boat is leaning over, top heavy with ice. But I believe they're going to be all right." I said, "Tomorrow morning, ten o'clock—you look out the harbor and you'll see your husband bringing in the towboat towing a barge." Oh boy, she started to cry. I was looking too. And, yes, the boat was sure enough coming down the harbor, about ten o'clock. I knew it was all right. I knew the boat was going to come down the harbor—because I was told from God's world, and they're never wrong. If there is ever anything wrong it's me, not the people from that world. They're never wrong.

*Cleve Townsend of Louisbourg*

I joined the *Troja* I think it was, yes, right here in Louisbourg. Another fellow and I joined the boat the same time. And we went out in a storm—oh, what a terrible storm—and coming out from not far from Grand Manan—we were heading for St. John's, New Brunswick—and we were sixty miles off our course—and we ran on a reef sometime in the night. The engine room was the first to fill with water, the boiler room dead—so there couldn't be a message sent. I was the wireless operator. I couldn't send and I couldn't receive. And the captain called all the hands together. "If the boat stays on that reef and the wind doesn't change—we're all right. But if the wind changes and a gale of wind comes and blows us off, the boat'll go to the bottom. So I want you to prepare for the worst." But a message was received in New Brunswick giving the exact longitude and latitude—our exact position. When representatives of the steamship company came aboard: "We received your message. We knew exactly where to find you." And here was the message, from me, my name on it and everything. But we didn't send a message, couldn't.

There was once a man, sailing on boats, he was from Forchu. And he was told that I was on the boat. "Cleve Townsend's on that boat, I wouldn't go on there." During the First World War I was on a boat. A man from Louisbourg and myself, we joined a boat. We didn't sign on; we were to sign on the next day. I was just getting ready to go to bed, and I believe he was in bed—and I said, "Come on, get off this boat. They're gonna sink the boat. And it'll be somewhere in the North Sea." He said, "Cleve, just wait a minute, where the hell am I going now?" "I know a house to go." So we left the boat. And we said to ourselves, Now we'll watch the papers—see if that boat is torpedoed. And it was, sure enough. It went down, sunk by the Germans, in the North Sea.

I was working on a building in Detroit. It was the new Ford building. Fifty stories high. I was living at that time in Windsor. We were working overtime on Saturday. We worked our day but wanted to come back and work till twelve o'clock at night. "Townsend, you go up right to the very top fifty floors up, and you'll start installing radiators." All right. I went up there. I didn't install very much. Eleven o'clock came around. I was the only one at the top of the building. All the others were down below. The boss says, "How's about all going home at eleven o'clock? All satisfied?" Yes. But I didn't know anything about it. Eleven o'clock came they switched all the lights off. I was left up there. A great large room. And a place for a freight elevator right in the middle. You go in there there's nothing to keep you from going down fifty stories. A hole for a passenger elevator was also there. A hole through every floor. I got to thinking, By gosh, I can't move. I wouldn't *dare* to move. So I doubled up my coat into one corner. I made a pillow of my lunchbox. I didn't go to sleep. I didn't have time to go to sleep. When a great mighty light came in front of me. Oh, no light, no electric light was as bright. Came over close to me. Then it started to move away. Nothing said. I knew what that meant: for me to follow that light. I got my coat on, the lunchbox and went over to the ladder. And that tremendous light stayed with me almost all the way down the fifty floors. There was only three floors and the powerful light left me. God was taking care of his own. Showed me the ladder, every ladder—no steps, all ladders. I came down fine and dandy.

About 1955, somewhere along in there, I started a business in Sydney, on Charlotte Street. A healing centre. God's healing centre. Really, divine healing. The healing power of God. There's no other to beat that. But I had been healing before that. People pushed me to it. They said, Come on. I was working at the steel plant—I was on the railroad. I was hanging on there. The people wanted me to quit the plant and charge them for treatment—enough to make the same as you make at the plant, or more if you wish. Well I couldn't see it. I thought I better stay on the plant. But I got a warning—got more than one warning. "You stay on the plant much longer, and you'll be leaving your bones here." I pretty near got killed one night. Then another time I pretty near fell off of the engine. Then my father came along. "Close the gate. Now," he said, "don't ever open it. Let it stay closed. Keep away from it. Get away from that place and do what the people want." He meant the people that wanted the treatments.

But I was treating people before that. Started in my home. So many started to come I couldn't handle them, so I thought I better get a place on Charlotte Street. And I had a mighty waiting room—twenty-one by twenty-two. And there'd often be twenty people waiting, while there'd be one receiving a treatment. I used to charge for treatments—three dollars. That was a long time ago. I was told from the other world what to charge—and I never changed it. Twenty minutes and three dollars I would just place my hands on them. And prayed. I'd find out where their trouble is. They would talk to me and tell me, and very often I would feel around and know myself because I would feel and know just exactly what's there. All right, there's something here that I want to explain to you. In diagnosing, how'd I do it? This was the way. When a sick woman or man is standing up before me, right close to them I would see their insides. All their insides. Clear and plain, and just where the trouble is. A growth or anything else. I'd see the bowels and the stomach, liver, lungs and everything. My cures were—prayer. Yes, prayer. Turn to God. And my hands. They called me Dr. Townsend. I didn't. After a time I started to put it in the paper myself. Dr. Townsend, Healing Specialist. Oh, boy, the medical doctors in Sydney loved me. They said, We'd chase him to hell, if we could. A Presbyterian minister said that I was fooling people. "In time he'll go to jail. And if I could do it"—a minister said this—"I'd chase him to hell out of Sydney." I quit in 1968. There is a strain on you, yes, a great responsibility there. In telling people certain things. In healing, it's a mental strain. Oh, yes. When I finished a day I'd be as tired as if I'd been out there digging ditches. A mental tiredness. And boy I'll tell you some tired. But I used to go to a tavern. I'd finish about ten or eleven o'clock at night and have a bottle of beer and that'd bring me back.

In plain English, I've lived in two worlds for over seventy years. I lived here and I lived over there. And I don't need to point up so high either. I lived with my feet on the earth plane and lived in the spirit world, right here. And still do. Yes. You see, there's two worlds. The spirit world and the earth plane. And when you, me or anyone else—when we're walking around—we're walking through the other world because this is it. You've got your feet on the earth plane but your body is in eternity. Right now. Yeah. You won't see them. Unless God gives you the clairvoyant sight. I can hear them, yes. At the beginning their words are like listening to a mosquito— and after a time it increases and increases—until it's clear. And I can speak to them. That world is not a different world than the world we see. Sometimes when death comes to the physical body, the man will go over and that world is so much like this that he doesn't know where he is. He doesn't know he's out of the body and dead. And his body, his physical body, is no more. But it's death of the physical body only. The inner man, inside of you, will live on. A million years. A hundred million years. There's no death, for the inner man. The inner man is what controls this body, not you. It's the inner man that's controlling everything. The fear of death, when they don't know what's ahead of them, it's tough. They don't know what they're facing, that's what makes it tough. And through religion they're going to heaven or hell. But, no sir, there's no hell. The heaven you take it with you. A beautiful plane of life over there. There's no hell over there. But of course, I'll tell you, if a man lives a pretty good life why he's gonna find over there it's really good and beautiful. But if he lives a life of sin and likes to kill or something like that—his home over there will be the same as down here—black as Egypt. And he may get one hundred years or three hundred years of that. He's got to pay for his sins. And I don't care what church you belong to, see? The important thing for you is spiritual progression. Not religion. Religion's good in this world—but listen, when you go to the other, spiritual progression is what counts. And once you get over there, in time, me, you or anyone else, once we get over there and established, if we want to move on, out of this darkness, we can. Turn to God, in prayer. Turn to the people of the other world. Ask for help. Desire help. And you'll get it. And they'll help you. Oh, yes. There's no such a thing as leaving this world and no one over there to help you. If I would have listened to people in my own home here I wouldn't have done any of that, because I was told by people, "Don't talk like that. They'll think you're crazy." I remember great mediums in Detroit and Toronto, and they used to say, "If they think I'm crazy I want some more of it, more of that crazy stuff." And I thank God for it. I'm thankful for everything I've got and what I could do for people.

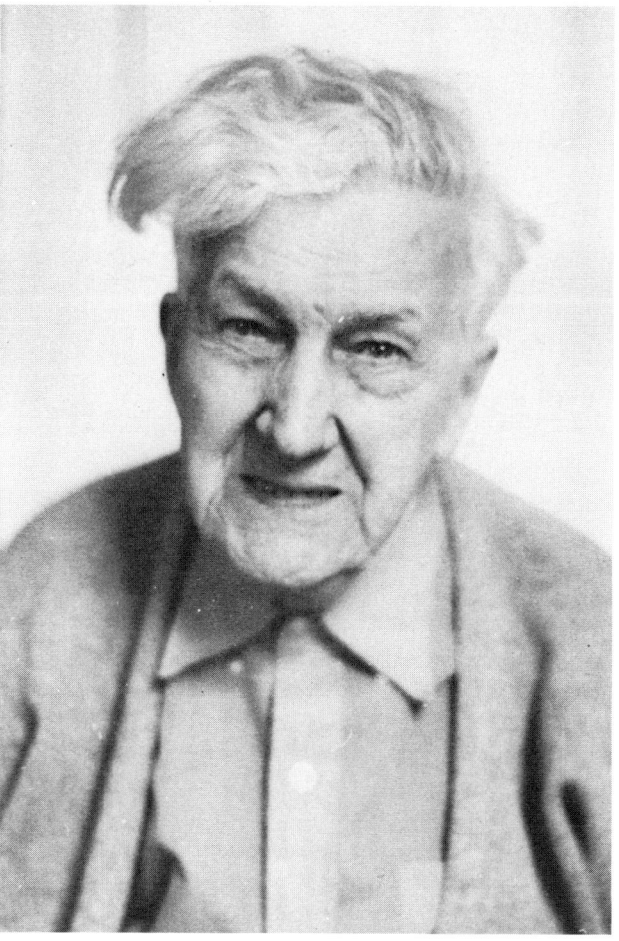

*Cleve Townsend of Louisbourg*

# How to Make Ceann Groppi

Sadie MacDonald.

Norman John MacAskill provided us with enormous codheads and livers, and Sadie MacDonald of Skir Dhu showed us how to make Ceann Groppi (Gaelic for stuffed cod head). Sadie's husband, Neil R., told us: "It would be hard to tell you how old I was when I first ate Ceann Groppi. They used to start making them in July. Well, the liver is no good until August. From then on up to Christmas. Stronger. I would eat it two and three times a day. The same day. I did that not so very long ago. This summer. You get up in the morning, make a cup of tea and bread and Ceann Groppi boy—you talk about your feed." Neil R. said he never heard of any songs or stories or even jokes about Ceann Groppi. "All they did was cook them and eat them, and they were only too glad to have them to eat."

To make Ceann Groppi, you'll need four or five cod livers and a good-sized head (one about the size of a tea kettle, though any head will do)—heads and livers, that's all you will need from the sea. Sadie said: "You want the livers as fresh as you can possibly get them. Get them right away and put them in the fridge in water, a little salt with the water. That'll keep them overnight. I wouldn't hold them longer than that.

The head of a codfish.

They'd get soft. They'll fall apart in your hands. You can't do anything with them." Put a large pot of fresh water on to boil. Take the head to the sink and wash it. You want to get all the blood out. Clean around the mouth and inside the mouth. Just open the mouth under the faucet and let cold water run through. Carefully wash the gills. Then take the livers separately and wash them in cold water. Drain the water off them and leave them in a large bowl or pan. You'll find them slippery. Rinse them again in cold water and inspect them. Sadie normally cuts away anything that doesn't look just right to her—especially any little greenish patch you sometimes find. Anything hard or discolored. Occasionally you

*Below: Squeezing the livers. Middle: Stuffing the codhead. Bottom: The cooked codhead.*

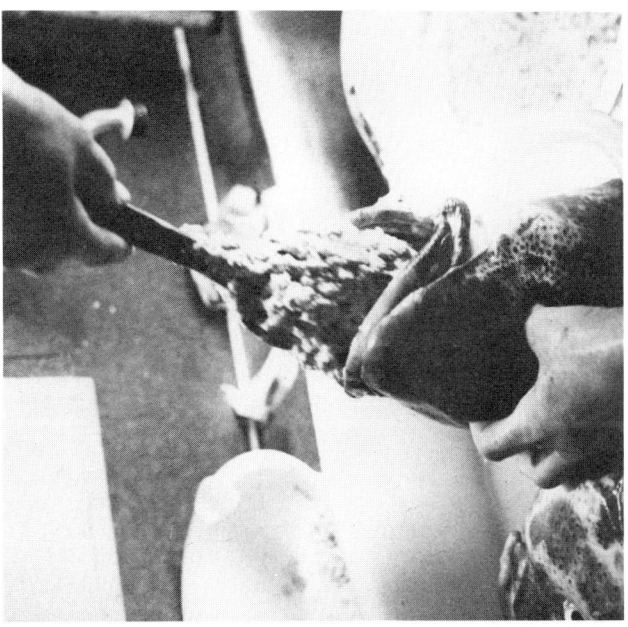

find a little brown spot just under the skin of the liver. "Perhaps there's no harm in them but I always pick them out." Then Sadie began to squeeze the livers in the palm of her hand, to get the veins out of them. You do this one liver at a time, squeezing it in your fist, the liver coming out between your fingers leaving the stringy matter behind in the palm of your hand. When you've finished that, mash them further so they won't be lumpy. The livers will look like a kind of porridge.

To the livers add one to one-and-a-half teaspoons of salt. Put two teaspoons of salt into the boiling water. And put a teaspoon of pepper into the livers. Sprinkle on top of the livers three-quarters of a cup of white flour, one cup of corn meal and (to start with) two cups of rolled oats. Mix thoroughly with a large wooden spoon. If it seems too soft and runny, add more oatmeal. You don't want the mixture too dry but you don't want it so thin it'll come out the head. Now fill the head through the mouth. Pry open the mouth and grip the head with a thumb and forefinger one in each eye—this will keep the mouth open. Once the head is stuffed put it in the boiling salted water. And if you have any filling left over, put it in a cloth (a piece of white sheet or flour bag) and put it in the pot with the head. The water doesn't have to actually cover the head. The steam will cook it in a covered pot. Boil for an hour.

You can serve it right from the pot or cool it in the refrigerator first. The taste is stronger when it's hot. Sadie said that you can freeze them. "You can't freeze livers very well, but if it's made up as Ceann Groppi it'll keep well in the freezer. We ate one this spring that was put in the freezer last fall—didn't know it was there till I came across it—just let it thaw by itself. I don't believe you could warm them in hot water again. I guess you could warm it in the oven. We ate it cold. It was just as good as fresh."

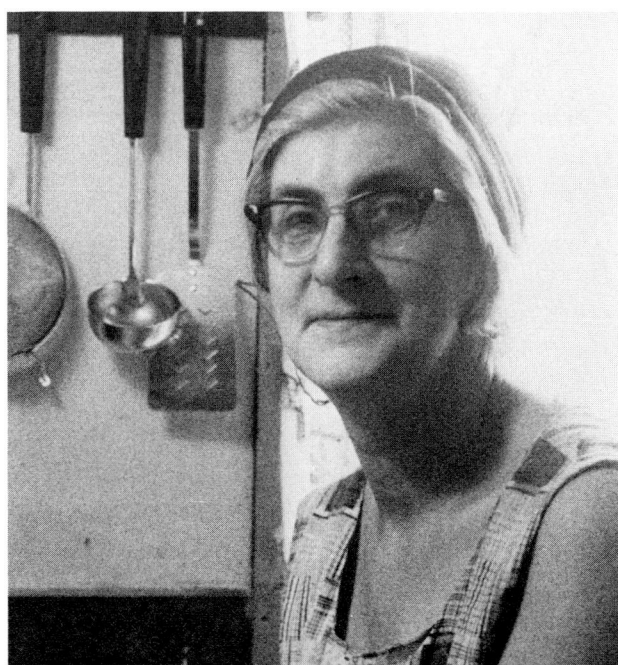

# The Life and Death of the *Aspy*

*There were actually three Aspys, each in turn (though to a steadily lessening degree) a main link for travel and goods between the island's commercial center of Sydney/North Sydney and the small farming-fishing communities down north. There were several other coastal vessels serving in this role all around Cape Breton. Here, it is generally the first Aspy that is being talked about. The second saw less work as the roads improved and there was finally very little work for the third Aspy as the big trucks took over. Henry Howlett told us that she ended her days as a youth hostel near Halifax. "They stripped all the engines out of her and made one big hold. Oh, they had bands down there and bunks all over the place. She was a hard looking sight then. And that was her last days." What follows are memories of when the name Aspy still meant a welcomed vital contact to the wider world.*

CAPTAIN SMITH: As far as I'm concerned, the *Aspy* was not only a little passenger and freight ship carrying everything you

*The first* Aspy *passing Englishtown.*

*Captain John Smith when he was mate.*

can think of to these communities—to me she was more or less an institution. You know, to the people of the north country—the *Aspy* was practically the only means of transportation and it was the only scheduled means of getting supplies in and out. And all the merchants would have their supplies in before the *Aspy* made her last trip. And no more supplies came in until the *Aspy* started to run again in the spring. Nothing. The roads were dirt roads and there were no snowplows at that time to keep them open. The only thing that went down that way in the wintertime was the mail—and that went by horse and sleigh . . .

LIDA SMITH: We used to have seventy-five for dinner sometimes. That's where I met my husband. I loved it. I wore a white uniform. I had to take care of all the cabins, and if there was anybody sick—lot of seasickness. Some people would be so seasick they'd just wish they'd die. It could be quite rough at times—quite bad storms. But it didn't bother me. I was never frightened. Never.

I have seen one morning when we left Dingwall—there was a terrific storm—sheep on board and everything, some on the deck. The boat was rolling so much the cook Angus Hines lashed the pots and everything on the stoves—iron bars to keep the pots on—the water coming in everywhere and finally we had to leave down below. The cook was up to his knees in water. Another morning, he just had to close the kitchen right down—it was full of water—bedroom and hallways downstairs all full of water. That's the worst in four years that I was on. Pottie was captain. Said to me, "The worst storm that I've ever been on. We just had nip and tuck." But he never gave in at the time. Said there were times he went down he never expected us to come back up. Those waves. And people in Ingonish were out with glasses, watching her come across. They said when she went down they couldn't see her, only get a glimpse of the smokestack or something. They never expected her to get back up out of those terrifically deep waves. And by that time, the boat was getting bad. She was taking water that day. And we had a crowd of passengers, going to Dingwall—and many were Catholic. I got into their stateroom somehow but it was hard slugging to get even in the door—and they had their beads out and they were praying. And some of them were so sick they couldn't even pray.

CAPTAIN J. D. POTTIE: Those were hard days. We'd come in to Sydney at night and have to bunker—put coal aboard—ten, fifteen, twenty tons of coal—then take on cargo after that. During the depression we had the Liberal government in in 1930. In 1932 there was a change of government and R. B. Bennett came in. Of course we were a subsidized company. So they cut the subsidy ten percent. So they cut our wages ten percent. Worked twice as hard. Twenty-five hours a day we

*Lida Smith when she was a stewardess; Captain J. D. Pottie.*

*The Life and Death of the* Aspy

used to work in that ship. I was on seven years. Worked my guts out.

There were a lot of things happened were ridiculous. You look back at it today you say no bloody way would I do it now. I mean, you're talking about working—nobody knows what work is—it was the same as back a hundred year ago in those days. We would go and open a train car of hay in North Sydney—you'd take hay by the car. I remember one Christmas Eve we went over. Well, it was in the afternoon of Christmas when we opened the car—Roy Bennett and I and another chap named Westbury. We got one of the firemen up to run the winch for us. We broke the seal and get in and start driving this hay aboard the *Aspy*. Forty-seven minutes from the time we opened the door till the time we had all the hay aboard the ship. Was all stowed and, jeez, one man in the hold—it was hard going. Big bales of hay right up to the deckhead. That was bales 147 pounds. I was only short you know. And I couldn't get my arms around them. I'd get the wires and drive them. Roy was up helping in the car. And of course he was purser, had to check each bale—so he'd help load them and then he'd check it off. And sometimes you'd get five bundles in a sling. Well you'd have four away in the hold but you'd still have one to heave—when they'd drop five more on top of you.

And finally this started to build up an extra one every time. Jesus, hard going. This was all stowed and going to put the hatches on and went and called the mate. He came down and he looked down the hold and he says, "Go down there young fellow, and check make sure none of those bales of hay are close to those pipes." Pipes running through the hold to the windlass and the winch. Had to crawl down through and move bales again. And they were nipping back a few. It was Christmas Eve. So we backed off of there and up almost to Point Edward and we turned around—and didn't we go ashore right there at the coal pier. And this is Christmas Eve. Stuck there not too long but long enough to frig us up. We finally got her in the dock and it was too late to go anywhere. One o'clock in the morning. Christmas Day. So we lost our Christmas Eve. But that was nothing. We lost every one. I don't remember being home for one in the seven years.

We started at seven o'clock in the morning, from Sydney. We'd go to St. Ann's and back—one day. Then we'd have to load for north, and bunker, wash down—wash the ship down. She's full of coal dust and hay. Then you'd go north. And going down north you might land a whole load of hay like that at one place. Or cement. A car of cement would be 1400 bags—highway construction, bridges. We'd have punchions of molasses and one man on deck—you'd have to up-end them yourself—1724 pounds. That's a lot of molasses. That's a lot of lift, too. You might have ten punchions on deck. You might have fifty barrels of gas. And a hold full of cargo. And there was a great deal coming out, too. Fish and cattle, sheep. You'd take the sheep out. They'd bring them out to you in boats at Dingwall and Bay St. Lawrence—boats twenty feet long, four or five feet deep—they'd take maybe fifty sheep at a turn. They'd have to go back and get more and you'd be anchored there, thinking about getting back and so much on the dock. You'd load them aboard the *Aspy*, put them along the side of the ship, on the deck. And they'd be there baa-ing till you got to Sydney. Then we'd put them in a pen. Sometimes they'd get loose on us and they'd run, and we'd have to go and chase them. All around the ship. All around the city. You better believe it. Sydney. All up and down the Esplanade and us going in big rubber boots chasing all those bloody things. It was real weird. And we'd have to get them back, put them in the pen, then go back aboard—bunker and load and wash down. Imagine washing down. Boy, they were hard hard times. They paid me thirty-six bucks a month. That's before we got the ten percent cut.

## The First *Aspy* in a Storm

DANIEL K. MORRISON: The night before the big storm, a Tuesday night, we came back to White Point after going as far as Bay St. Lawrence. That day was a pretty day on the ocean, as calm as a pond. But at five o'clock Wednesday morning the captain woke up all of the crew and both firemen to get the steam up and under way. He predicted that a storm was on its way. He said the storm glass was way down to the bottom. At that time, this was all he had to go by. There was no radio and no weather report.

So, we got the steam up, let the lines go, and away we went. Not long after, the wind came up and became so strong that if you went outside, you had to hold on to something or the wind would go with you. The wind was coming up from the south. The *Aspy* didn't have much rigging on, but you couldn't hear anything with the wind whistling through those ropes. It was getting worse all the time, and the waves were swelling larger and larger. The engineer was strapped in his chair by the levers. He would shut off the steam of the engines when he felt the steamer plunging down since the propellers would lift out of the water. Sometimes he would miss, and you would think that the stern would shake to pieces with the propeller going a thousand times faster.

At last, the steamer wasn't going ahead one bit. I'm sure she was losing ground. When she would come down from a

*Dan K. Morrison when he served on the* Aspy.

wave, the next one would bust down on her bow, hitting her with tons of water. You couldn't see anything but the forecastle mast. You would think sometimes she would never come up.

Just then, the whistle blew, and the captain told us to go around and tell the passengers to be on the watch since he was turning the *Aspy* around and heading back to White Point as soon as he would see a good lull. A good chance came, and we noticed she was turning. She was broadside when the first wave hit her and put her over on her side. I was holding onto one of the stringers for dear life since you couldn't stand on the deck because of the slant of the steamer. When the steamer started to come back I looked and saw how deep it was between the waves. I said to myself here she goes and sure enough I knew she went so far on her side that if you were on the other side, you could have seen the keel. But, what saved her was the next wave would hit her broadside and put her far to the other side. Well, she finally came around and we were going before the waves.

We didn't take long getting back to White Point with the waves busting down on the *Aspy*'s stern all the way. White Point was a great shelter from storms coming up from the south, but a gale from the northeast would come right in there. Anyway, we tied the *Aspy* up with plenty of lines at a new government pier. The pier had three big spools to tie her to.

Around eleven o'clock, the wind shifted from south to southeast and then to east-northeast. The *Aspy* started rocking back and forth. Then the lines began snapping. There was a big coil of new rope in the locker room, and we got that out and put four new lines on her. No sooner had we done that than you could hear shot-like sounds of the lines breaking. The captain came down and told us to get the steel hawser up from the aft storeroom. We had about eight fellows from White Point helping us. We always thought about how hard these men worked with us and without expecting any pay for their work. God bless them.

We put one end of the hawser out on the stern, tying it to the spool on the pier with ropes. We ran the other end of the hawser through the steamer and out on her bow. We were trying to secure the hawser at the bow as the storm was getting worse. The cable was so heavy we couldn't take up so much slack at a time. This one time, the undertow pulled the steamer out and yanked that big spool right out of the pier. The captain hollered to take the hawser in, and the White Point men had to come aboard to help us. Then when they got a chance they jumped back to the pier. Captain Dan came down and told us we would have to go outside and anchor. He ordered us to get out both anchors to the last link of the chain.

We had another captain with us by the name of York who had replaced MacDonald when he had an operation during the summer. When MacDonald returned, York stayed on. He was a good, able man who was not afraid of anything, and that helped us a lot to keep our spirits up. So, Dannie and Captain York went to get the anchors out after the *Aspy* was out quite a bit. They tied themselves with rope, and that saved them. A couple of times they had to jump into the rigging until the big waves passed by. One anchor had a very long chain on it, the chain on the other was shorter. Anyway, they both had a good hold on the bottom, and when the steamer would up on a wave, the chains would become so taut you'd think they'd pull the bow out.

We got out around two o'clock. I was staying up on the second deck, holding on. The wind was so strong, whipping the sea up like it was light snow. You couldn't see very far out on the ocean what with the spray. What frightened me was the big waves—sometimes in threes—would come together and break, then go some distance and break again. I said to myself if ever one of these comes down on the *Aspy*, she

*Captain Dan MacDonald.*

would never weather it. At last, I saw one of these waves coming right at us. You couldn't have timed it better as that wave busted right down on the bow. She was so slow coming back up that I thought she was sinking. As I looked down on the first deck, here the water was only a couple of feet below the second deck where I was. Captain Dan came out to see what had happened since they couldn't see through the spray on the windows. He said he thought for sure the housing, including the wheelhouse, was gone after the way the steamer had been shaken.

About nine-thirty at night, another wave hit her and a lot of water poured down the stack, the deck, knocking out the dynamo and all the lights went out. The people in White Point watching the *Aspy*'s struggle thought for sure she had gone down. They sent a telegraph to the owners in Sydney that the *Aspy* was lost with all hands. After that, they couldn't get a message out to confirm it since trees fell across the wires, knocking out all communications.

The wind had shifted again to northwest and swung around to west, and what a wind it was, putting the steamer hard on her side. Talk about rolling. I was put on the 10 P.M. to 2 A.M. watch. Around midnight I knew she was dragging anchor, although it was hard to make anything out in the pitch darkness. At 1 A.M. I went to wake the captain, but he was already putting his coat on. He agreed that the steamer was dragging anchor, and told me to go and wake the rest of the crew. I went to York's cabin and rapped at the door, but there was no answer. I opened the door and had to laugh at what I saw. He had propped the mattress up against the side of the bed so he wouldn't roll or fall out. I had to shake him before he woke up.

So we weighed anchor. Captain Dan said with the west wind blowing this hard it would calm the sea and the waves down some, and he was right. We made for Ingonish. About 4:30 A.M. we arrived at the entrance to the harbor. However, the entrance is not very wide, and the lighthouse on Ingonish Beach had been swept away. The searchlights on the *Aspy* were little good in that gale, and the captain couldn't pick up the channel. So we had to back out and anchor again in the shelter of Middlehead. We had a nap and a good hot breakfast. Later, we came into the harbor, and soon a crowd gathered to find out how we weathered that awful storm down north.

We left Ingonish around ten o'clock in the morning with the wind blowing from the south. Mother and father were pacing the floor waiting for some word on the fate of the *Aspy*. Father had been over to Alex J. Morrison's where they had the telegraph office, but the wires were still dead. They kept watching the ocean, and lo and behold the *Aspy* came into view, still battling the storm with white spray flying over her. The wind was coming from the south as it had the previous morning, causing the steamer to pitch in those waves while rolling in the waves stirred up by the northeaster. How glad we were as we steamed into Sydney Harbour. All the oldtimers from the North Shore down to Dingwall said they had never seen a storm like it. Fishermen had never before seen a wind come up around full circle in twenty-four hours with no let up.

I had my mind made up when I got my feet on solid ground that I would stay there. But then I read about the storm in the newspapers and how some big freighters for England had to turn back to Sydney for repairs with shattered pieces of lifeboats dangling from their davits. So I said to myself I must be a pretty poor sailor for quitting my job because of being in a storm. And I so much wanted to become a captain. I said to myself, If the *Aspy* was able to ride out that storm she'll ride out any storm. So I stayed on her until she tied up in January for the winter.

## The *Aspy* at Breton Cove

JANIE MACLEOD, *Baddeck:* The *Aspy* was our big event. In those years, the *Aspy* came twice a week. Before the

*Aspy* there was the *Harlaw*. The *Weymouth* ran there too for a while—not too long. The *Harlaw* was before my time. She made the one trip, a round trip—north and came along the shore or went to St. Ann's and went down along the shore to Ingonish. They didn't have special days. Somebody would see the boat coming and they'd notify the rest. My father had a general country store. There was everything from as they say a needle to a haystack. It was just called D. B.'s Store—that's all. I remember one time father had a Newfoundland dog—he used to run errands for him. This time they were working at the foundation of the mill and the dog came with a shingle—the *Harlaw* was coming, get to the shore. So they all made for the shore, took the boats and went to the *Harlaw*. There weren't so many travelling in those days. But you knew when the *Aspy* was coming. She came on Mondays and Thursdays to Breton Cove and St. Ann's Harbor.

If it was during the lobster season, of course, all the men would be at the shore anyway—they'd be there working the lobster factory. And my father had boats. First it was just rowboats. And then he got a motorboat and he towed the big scow that carried the freight back and forth. Like in the fall of the year they got their winter supply—they'd be there all day. That boat would come in the morning—it'd be after dark some nights when she'd leave there. Passengers on board; it was a terrible day. It'd be rolling and they'd be sick—waiting on the boat for it to go in to St. Ann's. They'd perhaps have two scows and a motorboat taking them back and forth—a crew on shore and a crew on the boat loading. They'd use two when they got their winter supply or when they got the first load in the spring. There was a lot came. There were big families. The first year I went to school at French River, there were sixty-five on the role. This was just a four-mile district. There was a school at Wreck Cove and one at the Plaster.

Of course all the neighbors chipped in. Nobody got paid for anything in those days. We never got paid for landing freight or anything in the early days. And they never charged to take passengers ashore in my father's day. It was after that they started to get paid—some places charged ten cents—but nobody ever charged passengers to take them ashore at Breton Cove. If the boat was late and it was noontime they landed, my father took them in and they had dinner at the house—and in those days you would never charge anybody for a meal like that. People came from Wreck Cove, Indian Brook—came to get the *Aspy* at half past ten. If she was delayed, perhaps didn't get

Left: *Janie MacLeod.* Below: *A crowd waiting for the* Aspy *at Breton Cove.* Bottom: *A small boat under tow, coming out to meet the* Aspy *with tubs of butter, homemade rakes and other goods to ship away. The boat will bring in goods and passengers.*

*The Life and Death of the* Aspy

The Aspy at White Point.

there till one o'clock—these people would have dinner either at our place or if they had friends around the district they'd be there. Till they'd see the *Aspy* coming—then they'd go to the shore. And they had to go out in the boats.

## The Wreck of the First *Aspy*

WALTER LEFRIEND, *North Ingonish:* I was going to tell you about the night we went ashore. It was on a Tuesday. We went down north and we stayed at White Point that night. Fine nights you could go in there and stay. You could stay there in a storm too. Wednesday morning we'd come up and go to Sydney. Well, we didn't stay that night. We stayed there for a while, went ashore there at White Point to a dance. The storm started after we went to the dance. Then we heard the whistle blow—Captain York blew three whistles—we knew then that he wanted us. He said he had orders to get out, pull out—either to Sydney or South Bay. That's where we used to go and put up lots of nights. So anyhow we run for an hour or more—then we hauled her up on her course for to go to Sydney or South Bay, wherever he was going.

We were all getting a lunch, passengers and all in the galley—and we were going along and all at once [Walter thumped his fist on the table] I could hear this, and I said, "That's very good, that one." And again [thumps his fist down again] and I said, "That's still better" to the passengers. [Thumps] There it is again and I said "That's still better—she's ashore." I knew it. She had to be striking the bottom because she started rolling. She was ashore just the same as you'd look at the land out there, right in underneath—an awful place boy. We couldn't see anything where we were. But we were lucky she went where she did—between Long Point and a place by the name of French Cove. If she went up a little farther and struck on what we call Long Point, there'd be nobody got ashore. Impossible. Because it was all breakers there.

*Walter LeFriend (left) and George Buchanan.*

Just opened the galley door and there was the sea coming, boy—coming right aboard of her. Went to see the captain to get the lifeboats out—but he wouldn't give any consent at first. He thought she was going to back out. But she wouldn't because her steam pipe was broken in two. Paddy Strumps, George Buchanan, a fellow by the name of Paddy Ryan, Tom Janes, the mate was Albert Nicholson and Captain York. He thought she'd back back—but when he left the wheel and came down he knew it was impossible. Then we got the lifeboat. We tied a rope to the *Aspy* and got it ashore—Tom Janes was ashore. He took the rope and tried to make it fast there—had to hold the rope in his hand—then he got it fastened around a big rock. You couldn't see, could just feel your way. Albert Nicholson was the man with me in the lifeboat—we'd pick the women up and hand them out to Tom Janes ashore. A man could just jump ashore from the lifeboat.

We pulled our way back and forth along the rope. We couldn't row. Only the lights of the boat and they didn't stay too long. The captain was the last one off. When he got out of her we went to pull the lifeboat ashore—and the sea just came up and away she went. Took it from us and that's the last we ever saw of her. Then we had to move up every time the sea would come up—we'd move up close to the bank. Couldn't start a fire. Was pouring rain. They got up on the bank there,

*Boarding the* Aspy *at North River wharf.*

somewhere through the woods, and stayed there. Till daylight came, then they left. They lost everything they had. There were women were going to the States. Joe Naddaf of North Sydney was on her—a pedlar—lost everything. They walked to Neil's Harbour. Then we went back and we stayed there. We must have been there a couple of weeks anyhow. Stayed till she went. Came in a storm that night and that was the end of her. We left when we saw she was breaking up.

GEORGE BUCHANAN, *River Bennett:* It took an awful storm to break her up—she was well built. Big timbers in her. That was a stormy night though. Wireless message from Dingwall to get out of White Point. There was a southerly gale coming. We had freight aboard, and thirty passengers. And the captain kept her out so many minutes of each course—the wind was blowing in on the shore—he kept her out and the wind was pushing her in all the time—and she struck on this rock. There was eighty feet of water at her stern and the rock came through her cargo, right through the forecastle—and she hung on that. And there was a man named Freddy Martell in there all the time. A fisherman, he was off of watch. And we put a bar against the door so the sea wouldn't open the door. He was up to his neck in the water when we thought of him and got him out of there. Vincent Welsh was the cook on her. I'll tell you what he did. The dining room had a lot of water on the floor and I guess a force of habit—he was gathering up to salvage crockery and there was one plate fell out of his arms on the floor—and do you know what he did? He went in the galley and got a dust pan and a broom and swept it up. And her in ready to smash up.

We had to try and get the lifeboats off. The first one got off the rope was rotten. The smoke from the galley pipe was hitting against it and it kind of burnt it. The rope broke and the boat went down. We had to lug the other one across the deck and she was rolling like that, back and forth. Just like hailstones, the wind blowing the water in your face. There were a lot of ships lost that night. We couldn't use the oars so we ran a line under the seats of the lifeboat. Got a line fastened to the *Aspy* and made the other end fastened to the cliff. That's how we got them ashore with the one boat. The rope was running under the seats so she couldn't get away. And there was one old woman she was way over seventy years of age. There were no old men. There was a cow and a calf on board, and there were ten sheep. Well the sheep will drown themselves; when the wool gets wet they go to the bottom. They went down the bottom of the engine room. They got panicky, you know. And they got running up and down the corridors and, you know, nobody to stop them and went in the engine room and down to the bottom. The calf drowned —she was tied too short—but the cow, she was tied loose, she was alive.

*The second* Aspy *at Ingonish.*

It was still dark when we got ashore. And I went behind a big rock to get shelter, soaked to the skin. I was in my sock feet. I had had a big pair of boots on. I threw them overboard. Daylight came. And the first job I got—see, the insurance does this—you put what's left of the passenger's luggage in a circle. And you sit down inside there. So nobody'd steal it. And the insurance called for this too: There was a man came down three times a day from Neil's Harbour—he was appointed by Lloyd's insurance I think—used to bring us down a plug of tobacco. And he made tea and he brought us three meals a day. And we had a tent rigged up then. She was there damn near a week and a half before she broke up. Took an awful pounding to break her up. The water's so deep there. But no one was lost—only that calf and the sheep.

# John R. and Bessie MacLeod Tell Stories of Their Old Home

BESSIE: No, no, it wasn't this house. It was just down below here. That house is taken apart. But I'm telling you, really, it was spooky. And then we moved out. I was never scared when I was there. I heard lots and lots and lots of things there. And after we left—we only moved up just across the road—I went down the next day for dishes that I left at the house and, it was so funny, when I got to the door—if there was a dish there covered with diamonds, I couldn't go in for it. I froze right at the door. And I just couldn't—and I was looking at the dish in the pantry, through the window—just at the door I could see it. No, sir. I was so scared I couldn't go in that house. And when I was living there I wasn't a bit frightened or anything. I'd stay alone there in the night. But when I left there, everything came, boy. That's the time I was scared. I could go as far as the door and I would just freeze right there. I could not go inside. Yet while I was there it didn't seem to bother me. I used to hear walking. And if you'd be in the kitchen, in the dining room, you'd hear somebody coming downstairs. And you'd be in one room and you'd hear whatever it was walking into the other room. When you'd be in bed upstairs through the night you'd hear the walking down below, pulling dishes and opening the doors. That's what happened that night we heard that man coming in. John R., tell it. You tell it better. Tell him about the night the man came in.

JOHN R.: I'll have to tell that the last of it. We had just moved in. Thirty years ago. The old people had heard stories about this house, yes, the old people did.

BESSIE: I think that's why they moved out of there, the family that owned it before. They never told till after they sold it that that's why.

JOHN R.: They used to see a woman coming down there.

BESSIE: Yeah.

JOHN R.: She'd go in the house. They couldn't see her. They'd see her going in, that's all. My aunt was over there one night playing cards. She'd be 150 years old if she were living. And Mr. MacDonald had a black horse. In the barn. She was over then, and she looked out the window—great big beautiful-looking horse—and she told Mr. MacDonald, "There's a black horse looking in the window." "Oh, hell of it," he said, "the little black horse must have got out." And he took the lantern and went out and went over the barn and he came in and he said, "Oh, I put the horse in." But the horse wasn't out—but Mr. MacDonald put it that way so the women wouldn't get scared. Yes, they were seeing, hearing things before I went there.

My uncle Joe MacKinnon bought that place. He came home from out north. He bought that farm, from MacDonald. I used to be over there with him. I wasn't married then. We were shingling and painting the barn. My uncle this day went to town—went on a little toot—he came back, he drove down to the place and he put the horse in the barn. He went over to the house, he opened the door. Sometime in the night—I don't know when he came home—but whatever met him at the door, he didn't go in. He went out to the barn and he took the robe out of the wagon; and there was hay on the threshing floor—and I caught him there in the morning and I asked him what happened. "How is it you're sleeping here and a big, beautiful house over there?" "Look, John R.," he says, "I'll never, never sleep in it. Or go in it." And neither did he.

BESSIE:   And they were awful good people.

JOHN R.:   The people who owned it were very, very good people—whatever was wrong there.

Well, anyway I moved from a place they call Egypt. Upper Margaree. Southwest Margaree, Egypt. Moved down and I wrote to my uncle and he gave me the house. And we moved in there. This noise was going on. When we'd go to bed we'd hear everything moving and going and a table move and dishes moving and—anyhow this night my Aunt Teresa made the card playing. Bessie says, "John R., we're going to the card playing." A snowstorm on. I didn't want to go. I was working in the mines and I didn't want to go. She coaxed me so we went. The storm was so bad we got as far as my father's. My father and mother were in, living alone. Went in. And my father said, "God, John R., you getting crazy, out on a night like tonight." I said, "Aunt Teresa got a card playing and I'm going to go." "T' hell," he says, "with the card playing—you'll get lost." So my mother made tea and we were in talking. Went back over to the house. Walked back. Oh, we couldn't hardly see a hand ahead of us. We got down there. Went in and her mother was up and she had fires on and we had tea and went to bed. Her mother went upstairs ahead of us. And she told me, "John R., lock the door." "Ma," I says, "I'll lock it. The *bodachean* won't get in tonight."

BESSIE:   That's the little old man.

JOHN R.:   My uncle had a Yale lock on the door. There was a storm door and there was a big hook, heavy hook on it. I put the hook on the storm door. I shut the door and I put the Yale lock on it. Well, this dog, this German police dog was down in

*John R. and Bessie MacLeod Tell Stories of Their Old Home*

the kitchen. We just got upstairs and I put my foot across like that—I was opening the laces. Well holy jumping God. We thought the side of the house came in. And this went through the house, same as you took a 1700-pound horse and went right down through the hall, right down into this old kitchen. My mother-in-law said to me, "John R., there's somebody in." "I'll tell the world there's somebody in. I'll go down." Her grandfather's tool chest was over the attic; little wooden mauls in it they used to have long ago to drive pins. I went over and got this maul, boy. She followed me down with the lantern. Looked at the door. Same as I left it. Same as I left it. There was a little place underneath the stairs there. Opened that. I went underneath that and I searched it. Searched every inch of the house—well, the old kitchen you couldn't get in there; I had it all boarded up. We searched every bit of down below—nothing. Went upstairs back. I just set on the bed boy.

BESSIE: The little dog.

JOHN R.: Oh, the dog. Yes. The dog came upstairs. And he was so scared he went to get in the bed and he hit his head in the bed and he jumped back and he dove and he went underneath the clothes. And he stayed there. Well, we went upstairs. And Mr. Man went through. And he took the same thing going out with him.

BESSIE: Yeah. Came through the dining room, down the hall. He was just like a horse that would have iron shoes on him. And the house shook, just shook. The bed shook. I was sitting on the bed and the bed shook when he went through the two doors. Went right back the way it came. That's a true story.

JOHN R.: Anyway, one night, this MacNeil came over. Aw, they all knew we were hearing things in the house. And MacNeil came over and this night we were talking. And this man came in the door. I guess he was six foot, four if he was one inch. And he filled the door. He just filled the door there, coming into the dining room. And he was there and he was staring right at me. He had this long slicker on right down to his ankles. And he had his slicker all closed up. And he had two straps and two brass big buckles for those straps to go into to keep it shut. And he had a cap on him—I'd say it was a captain's hat—with a great big badge in front of it. And he stood there for about twenty to twenty-five minutes in the door and I was watching him. And MacNeil jumped from his chair and he went over behind the stove. And I was watching the man, see would he move. And whatever happened I took my eyes off the door, I went to look at something and I looked back and there was no man. So MacNeil wouldn't go home alone. And the lantern was on the table there and he went and he lit the lantern and I told him I wasn't going over there. It was as bright as day outside. "You're coming," he said. And MacNeil's a man not scared of nothing. So, I had to go with him. Walked along the road—the lantern between us—to his place. I put him in the kitchen. I left the lantern there and I walked home. Somebody would have thought I was crazy with a lantern, the night as bright as day. Went to bed. And that was it.

BESSIE: That was it for the night.

JOHN R.: That barn was about as far as this trailer from the house. I came home from Margaree with a load of hay. I go in the threshing floor—open the threshing floor doors and I drove in—took the horses out of the wagon and I put them in the stable. Fed them and went in the house. Bessie said, "John R., I didn't milk the cow." "Well I told you Bessie to milk those cows before dark. Not to be going near that barn after dark." So there was no milk for one of the children—one of the babies. So we had to go. And the lantern was in Upper Margaree. I left it up there. And we went out, took a handful of matches. And got our way and got the cow and I milked the cow. Told her, "I feel funny. There's something wrong here." And she never said a word. Left the cow and went out and I shut the barn door. And there was a hollow right near the barn close to the door. And it was always full of water. And here, I had my head down and I was walking. And I looked and I said, "Bessie, look where you're putting your foot." There she was, she was going to put her foot right on a man's throat. And she looked and she started squealing and hollering. I went straddle legs on the man. And I told her, "Go in the house. I'll hold him here. Go in." She wouldn't go. She started screeching and hollering. And pulling me. I said, "Go, go in. I'll find out who he is." He had a khaki pants on, a pair of brown shoes and a jacket. Nope, she wouldn't go in. So I had to go in with her. And my mother-in-law came out with me. And when we went out there was nothing.

BESSIE: And it was so funny. When we went out it was so dark that you couldn't see your hand ahead of you. And when we came out of the barn, everything was so bright that you could see him so plain. And I can see him there yet. And I was just picking up my foot—I can see him yet lying down in the water. He had his hand under his head. And it was his head, mostly, that was in the water. A big puddle of water. I didn't know him.

JOHN R.: The same man I saw in the doorway? I wouldn't say yes, and I wouldn't say no.

BESSIE: What was so funny, how bright it was. I said when we were coming out of the barn, "Gee, didn't it get bright!"

JOHN R.: When I left that place, John Simon took it—and I told him to be careful, not to go near the barn after dark. He said, "I know everything that you were hearing." John Simon was from Cape North. Wasn't scared of nothing. Didn't care what it was or where the hell or what. "All right," I says, "you'll see for yourself. But," I said, "keep out of the barn." But he was hearing things in the house himself—John Simon was hearing things and he was telling us. John Simon was fishing—and this night it was raining and pouring and his wife wouldn't go for the cow. I would not blame her a bit, raining and pouring. John Simon came home and no cow and he had nine or ten—he had ten kids. And they were only small. Well he had to go and get the cow. He got the cow. Put her in the barn. And he went back home to the house. When he came back, boy, this animal was in the drain. It came from behind the cows and the horses. His two eyes, John Simon said, his two eyes was a fire as big as buckets and fire coming out of his nostrils and out of his mouth. The wagon was across the horse stable door, little ways from it. This animal was coming out and John Simon start backing out—and the stretcher of the wagon caught him right in the knees, and turn a somersault on him. He said that beast went right through the wagon; he said it went right down into the brook. The next morning I was going over and John Simon was out. He had a bottle and he was slashing at the barn with this. I seen him in a couple of days. I said, "What were you doing when I was going over the other morning there, you had a bottle." "Aw," he says, "you had the truth, John R. The devil came out of there. You'll never catch me again in the barn."

BESSIE: He was splashing holy water.

JOHN R.: Yeah. He thought he was going to put the devil away, but I don't think he did. And in two days time John Simon packed up and moved and went up to Cape Mabou.

I don't know what it all might mean. I don't feel any of it was trying to do us harm. No, not a bit. Didn't hurt me, didn't do nothing... Fred MacIsaac, himself, and Joe MacRae was up there. They're both dead. When we'd go to bed, we'd take the lamp with us upstairs. And when we'd put the lamp out, they'd watch. When we'd blow the lamp out they'd know, well, they're in bed. Down the kitchen and the front room and dining room would all light up. What was doing it I don't know. They didn't know.

BESSIE: The house was torn down.

JOHN R.: I tore it to pieces. I found a glass jar down in the silling. Full of ashes. I took it up here. And they went out of their minds. They said, "Throw that in the brook. Get out, get with it, get, get. That's somebody that died. And he was burnt." I said, "You're crazy." I went and I threw it in the brook and the bottle went to pieces and the ashes went down the brook. I hauled a piece of the house up here. I had it below there, had it for a barn. Tore it apart. All went. Nothing ever happened. The old barn fell down. Nothing ever happened.

BESSIE: Whatever it was, it was somebody that was... troubled.

# Evidence of Early Man on Cape Breton

## An Incomplete History of Cape Breton Indians
*by John R. Erskine*

As I could not learn from books about the predecessors of the Micmacs, I asked any older Indians whom I met. Those of the southwest knew nothing, except that one said that the Micmacs had driven the Maliseets from Bear River. At Pictou Landing a very helpful Indian told me that the Micmacs had found the Red Indians in Cape Breton and had driven them out to Newfoundland. At Whycocomagh I was told the same. The "Red Indians" were the Beothuks of Newfoundland, whose men and women covered their hair, face and clothing with red ochre. Old Indians told me exactly the form of the Beothuk winter house, dug into the ground and with a groove for each sleeper, but all agreed that no such hollows had ever been found in Nova Scotia. For some years I thought that the "Red Indians" were the "Red Paint" Indians, also called "Archaics" and "Laurentians." They were called "Red Paint" because their graves contained only a few of their tools and an amount of red ochre, but so were the graves of many other Indians and as well also on the Cave-Men graves in Europe. Some of these Laurentian tools were illustrated in a book on the Beothuks. Gradually it came to me that no one knew anything about the Beothuks except in the last years before their destruction. I had to attempt to dig for their history.

My first effort was at the well-known camp at Little Narrows. It had suffered from the building of a mill, and thereafter by digging for curios. I found some bits of Indian pottery and broken tools among gin bottles, but I was looking for a home which would give me an idea of the people who had used it. There were no bones to tell of hunting, but bones do not last in this limeless soil unless shells come to remedy it. There were oysters in the water beside the camp, but only four oyster shells appeared in the site—and these had been used as scrapers. At last I found two-thirds of a wigwam site, the other one-third having been destroyed by a building. The depth of the site was never more than six inches, but the few

*John Erskine.*

arrows or spear points were of three cultures: the uppermost Micmac, below it another belonged to the Shield Archaic, and below this was a point of the Archaic (or Laurentian), not less that 3000 B.C.

## The Laurentians

This tribe reached Nova Scotia at about 3000 B.C. They seem to have come by way of the Great Lakes, but their tools and their artistic sense suggest contact with the Eskimos. Their canoes were dugouts—the logs dug by means of fire, the charred wood cut away with stone gouges, and then the inside was scraped with a broad chert scraper. In the winter they hunted moose or deer in the snow, their lances tipped with points with triangular stem which would inevitably leave the point in the wound. They must have had snowshoes, but no trace of these has been found. With the coming of spring they moved down a river to a convenient place to catch smelts, gaspereaux or salmon as they came up the river. Their nets were weighted, at first with square flat stones with opposite notches, but later with neat plummets. Later they might move out to the sea. They did not eat shellfish and had no pottery. They made a few small stone-carvings of fish or turtle, but their specialty was the making of slate knives which varied from simple fish-knives to elaborate or long knives not intended for use.

Our study of their sites in Cape Breton has been poor, as the few camps had been ploughed. One was in Scotsville and another at Margaree Forks. By 2000 B.C. Laurentians were established in Newfoundland, but a diminishing part of this culture lingered in Nova Scotia for another thousand years.

## The Shield Archaic

This culture had been first discovered far north in the Canadian Shield. For many years this culture was not mentioned in books, perhaps because instead of a standard type of points, it had many and uncertain ones. In Ottawa it was decided that the more interesting finds from Little Narrows were of this culture. At the same time I had noticed that the larger tools from this site were similar to "Beothuk" tools found in Newfoundland. Could this be the people driven away by the Micmacs? At this time, about 400 B.C., a number of strangers landed in southwest Nova Scotia, and this band seems to have come from New England. Some ate clams and others only oysters. The Shield Archaics did not eat either. The other bands made Owascoid pottery, suggesting contact with the Iroquois. The Shield Archaics had no pottery.

On the face of a sandy low cliff by the beach was a strip of black. We dug it, and found that it was the grave of a woman. Nothing remained except two teeth. The molar was flat on top, which showed that she had not been eating clams, as the sand in clams scoops out the molars. The incisor had been worn down to the base. This is usual among Eskimo women who must chew the fat out of skins. It seemed possible that all these newcomers had been in contact with the Iroquois and had preferred to be farther away from them. Some had even started an industry of smoked clams, a practice among tribes in Maine. One last campsite of the Shield Archaics was excavated by Dr. MacDonald on the North Aspy. The Micmacs are a branch of the Algonkian Abnaki of the Laurentian shores. It seems that the Mohawks, the most dangerous of the Iroquois tribes, were also stretching their country eastward as far as good agricultural land could be found. The legends of the Micmacs include raids which describe the Iroquoian longhouse accurately. Another story tells of a summer of planted corn, and then the harvest was all eaten, leaving no seed for the coming summer, so farming was ended. Other tales tell of the battles in which the Micmacs always triumphed—but it seems more likely that the Micmacs were gradually pushed southward. Their arrival seems to have been not much from 1000 A.D. The story of the driving of the Red Indians out of Cape Breton fits the period well, though not of the Beothuks. At that time there was the shellfish culture in the south half, but shell-heaps stop abruptly at Merigomish and Musquodoboit, as though here was a dangerous line. It seems that the Micmacs divided, one party taking the south, the other the north. The Micmacs had the advantage of bow and arrows. They did not kill women of other tribes but added them to their families. In the south the women had been accustomed to shellfish and to making Owascoid pottery. We find the Micmacs of the south eating clams and oysters and making pottery in both techniques of the Owascoid and of the Cord-pots of the Algonquians. It seems that the Micmacs had not eaten shellfish at their home. Those who went to the north acquired women who knew nothing of shellfish and nothing of pottery, so their only pottery was the Cord-pots, as made by Micmac wives.

## Unknown

There is a great deal that we do not know. In 9000 B.C. a band of Clovis hunters made their base on the sands of Debert, Nova Scotia, coming with the caribou in the spring and going back before the winter and following the caribou. During the summer, wandering hunters lost spear-points or dropped broken ones. One has been found in Kings County, and two broken ones in Prince Edward Island. Probably at that time the crossing from Havre Boucher to Paddy's Island was still passable. It is not impossible that a random Clovis might turn up in Cape Breton. There still remains the Plateau (the Highlands) where no one has studied the Indian trails to see the remains of the bands which spent the summers there hunting for caribou.

## Discovery on Ingonish Island
*told by Dr. Ronald Nash*

*Shortly after we received John Erskine's record of the status of information about Indians in prehistoric Cape Breton, archeologist Ron Nash made a significant find at Ingonish Island. In the summer of 1975 he and his staff had a chance to search a portion of the Plateau (the Highlands), the area to be cut over and flooded by the Wreck Cove Hydro-Electric Project. They found the area too overgrown for effective search, but tried other areas, mainly along the coast, and made a find that begins to fill the gap between 9000 B.C. and 3000 B.C. that John Erskine points out. Dr. Nash believes it will rank as one of the major finds in Nova Scotia.*

Here's how I found the site. I have a map out of Hoffman's thesis [B. G. Hoffman's *The Historical Ethnography of the Micmac of the Sixteenth and Seventeenth Centuries*]. And there's a place called Geganisg, which is a Micmac name meaning "remarkable place." It's at Ingonish. I figured there must be a site there. I went out to Ingonish Island, got off the boat and started looking along the bank there, where there was some erosion taking place. And I saw these flakes, chipping debris, eroding out of the bank. Now when you manufacture stone tools, you start with a huge block of stone and you end up with some small part—and in the process you throw away a thousand flakes from the process of just chipping it into shape. Just waste pieces. This is the kind of material that I first saw.

So I call the site Geganisg—and it is a remarkable site. In parts it appears to be a quarry site. There's an outcrop of basalt on the island and people could go there and manufacture their stone tools. Some of the other functions of the site I'm not sure of. I'm not sure why people were camping on the Island. I want to talk to geologists and find out whether the island might have been connected to the mainland at the time the site was occupied. On the other hand it might have been a particularly good place for codfish. This was the case for the whole Ingonish Harbour at the time of Louisbourg—a fantastic codfish place. Unfortunately there's very little bone preserved at this site, so it's difficult to say just what was going on there—but it was a large site and people were certainly living there over centuries.

You're holding a point that I would say is something on the order of 8,000 years old—something that's not far removed from the Clovis points, typical of the Debert site. Now the Debert site dates 10,000 years ago. This point is slightly smaller than the Clovis and it's only fluted [a characteristic deep groove] on one side—and I would say it's slightly later. Fluting is definitely a characteristic and in fact it's a very

*Left: Dr. Ron Nash. Below: Fluted, Clovis-like point, about 8,000 years old.*

*Part of the crew digging at Ingonish Island site.*

delicate operation to extract that kind of flake from a very narrow striking platform. These early points are characterized by not crude stonework as you might expect but excellent stonework. The main kind of tool found are large knives, stone knives. Knife is a kind of blanket term that covers a lot of functions. I'm finding hundreds.

*Then they were used in the place they were made?*

Yes.

*And people were coming here?*

Yes. The projectile points suggest some time range. I would say probably two or three thousand years. We were digging down at the thirty centimeter level today—and when you see that much stuff and that much depth leads you to question just how much nomadism is there? Or was it as some people have defined it as a sort of base camp and people lived out from there?

What we are talking about is at least two occupations of this site. One is a Paleo-Indian, Early Man occupation with the Clovis-like point. And the other I'd call Archaic, and it forms a rather substantial range of time as well. There may be continuity in the general area. And, in fact, these things may fall one upon the other. There's no, say, stratigraphic breaks in the site. No occupation then sterile sand then another occupation—nothing like that at all. So I wouldn't reject out of hand the idea of local continuity and evolution.

*Are we confident we're talking about direct ancestors of the contemporary Micmac?*

No, we can't say we're confident. How far Micmacs descend

*These are of the Archaic Period (that is, before pottery)—about six to seven thousand years old. Evidence was found indicating continuous occupation of the island until 500 A.D.*

back is something the Union is very interested in from the point of view of their land claims. I would be favorable to the idea of a very lengthy time for the Algonkian-speaking people to have been in here—of which the Micmac are associated. As archaeological work increases in North America we are finding that you can make long, long-term connections. At least this site at Ingonish fills a gap. We knew about Debert at 10,000 years ago. We have a couple of John Erskine sites—ceramic sites—dating in the last 2,000 years. We had a site at Gaspereaux Lake of which nothing has been published but there are some artifacts in the provincial museum. Then there was a large gap you see between 5,000 B.C. and 10,000 B.C. I see this site as being extremely important because it fills this time gap. It's one of very few sites that has this quantity of material in it. I think it will remain one of the most important sites in Nova Scotia pre-history. It'll rank along with Debert and a couple of others.

The best scenario I could envision for the island would be for the government to take some interest in it. I see much more there than just archaeology. It's sufficiently important and of interest to all people of the province. I would like to see some sort of interpretation center set up—to display some of this material. Also, across the bay there's a French outpost. It's also a place where just thousands of gulls were hatching out—all spring. And it's a beautiful bird sanctuary. It's an unspeakably beautiful island.

# A Theory of Vikings on Cape Breton

*In the late tenth century, a Viking settlement was established in Greenland. Very soon afterward, a merchant named Bjarni Herjolfsson set off to supply that colony. He was blown off course and sighted new lands. Some time later, Leif Eriksson with one of Bjarni's ships deliberately set off in search of those lands. As the sagas report it, "By God's will, after a long voyage from the island of Greenland to the south, towards the most distant remaining parts of the Western Ocean Sea, sailing southward amid the ice, the companions Bjarni and Leif Eriksson discovered a new land, extremely fertile, and even having vines, the which island they named Vinland...." This is all reported in what are known as the Vinland Sagas—but the sagas are not sufficiently detailed to locate by the texts alone precisely where this new land was. Different people have argued it was places as far apart as Hudson's Bay and New England, and several places in between. H. L. Livingston of Marble Mountain is apparently the first person to declare that Cape Breton Island was Vinland. He feels he has gone as far as he can guided by the sagas alone. We present this discussion with Mr. Livingston to help keep his theory alive until proper archeological research can supply the artifacts proving the location of Vinland.*

*H. L. Livingston.*

All signs point to its being Cape Breton Island. There are so many clues combined. F. J. Pohl has been writing for years, trying to prove that Vinland was in Massachusetts—and it could have been. That's the tantalizing part of this whole thing. Any one of us could be right or wrong. We can only take the evidence and see how well the sagas fit the district. It may seem strange that no one has ever thought of Cape Breton before as Vinland. But it has never been proposed because to compare two persons, two things, or two conditions, you must be familiar with both. And the people so far who have been interested in the Vikings and wrote about them didn't know anything about Cape Breton. But I went to school and in the spring and summer I fished. Lobsters first. Then we set out a fish-trap to get the mackerel run. Then we went swordfishing. All the way from Scatari around to Flint Island. That's the way I got my knowledge of the Cape Breton coast. Weather conditions and so on. And that knowledge is essential to an understanding of the location of Vinland.

The first voyage of the Vikings in 985 A.D. was accidental. Bjarni was blown off course going from Iceland to Greenland. When he arrived from Norway at his home in Iceland, he found that his father and mother and whole family had gone with Erik the Red to Greenland. So getting the consent of his crew—he had to do that because they were going to stay in Greenland—and without unloading his ship, he set sail for the Green Settlement. And for three days they had good weather. And then they ran into a northeaster—north wind—and overcast skies—so he didn't know which way he was going—and the saga merely says that happened for many days. We don't know how many. He just ran before the wind. This is an important point with the sagas. I don't believe their ships could beat to windward or that they ever thought it possible to beat to windward—but they went cross-wind very fast. They were faster than anyone thinks. And if a storm came and they didn't know what direction they were traveling, all they could do was just leave a man at the steerboard and let the thing run before the wind. That's why they were so constantly getting hundreds of miles off course.

So after the gale blew itself out and he got latitude—they couldn't get longitude—he sailed for one day until he came in sight of a low-lying land that was heavily wooded. He left that land to port—so it must have been on the west side—and sailed for two days till he came to a second land and he got becalmed there and his crew wanted to go ashore—also

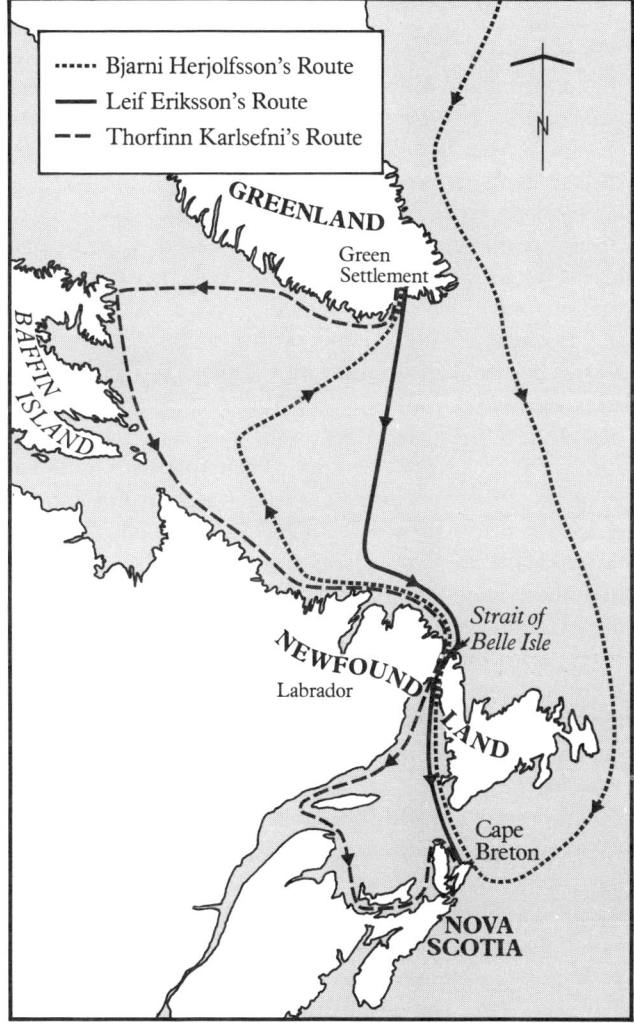

low-lying land heavily wooded—and I think that was probably the peninsula at Cape George on the west coast of Newfoundland. Now what direction they went depended exactly on the way the wind was blowing—and it's impossible for anyone that's not familiar with boats to understand the sagas. For instance, this Danish writer, Krogh, says that Helluland is southeast of the Greenland settlement. And then goes on to say that Baffin Island must have been Helluland. That's ridiculous. Because Baffin Island is not southwest of the Green Settlement. It's northwest. And moreover, I think that Farley Mowat's greatest contribution is that he shows almost conclusively that Erik the Red and all of his people were familiar with Baffin Island—they hunted there—so Baffin Island couldn't possibly be Bjarni's third land.

Now there's still something to be said for New England as Vinland—because when Leif travelled from Bjarni's second land to Bjarni's first land—Markland to Vinland—he ran before a northeaster. Now that couldn't possibly happen either on the east coast of Newfoundland or of Labrador—because the geography prevents it. But it could happen from Newfoundland to Cape Breton. Or at least from Cape George till he sighted the high hills around Cape North—which would be the first land he'd sight after leaving Newfoundland. Then if it was still northeaster he'd have trouble coming into either St. Ann's or Big Bras d'Or—but the wind changes frequently here. A gale usually starts from the east, southeast, and swings around to the north. So you have to understand the prevailing winds. You have to know the geography of Cape Breton and Newfoundland before you can make sense of the sagas. And then when you do that—everything falls into place. There are no contradictions, or practically none. Everything just fits.

The southernmost land was Bjarni's first land—that was the new land, Vinland. And my idea is that it was Cape Breton. It couldn't possibly—as far as I can interpret the sagas—it couldn't possibly be north of here. It could be south of here, in New England—certain things point that way. For instance, there's running before a northeast wind from the second to the first land fits New England, and the wild grapes fit New England. But there's no *Straumsfjord* [fiord with a very strong tide] in New England. There's no river flowing westward. None from Minas Basin or Apple River in Bay of Fundy right down to Florida—there's no river flowing westward. So that doesn't jibe.

Farley Mowat [who argues in his *Westviking* that Vinland is Newfoundland] thinks *Straumsfjord* was the Strait of Belle Isle—that's awfully farfetched, it seems to me. A strait ten miles across at its narrowest point and *knowing* that it was a

*A Theory of Vikings on Cape Breton*

strait—they wouldn't call it a fiord. They had their own names for channels and for bays, and a fiord is a narrow entrance with a hill on both sides. So I don't think it could be the Strait of Belle Isle. Now, Ingstad has proven that the Vikings were there [at L'Anse aux Meadows, Newfoundland, the northern tip of the Strait of Belle Isle] but he hasn't proven that that place was either Vinland or Markland.

*And you yourself see that site as a kind of a halfway house?*

Yes, it's a natural place for a halfway house. If they delayed too long around the Gulf of St. Lawrence and winter or October overtook them and they couldn't get back to Greenland on account of storms—that would be a natural place to have a halfway house. I think Ingstad has strengthened my theory. Because they are not the kind of people who would stop for two hundred years at the Strait of Belle Isle, with these two shores extending southward. The whole idea is absurd. They couldn't. They'd have to go down the strait and see.

F. J. Pohl [who argues that Vinland was in New England] says that *Straumsfiord* was the Hudson River. But in my opinion the sailing time given for Bjarni's return to Greenland rules out the whole American coast. It just couldn't have been done in ten days, without a compass and without any means of finding out where he was in overcast weather. They not only didn't know where they were, they didn't know in what direction they were sailing. They had to get a sighting off the sun or the north star to find out their location. If Bjarni had sailed up the coast of Maine, he would certainly have gone into the Bay of Fundy, because he was trying to go north and he certainly would have gone up until he saw that there was no exit—that Nova Scotia was not an island. Then he would have to retrace his steps down around Yarmouth and keep well offshore. And he couldn't travel at night except out to sea—it was too risky—and he was no Viking. He was a careful merchant-trader—and with all the islands and reefs along the Nova Scotian coast with a good strong breeze, he would have been lost.

But he wasn't lost. And he did return to Greenland within ten days. He did report finding three lands—the three lands could have been almost anywhere. Could be Massachusetts, but they are not likely to call it three lands unless they were separated by a body of water. Must be some distinct difference. That would give us Nova Scotia, Newfoundland, and Labrador. Now there is one contradiction to that in the sagas. The sagas report that when Bjarni came to the third land, he "saw that it was an island." Now he couldn't *see* that the Ungava Peninsula was an island. He couldn't *see* that Baffin Island was an island. It was, but they'd never circumnavigated it because of the ice. Now that supports the American theory, that the third land was Newfoundland. But remember that the sagas were written down almost two hundred years after they were first told. And if we substitute the three words "the second land" for "it"—that establishes definitely Vinland in Nova Scotia. Because as soon as they got through the Strait of Belle Isle, they would see that Newfoundland was an island.

Here in Cape Breton all these things combine. We have the low-lying land for Bjarni's landfall from Canso to Flint Island. Here we have the "rivers flowing westward" (the Cheticamp, the Margaree, and lesser streams). Here we have the long sandy beaches (*furdustrandir*) at Bay St. Lawrence and Aspy Bay. Here we have the "wild wheat" still growing along the beaches of the Bras d'Or Lakes. Here we have "*Promontorium Winlandia*" between St. Ann's Harbour on the southeast and Margaree on the southwest. We have also that remarkably accurate description of Bird Island and the entrance to Big Bras d'Or in the Erik the Red saga: "They laid the ship's course up into the fiord off whose mouth there lay an island. This island they called *Straumsey* (island of the strong tide). There were so many birds there that a man could hardly put his foot down between the eggs. They held on into the fiord and called it *Straumsfiord.*"

*Straumsfiord* is in my opinion the entrance to Big Bras d'Or. They would not call any inlet *Straumsfiord* unless it had an *exceptionally* strong tide—and this the Bras d'Or certainly has. With a full moon, it sweeps inward for six hours at a speed of approximately six knots. Then, with its volume and velocity increased by numerous fresh water streams, it turns quickly in fifteen or twenty minutes and runs outward even faster. There are many places on the coast where for a few minutes the tide flows in and out of a basin—Digby Gut is one of them, Hamilton Inlet is another one—but there is no other place where the tide runs as fast or as long as at Big Bras d'Or. And, moreover, the Norsemen used the plural in speaking of *Straumsfiord*—and there is, of course, another entrance on the South Side of Boularderie Island with the same six-knot tides.

The description of Bird Island is another good clue. They used the singular and spoke of only one island. But it would have been only one at that time. If you go between the two islands it's still only about ten feet of water at low tide. And in a thousand years with the Atlantic going up six to eight feet or perhaps two meters—then that would have been one island 970 years ago. The island with so many birds' eggs they

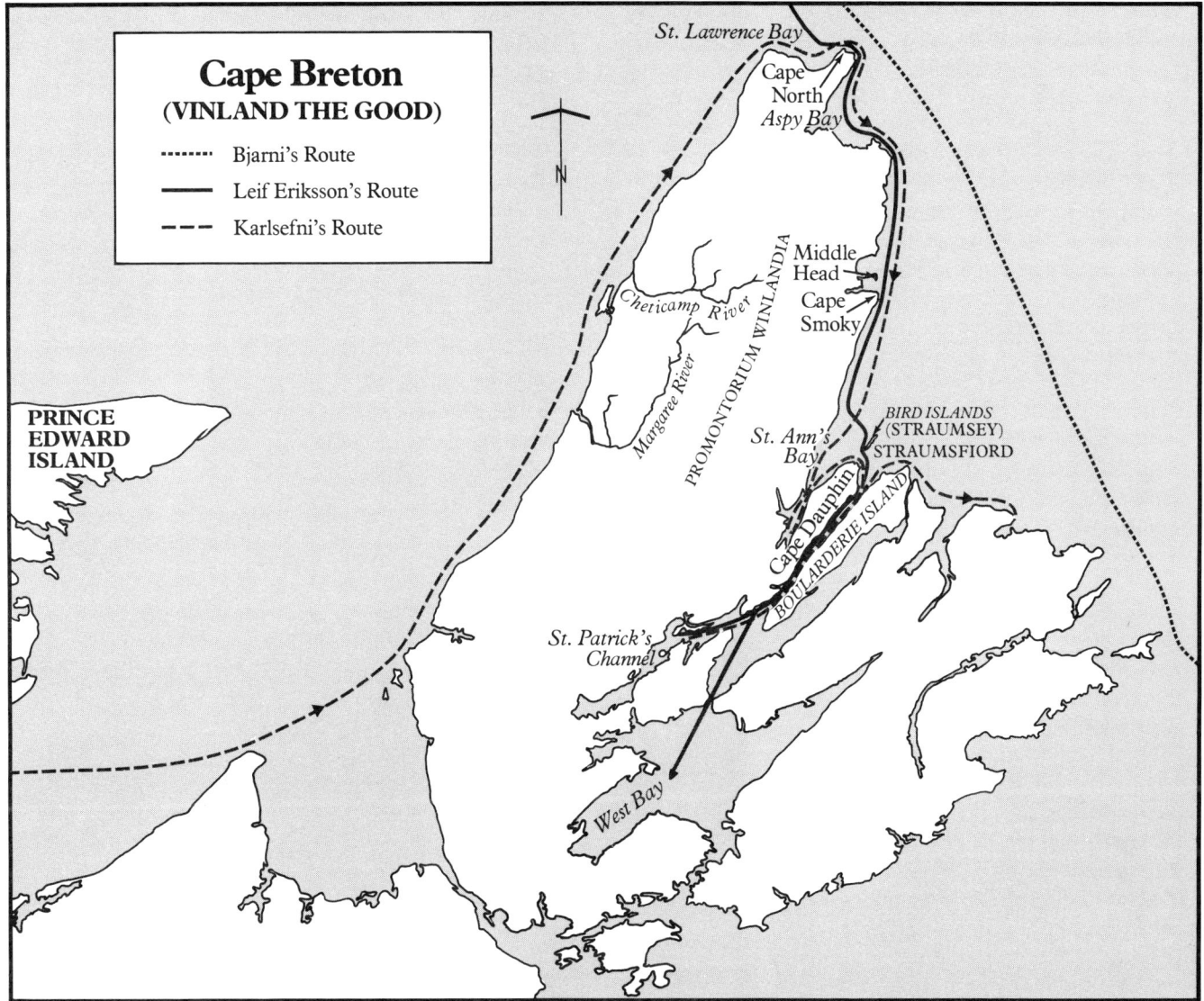

couldn't put their feet down between the eggs. They left the island—presumably they explored for a harbor. They were looking for several things. One was a place easy to defend. Another was a place with fodder for cattle—that they had to have. And a place where they could haul up the boat and build their house within view of the boat so they could watch it all the time. They hauled up their boats in the winter, even those larger ships.

Perhaps the most important clue of all is the ease with which Leif Eriksson found Bjarni's first land and subsequent expeditions found Leif's buildings. This would be possible without charts and from simple sailing directions, but it would be extremely difficult on any other part of the coast. We must remember that Leif sailed a ship that would beat to windward scarcely at all, and the prevailing winds were westerly, sou'west, or nor'west. If Cape Breton were Vinland, however, and Bjarni's "first land," all Bjarni had to tell Leif was to wait for a fair north or northeast wind and then steer a course to the sou'west until he hit the broad coast of Labrador, follow the Labrador coast, go through the strait [Strait of Belle Isle] and down the *west* coast of the *second* land (Newfoundland). In clear weather he would never be out of

*A Theory of Vikings on Cape Breton*  187

sight of land and would have the advantage of prevailing wind from Nain to Cape North.

It is easy to imagine Leif Eriksson coming close inshore at Aspy Bay after leaving St. Paul's astern; setting his square sail to port, and with a fair northwest wind, sailing along the shore to view the land, as closely as safety on a strange coast would permit; past Neil's Harbour, Ingonish, and Cape Smoky; then turning southward to investigate Bird Island (*Straumsey*). Here he would find thousands of birds, an easy place to defend against "the *Skraelings*," and plenty of fodder for cattle, but no harbor for his ship. He would then sail on "between the island and the cape," past Cape Dauphin and up along the shore through what sailors of a later day would call the "false channel," until the ship grounded on a bar at Carey's Beach. When the tide got slack to turn in, he would re-float the *knorr* and helped by wind and a strong tide he would sail up the fiord until he came to "a large lake." They explored Lake Bras d'Or to "the land to the westward." That would be West Bay. If you travel to the westward there's no other place that completely fits the description. When Thorvald (Leif's brother) came down, he spent the summer exploring right around Leif's camp. And if my theory is correct they probably explored St. Patrick's Channel pretty well. But the next season—they stayed there that winter—they decided to do further exploration and a crew of perhaps eight or nine set off in a longboat to explore to the westward in the Bras d'Or, to where they found many shoals and islands, and a white sand beach. Now the only real white sand beach on this east coast is at Marble Mountain. It's the marble from the hillside that's made it white, completely white. And there they found a corn crib made of wood that the Indians had used for storing corn. One translation says there were mountains there and the land was beautiful to behold—it's still beautiful. That's one clue. They explored to the westward, and West Bay fits the picture perfectly.

At the same time Thorvald set off in the large boat, the merchant ship, the *knorr*, and went south and then east along the land till he came to a cape where he ran aground and broke the keel of the ship. I think that was probably Smoky though I've no evidence of that. Then he came a little further to a fiord with a long headland extending out between two fiords—Middle Head [where Keltic Lodge is today]. He tied it up to land, so it must have been a very sheltered cove. There are both North and South Bay at Ingonish. They found Indians asleep under a canoe. They murdered all but one who escaped. Next day the Indians attacked. And although the Norsemen put up their shields along the gunwale of the boat for protection, an arrow came in between the shields and fatally wounded Thorvald. Before that he had expressed the wish to build his home here because it was such a beautiful place.

There are still problems. The wild grapes, for instance, are important. They are not here now but they might have been in former times. [Mowat claims that they grew wild in Newfoundland.] Grape pollen is so small and so rare that even a proper pollen analysis would still be like looking for a needle in a haystack. But I think I've gone as far as the texts will take us. We need to find artifacts. I see a settlement here in Cape Breton—but only for four years. Snorri, Karlsefni's son, was born here. That settlement was somewhere in the vicinity of Nyanza. I don't think Cow Point is necessarily the place—but the river mentioned is Middle River or Baddeck—or both. We can be reasonably certain because they found big salmon in the rivers and one of the translations uses the plural, speaks of rivers.

My whole object is to encourage further investigation. I'd be glad to be proved wrong if it can be done—but it can't be done from the sagas. And the sagas are all we have so far. My principal object is to keep people interested. I believe a proper archeological search will find something.

# Pirate Shipyard on the Mira River

*by David Dow*

Starting with known facts, we find that until the English and French arrived in force around 1720, all attempts at settlement in Cape Breton failed.

First, there was Fagundes, a Portuguese explorer, around 1521-25—some say he tried to settle at Ingonish, others at St. Ann's. It lasted eighteen months and is the first recorded attempt at settlement in North America. John Rut tried in 1527, and left. Jacques Cartier met fishermen between Newfoundland and Cape Breton and had an argument with them in 1534. Humphrey Gilbert in 1583 visited the Island but was persuaded to go to Sable Island and not stay in Cape Breton.

Stephen Bellanger in 1583 reported an unknown town of four score houses somewhere along the coast of Nova Scotia "upon a river side."

In 1594, Sylvester Wyet visited, was impressed by the natural resources and left. But in 1597, two English ships, the *Hopewell* and the *Chancewell,* found that men were living on the Island who came out in shallops and pillaged the *Chancewell* after she had been slightly damaged by a rock. They came and "robbed and spoiled all they could lay hands on, pillaging the poor men even to their very shirts and using them in a savage manner." Only the timely arrival of the *Hopewell* saved the ship and crew. Later they put in at New Harbour on Scatari where they met the "Admiral of the shallops" and persuaded him to get some of their stolen goods returned. This caused so much anger amongst the crews of the shallops that the ship took an early opportunity to slip away undetected and head for home, counting themselves lucky to have escaped with their lives. New Harbour on Scatari is now Eastern Harbour.

There are two very important notes in Nicholas Denys report on Cape Breton written in 1672—nearly one hundred years later. He writes that all the Indians had left the Island because all the moose had been shot and that he too had been burnt out of his well-established fort and settlement, some fifty years earlier. Lord Ochiltrees' Scottish settlement at Baleine in 1629 also failed as did Sieur de la Boularderie's farm.

Now the chance of so many attempts failing from purely natural causes seems remote, even allowing for Cape Breton's long winter, so it seems that there was some sort of conspiracy to prevent permanent settlement. Bear in mind the unknown town of eighty houses which was never located and the base for shallops at New Harbour. Someone *was* living on Cape Breton during those two hundred years and they could have driven the Indians away by usurping their hunting grounds. But, why the secrecy?

In 1974, R. MacKinnon, a scuba diver from the Mira area, told me that he had located the Old French shipyard in the Mira and escorted me on a tour of it. I was so impressed with the workmanship that I immediately went to Louisbourg to find out more about it. To my astonishment, there was no record of the shipyard in the archives and I was assured that it was not French. The shipyard must have cost a fortune to build (I will describe it later), so surely there must be a record of this expenditure somewhere, I thought. It took months of work but I found no mention of it anywhere; British, French, Dutch and Portuguese archives yielded nothing.

Enquiries among local families proved frustrating. They knew about the shipyard which had ceased operation around 1810; between 1810 and 1820 it had been briefly used as a sawmill, but abandoned because of ghosts!

Then came the breakthrough. Talking with first one and then another of the older families along the Mira, it came out that their great-grandfather was the Mira Pirate. Hearing this so often I jokingly remarked that the Mira must have been a nest of pirates!

About fifteen miles from Mira Gut down the Mira there is a carved stone memorial to Captain Kidd, obviously carved by someone sympathetic to him since the inscription reads "Deprived of mercy 170.." He was executed in 1701. There was a Captain Roberts of the Mira who sailed into Trepassy Bay, Newfoundland, and looted twenty-two ships in one day according to the people of Trepassy. In 1801 special laws were enacted at Halifax to protect shipwrecked mariners and the official Receiver of Wreck was given—and still has—powers to shoot-to-kill anyone refusing aid to shipwrecked seamen. Tough laws for tough times. Pirates raided Sable Island even when Rescue Stations were established there. By 1830, so many buoys had been cut loose around Cape Breton that extreme penalties were ordered for anyone approaching a navigational buoy. It is still illegal to tie a boat to a Navigation Buoy.

So the very blurred picture begins to stabilize and we see that Cape Breton may well have been one of the main bases for pirates. If so, it would explain why settlers of any nationality were unwelcome since a settlement meant the advent of law and order.

Why would pirates choose Cape Breton? If you look into the sky on a clear summer day in Cape Breton, you can see the answer. At any time there will be at least four vapor trails visible as high-flying planes travel between America and Europe. It is on the main great circle route of the air and of course the sea too. Treasure ships bound for Spain, using the Gulf Stream and the Trade Winds, would pass a few hundred miles off Cape Breton. All the commerce of the Caribbean would be within easy reach as would Florida and the riches of the Spanish settlers. Ships voyaging up the St. Lawrence were less than a day's sail away, and the rich trade with Newfoundland was similarly placed. Strategically it is well placed to control the commercial lanes, and of course that is why the French erected the Fortress of Louisbourg and why, in the Second World War, Sydney was heavily fortified.

The pirates left few records of their activities, but those that did, refer to the safe harbor north of Florida called St. Mary's. Old maps show the Mira as St. Mary's River. Near Mulgrave is Pirate Harbour, and there are several other clues of this nature. But let's return to the shipyard in the Mira.

Even today you can walk along the north bank or sail on the river and not see it. Actually, it is on the south bank about three-quarters of a mile up from the sea, and you can most easily reach it from Brickyard Road.

The entrance as seen from the river is apparently a small cove, in tall cliffs probably fifty feet high, with nothing in it. If you go inside this cove, you find it turns sharply to the right and then to the left and is surprisingly long. Although it is now filled with silt it was very much deeper in living memory and was certainly deep enough and wide enough to take a ship of one to two hundred tons. Ships of this size could be towed around the first bend and would be totally hidden from view becasue of the trees on top of the cliffs. The canyon is big enough to hide at least three or four ships at once, more if they were smaller.

At the far end of the canyon we find a gently sloping sandy beach, ideal for careening a ship, to the western side. Centrally placed is a steep ramp, obviously man-made and big enough to handle ships of, say, fifty tons. On the eastern side is a long, beautifully constructed mill race at the far end of which is the remains of an axle of a water wheel. When we visited the site the stream feeding the race was dry and the race itself was full of debris, but the set-up was quite clear. Archaeologists told us that the water wheel was typical of those used to power a trip-hammer forge.

On the clifftops overlooking the river we found hummocks which could have been gun emplacements in exactly the right place to interdict the river. Nothing could have moved on the river without coming under the guns of these hidden batteries. The canyon was out of range of any warship at the mouth of the Mira or in Mira Bay because of the flat trajectory of the shot, and the forest which would have prevented observation of hits. Even if the forest had been set afire, anyone in the canyon would have been safe. It is almost impregnable to any normal form of attack by land or sea.

The canyon is sometimes called Echo Canyon, and we noted that when we were on the cliffs we could not hear our companions at the bottom, whilst they were in the inner part. Any sound made inside bounces back and forth between the walls and no matter how much noise you make, hardly any reaches the actual river. It seems likely that even when the trip-hammer was working, nobody on the river would have heard it.

It was, and still is, a mysterious and very secret place, and if I were asked to design a pirate shipyard, I could not think of any improvement which could be made to the site in the Mira. It is perfect for the purpose, so perfect, in fact, that I cannot imagine it being used for anything else.

Normally, a well-equipped shipyard would welcome business, certainly not hide itself away. There would be merchants, chandlers, shops, taverns, hotels, lodging houses, and entertainment of all sorts. Nothing like this existed near our shipyard. Around the area of all well-known shipyards the forest disappeared—being a handy source of timber; the forest on that side of the Mira appears to be untouched.

Far down the Mira are very old farms and presumably the pirates victualled the ships with farm produce from these, so it is probable that the entire area was organized for their benefit. The Mira farmers would have been well rewarded for their produce.

The forge is very interesting. In the early days of sailing ships, the only items of iron or steel were weapons, swords, guns, etc. Later there was a shortage of hardwood for knees and other essential hull parts and iron was substituted. Cannon needed frequent repairs because the acids produced by the exploding powder and the abrasive blast wore the touch holes until the loss of explosive power drastically reduced the range of the shot fired. They were continually being rebushed, and this required forged bushings. Mira is within easy reach of the coal seams which outcrop on the neighboring cliffs. A forge could get all the coal necessary without having to used charcoal. Doubtless their shacks were heated with roaring coal fires too.

Then too, the Mira never freezes completely. Occasionally, the entrance plugs with drifting sea ice in an easterly gale, but soon clears as the prevailing westerly wind sweeps it to sea again. The area in summer is frequently fogbound, and what better cover could a seaman who knows the coast require? There are sufficient islands and capes around the area which could have been used as signalling points for night approaches, safety for friends and in all probability destruction for enemies. Wrecking was part of the scene in Cape Breton until the latter part of the last century.

So I believe that this was the pattern of life in Cape Breton until 1720, when the British fortified Sydney Harbour and the

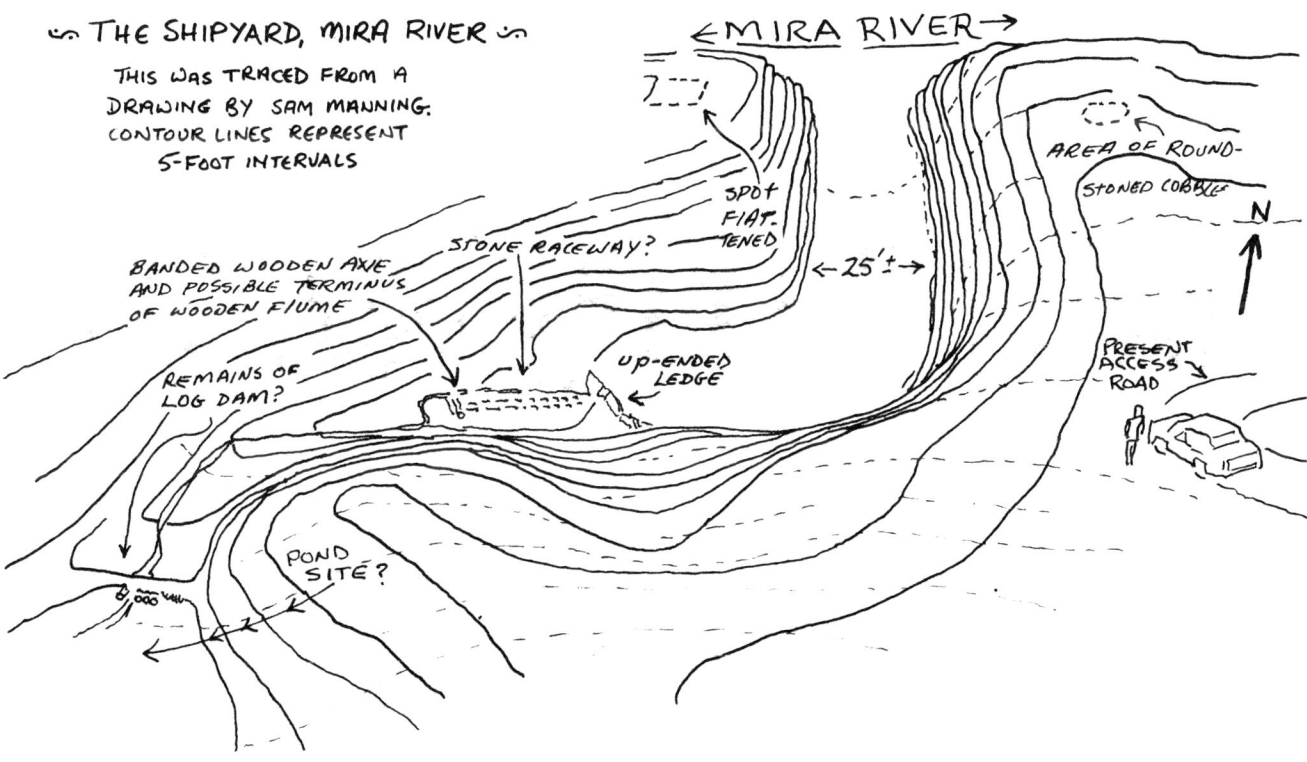

French built Louisbourg. The Fortress would not have interfered with the pirate base to any great extent. Pirates were of all nationalities, including the French. Deserters from the Fortress would find a ready welcome and a safe haven only twenty miles away, and no doubt much information about expected shipments to Louisbourg was obtained from deserters to everyone's benefit except the proper owners. Could this be why the fortress cost so much to build? As long as the British and French were fighting each other or someone else, the loss of a ship in good weather could be attributed to enemy action. However, when peace finally came in 1815, people would start asking awkward questions, especially if many ships mysteriously disappeared in the same area. Then, too, around 1800, settlements protected by British forces were spreading and commerce in the shape of coal mining came to the area.

There were too many outsiders for comfort and, most serious of all, the British had perfected the bomb ketch which could lob an explosive shell fifteen hundred feet in the air and drop it exactly on target up to a mile away. The descent of the shell or bomb was almost vertical and so the canyon was no longer safe from attack. Around 1810 the pirates left.

*In a recent conversation David Dow added the following comments.*

Actually, pirates started way back in about 1450, I would think, when the Portuguese under Henry the Navigator first sailed out this way, got to the cod banks off Newfoundland and started taking fish back. That's before Columbus. And a ship's captain had to sign a sort of bond and put up quite a lot of money before he sailed, guaranteeing that there would not be settlement of the land over here. And if they did not return with the men they hired, they either had to prove their deaths or lose their bond. Of course, the boats they came over in were very small—not much bigger than lobster boats today—across the North Atlantic in springtime, which isn't very pleasant anyway—and a lot of guys deserted. Their heads were on the block literally for desertion.

They ran away just in what they stood up in, and perhaps a knife—ran into the woods—and of course they had nothing. So over the years there were dozens of them, collected in the woods both here and in Newfoundland—and we know them as the Masterless Men. Their existence is fact. A boat would come ashore—like the *Chancewell*—and these Masterless Men would come roaring down for the sake of the boat and clothes and things they could get. They would kill the crew. Then once they got a boat it was very easy to become a pirate.

*But, David, you don't see Cape Breton as a place for buried treasure?*

That's right. It may have been buried earlier on. But the pirates faded out; they weren't suddenly chopped out as they were elsewhere—so there was no reason for them to bury their treasure and leave it there, provided they survived. I think they took it with them.

# Sowing Oats and Hay

New fields of oats and hay are rarely sown by hand anymore. And yet, even in this, there is traditional method to be observed. We had a field that hadn't been plowed in twenty years, and we asked Dan Murdoch Morrison to come and sow the oats and hay. The field was plowed with a tractor and then Roddie Hector MacDonald went over it with his horse-drawn spike-toothed harrow. Then Dan Murdoch came.

The problem, of course, is how to sow something as fine as hayseed and get it evenly spread. Dan Murdoch's method was to mix the hayseed in with the oats—the oats coming up

*Dan Murdoch Morrison at the barn with a bag of oats, a bag of hay, a tub for mixing and two buckets—one for water and one to carry the mixture when sowing.*

*The oats go into the tub first. Then sufficient water is sprinkled to make sure the hay will stick to the oats. Now the tiny hayseed is sprinkled onto the oats.*

Sowing Oats and Hay   **193**

*Above: The seed is thoroughly mixed until inspection shows the hayseed stuck to most of the oats. Right: Roddy Hector MacDonald helps Dan Murdoch carry the mixture to the field.*

tall and serving as a kind of nurse crop to the much more delicate hayseed. The oats will be cut in the fall and the hayseed will come into its fullness in the next spring and summer and be cut the first time that fall. Dan Murdoch figured the field would take about a bag (100 pounds) of oats. To that he added between three and four pounds of hayseed.

First he wet the oats very slightly, mixing the little bit of water throughout the oats. He didn't want the oats to swell and he didn't want the seed to stick together in clumps when thrown—he wanted just enough water to have the oats moist enough for the hayseed to stick to them and, literally, go for the ride. He sprinkled water on the hayseed and knifed it down into the oats with the ends of his fingers. Then he began reaching deep and raising and mixing handfuls, scooping it up and stirring, stopping now and then to look at the seed. He did this until he saw hayseed afixed to nearly every seed of oats. Then it was ready to take to the field. We asked Dan Murdoch what he would have done if he did not want a crop of oats and still wanted to sow hay by hand and evenly. He told us he would use the same method, replacing the oats with sawdust.

It is difficult to describe his every move. We hope the photographs help convey some idea of how it was done.

Clearly, there is room for a wide range of personal variation in this—but it was interesting to us that just as Dan Murdoch started, with his very first toss of seed, Roddie Hector said, "That's it there, boy"—and you could tell by the way he said it that it'd been a long time since he'd seen that done, and that it was being done exactly right. Dan Murdoch was out in the field alone. He started from a corner, working along an edge of the field. Throughout the sowing there was nothing random or wild in his motions. He'd take a step, pause, and throw—working his way back and forth across the field. As he moved across, he picked out marks in front of him and behind—a rock behind, say, and a fencepost in front of him—so as not to go astray.

The typical image of broadcasting—handfuls being thrown in a wide arc out to the side—was not the method Dan Murdoch used. The idea was to have the seed leave his hand in a spray—so that no two seeds would fall on the ground together. He worked from the elbow, not the shoulder. His aim was toward a narrow swath in front of him. He'd take up a handful of seed and begin (usually) with an upward and outward cast—the seed going about eight to twelve feet from him, the swath about six feet wide. The shooting forward on a single finger on the first toss—the thumb and other three fingers still holding seed—was a basic technique, whether tossing overhand or underhand. He might toss twice under-

*Three separate tosses and a close-up of how the hand is held each time. This sequence of tossing away a single handful in three swings was repeated over and over.*

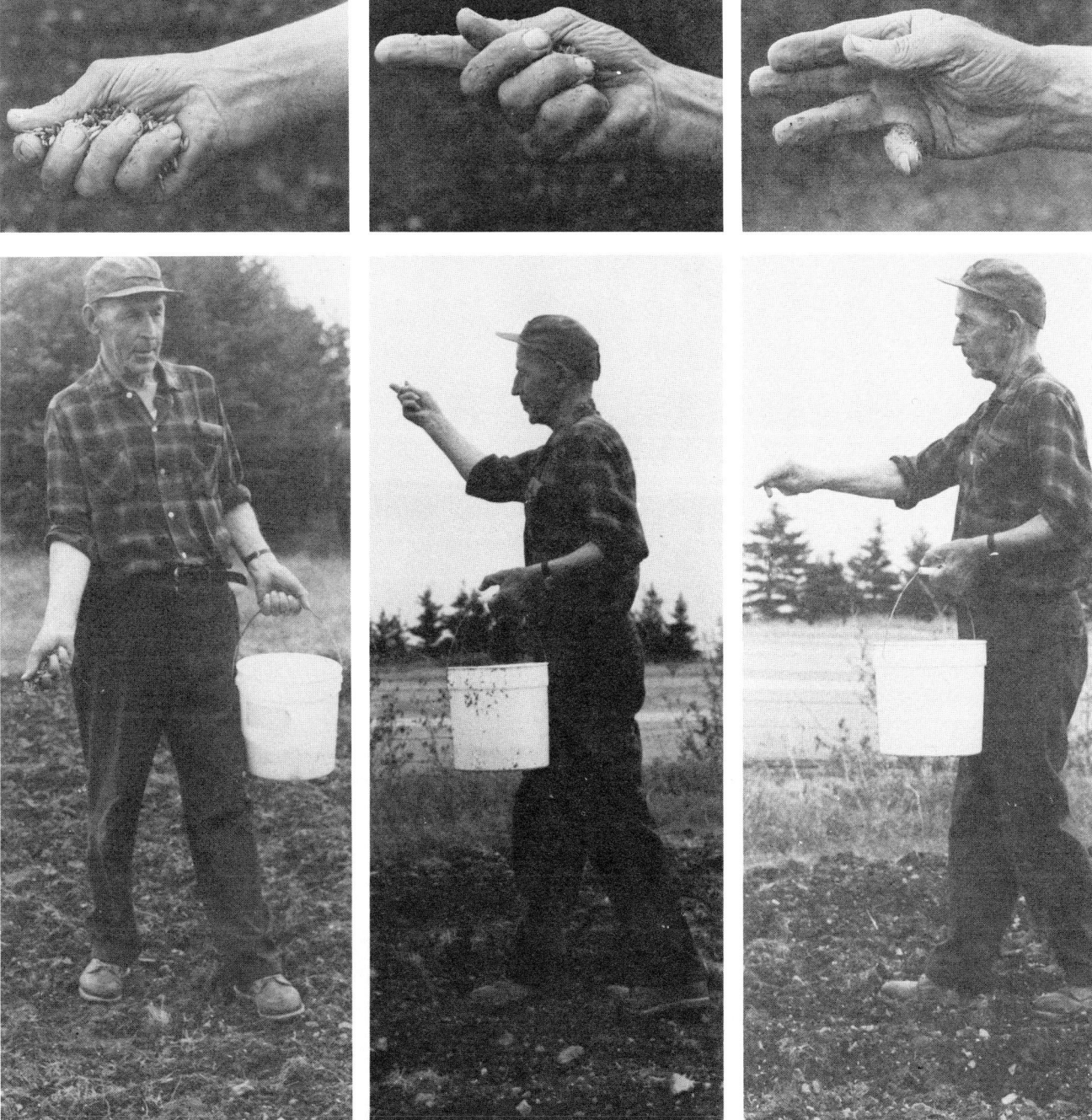

*Left: The seeds fly out in a spray, not a clump. Below: Roddy Hector harrowing the sown portion of the field.*

arm and if any was left in his hand, throw it away overhand and reach in the bucket for more. He'd take a step and pause. He'd make (perhaps) a long first cast of seed, underarm—and then firing forward from the elbow would release another spray of seed overhand and at a shorter distance.

Then he'd fire the rest of it, usually into a patch of ground that was seedless. He'd take up more seed and if there wasn't enough in the area, he'd do a few quick, circular motions of his hand, releasing seed as the hand turned, the seed falling in a way that filled in the obvious blank spaces among seed already on the ground. Then he'd take a step or two forward. And as he walked he'd watch at his side toward the area already seeded, and when he'd see a blank he'd fire at it overhand—a spit of seed filling the area, the seeds always neatly spaced.

Roddie Hector started in with the harrow again when Dan Murdoch was about halfway through the field. He followed Dan Murdoch's route up and down the field; and finishing that he turned and harrowed the entire field crosswise, burying most of the seed.

# The Dump Cart and Hay Truck

*Roddy Hector MacDonald making hay in a field below his home.*

*Above: The heavy wheels come out of the barn first. Then, with the axle in place, the pins go in to lock the wheels on. Now either the dump cart or the hay truck can go on. Below: The dump cart ready for use.*

198  The Dump Cart and Hay Truck

The dump cart and hay truck continue to be tools in Roddy Hector MacDonald's life. Both cart and truck use the same set of wheels. The vehicles are disassembled each fall and spend the winter in the barn—the huge wheels side by side and the steel axle upright, leaned against the trams and the hay truck; the cart box also stands upright. All the metal pieces are tied together (the ringed pins to lock the wheel onto the axle, the long straight pins to hold the trams or hay truck to the axle, and the rod that goes horizontally through the timbers of the cart box and the trams—it is on this rod the

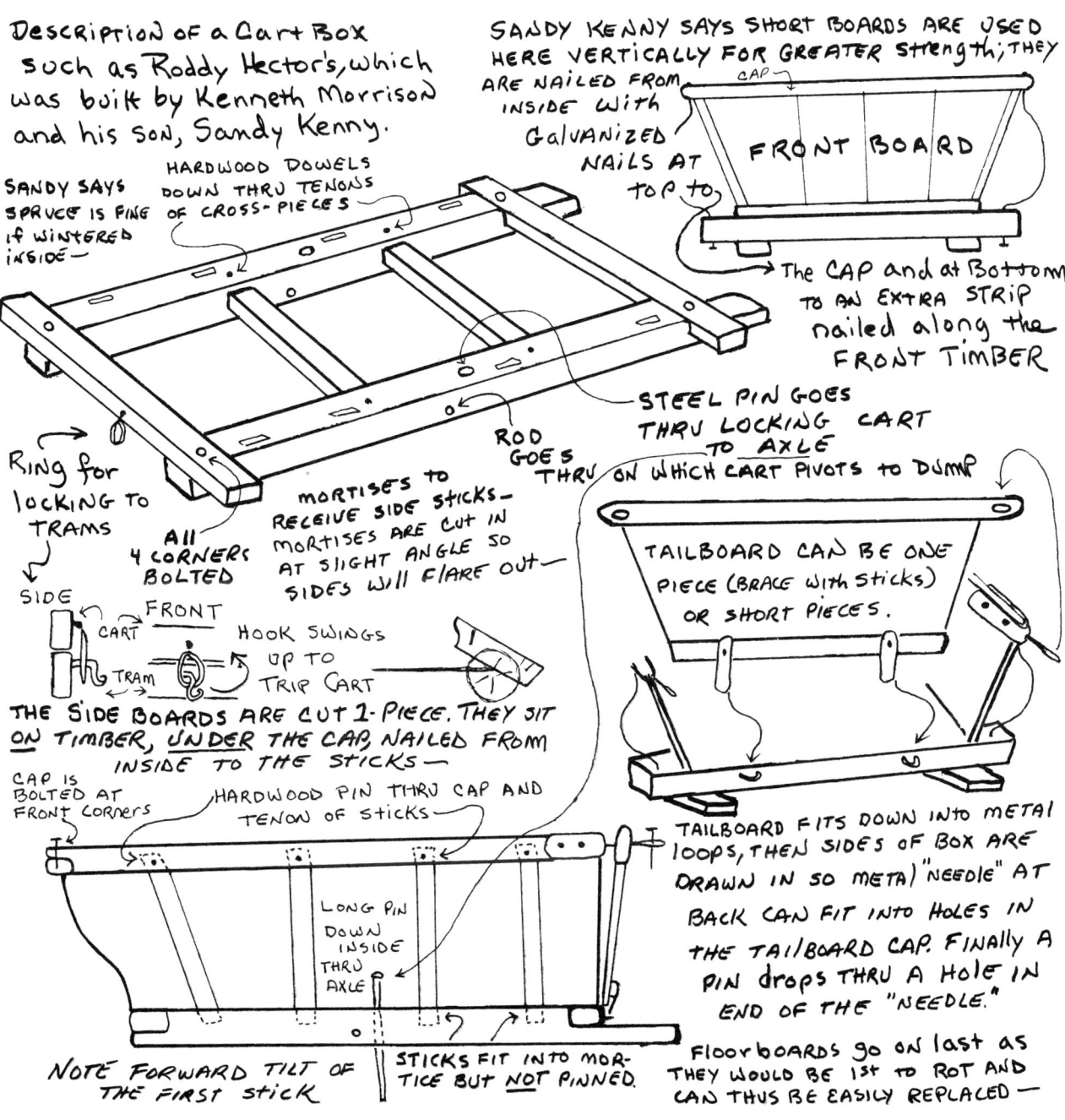

*The kind of wooden wheels and axles used before the high, spoked wheels came to the farm.*

*Above: The dump-cart box comes off and the heavy trams and planks of the hay truck go on. Right: Pins go down through, fixing the hay truck to the axle.*
*Opposite: The dump cart with a horse in the trams.*

cart pivots when it dumps). In the spring Roddy Hector puts the cart together, primarily to spread manure, and in late summer he exchanges the cart for the hay truck.

The hay truck is essentially a long set of trams—straight except for the curve where the horse goes between the shafts. The big timbers are usually cut from a single stick of wood that already has the necessary curve. Between the timbers are rough boards, widely spaced. A stick goes upright into holes bored at the four corners of the truck, and the sides are made

of two sticks and two boards. Enormous loads of hay can be transported if it is forked on properly—building up first at the corner-sticks and sides, tramping the load often and forking the hay to the front and rear to keep a balanced load.

Roddy told us that before the cart and truck and the large spoked wheels came to the farm, they used to make a trolley for hauling manure. The wheels were sliced from a hardwood trunk about twenty inches in diameter—the finished wheel about six inches thick. A hole would be bored through at the center and a wooden axle passed through. The trolley had two wheels but as it was low to the ground, it was not built to dump. You shoveled into the simple box, and you'd shovel out. The shafts would have a curve something like the rough drawing here. For the hay they would use a sleigh (essentially a drag) with runners nine or ten feet long—the longer the better—and straight shafts as shown in the photograph. There would be three beams nailed across the runners. The sleigh was a lot easier to load with hay than the hay truck but because it was so low it was just that much harder forking the hay up in the barn.

# A Story of Christmas Island

*told by Dan MacNeil*

I'll tell you one story and you won't believe it. And it's as true as anything.

There was a little girl, a MacKenzie girl, up in the rear of Christmas Island. There's nobody knows yet what was the meaning it had. She was quite a little girl, and in the nighttime there'd be a knock come at the door (knock, knock, knock, knock on the table top) and a little hand would show. The hand would show on the wall. And she'd go in what you'd call a trance. She'd faint. And she'd go across to the other side, she'd go to heaven. And do you know the one that was taking her around in heaven, by the hand, was Mary Magdalene. And when she'd come out of that trance, when she'd wake up from that trance she'd tell them everything. She'd tell them a neighbor of hers, she says, "My neighbor died just a few minutes ago. I saw him entering into heaven." And by gosh the next morning they inquired, boy, and the neighbor died at a certain time, when she'd seen him going into heaven.

And that was going on. They took her to priests and they took her to the bishops and everything, and it was no use. And she used to be like that every night. Pretty near every night, anyhow. And that Huey MacKenzie we were talking about, that Huey MacKenzie who had the Gaelic and everything, had a book, boy, stories—this knock came one night and the door opened and this hand came on the wall and Huey was sitting somewhere and he had a pillow and he just aimed on the hand—and the hand, boy, threw the pillow back in his face. That was going on, boy, and she was to priests and she was everywhere—no use.

And this once—this last time—she went in this trance and she went to heaven, and she always went around with Mary Magdalene in heaven—Mary Magdalene took her by the hand around heaven—and this old lady that died up there rear of Christmas Island, she was a MacKenzie too, she was in heaven. She was dead, she was in heaven too. And she told her, she says, "You tell your father to go to my son, and look in an old trunk in the attic and you'll find a ring there," she says. "And get that ring," she says, "and put it on your finger. And this'll never happen to you again."

By gosh, she told her father what the old lady told her. And he went down—it was only a couple of houses from them anyhow—he went down and told the man of the house the

story about his mother, that the little girl was talking to his mother in heaven. Well he says, "There is such a trunk upstairs all right." And the old woman, in heaven she told her, she said, "That ring is wrapped up in a rag. It is in the bottom of that trunk." And by gosh the man of the house went upstairs to the trunk and they found the rag in the bottom of the trunk with the ring wrapped up inside it. And she was only about five or six, and the ring was big, a woman's ring, and they had to tie that ring with string on to her hand. And she never saw anything after that. And she got married, she only died about three years ago.

She didn't want it but it was coming to her. And they never found out what was the cause of it. And this story is true.

# A Visit with Marguerite Gallant

Marguerite Gallant lives at Cheticamp, at La Pointe on the island. On Hallowe'en [1980] she will be ninety years old. "I came into the world with the goblin and the owls and the pussycat." She makes wines and vinegar, has onions in the ground as soon as the soil can be worked. Her home is known as a place where things will receive a welcome reception: shells and old dolls, photographs, bits of glass and rock, antlers, book ends—things that others do not want and yet would not want to throw away, these things they bring to her. And to what comes to her, she adds things she has made, such as dried apples and potatoes she has painted and dressed like animals and small men. And as things gathered here, and were loved by Margie and displayed,

*the very walls of her house became her creation, developing into extraordinary collages. And it is in these rooms she lives, welcoming whatever comes to her, discovering the best in each thing. And it is here we have visited her over the years. The following is taken from our conversations.*

If it wasn't for nature I don't think I would have bothered to learn to read. I didn't like to read. But nature, oh, I don't know, I couldn't explain to you what nature is. When you look at a thing. When you want to look at something that is really wonderful, you look at the wild geese when they come. There may be a dozen different flocks of them, and they all fly different ways—some fly straight, some fly in a vee, some fly in a triangle. And they always have a leader. And the minute that fellow the leader gets tired—oh, it is done so wonderfully. They just change that position. It's unbelievable. It's a miracle and a mystery. It's a Godgiven power of nature. That's what it is, to me.

There used to be a blue heron. He used to follow me. And never moved when I came near. But I guess he died. Then there was a little blue kingfisher. I used to have an old table but the wind just blew it away. It was rotten really because it was made with old planks form boats sunk to the bottom of the harbor here. And the little kingfisher used to come and sit while I'd be shelling peas. She'd sit there and she'd go br-r-r-r-l, br-r-r-r-l. And one day she brought me—I believe she did it on purpose—a little yellow pebble. It looked like a pea. And then all of a sudden I suppose she died. I have the pebble in a little box here. It's unbelievable. I will show it to you. This is what my little kingfisher brought me.

I like gifts. Yes. But what people bring me, they're not gifts. Everybody that doesn't want a thing, they bring it to me. They know I'll take it. Here's the picture of a person, I don't know who it is. And those are just beads. They used to be on old lamps years ago. They just bring them to me. They mean a whole lot to me. And look, my cousin he made all those kinds of knots. And a boy brought me that when they were first making the national park—a sea urchin, I think. You look at them and then I'll put them back. Now look, these little boxes, you may not think much about them, but they were spice boxes the old ladies used to have. See, it's sewed with wood. I've collected things since I was a child. If I had everything I ever collected you'd be afraid of it. And I never lose anything, anyone that ever gave me anything. I know where everything is.

The first thing someone gave me wasn't a gift. It was a dress. It was beautiful. Kind of all rose and pink. It was kind of tweedlike. In the olden time, the material was unbeliev-

*Opposite (top to bottom): Three views of the walls in Margie's home.*

able. Well, I went to school and I came home and my uncle and my aunt had come, and my mother had sent my dress to Mary Ellen, my cousin. And the first gift I remember I got was a set of dishes. It's not yesterday. Now what happened to my dishes? It was four little cups and a teapot and a pitcher. Well, one day I came home from school and a great bigmouthed woman had come and she had broken one of my little cups. And I guess it's the same time my mother had given my dress. All I had was a teapot and a milk pitcher. And three cups and four little plates. And, ah, I was heartbroken. I cried. Well, the woman who broke my first little cup, she died last fall. And when I came back from Pennsylvania after all those years I had to go to her and beg her pardon because I had a grudge against her for all that time.

Once I saw a little glass case and a little man in it in a California museum. There was a little loom and a little woman sitting at the loom and the little man was making a birch-bark rope. And it said below, made somewhere in Acadia, Nova Scotia. Well, look, if ever I envied a thing, that was it. I could have cried. It was the most beautiful thing. Oh, yes, I appreciate a gift. Well, look now, little children come and they bring me a rock—well, some would just chase them away but I love it. I have a bagful there. I have a big bag upstairs. I have two or three boxes. I have beautiful rocks. I'm not exaggerating. Now you tell me what *that* is. The children brought it to me years ago. They found it in the surf. I don't know what it is. It's so marked, and it floats. And here is a fossil. Take it off my knee, it weighs a ton. And look, that's a handmade brick. And if you were a witch, you would have to have this: it's a brain coral. They used to say there were all kinds of witches at The Point when the Jerseymen were there. If not, then there must have been coral beds there.

And these are all old pieces of wood. Every once in a while people come and they want a piece of wood. I give them this. Oh, I'm crazy. I'm crazy, you can tell me. It wouldn't hurt my feelings. I'm happy. Everybody's good and kind to me. You know, I think I'm the happiest woman on earth.

Here is a song we used to sing:

Mon père n'avait un âne
Tout comme vous
Semblable à vous
Je crois qu' c'est vous
Mon père n'avait un âne
Tout comme vous

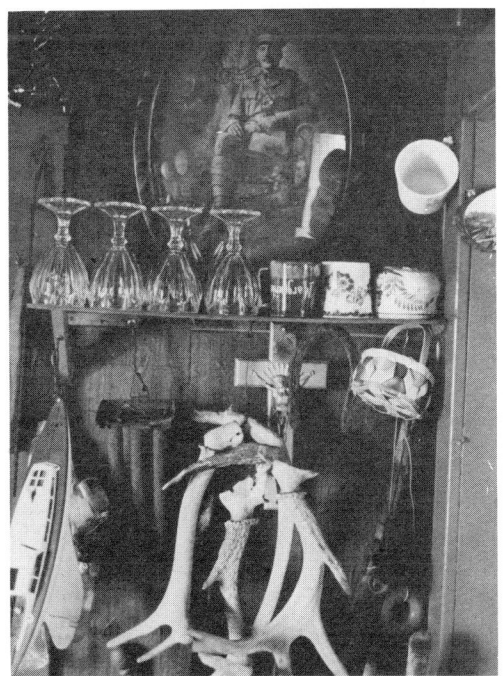

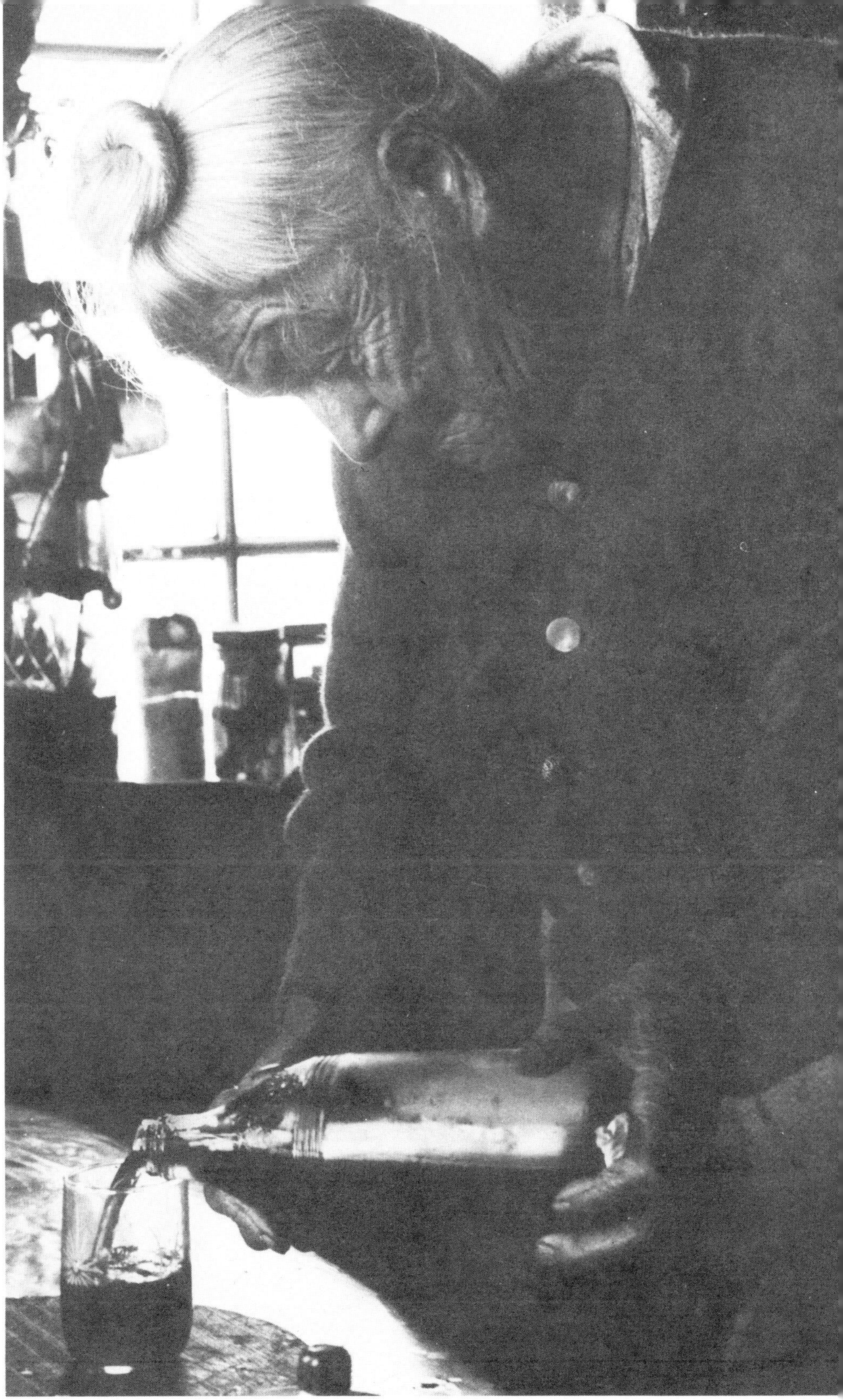

*A Visit with Marguerite Gallant* 207

Il avait des grandes dents
Tout comme vous
Semblable à vous
Je crois qu' c'est vous
Il avait des grandes dents
Tout comme vous

Il avait des grandes pattes
Tout comme vous
Semblable à vous
Je crois qu' c'est vous
Il avait des grandes pattes
Tout comme vous

 Do you know what that is? "My father had a donkey, just like you, the same as you, I think it's you." Now isn't that nice? "Well, now, that donkey had big long ears, he had big long teeth, he had big long tail, he had fluffy hair, he had big long legs, funny hooves—just like you!" Oh, that was the nicest song to me. Everybody used to sing it. And then you'd get the stick for all your nice singing. I used to sing and my brother used to say, "Hey there, if you want to be lonesome, why don't you be lonesome to yourself!" Now wasn't that a compliment? But I didn't care. I'd sing anyway.

 People ask me, what do you do when you're alone? Well, sometimes I tell myself stories, sometimes I sing, sometimes I remember all the old jokes in the olden time. Listen. Oh, this was years and years ago. I suppose I wasn't even born. They were having a party. And they were crying for liquor. And look, my cousin, that fellow could steal the eyes out of your head. They said to him, "You haven't got any brains." He said, "If you give me two dollars I'll give you all the rum you want." And an old man in Margaree used to sell rum. And this night, I suppose it was a night like tonight, I suppose it was kind of stormy. So there comes my cousin, a knock at the door. He said, "I saw your light shining and I was so cold, I thought I'd come in and say how do you do to you." And he says, "That's not all." He says, "Years ago you sold me a bottle of rum, and I didn't pay for it." "Oh," the old man said, "that isn't anything." "Oh," my cousin said, "I came in on purpose to pay you." "Well," the old man says, "you're an honest man."

 Then after he got warmed up, he stood to button his coat, the old man said, "Aren't you going to buy another bottle of rum?" "Oh well," he said, "that two dollars was all I had. I have no more money." "Well then," the old man said, "I'll give you all the rum you want to take home, because you are an honest man." Well, he went back to St. Joseph du Moine there and they had the time of their life, for two dollars.

 You know, these things should not be forgotten, the old stories and the old songs. Sometimes they come back to me.

Pourquoi me fuir, passagère hirondelle
Ah viens fixer ton vol auprès de moi
Pourquoi me fuir lorsque ma voix t'appelle
Ne suis-je pas en exile comme toi?
Ne suis-je pas en exile comme toi?

Dans le désert le destin nous rassemble
Ah ne crains pas de rester près de moi
Si tu gémis nous gémirons ensemble
Ne suis-je pas plus à plaindre que toi?
Ne suis-je pas plus à plaindre que toi?

Tu revoirras ton ancienne patrie
Le premier nid de ton amour helas
Un sort cruel qu'on fit ice ma vie
Ne suis-je pas plus a plaindre que toi?
Ne suis-je pas plus a plaindre que toi?
Ne suis-je pas plus a plaindre que toi?

Viens déposer ton nid sur ma fenêtre
Un jour cruel peut chasser si que moi
Viens deposer ton nid sur ma fenêtre
Ne suis-je pas en exile comme toi?
Ne suis-je pas en exile comme toi?

That's a soldier singing to a swallow at his window, asking, "Am I not in exile, just like you?" It's a beautiful song. That song was made from the Dispersion of the Acadians. They sang it long ago when I was a child. These are the kind of songs I'd hear right in the house. My mother was a beautiful singer. I think this is a nice song:

Qui est-ce qui me passera le bois
Moi qui est si petite
Ca sera monsieur que voilà
Oh, qu'il a bonne mine

Sommes-nous à la rive des bois
Sommes-nous à la rive

Ca sera monsieur que voilà
Oh qu'il a bonne mine
Quand on fûme au milieu du bois
La belle s'est mise à rire *(Refrain)*

Quand on fûme au milieu du bois
La belle s'est mise à rire
Quoi qu'a vous belle oh qu'a vous donc
Oh qu'a vous à temps rire *(Refrain)*

Oh qu'a vous belle, oh qu'a vous donc
Oh qu'a vous à temps rire
Je ris de toi, je ris de moi
De nos folles entreprises *(Refrain)*

Je ris de toi, je ris de moi
De nos folles entreprises
C'est de'n m'avoir passé le bois
Sans petit mot lui dire *(Refrain)*

C'est de'n m'avoir passe le bois
Sans petit mot lui dire
Oh revenez belle, oh revenez
Je vous donnerai cent livres *(Refrain)*

Oh revenez belle, oh revenez
Je vous donnerai cent livres
Ni pour un cent, ni pour deux cents
Ni pour trois, ni pour mille *(Refrain)*

Ni pour un cent, ni pour deux cents
Ni pour trois, ni pour mille
Y'a fallu plumer la perdrix
Tandis qu'elle était prise

Well, in that song there was a young girl and she had kind of a forest to cross and she wanted a young man to cross with her—and there was one there she liked him very much because he had a very good appearance. And then when she was in the middle of the forest she started to laugh. And she laughed and she laughed and laughed until the man asked her what was wrong. But by then they were out of the forest. She said that she was laughing at him and that she was laughing at herself and the foolish enterprise. That he had crossed the forest without opening his mouth, without saying anything to her. He says, "O come back, come back, I'll give you one hundred pounds, two hundred pounds, three hundred pounds." And she says to him, "I wouldn't go back for one hundred pounds, not for two hundred pounds, not for three hundred pounds. You have to pluck the partridge when she was well caught."

I like this song: "When my wife goes to marketing/a man by the name of Nicholas/used to sneak along and he'd go with her"—and the man would have to stay home—"They eat the best there is/and I have to pick the bones/if you were in my place my dear friends/what would you do?/would your heart be in peace/or would you be jealous?/would you lend Nicholas your sheet, your bed, also your wife?/I don't know if they're doing any harm/but I don't like it."

Quand ma femme s'en va-t-en ville
Pour acheter des provisions
Mon Nicholas s'y faufilé
Et moi je reste à la maison
Derrière chez moi font bon fricot
Moi par derrière je ronge les ous
J'ne dis pas qu'ils font du mal
Mais ça 'm plaît pas

Si vous étiez à ma place
Chere amie que feriez-vous
Auriez-vous l'esprit tranquille
Ne seriez-vous pas jaloux
Prêteriez-vous à Nicholas
Votre lit, votre femme, aussi vos draps
J'ne dis pas qu'ils font du mal
Mais ça 'm plaît pas

Par le trou de la serrure
Devinez quoiceque j'ai vu
J'ai t'aperçu mon Nicholas
Qui tenait ma femme entre ses bras
J'ne dis pas qu'ils font du mal
Mais ça 'm plaît pas

Now the last verse is: "By the keyhole/guess what I saw/I saw my Nicholas that was holding my wife between his arms/I don't say that he's doing anything wrong/but I don't like it." Oh, the ragtime songs. It's beautiful. But no one sings them. The children don't sing them.

I wish I could remember the story of Richard le Cordonnier. How did it go? There was a man and he was married to a woman and she was very very bad. And finally the devil came after her. So, he was a fiddler and a shoemaker. So after his wife was away for quite awhile, he became very lonely. So he started to hunt for his wife. First he went to heaven but she wasn't there. So he went to purgatory and she wasn't there. So he went to hell and there she was. He said to the devil, "I want the soul of my wife." "You can't have her," he said, "she's here for eternity." He said, "I'm going to have her anyway." "Well, if you're going to have her, you'll have to come in with her." "No, I'm not going in there. It's too hot. It's not a place for me, and I don't like it. I want a cooler place than that." So Richard has his bag and his fiddle and he said to the devil, "Do you like to dance?" "Oh yes, I love to dance. Waltzing is my favourite dance." So Richard begins to fiddle. And he plays for nine days. And at the end of nine days the devil was so overheated that all his fur was red hot. And so another devil came—and he said, "I want the soul of my wife." "You can't have her." He said, "If you don't give me the soul of my wife, I'm going to put you in my bag and I'm going to hammer you until the end of days." So he put him in the bag and he hammered on him—maybe a week, two weeks—but at the end of two weeks the devil was so flat he couldn't breathe. The story goes something like that. I think I can tell it right in French.

Il y avait un homme et une femme, l'homme s'appelait Richard, le cordonnier. Sa femme mourut. Elle avait été au paradis p'is il l'avions pas voulu là. Elle a été au purgatoire p'is il la voulions pas encore. Mais il l'envoyire en enfer et il la gardire. Ca fait que Richard le cordonnier n'aimait pas rester seul. Y se mettions en chemin pour aller en enfer pour charcher l'ᶜme de sa femme. P'is c'était un bon joueur de musique. Il arrive au paradis, sa femme n'était pas là, au purgatoire sa femme n'était pas là, mais en enfer sa femme était là.

"Que veux-tu? Que charches-tu?" Y dit, "Je veux l'âme de ma femme." "Ah, tu peux pas l'avoir." "Bien," y dit, "si tu veux pas me donner l'ᶜme de ma femme, j'm'en vas te mette dans mon sac."

Il l'a emprisonné dans son sac. P'is tout, d'un coup il y a un autre diable qu'arrive. "Qu'is qu'est là?" "Il voulait pas me donner l'âme de ma femme. J'l'ai mis dans mon sac. Eh bien, p'is toi si tu veux pas me donner l'ᶜme de ma femme, j'm'en va te mette sur mon enclume, p'is j'vas te marteler jusqu'à la fin des siècles."

Ça fesait pas bien. Là, voilà un autre diable qu'arrive. Eh bien, y dit a Richard le cordonnier, "Que veux-tu? Que charche-tu?" Y dit, "Je charche l'âme de ma femme et je veux l'amener avec moi." "Mais," y dit, "tu l'auras pas." Y dit, "Est-ce que tu peux danser?" "Ah," y dit, "oui, je peux danser."

Eh bien, Richard pris son violon p'is le vela à jouer du violon. Y dit, "Comme la valse est la danse favorite du diable." Le diable se mis la pointe du pied gauche en dedans et se mis à valser. Il valsit pendant neuf jours et au bout des neuf jours le diable était tellement échauffé qu'il en avait tout le poil rouge. Ça fait y donnir la femme à Richard le cordonnier, p'is les diable s'enfuirent dans le fond de l'enfer. P'is c'est toute, j'crois.

You know, I was very sick one day, and I was supposed to die. I was thirteen days on the dangerous list—and Leo came in to see me. I said to him, "After I'm dead I will follow you to The Point. And you will see my soul on pebbles, on grains of sand, on little pieces of straw—any place you look. I will be in front of you in fifty different shapes." And there I look. And there was Leo, crying. And I said, "Leo, I was going to tell you a story but in that case I won't tell you. You're ugly enough as you are." "Keep quiet," he said—and he was laughing through the tears. And in the afternoon another person came and I said to them, "If you came here to cry because I'm dying, go home." And then she was laughing, she was crying—and you know, she died suddenly afterward. And the nuns—I told them to get out of my room. They were all in there saying the rosary. But I didn't die. I wouldn't give them the satisfaction.

*"This is my cart. Isn't it beautiful? I want you to take a picture of it. That will be something for your magazine."*

*A Visit with Marguerite Gallant* **211**

# The Sinking of the *Caribou*

*Cape Breton Island was deeply involved in the Second World War. Sydney Harbour was the most heavily defended port in North America. It was in Sydney Harbour that the SC Convoys formed up. These were the convoys that were slower and more vulnerable to submarine attack. But these were also the convoys that carried the food and ammunition and everything else necessary to sustain the troops in Europe. To the men of the merchant marine, Cape Breton was the one place they would return to again and again, the place their next convoy would form up—if they made it across and back. A good many of them never made it. But the sinking of these vessels by the enemy was to some extent an accepted part of the war. The sinking of the* Caribou *ferry was something else again. She was a civilian vessel carrying passengers and goods on a regular schedule across the Cabot Strait, linking Newfoundland and Cape Breton. On the night of October 14, 1942, there were 246 passengers and crew on board. She was torpedoed and 137 died.*

THOMAS FLEMMING, *North Sydney:* The first sinking that we knew of on this side of the Atlantic was in the Cabot Strait in May of 'forty-two, when a German submarine sank a cargo ship in the mouth of the St. Lawrence River. Occasionally we were escorted by patrol boats of the Navy and they notified us on several occasions that we were being chased by submarines. We were ordered to change our course, take a zig-zag course. We did avoid them but they were in the strait long before the sinking of the *Caribou*—because fishermen saw them in the coves charging their batteries at night. We left North Sydney the previous trip and we were escorted by two naval vessels and we were chased from North Sydney to within ten miles of Channel Head, Port aux Basques. That was the Sunday morning before the sinking. And that morning after we arrived in port a paper boat out of Cornerbrook was sunk.

The night we were hit, the total complement of passengers and crew amounted to 246. We had a lot of servicemen on that trip—American service personnel, Canadians on leave, soldiers going home before they went overseas—and the ordinary passenger list. We had the escort vessel but the escort vessels were slower really than the ships they were escorting. We had a perfect night. It was bright, which probably led to the sinking. Because the Caribou was a coal burner and you could see that smoke for miles and miles. I was in the wireless room with my assistant, William Hogan of Carbonara—we were working till one-thirty. Then we decided we would have a sleep. Just as I was getting ready a tap came on the door and the captain came in. He asked me whether I saw the escort. I went out with him and we walked the bridge deck for probably half an hour. It was near two when I left him. We didn't see any sign of the escort. It seems I had just fallen asleep when I heard a thump—the explosion. I knew what it was right away. The ship rolled over to port and all the ceiling and wiring came down in the wireless room. We were all prepared as far as uniforms and lifesaving equipment. It was just a matter of to reach for it. The ship rolled over and

*Thomas Flemming.*

settled back. Hogan and I came out on deck. The captain was there. He was trying to get his coat on. I tried to help him to put it on. That was the last I saw of the captain. I saw him go to the bridge. Hogan and I went to the boat deck—one deck below—to release a raft. It wouldn't release... there wasn't much we could do. I saw our chief engineer, Jim Pike—he passed in his shirt sleeves. And I saw our stewardess who asked me where Number One lifeboat was. Apparently it was blown away. That's all the crew I saw. The second officer was on that watch—James Prosper—he was never seen after the torpedo hit. Must have been blown off the bridge.

By that time the ship was taking in water on that deck. It was almost up to my knees—the ship was sinking so fast we couldn't wait for this raft to release. I decided for myself I was going to jump overboard. She was going down and as she was going down she was steaming ahead just the same. Her engines were still working. The steam was just gradually leaking off. I jumped overboard. If I had waited any longer I wouldn't have a chance. I thought it was everybody for himself then, if you could get clear of the ship. I don't know what became of Hogan. He was lost. The ocean was cold but I didn't mind the cold. The excitement—I didn't feel the cold. I suppose the shock made that much difference. I tried to get away from her as far as I could underwater. When I broke surface all that I could see was a sort of fire. I thought it was the ship but the ship was gone. It might have been an explosion. It could have been a depth charge.

The escort vessel was up to us then and they were throwing depth charges all around. I didn't see any lifeboats at all. A liferaft passed me and I tried to get on it and somebody sang out it was overcrowded. Eventually I got on another one. I was on that five hours and we drifted five miles. And the raft was sinking. We could just keep our buoyancy by remaining still. It was overcrowded. We kept still and we kept our positions—otherwise it probably would have turned over. These are wooden rafts with oil drums for floats. They talked. They sang "Nearer My God to Thee." You could hear hymns in the distance. They didn't talk too much to one another. When daylight came there was nothing in sight. The escort was gone. We were sighted by a bomber. They dropped smoke flares for the escort ship to pick us up. It picked us up about eight-thirty and took us to Sydney.

MRS. THOMAS PEARCY, *North Sydney:* In the morning when I went out to the clothesline everybody kept looking at

*Mrs. Thomas Pearcey.*

me, looking at me. And I figured it was because I had been so sick. I had had meningitis and I had just got... well, I guess it was the first time I ever got outdoors afterwards. There was a haze. It was something like when the sun is going in eclipse—that greeny haze—like when it's hot and it's hazy—well that's how it was. And I wonder if it was the day, the kind of a day it was—it was in October—or if it was because so many lives had been lost. Who knows? My son was very young. He was only sixteen. And he was working at the Marine Railway—it was called The Slip then. And he came home to dinner at twelve o'clock and he said, "Ma"—nobody had told me before—he says, "Ma" he says—and he started to cry. "Did you hear the *Caribou* was lost?" And I said, "No. I don't believe it." And he said, "I don't believe it but everybody downtown says it's true." And I said, "I'm not going to believe it." And that evening I went outside and saw old Captain Critchell—he's dead now. And I said, "Is it true, Mr. Critchell, that the Caribou is lost?" And he said, "Yes, my dear." And I said, "I heard it, you know, but I would not believe it." Well, then you know anxious moments and anxious moments—and about eight o'clock my husband came home. He came in the house first. And it was my son I was thinking of. So young. And I said, "Where's Billy?" And I think I died a thousand deaths in that minute. You know, he came in without him. He said, "He just stopped off at a neighbor's to tell the woman that her brother was still living." So he came in then. And the house was full of people.

JACK HATCHER, *Neil's Harbour:* Oh, they got lies—lies that they put out about the *Caribou*—but I'll tell you the truth. When the steamer leave North Sydney to go across—you know where the Farewell Buoy is to? The Farewell Buoy up off Low Point—she's there. When he'd go to Newfoundland and he had to stop there—the war was on—he had to get his course from the Navy at Sydney before he could go across. He couldn't steer where he wanted to steer. He'd get his course, and then he'd go below—stay there till about four o'clock in the morning, before he'd come on deck. The captain. He'd go to bed. I know this is true because I had a friend, he was at the wheel, was steering. When he was to leave and go below, the captain said to his men: "This is the night we're gonna get it." He said that, then he went below and went to bed. And he's up—every five and ten minutes he was up. In the wheelhouse that night, could not rest. He steered across what orders he had.

THOMAS PEARCEY, *North Sydney:* The captain had a hunch, but he couldn't say for sure. He had a hunch she was going to be torpedoed all right but he didn't know if it was that night or some other night. I was up in his room at three o'clock in the morning and he wasn't in bed. He always used to go to bed after we'd leave North Sydney. He was up. I asked him, "What's the trouble?" He said, "Aw, I've got an uneasy mind. I think we're going to get hit tonight." That's the words he said to me. I didn't expect that from him. And he had two sons, they were lost that night. Chief steward, second steward, steerage steward, stewardess, three mates—all them fellows were gone. And all the engineers. Thirty-one of the crew was lost.

I was in the pantry when she struck. I had just cleaned up the place for the boys who would come on next morning. I had it all cleaned up and I sat down and five minutes to four, blippo! all the lights went out. Couldn't see. But I knew where I was to, I knew what way to go. Second steward—called into him that we were torpedoed and he came out of his room and he went down on the port side and I went out on the starboard side. He was lost and I was one of the survivors. When she got hit she listed over, took water aboard. Well, the people that were down in steerage, they never had a chance. They couldn't get up because she was all flooded with water. They were drowned like rats down there. But you're not supposed to close a door. Anything happens aboard ship you can't get the door open, it jams, see. And all them doors was closed downstairs. They were all warned that night—the captain warned them—be ready for the lifeboats and keep their clothes on, don't take off their clothes. He had an idea. He could have been saved—the captain could. He could have gone with Tommy Flemming. But no, he went down with the ship. There was no need of it. There was nothing he could do.

I got out on a raft—they had drums under them. I was on that raft four hours and a half. There was six of us—a woman and four men. That's all it would hold. You could not see anything. October, four o'clock in the morning, it was dark. But you could hear people screeching. All over. And then the cattle drowning. Three cars of cattle going that night—Number One hold. There were three hatches off to give them fresh air. They went down with the ship. There were oars on the raft but you couldn't do anything. When you started

*Jack Hatcher.*

*Thomas Pearcey.*

rowing she'd be going around like a spinning top. A raft is not like a boat, you know. We covered up the woman with tarpaulin, keep her from getting wet. The water was coming in over her—a little lop that night. We were all soaking wet. We didn't talk much. You had to watch yourself, she didn't tip over or you didn't get washed off. Pretty quiet. We were picked up half-past-eight in the morning.

It was my son who dove in the water for the baby. Yes. He had the baby in his arms. He had it about an hour and a half, passed it over to somebody else. That was the youngest survivor—about a year and a half old. Billy was in the water two hours. He had a lifebelt on. He was on a boat and the boat broke up—leaked, see—our boats were old. And then he was on a raft. I was aboard two hours before he was picked up. I didn't know whether he was gone and he thought I was gone.

JACK HATCHER: When they got the bodies they had lifebelts. I had no lifebelt. If I had a lifejacket I wouldn't be here today. I'll tell you why. The boat I was on—the first boat—she'd accommodate forty-five. That's what they told me in the immigration office. Forty-five. There was eighty on it. Eighty. I got on the lifeboat. You had to squeeze yourself to get in—there was that many. And boy, over she goes. I went down under water. I went down under water. But if I had had a lifebelt I wouldn't've went under water. I'd've been caught in under her. After I broke water, I made a few strokes and my chest brought up to the boat. I got on the bow—well, I never got on the bow but I got a hold onto her keel. And in the water three or four others, and they had hold of my legs, tugging at my legs. As the sea struck her, I was fading out, fading out and then—I got ahold again. Yeah. A hard sight. Only six of us saved out of eighty. I could hear them in under the boat, tearing the strips out of her. You see, when they turned over with lifebelts on, they had to stay there. They couldn't get away. I could hear thumping, thumping ... When she come over—there was so many people, drowned, in their lifebelts. They floated away afterward, I suppose. I saw a woman, or a girl, next morning—and if she come out of the beauty parlor her hair wouldn't be no better. She was shot up in the water, her lifebelt took her up. But she was dead. Ah, it was tough times, my son. Tough times. And I've had tough times in my days. Oh, yes. I seen the ship go down. Head first. She was some boat. Awful explosion aboard of her. You know, that was when the water got to her engine. Boilers. The lifeboat had turned over—then she come back and we got into her. It was only six of us got into her. She turned over again and I got onto her again—on her bow—they had big tanks on the lifeboats, so they wouldn't sink. And the starboard tank come out of her, and she was on her side. She was sunk down but the one tank kept her afloat. I held onto the boat all the time. And that's what I was took off of, the next morning.

THOMAS FLEMMING: People that didn't survive were picked up by fishing boats sent out from Port aux Basques that morning. They were all taken to Port aux Basques, identified and sent to their homes. In Port aux Basques there is a monument erected by the railway in memory of all those who were lost. And after the war they found documents relating to the sinking of the *Caribou*. *The Laughing Cow* was the name of the sumbarine and she was commanded by a Captain Swartz. After sinking the *Caribou* she went home to Germany for refit and in February of the following year she returned to the Atlantic for patrol—and she never returned.

THOMAS PEARCEY: I was home five days and went back

*The* Caribou *ferry and those of her crew that were lost. The larger photo (top center) is B. Tavernor, Master. Beginning at his left the smaller photos around the* Caribou *are Miss Bride Fitzpatrick, Stewardess; W. Hogan, Asst. Purser; C. Hann, Donkeyman; G. Gale, Oiler; Israel Sheaves, Oiler; Joseph Richards, Fireman; W. Samms, Fireman; Jerome Gale, Asst. Steward; L. Carter, Asst. Steward; C. Humphries, Asst. Steward; M. French, Second Steward; A. Strickland, A.B.; B. Coffin, A.B.; Israel Barritt, A.B.; Elijah Coffin, Bo'sun; V. Lomond, Trimmer; G. Thomas, Fireman; A. Thomas, Fireman; G. Strickland, Fireman. Larger photos left: S. Tavernor, First Officer; Harold Tavernor, Third Officer; J. Pike, Chief Engineer. Right: J. Prosper, Second Officer; C. Percey, Third Engineer; T. Moyst, Second Engineer.*

again on the *Burgeo*. But after the *Caribou* was lost we never sailed at nighttime. When the *Burgeo* took the place of the *Caribou* all the crew went on the wharf— they wouldn't sail the nighttime. That's when they made it a day run. And the first trip we made on the *Burgeo* we were chased that day by two subs, one on each side of us. We had two corvettes. Once they dropped the depth charge the subs were gone. That drives the subs away.

# The Berthing of Supertankers

*"Shiphandling is an art. It involves combinations of variables so numerous and complex that no amount of detailed predetermined instruction can bring a ship through a canal or dock it. Each time a ship moves, the precise influences acting on her are different than they were at any other time; and the ship responds to every one of them. A great many procedures and processes in the industrial world lend themselves to the kind of training in which definite actions at specific times can be taught in advance, and anyone with a good memory and a little practice can perform as instructed and obtain minimum results. Shiphandling is not one of them." From the Manual of Shiphandling, Port Revel Centre, where pilots of supertankers train.*

PILOT ROY BENNETT: From the time those ships leave we'll say the Persian Gulf, we begin to hear that the ship is due at such a time. Personally I've never seen one arrive according to the computer's estimation yet. A year ago last February I went out for a Norwegian tanker of 230-some-thousand tons and we waited hours and no sign of her. Came back in and then got word she was delayed and the master was so concerned he forgot to notify the pilots. Next morning went out and got him and she was encased in ice on one side of her—ice a foot thick—and it took about two hours work coming up the bay there to free the windlass and winches to be able to work lines when you got into the dock. He told me as she came up over the continental shelf, a tremendous sea running—the seas were coming right aboard him, he had to slow her down. Talk about those ships are like floating islands. They're not floating islands with a sea raging and solid water over the bow and spray further back turning to ice and adding greatly to the weight. They chopped an area by the ship's rail wide enough for me to get aboard. But she wouldn't completely encase because that oil is kept at a temperature of 135 to 140 degrees. It might be freezing on the deck and railing, but the ship is a heating element in herself.

It takes a long time for that ship to lose her way [slow down] so the pilot can get on board. We have a slow pilot boat—eight knots—so the master of that ship must take action some distance out to slow the ship down to five or six knots. When you come aboard, you meet the captain and you

*The T. G. Shaughnessy, 1,105 feet long and 170 feet wide, 285,000 tons deadweight, at the Pilot Boarding Station in Chedabucto Bay, about to enter the Strait of Canso.*

*Pilot Alex Huntley during the nighttime berthing of the* Shaughnessy *at the Gulf Oil Terminal, Point Tupper. (Right) Pilot Roy Bennett.*

make sure that certain regulations have been observed—that he's requested a pratique—that his ship is healthy. You should know that before you go on board so you don't become quarantined. We don't follow it all the time but what you should do is give your name, the master will give his name. Give him information whether he'll be going alongside or anchoring. If going alongside, how many tugs, where they'll be located, ask about what type of engine, whether turbine or motor, and with the large ships ask what the maneuvering speed is. For smaller ships we generally ask for seaspeed because that can be a difference of two and three knots and we can come up with a ship of 20,000 tons faster and save time. But with the large ones you're not interested in saving time. Just a matter of getting there safely. When you're going slow enough you have control of it. Then if it's required for any turning on the helm you can ring Full Ahead, Half Ahead, whatever—and you're getting that

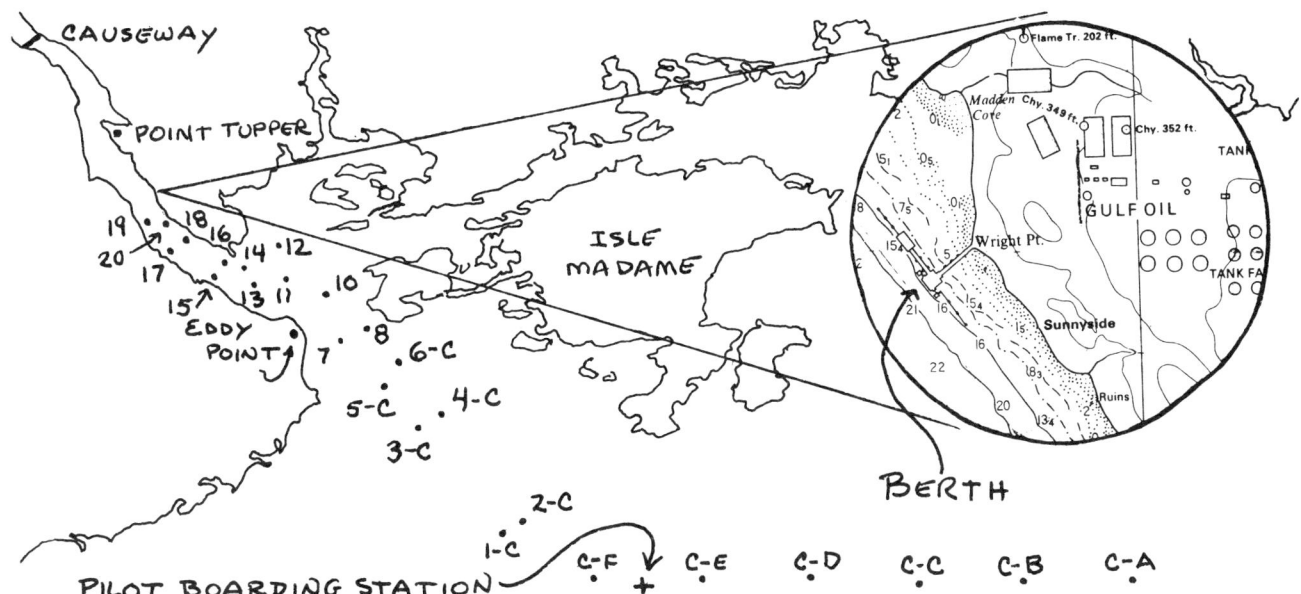

*The tanker reports to Eddy Point at Alpha and Delta buoys (C-A and C-D). The pilot boat meets the ship at the Pilot Boarding Station between C-E and C-F, and the pilot is now responsible for reporting to Eddy Point on reaching C-F. He gives an Estimated Time of Arrival at 6-C. At 6-C he gives an ETA for 10-C, and at 10-C an ETA for 14-C. After passing 11-C he takes the ship through a Dogleg Turn: traveling at 320 degrees he alters course to 268—52 degrees to port. At 14-C he gives ETA for 20-C. Then at buoy 16-C—off Bear Head— he orders a turn to starboard 37 degrees—from course 268 to 305. Buoy 20-C is the last one before docking. Depending how close the tanker is to 20-C, and considering wind and current conditions, the pilot will determine how far off he wants to steady the course. He is now three-quarters of a mile from the berth.*

increased thrust on your rudder—and those ships handle unbelievably well. They are the best maneuvering ships built, those large ones. Hard to believe, but that's a fact.

You ask the master the ship's handling characteristics—and you determine this yourself. A ship coming in when you board her is on a course of 270 degrees. Well, the first alteration may be twenty degrees working up toward the buoyed channel—270 to 290 or so—and you have three miles there to see how the ship will handle steering. And of course you have that straight run up the buoyed channel. Then we have a fifty-two-degree turn to port. That is where you really get the feel of what the ship will do—and that is where I make sure—not attempt to at all—I *make* sure—what I consider an element of safety—that when I'm arriving at the area where I'm beginning to make this turn that ship is not going any more than four knots. Then if the ship should be sluggish on making the turn you can increase the revolutions. You can increase the revolutions of the engine and yet not increase the speed noticeably, because it's only for a matter of two or three minutes and that tremendous wash against the rudder will turn the ship and, as the rudder is put the opposite direction, steady her up. The thing is, going slow, if that ship has a breakdown in her steering equipment you ring Full Astern and you can stop the ship and hold her. And you have the tugs alongside—the tugs are alongside before we make that **dogleg turn on the big ships—but if you were doing six or seven knots I wouldn't guarantee what would happen. They** *might* handle just as well but I have no intention as long as I am on the job of ever finding out. I have used the tugs on the turn but that was just to see what they would do—they were new—but now I never use the tugs on the turn. I took one in a couple of weeks ago, she was 1141 feet long—made every turn herself.

PILOT ALEX HUNTLEY: The engines were stopped when I went aboard the *Shaughnessy* Sunday night. I asked about that, and I informed the captain of the problem we were having with the tugs. [The Chief Engineer on one of the two tugs coming down from Halifax had slipped, injured his head, and thus the tug was delayed. The Halifax tugs—

*Foundation Vigour* and *Point Spencer*—were to join the *Point Melford* and the *Point Tupper*, the tugs in the Strait of Canso.] I told him I didn't want to anchor if possible. But I wanted the four tugs. I definitely think it's safer. If those ships get out of hand, you have to understand that we're talking about hundreds of thousands of tons and it takes a lot of pushing and pulling to show any movement on these ships. So if they take a sheer on you—a sheer means that a ship just goes off her course—all ships are built different—some will take a sheer under circumstances another ship wouldn't—so to counteract that we have the tugs. The ship can go ahead from stern, but for side movement you want the tugs. Now Sunday night was incredible, the weather was incredible. You don't always get those conditions. You can get some pretty scary conditions at times. The last one I had in we had real dense fog, for a while I couldn't see the deck from the bridge. I've docked one in a storm up to fifty-five miles an hour. Strong

*Left: The pilot boat heading out to meet the* Shaughnessy. *Below (left and right): Huntley climbs aboard the supertanker. View from the* Shaughnessy's *bridge.*

The Berthing of Supertankers

winds. Strong currents, setting on the dock. You don't worry too much if it's setting off the dock—but if you have the current setting on, the wind setting on—it can be a little scary. We've had a survey of the currents in the strait area by the Bedford Institute. There's no set pattern. You simply have to be prepared. You have to *feel* those things on board. Absolutely, on board. Sunday night I stopped the ship's engines when I passed number one and number two buoy. I was very close to number two buoy and I figure by the time I got up to number three and four that I had gone sideways a thousand maybe 1200 feet in two miles—that's the current setting from the westward.

When they come up to the ship the tug captains are in control of their tugs. They're under pilot's orders and we tell them where to position themselves. Once they tie on they're under my control. Pilots handle this differently. For this particular berthing I used two tugs in each position, paired off—so when I give orders I call the pairs One and Two. Under certain conditions (such as high winds) you might have them all in a line and have One, Two, Three, Four as designations. I can use the power of the tugs and the power of the ship itself. I can have one pair or the other pushing.

Or both pushing. Or pushing and pulling. Some ships give more problems than others. You have to get a certain amount of speed up before they'll respond. And that's no good. In fact one alteration, the *Shaughnessy* was a bit slow responding. But I did not use the tugs very much. I was practically alongside the dock before I used the tugs. Other times you use them a lot. Sometimes you need the tugs when you turn the ship—where you come in below Eddy Point—some ships you have to use the tugs in order to swing them. Sometimes you can't put the speed that you have. I mean, if you rev these ships up you could swing them quicker but I prefer to take them around those turns pretty easy.

*The tugs* Point Spencer *and* Foundation Vigour *paired for pushing the* Shaughnessy *to the dock. Pilot Huntley (right) out on the wing of the bridge as the tanker closes with the dock.*

*Tug Captains Chaisson and Anstey.*

TUG CAPTAIN ANSTEY, *Point Melford*: There is no specific special training for the tugs that handle supertankers. We found ourselves that we'd handled vessels in Canada up to 150,000 tons and this was no great difference to what we'd already done. It's not so much special training as experience over a number of years. The pilots do go to a special school in France but they haven't got a school for tugs. You're brought up on tugs. Our responsibility is to be there in time to meet the ship, and to put our tug in the position the pilot wants. Then we put ourselves under his orders for docking. We do not do anything on our own. The only time that we can work contrary to the pilot is when we see our tug in danger.

TUG CAPTAIN CHAISSON, *Point Tupper*: We've never had difficulty with a supertanker. We've had difficulty, such as high winds and a light tanker. A 20,000-ton tanker coming in is coming in for cargo. They draw only about fifteen feet back aft and about nine forward. So you haven't got the draft and the least little thing on the wind and it just goes sideways. If the ship is about stopped like a supertanker, we have only the weight of the tug and the horsepower—but with a smaller vessel we're being towed through the water—and all that comes on the line. With a small ship everything happens quicker—when we push them they go like all heck. A full speed push on a supertanker of over 200,000 tons takes time to come into effect.

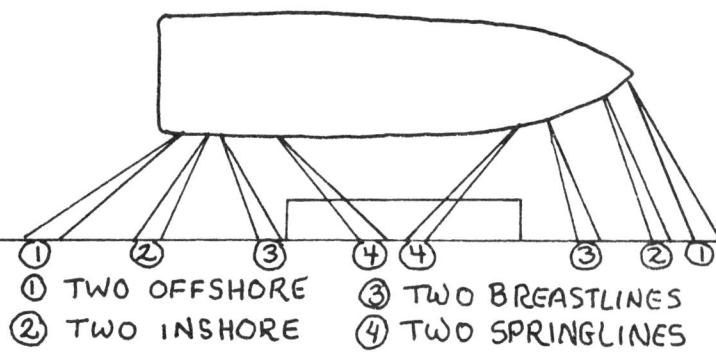

PILOT ROY BENNETT: The small ships are a danger because they're often worn out. They may be sailed under the Norwegian, British, Dutch, United States flag—and they sell them and they come up with a Liberian flag more often than not—flying a flag of convenience. What I brought in last night was 60,200 and some deadweight tons; that would be 420,000 barrels of crude. Gulf doesn't consider that a large ship. The agent at Point Tupper, John Shaw, has a tanker register book—and it's amazing the number of ship of over 200 and over 300 tons today. But I think the ecological problem is with the smaller tankers, ships upward of 20,000 tons—same as the *Arrow* a few years ago. That type of ship if it's operating under a flag of convenience, hard to find out who the owner is, the navigational aids are malfunctioning—that was the report on the *Arrow*. But the ship came up from

222    The Berthing of Supertankers

*Opposite (right) and above: "The navigator comes on the bridge well before docking and asks the pilot what lines he will want out. Then the crews prepare the lines on deck. The tugs hold the tanker to the dock while the bow lines and stern lines are run ashore. It could be two offshore, two inshore, followed by two breastlines, and the same thing aft—for a total of sixteen. This would be considered minimum. If storm conditions threatened, possibly twenty lines would be put ashore. Also, the order of the lines will vary with conditions. If a northerly gale was blowing, you would put out two head lines first and then the after springs. But if you have a southeast gale (strong following wind) you put out two stern lines first and the forward two springs." PILOT ROY BENNETT*

Venezuela and made the turn into the bay—it was a clear day—there was just a slip-up somewhere. But as far as the pilot is concerned, you handle the humblest of ships with as much caution as you handle the greatest. You have radar and other aids. Since this past winter the Eddy Point Traffic Regulating System is there. And you have your clues: We watch the buoys. You can see the tidal effect on the buoys, the swirling—that's a good clue. When I'm docking the ship I get various objects ashore in transit to give me an idea of how rapidly the ship is going sideways when I'm going sideways. You *must* do that. You can't just look at a fixed object. It must be two in transit. You'll see if you are closing them. The same thing the last ship, just have her barely moving ["Over the last hundred yards velocity must come down from fifty feet per minute to no more than five feet per minute"—British Information Services]. I don't want to comment too much on the future, but I do believe it's a good safe port.

ANDY GIBB (*down in the engine room*): I joined the ship in Bantry Bay, in Ireland. This is my first trip with a supertanker. I was on general cargo before. I enjoy this, but right now it's hell. Everything's going haywire. Boilers and one generator. You see, you've got two boilers and they are provided mainly for the discharge of the cargo—there are four steam-driven turbine cargo oilpumps—this ship can discharge in thirty hours with those pumps going flat out. The boiler is mainly for those and the tank heating of the cargo. Around all the cargo tanks you've got coils, steam coils with steam passing through. Sea temperature right now is fifty-seven degrees. That's too low. That'll make the oil too thick to pump. They heat them up. That's what boilers are mainly

*Part of the crew in the engine room. Andy Gibb is second from left.*

for. Now without the generators the boilers won't go—it relies on electric to work. Normally it's fully automatic. Normally. It isn't at the moment. It relies on prayers and things like that. The thing is, at sea you get everything settled down nicely. Once you arrive in port you start getting demands for extra steam, the engine movements, everything else—everything goes haywire. That's common. It's just the way it goes. It's difficult to explain what I do to correct it. Even I'm not sure what I'll do. It's sort of instinct. You run around and shut this and open that and sort of say oh well that's fixed up.

DAVE WEST-WATSON, *Navigator:* The engineers aren't precision engineers. They can't be on this sort of thing. They've got to keep her running. A precision engineer, you've got to stop in, make repairs. But on this thing time's money. I'm the navigator. If I made a mistake in the general average speed point one of a knot [.1 knot], amounts to about $10,000 to $25,000—depends on how it goes over the year. I mean, point one in a knot is nothing really. It's money, everything's money on these.

I've been on five months with the prospect of another month. I haven't spent one hour ashore. Oh, I made a phone call in Bantry. I reckon that you reach a peak at about a month and then you start fading away. You know, it's not bad. I asked to come on this ship and I asked to stay on. This is the sort of thing I wanted because I'm going after my ticket—my mate's ticket. The life obviously isn't like anything to compare with ashore. And it isn't like any other ship that you'll go on, these supertankers. Even on the smaller supertankers in this company—75,000 tons—you get an opportunity to go ashore. You might not go but you've got the opportunity and that's all you want. The opportunity gives you sort of relief, you know. Ah, I could have gone ashore there. You're free. You're still doing your watch—you're doing eight hours a day, seven days a week—and this is the first port in five months where there are people.

I don't know whether you remember the article they wrote in the *Daily Express,* the one about the supertanker going up the channel—"The old man's eyes were red-rimmed with looking through his binoculars"—and all this sort . . . —"and the radar was picking up a seagull on the water at ten miles"—and there was a ship on the starboard bow and everyone on the ship stood still in a moment of tension. Do you know what this is? It's a job. All right, you are carrying 250,000 tons—you don't think about it. You're just doing a job. It might as well be bananas.

And this is where I say you could write a much more interesting article, instead of what's normally written—about us at sea on these supertankers who when in ballast, in dirty ballast, are wandering around with a live bomb on deck. And it is. If this thing went up once we finished discharging, Port Hawkesbury would be wiped off the map. [Andy Gibbs held up a bottle and said: "We'll say for instance that's crude oil and you had a match—you'd be pretty safe. But if you emptied that and you shook it up and put a match in quick, it would go."] All right. People are *aware* of it. But we're not sort of tremble, tremble. I mean, we've got articles, safety things on the bridge, stating that a drop of water in a tank when you're tank cleaning, just dropping from the deckhead—can cause an explosion. They call this a water slug. What happens is that it drops from the deck head, builds up a charge, passes a protruding bit of metal and sparks, arcs across—then boom. That's what they think happened to the supertankers off South Africa. There were three within a month. Well, all right. We're aware of this. We know what we're carrying—but can you imagine we'd be nervous wrecks if we worried about it, because we'll be tank cleaning on the way back. And when you're tank cleaning it's a tricky time. And you still go for your walk, look over the deck, see if there are any dolphins about. You know, you just carry on. They try to force the fact that you're living with danger. You're not. You're doing a job.

*Dave West-Watson, the navigator.*

*Above: The* Shaughnessy *docked and two tugs that will take the empty tanker away. Right: Part of a series of pipelines carrying oil from the tanker to the refinery.*

TUG CAPTAIN ANSTEY: When we're taking the ship away it will be done in a different manner. We'll not be made fast alongside the ship—we'll be on tow lines, one forward and one aft. The *Vigour* and the *Spencer* will be alongside. They'll push up against the ship and hold her to the wharf while they let go her lines. When all the lines are clear and in, then we'll pull them off with the tow lines—straight off the dock. Then under his own power, with our assistance, he'll move up ahead clear of the wharf. Then we'll turn him around in the turning basin. He can't go out backwards.

TUG CAPTAIN CHAISSON: One tug will pull one way, the other the opposite way. Then we'll let go and we'll escort her back to Eddy Point. If the pilot feels she's not handling as well as she should, we'll come back in and make fast again. Once the pilot's satisfied, he gives three long blasts and a short. We give a farewell whistle of three long blasts and he gives three long blasts and we give a quick short and he answers with a short—and that means farewell, goodbye.

# Johnny Murphy of North East Margaree

You know, we were very poor. In order to exist, you had to pretty well learn sound. My grandmother, she used to make a lot of cake and cookies for a daughter of hers that lived two miles out here. And she'd hide them—in a trunk she had. She had a bunch of keys, the keys for these trunks and the keys for the door. My brother would want to find those keys. He stood up on the table and I put my ear on the floor and he'd jump off the table and I'd hear where the keys were at. Sort of a matter of survival. If the keys were hanging on the wall anywhere you'd hear them rattling. If they were on the floor, if she hid them under a mat—we'd find those keys, it didn't matter where she ever hid them.

My father used to play music. Used to play the violin. I was only a year-and-a-half old when he died. He was only thirty-two or thirty-four—got cold I guess. He had had a bad experience before. Him and my cousin got lost, looking for cattle. It was in June or July. The cattle used to go chase what they call this cow cabbage. They followed till they got way

*A portion of the wall in the Murphy living room.*

back and they got lost. And I don't think that he ever got over that night in the woods. He was a carpenter as well. I know when they built that big barn he could walk the ridgepole before there were shingles. But he couldn't go up after that night in the woods. Then after that he took sick. There was an old O'Ryan fellow, he was going home with a load of hay—the road was right below the house—and the wheel of the cart broke. My father went to help this old fellow with his cart. And he had the cold. I believe he had been working making something in the forge—and he was warm. And he got cold then. He helped this old fellow get the wheel on the cart so he could get home—but he didn't live too long after that. Turned to pneumonia, I imagine. And that left my mother with three of us. I was only a year-and-a-half old. I often wondered, how did she raise us?

When did I first hear music? Well, this Dan Young was building my mother's house. He played the violin and he was a beautiful singer too. He happened to come to the house, brought his fiddle. And I was crazy about it, I just loved it. That's how I came to play. But he didn't teach me. I just picked it up on my own. My father had had a violin, and I was awful anxious to hear what it would sound like. So I told my brother if he'd learn to play the fiddle, I'd steal the eggs on my mother and take them and sell them and get fiddle strings. And he'd get my father's fiddle. And I got the strings and got old Dan Young to put them on for him—but he didn't make a very good success of it. So I decided to try. So first time I tried I could play a tune on one string. But I couldn't tune the thing. But I started from that.

I had to steal about three or four dozen to get the fiddle strings. Just keep gathering a few at a time. But there were two girls out here, their mother used to give them eggs in their lunch—but they didn't like eggs. But they come up with this idea one day—boiled eggs—they kept them for three days, two each—they had a dozen. Said they liked them in their lunch, I'm not going to say their names. Three days they had a dozen eggs. Hard boiled. So they took them down to the merchant for good eggs and got the worth of them in candy. And oh, they got away with that a few times. But one day he sold a dozen to some woman for to make a cake—and they were already cooked....

I used to hear old Malcolm Gillis and his son—they used to play at the hall out here. I was I suppose nine or ten. I loved the music. Oh yes, and my mother sang. She had an organ and used to play by ear. And we used to go from one house to the other. There were a lot of musicians. One night we'd be at Kenny MacKenzie's. They had fiddles there and piano. And then another night we'd go to what we called Clem Ingraham's. And then we'd go to Ernest Fraser's, and Ralph MacPherson's, Johnny Burton's over there, and spend a night there—one house to another. It was a great pastime. Time didn't matter. Twelve or one o'clock. At that time there was no television and not too much radio. We'd be in bunches. We wouldn't take fiddles. They'd generally be in the house. And there'd be an organ in every house then. And they'd sing. Some of them were beautiful singers. I remember one song—I wish I had a copy of the words—Clem Ingraham used to sing one: "The Shooting of President Garfield." There was a beautiful air on it. I suppose you'd never find that today.

*Above: Hilda chords while Johnny fiddles. Above right: Hilda with the autoharp, Johnny playing the ukeline.*

But my real interest was fiddle music. I'd learn tunes hearing them. That's why I'd go to dances. Then I'd come home, try playing them. I never danced too much. Then I did learn to play and then I didn't get a chance to dance because I had to play for others. I'd just sit somewheres handy to the fiddler. And I never could learn a tune that way. If I heard a tune maybe it'd be two weeks afterward it would come to me. You could play a tune a hundred times and I couldn't learn it that way—but maybe in a month's time it would come to me. I don't know why.

When I was thirteen I left home and went to Nyanza, worked at a sawmill with my brother, Mike. I often think what people did at that time. My god, it was a long walk. I left in there in the month of April and I walked to South Haven at the foot of Kelly's Mountain—right below the graveyard— that's where the mill was at Fowne's. Ten hours a day—I often think—and the sawdust piling up higher and the smoke blowing in your face, trimming lumber and tallying and putting it out. I think we got twenty-six dollars a month, a dollar a day. But people walked in those days. A Deveau, he left Cheticamp, he and two other fellows, and they walked every camp at St. Ann's—every camp. He got a new pair of boots before he left down there. They didn't get work and they walked to Baddeck and slept in a barn all night and walked back—and his feet were on the road—he had to walk from Belle Cote to Cheticamp in his bare feet. And there was a trapper—Frank Walters—he was only a thin, thin fellow— about six feet tall but only weighed about 120 pounds. He used to trap all in the Highlands. Used to walk from Ingonish to the head of the Margaree River on his trapline. And he thought nothing of leaving the head of the Margaree River at ten or eleven at night and walking back to Ingonish.

It took what little I had to marry Hilda and buy this place. We had fourteen children. One child—I gave the doctor two barrels of carrots and a ton of hay to pay him. Imagine. I never had any trouble making a living as far as eats, such as it was. It was these doctor bills and taxes—that was the two headaches. There were six of mine operated on for appendix.

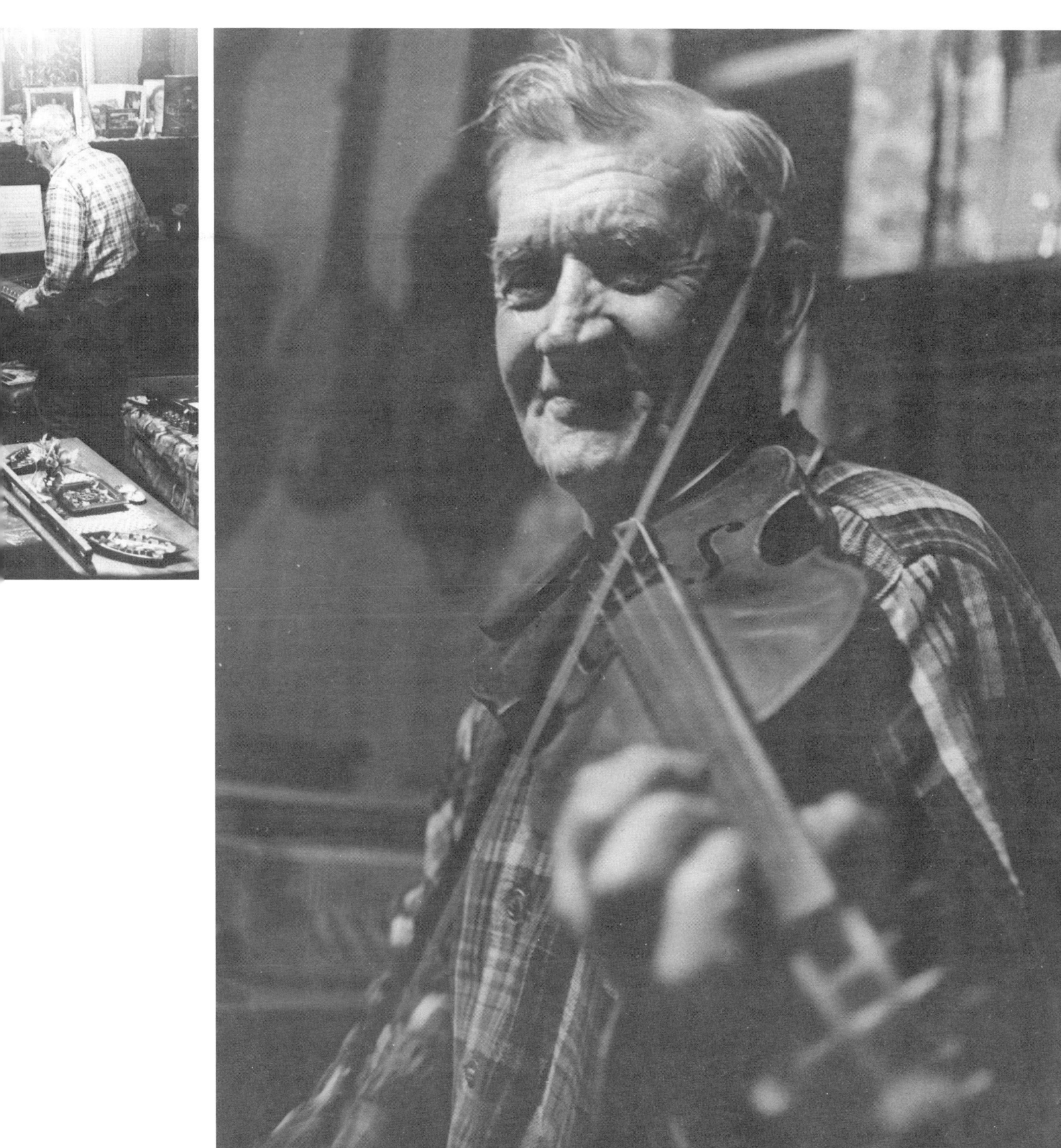

For a living, I did everything. Played for dances, lumbered, farmed. One summer I got up at half past three in the morning and I milked six cows, loaded a load of manure and went into the Normaway and spread it before seven o'clock and got two dollars and a half for the load of manure. Then I hooked into the walking plow and I plowed eighteen days there—ten hours a day. I got $5.85 for the ten hours. One summer I got fifty cords of pit props for the old country, England. Six feet long. Draw shaved. And at the side of the road we got six dollars a cord. And they couldn't be over six inches at the top nor couldn't be under three inches. Now can you imagine? I got 53,000 feet of boards for the Forum in Sydney—and put over the rail onto a boat at Nyanza I got fourteen dollars a thousand. I paid seventy-five dollars for that strip of lumber. I cut it and hauled it, put it over the mountain into a pile—2,100 logs. Sawed it. Loaded it on a truck, hauled it to Nyanza and put it on a boat for fourteen dollars a thousand.

Of course, for food we used to buy different then than we do now. For winter, get in ten to twelve barrels of flour, get ten or twelve gallons of kerosene for the light—and one year I got 1300 pounds of sugar. And as far as cheaper, I know for one hundred pounds of sugar I hauled logs two days with a team of horses to pay for it—around seven dollars a hundredweight. Thirteen hundred pounds of sugar sounds like a lot— but when you go feeding forty-five meals in a day. And tomorrow the same thing. You can figure there was fourteen of us. Three fourteens is nearly forty-five—and there'd be extra meals even if nobody came—children have to eat before they go to bed. You can figure Hilda was getting at least forty-five meals a day. A 200-pound barrel of flour—she cooked that in a month. She was slaving. And can you imagine carrying the water for to wash for those children?

Christ, makes a lump in my throat when I think of what she had to do. And the money that they're throwing around now. People are spoiled today. It's outrageous when you think back—no lights, no hot water, carried water and heat it on the stove—that's hellish. She worked like a slave. She'd do the laundry and ironing at night—you imagine washing for all those kids just on a scrub board. I don't know how she did it.

Hilda and I would play together. When the kids were small Mrs. Connors would come down and she'd look after the kids for us, poor old thing—and stay till two o'clock in the morning. We'd play for showers and weddings—and I'll tell you. I never want to take money for showers or weddings—I never would do that. But then we played for school dances and people would dance. That was an awful job. No pick-up or anything. You'd be played out, press so hard on the bow so they could hear it. We'd get paid ten or twelve dollars for a night.

Compared to Hilda's, my work was just ordinary work, you know. You just went out and worked. But hers was *care*. My God, look here, you take the care of those kids, up at night. There was one, the little girl that died—she was sixteen months old—I am sure Hilda didn't sleep two hours in six weeks, up with that child. She was sick for six weeks. And she never smiled nor never cried from the time she took sick. I was never any good in the house. Like I told her when we first got married—she wanted to learn to milk—your work is in the house and my work is outside and you're not doing anything outside because if you start doing anything outside, then I'll be expecting it.

Hilda was very religious. She'd walk to church and take those kids by the hand in deep snow and, look, stay up all hours of the night to teach them their catechism—nobody knows. Somebody'd come in and perhaps stay till ten or eleven o'clock. I'd go to bed. I'd say, "Hilda, get in bed." "Go to sleep," she'd say, "I've got my prayers to say." She'd pray for hours. I'll bet she'd stay up till two o'clock some nights praying. And she'd light those candles. And if we were going anywheres for a drive and she forgot her beads—if I was halfway to Forks I'd have to go back and get them.

She did the praying and I did the cursing—that's awful but it's the truth. I wish she was still living today, when we could enjoy—that we could go driving, you know. She worked too hard. She would not stop. She wouldn't stop. We had fourteen children. There's twelve living. And there's fifty-four grandchildren. And I think it's fourteen great-grandchildren. She never growled nor ever complained. You imagine. I'm not bragging, but by God, she was a great woman.

# How We Buried Our Dead

Port Hood Island. March 9, 1890

Dear Nina:
It is quite a time since I got a note from you, but it is so hard to write when you cannot write good. We are all pretty well at present. I am troubled with rheumatism. Sometimes I cannot walk but such is life. Old age brings infirmities to be ready for that life where God has gone to prepare a place for loved ones that where he is they may be also. I want to be ready with my lamp trimmed and burning and ready to go in and meet my loved ones that have gone before. They are happy and we soon their happiness shall see. Pray the battle is never over till we enter the pearly gates. Richard is there. Grandfather is there. He left that old body here buried on the land but he had a beautiful mansion over there. Oh what shall Jesus' Father when ... our face like his shall shine. Oh what a glory when saints and angels join there.

All are well on the island. I don't go out much this winter. There is no snow to make roads worse down to Aunt Phoebe's. John Fraser is married and got a son. Charles is married, went home the same night. Everything is quiet. You are coming home in the summer. Give my love to all the folks up there I know.

From your affectionate grandmother,
Anne Smith

MRS. WILLIE D. DEVEAU, *Belle Marche:* Then, they used to have the body right in the house. It would be the front room. If it had been that they had no front room, they'd take all the things from the bedroom and it'd be in the bedroom. There'd be nothing else—no furniture—maybe a table to put a lamp on it. We've only had the funeral home since a few years. Even some today, when they die, they say don't put me in the funeral home. Still, they get embalmed. But before they weren't getting them embalmed. They used to keep the corpse two days. Me, I've always been in doubt. I've always said, if I die, be sure that I'm dead. When you're embalmed you're sure then. But it's not necessary. They only keep them a couple of days. Even if the person is very fat, well, you can keep the corpse a day anyway. If you see something change, you know very well that he's dead, the change shows you he's really dead. But in those days there was no embalming. Nothing at all. My mother-in-law and my father-in-law and my husband weren't embalmed. They were right here, in the front room. When they were making the coffin, used to keep them one day like to give people the time to make the coffin. There were certain men who did the coffin. And then the last night, well, they used to put them in the coffin. But after, we used to buy the coffin. We used to go and get them, and wash the person nice. Like my mother-in-law—you would never think she was dead. Put a little color to her and everything. We kept her two days: from the morning, all day and night and next day, and all night and she was only buried on the third day. And it was in August and she was as—I often thought if she was dead. She was, yes, she was so pretty. She went so long, for an old person. A young person it wouldn't be so—I mean, she's young and she's like a flower, a rose, a young person, but an old person like that, she was eighty-five, and she was so pretty, I hated to part with her.

But I remember long ago—lately they didn't do this—when a person was very, very thin—it was almost frightening for some—me, now, I didn't mind, but some did—so they used to put a piece of cloth like a large handkerchief on their face. And whoever wanted to see them used to lift the handkerchief.

And people would come to visit. Oh yes. A full house, every night. We used to stay up night and day. You wouldn't leave the body alone. Like if you were five or six in a house, two or three would go to bed one night and the other night the others. And sometimes there was always some neighbors who would come. And they would sit with the body, they would sit some in the kitchen. It was the style then. Never to leave the corpse alone. I guess it would be done now if we didn't have any funeral parlor. I guess if there would have been a funeral parlor twenty years ago they would have had to allow the people to stay all night because they would never put their dead in the funeral home if they couldn't stay with them. But now they're accustomed.

In those days, all night, the people were talking. Before midnight, there was always a lot of people. So we'd set a lunch by eleven o'clock for everybody. And then whoever would stay—and some would come—and by two o'clock in the morning another lunch—two or three, maybe four lunches during the night. They had to drink some tea or coffee, and plenty to eat. They'd stay all night. And they'd talk of everything. Except the family, they wouldn't talk much. After midnight maybe a dozen would stay. Seven or eight, maybe more. Oh, yes. And they would laugh too. Yes, yes, yes. I mean, some people used to like to go to a wake. In the last years there would not be singing, but before they used

*Mrs. Willy D. Deveau.*

to sing hymns. All church hymns, through the night. Not all the time. And they would say the prayer, always used to say the prayer before midnight.

Today, there's a lot of old people that prefer going there [the funeral home]. They understand how nice it is, for the people of the house. Me—first, my husband, my father-in-law, my mother-in-law, my daughter—if it had been in a funeral parlor I don't know how I would have felt to leave them from ten o'clock at night till the next morning. Maybe I would have felt worse that I did here. There's not as much remembrance. In the house, you remember everything. Every time I'd go in that room I could see everything. And I was sad, I was crying. If a person dies in the hospital and you think of them as though they're still in the hospital—and you don't feel so sad at the wake. You see nothing in the house. The house is like it was before. But, then, for me it wasn't the same. I couldn't find myself comfortable here after that.

Today they got some people to dig all graves. Before it was the family or the neighbors who dug the grave. But now you don't have to worry. You go to the undertaker. He has everything done for you. It's so easy.

MAURICE DONOVAN, *Ingonish Beach:*  In the days of old, then, the caskets were all handmade here. And there's one of the casketmakers sitting down over there—Robinson. He used to make caskets up until money got more plentiful and they started getting the undertakers in. [Mr. Donovan introduced us to Mr. Robinson.]

PATRICK ROBINSON:  There was a man here that used to make coffins by the name of Tom Austin Young. So he got me to go with him one time, making coffins. And then I did go with him every time after that, him and I, he'd make the coffin. And when he was dying himself, he sent them and asked for me to make his coffin. So I made his coffin.

Used to make out of three-quarter-inch pine. We didn't have a mold. No, we just went by measurements according to the size of the person. We'd take the width of a person, you know, from shoulder. Leave a couple of inches for room, and a few inches longer than the length of the person. And then we shape the bottom of the coffin from that. It would be anywhere from twenty-two to twenty-four inches in the breast, across the shoulders. It would come in to about fourteen inches up by the head and about eleven inches at the foot, coffin shape. Just clearance all around. You wouldn't jam up a person. Oh yes, they looked beautiful. Well, then, we could go to the store and we could buy this black cotton. And we'd line it outside with black cotton. Yes, outside. We'd

*Patrick Robinson (left) and Maurice Donovan.*

cover it with black cotton. You wouldn't see the wood at all. We'd cover it with cotton and turn it down in over the sides with carpet tacks. Turn it in under the bottom and nail it with carpet tacks.

Then the women would make a—what did they call that that went around the headpiece?

MAURICE:  It was called a tucker.

PATRICK:  Yes, they took a nice silk and they tucked it all on a machine and put it all around the inside on the edge. It would be all pleated. Used to look very nice, too. That would be white. It would come in snug all around the body. They used to put cotton wool in behind it and try to puff it out.

MAURICE:  I wish you could have seen one, see how well it was done.

Just the plank boards on the bottom. Didn't cover the bottom, just what you could see. A small pillow went under their head. The rest would be the pine bottom. Then we took the cover of the coffin and we covered that with black and turned it in underneath and nailed that with carpet tacks. Our coffins were all covered with black cotton. We could buy the handles. And there would be a cross that came with the handles—called the breast plate. That would be laying right on top of the coffin until burial—then take it off. The people would take it themselves and keep it.

The coffins would all be black, except the children's. Children's coffins were always covered with white.

PATRICK: After Young died I was the only one around here.

*Was it understood that if someone needed a coffin they would come to you?*

Yes.

*Would you make a coffin at home?*

Yes, usually. Sometimes you'd make it there, if they had a place you could work you'd make it there. If they didn't you'd make it at home in your own workshop.

*You always had boards waiting?*

Oh, yes. The sawmills around here always had pine.

*Do you remember what you would charge?*

Nothing. Never no charge. No, I always did it no charge. And it was a big day's work to do it. People now all buy their coffins.

*But why? Yours were certainly cheaper.*

Yes, and a hell of a lot better. The ones that I'd make, they'd last longer. Now you go over to the old graveyard and go around where they had old pine coffins— you don't see no graves fell in. Three or four years after you bury a person with these coffins you buy, first thing you see a big hollow. She just falls apart. They're only just glued, just stuck together—when they go in the ground they all pop apart. Yeah. More style than anything now. They pay eight hundred or nine hundred dollars for a coffin—it's a shame.

PETER WILLY MURPHY, *New Waterford:* Here's what I'm going to tell you, and this is a terror, this one. I used to like the graveyard so much, I don't think I told you. I wasn't a young man then. I was married. My domestic career blew up. And it was in 1931-32—and boy, they were hungry years. Hungry years. Father coming home with ten dollars, nine dollars, eight dollars a week to a family—eight to a family—no damn wonder. They were bad years. And there were no undertakers here then. The government appointed a man to bury you. Pick you up and bury you—unless you had money like to go and hire another that was in the undertaker business with parlors and embalming systems and whatever. But in New Waterford the early system was just they'd get the body and they'd wash it and they'd stick it in the box and bury it and that'd be it. And I was around the bodies—I shaved a dozen people for heaven's sake—and there was something about a body I didn't seem to mind—I still don't—and the graveyard I didn't seem to mind.

This friend of mine—he was for years a TB. That's before the sanitorium was popular. My uncle was the one to introduce the sanitorium—the TB treatment— into the hospital. You either went to the woods and died or stayed home and spread it in the home. Anyhow in this case this boy died at home. My friend, Charlie. And there was an upstairs in the house and the stairs were less than two feet wide. You get what I mean? A narrow stair with a turn in it less than five feet up because it was a low house. About four feet up and a turn in it—a square turn—and Charlie was over six feet tall. A tall man.

His mother kept boarders. There was a big husky man there but he had no wind. And there was another fellow there, stuttering—de-de-de, he-he-he wouldn't have anything to-to-to do. Wouldn't touch the corpse at all. That was it, by God.

So they called for a coffin, for Charlie. Well the house was way down by the shore. They couldn't get up with a coffin. And I was down at the wake. I was down to get Charlie washed up and fixed up—the others got him shaved—I was going to do the rest. Well, damn it, there was nobody to get the casket in from where twelve pit is now down to the body at Lane Street, where that dump is—was the route you have to go. And the snow that year was the kind of snow that was drifting eight feet, ten feet, banking and things like that. So they made it to twelve pit with the casket and couldn't come any further. Down that far the roads in town were shovelled—not plowed—shovelled. They came that far with a truck.

So this boy's mother, she said somebody'll have to go show 'em how to get in here. I went, out in the storm. I didn't mind weather. Tough as nails. And sure enough, the lights were beaming in the snow. The big rough box with the casket and everything on the back. Well, I couldn't handle the goddamn rough box. They said don't you worry about that. We'll get

*Peter Willy Murphy.*

the rough box to the graveyard when this storm clears away. How are they gonna get the grave dug? I said, let us worry about that. That time you dug your own grave, neighbors gathered. Pick and shovel. Frozen ground. Oh, yeah. I could give you another story about that.

But anyhow, I haven't got any rope. Took a rope from the truck. Took the casket out of the rough box, and out on the snow drift. Put the rope through the handles of the casket and put it over my shoulders like a dog sleigh. And I pulled that casket down to the house. By the time I got to the house the bottom of the thing was worn pretty near smooth, almost like a sleigh, dragging it. Dragging it. Only a little over a quarter of a mile but I almost wore the bottom out of the casket dragging it—on the snow and the crust and over hills and banks—and a storm blowing. This was a manufactured casket, not homemade.

Got to the house and my gosh, everybody was glad to see me, so the first one that was looked after was me. Give me a hot cup of tea and take off the icicles. Clothes changed. Casket was brought in and put flat on the floor in the living room. Everything opened up on it so you could get it dry—it was soaking, wringing wet. Okay. Big roaring fire going on. Everybody was looking at it. The casket was well-examined. No corpse in it.

Well, what are we going to do next? Well, you can't get the casket upstairs. We'll have to get him down. Well the strongest man there—he'd be the only one who could pick him out of bed and get him down. Who's going to help him? Well, damn it all, I'll help him. But the strong man was so big that no matter what he did with the corpse there was no way that he could get down the stairs. It was then agreed that if they'd put Charlie on my shoulders—and the corpse by now was stiff as a pole and wouldn't bend. Too long laying in bed. I couldn't lift him out. So they planked him on my shoulder and got out in a kind of a hall and tried to swing him out—head sticking out here, feet sticking out there.

Look, I said, never mind the natural way. Let's carry him belly down and I'll get my hands in between his armpits and you balance the feet—up or down—we all agreed. Okay, started. Down. But I couldn't hold him on my shoulder. I got my head right down so the body could go right over my head then reached up and got the hands in the shoulder pits. The stairs were too narrow. Couldn't get him on my shoulder and couldn't hold him on my shoulder, so I got him on the back of my head. And the steps. Come one. First step things is all right. Pumped up. Two. All right up there? I said, you keep holding him back. Come to the clearing in the stairs. Wooooo. The body croaks over. And the roar. Holy jumping Moses, I often think of it. If I was a nervous guy I would have been dead under the body.

The head was stuck out ahead of me. The pumps of the step pumped the wind out of the stomach. See. And whooooo—the body collapsed into a big hinge. And here I was stuck in the turn of the stairs. The body was over my head. Couldn't get it up. It was heavy. They couldn't get it up. We were practically knocked out with the roar of the body and the wind and everything. Anyhow, after I got my wind—another fellow, George, he's dead now, was waiting for us down at the bottom of the stairs. George called, are you all right? Yes, I said. And yes from up top—but the fellow said I don't know how we're going to get it down. I couldn't even see the steps by this time. The body had me jammed in front. The legs were behind me and the arms in front of me—and the fellow above still holding back so I wouldn't fall on my face. So down the next step. And the next. And finally down. And that's how we got the corpse down the narrow stairs.

And then get to the casket. And everyone was willing then to give a hand. It looked like I was going to have a broken neck. Pretty near two days to get the stiffness out of my neck—that body hanging on my head. Narrow stairs and boarded in. No railing. Gee whiz, an awful experience.

Anyhow, they flattened him out on the floor then and everybody took and put him in the casket. Put him up on two kitchen chairs. And the wake is on. Then everybody gets religious and starts praying. And what they would do in those days—everybody would gather round and say the rosary—that's the beads. From then on it was tee-total respect. The priest got there. Then up to the grave.

WILLIAM G. DOOLEY, *North Sydney:* I was born in 1881, twelfth of September. I started in as a funeral director in 1897. One time there were no funeral directors at all. My father started the first one. He was one of those fellows, everyone was a neighbor like. And a person would die they'd call him—and he'd wash them and dress them and make the casket by hand. He was in the carpenter business, picture framing. He went on till he became an immigration officer—then I took over. I didn't make coffins. By that time you could get them. There was a firm started in Amherst—I think in 1892—and later on a firm started in Antigonish.

MRS. DOOLEY: You be sure and tell him those were the hard days. Half-past two and three o'clock in the morning, the hospital would call. Mrs. So-and-so died—come down for the body right away. Today you can wait till the morning.

MR. DOOLEY: And it would be all excitement. Death in the family wasn't very often. And they'd feel you must get them fixed up right away. In those days, you see, we'd take our grip and equipment and do all the work at the house and even at the hospital after the hospital started here. What we had then, you wouldn't call it a funeral parlor. In a way, it was the only thing—if, for instance, a sailor died on a ship. Well, we'd take him home and fix him up. But the bodies were normally at their own homes. People wouldn't listen to funeral home then anyway.

I learned by just being around my father. And when we'd get a chance we'd practice. Get an idea and if it turned out all right, well, that would be all right. Get an idea we could make that fellow look a whole lot nicer than he's looking now. Little

*William Dooley.*

touch here and there, you know. Then the embalming fluid got on the market. They didn't have that at first at all. Used to get it from the Egyptian Chemical Company, about the only ones who made it in Canada.

How we learned—say we'd buy a case of fluid, there'd be a circular come with a case of fluid and you'd try it out first chance you got. And some of those sailors, as I said before, we could do a little practicing on them. Because there'd be nobody to say he don't look like himself. We'd try methods, take notes—and if we'd get a chance we'd hold them over for a week or two, see how they'd take it. There wasn't a school then. But there was a firm in Saint John, N.B., that built a factory to make caskets and sell fluid. And to make a start they got Dr. Renouard. He was a famous fellow in the States there. He'd come down and give them ten-day lectures. But this firm didn't last too long. But this Dr. Renouard, his father was a doctor in the Civil War and he was looking after the people who were killed and fixed up and sent to their original home for burial. And the way it was, before the train would take the body they'd have to be sure there was no smell—so he was his own boss, ship when he was ready—that's really the start of it. He made his own fluid.

*At first, did people object to embalming fluid?*

Well, they want the body looking as natural and no swelling or anything like that. They don't care how you do it but do it.

MRS. DOOLEY: In those days, dear, there was diptheria. And there was a place way down here in North Sydney by the station where they kept them. If someone died of diptheria then, Will would have to go.

MR. DOOLEY: Yes, and tuberculosis, and smallpox, and just one case of leprosy. But somehow or other, we didn't get frightened of anything. There was no way out of it. Say you had a death and I drive up in the wagon—and ten or fifteen people standing around. You wouldn't get one of them to help you. Because of the disease and fear of the dead too. You'd just have to move it inch by inch to the door. And people those days were frightened of ghosts. I was frightened of nothing.

VIRGINIA DOOLEY: Daddy always told Mama not to worry about diptheria. He cited this incident. In Saint John, N.B., they were building a new hospital and he was helping Mr. Fitzpatrick transfer the patients. Apparently they were going with this horse and wagon, this Fitzpatrick and Daddy and a Negro woman driving it. So one of the patients died. When they went to the doctor they found it was diptheria. So they quarantined Fitzpatrick and Daddy. They put them all alone in a room in the hospital for twenty-one days. They shoved the food in to them through a slot.

MR. DOOLEY: We were there eleven days. And my buddy died. And they gave me the whole twenty-one days again. Took this other fellow out. So I always told her not to worry. You know the disinfectant? Chewing tobacco was considered the disinfectant. And I'd chew when I worked. All the fellows did.

*When did you start having local people kept in your place?*

Well, that was kind of a gradual thing. If they died home they'd be fixed up home and left home. If they died in the hospital you took them home and they were fixed up home. That was the family rule. But it gradually wore away, you know.

VIRGINIA: It had already started in the big cities long before it came here. See it was about 1952 or '53, he started the funeral home. He didn't start keeping bodies till around 1950.

MR. DOOLEY: I remember a little fellow—perhaps a year old—a little casket. Well, the people lived up the creek there and they didn't have much of a place and they didn't want the baby taken home and they didn't want the baby taken down on Front Street there—that was just kind of a rough place there, pictures and framing hanging around—so we took that home. And that was the first body that was in our house then. That kind of started it away. And the next one or perhaps the second one after—oh, take that out of my sight. But there's few babies die now. One time we used to buy coffins from Amherst: send down a dozen two-foot, and a dozen two-foot-three, and a half-a-dozen two-foot-six, and all that. And you'd sell them before very long.

*What's the longest you were ever required to keep a remains?*

I don't know. There's no time limit. We had one fellow there, his boat upset out—they were rum running. Two went out in little vessels and something happened and she upset. One fellow got his feet caught in the ropes and drowned, and a tug came along and saw him and got him clear—but the other fellow wasn't seen yet. So they brought the first fellow in to me. Couldn't find out who he was. Left word around police stations and one thing or another. So someone thought, why don't we just stand him up in the corner there and people'd come in, they might recognize him. So we did that.

Not in a coffin. No. Stood him up, just put a suit on him. Like if you stood up there. I come and I'd know that fellow. That was down at the old place. He stood there eleven months and some days, not saying a word, and nobody recognized him. We kept an eye on him. He didn't smell. We kept enough fluid in him—but we never had any trouble with him. You know, people began to think he was one of us. Well, we buried him then. Old Dr. MacLean was coroner and he said, Aw, we might as well, we'll never find out who he is. So we buried him. And in another month or so we got word from some fellow in Maine—and he was missing. They sent a letter to the chief of police in Sydney and we had snaps taken different times. So we took him up then after being buried a couple of months, washed him up a little bit and sent him home—put a little notice on the coffin—they could open it if they want.

We've had them come in here—you now, all those vessels going down to Labrador—they have a lot of loose salt in the hold. And they salt their fish when they catch them. Well those fellows that died there, they put them in the salt and covered them up and they're there till they get here or St. John's, wherever they're going—and they're all right. They're pickled, you know. Oh, it was done, lots of times.

One time the older crowd would come around and pick out

their own casket, take it home and keep it under the bed until they'd need it. Perhaps after a couple of years they didn't die, they'd come in for a trade-in. This fellow a good while ago bought one, the old coffin shape. It got out of date. He brought it in one day and wanted to trade it. We traded it. He had that a couple of years. And that went out of style. And he wanted to trade again—but he wasn't too keen on the new prices, so he kept the old one there. And he used it after a while.

BOB FITZGERALD, *Dingwall:* You know, a man's love for his neighbor should be the same today as it was then. And after all, the best man that ever walked the earth was buried without a casket and no undertaker.

At White Point years ago, they would gather in four or five

*Bob Fitzgerald.*

carpenters. At that time there was no such a thing as an undertaker. And there shouldn't be any today. Not in those places. Not in a country place. So four or five carpenters gathered in a house, whether it was a woman or a man that passed away. It didn't make any difference, a child or whatever it was. Took the measurements and went to somebody's workshop. Got the lumber. Made a beautiful casket—and they were good carpenters. Covered it and bought mountings for the casket. Lined it inside.

Beautiful. Took it there. Put the creature in it, whatever it was. The neighbors took care of everything. They went and dug the grave and they saw to it that there was a team to take the remains to the cemetery and everything. That was all arranged by the neighbors. There was neighborly love then. And it was better then, of course. Why wasn't it? There's not half enough of that today. We've lost that part of our heritage. We have lost neighborly love. That's one thing that's gone. That's no more. Burials were a good example of neighborly love. It showed that you weren't alone. When you had trouble and misery and sorrow, the whole community shared it with you—and it made the burden very much lighter. When there was somebody died, the whole community mourned the loss of one of their number. Regardless of what religious denomination it was—it didn't make any difference at all. It was all the same. The people made caskets. Everyone was used the same. It was far far different than it is today.

There's a tremendous lot of people buried that don't have any stone, sad as it might seem. And you know, all of those old people, they all deserved one—they all deserved a stone.

They were tremendous people. We don't have anything like them. And God bless your soul, I have nothing but respect for them, yes—the most profound respect for them. Everyone of them. There's no more left like them and no more to come like them. All you need do sometimes, if you have a little imagination, is roam through the countryside and let your imagination run wild. And you'll travel some of the old farms in this country and you'll stop and look at some of the great rock piles here and there—and how many, when they look at them, how many stop and think of all the sweat and toil and tears it took to put that rock pile there? How many think of it? Very, very few. But if you drive along by one of those old farms some time, and you see one of those old rock piles, just get out and walk over to it and see the thoughts that will go through your mind—and picture the old slaves that dragged those rocks and stones from all around, the land that's cleared, and piled them there. We don't have no more people to work like that today. Somebody'll say we got wise. No, we got foolish. They were the wise people. They had to be.

# Acknowledgments

Hundreds of people have contributed to the making of *Cape Breton's Magazine*. While specific contributions used in *Down North* are easy enough to acknowledge, there should be some recognition of the encouragement of readers, advertisers and merchants, that has served as underpinning to the work. Englishtown Postmistress Katherine Robinson and Mailman Roger Edge have had their workload increased enormously. And, against the difficulties of making a publication in rural Cape Breton, there has been the ready help of the staffs of the MacConnell Library and Beaton Institute, both of Sydney, the Miners' Museum, Glace Bay, and several smaller, local archives around the island.

Most of the photographs for *Down North* were reprinted by Carol Gibson, Ottawa. Owen Fitzgerald, Sydney, took most of the milling frolic pictures. George Thomas, Margaree Harbour, took the photos of Mose Mose Chiasson mending a gaspereaux net on page 155 and the opening cemetery photo for "How We Buried Our Dead" (page 231). G. M. Somerville took the photos of the harpooning of swordfish and they are printed with the permission of Dr. Robert Cook, St. Andrews Biological Station, New Brunswick.

For the older photographs, thanks to Hilda MacDonald of Glendyer, Jim McEvoy of Cape North, Barry Dixon of Effie's Brook, Milton MacKenzie of North Sydney, Bill Fraser of Baddeck, Katherine Robinson and Robert MacDonald of Englishtown, Mr. and Mrs. Kevin Donovan of Ingonish, the family of D. B. MacLeod, Breton Cove, Helen Howatt of Sydney, Duncan Morrison of North River, and Mrs. George Hamm of Baddeck. Several rum-running photographs came from a scrapbook in the care of the Corporal's Mess, RCMP, Halifax.

John Shaw collected, transcribed and translated Joe MacNeil's story. The Gaelic of "Reiteach" was transcribed by John A. MacPherson, and Effie Rankin transcribed and translated the songs in Hector Carmichael's story. Jocelyne Marchand transcribed Marguerite Gallant's French, Christiane Tanner translated the song of the Chandeleur, and Christiane Paquin transcribed the stories told by Sophie Deveau.